POLICY WORLDS

ISBN:
978-0-85745-241-2

W0008740

EASA Series
Published in Association with the
European Association of Social-
Anthropologists (EASA)

1. LEARNING FIELDS
Volume 1
Educational Histories of European Social
Anthropology
Edited by Dorle Dracklé, Iain R. Edgar
and Thomas K. Schippers

2. LEARNING FIELDS
Volume 2
Current Policies and Practices in
European Social Anthropology Education
Edited by Dorle Dracklé and Iain R.
Edgar

3. GRAMMARS OF IDENTITY/
ALTERITY
Edited by Gerd Baumann and Andre
Gingrich

4. MULTIPLE MEDICAL REALITIES
Patients and Healers in Biomedical,
Alternative and Traditional Medicine
Edited by Helle Johannessen and Imre
Lázár

5. FRACTURING RESEMBLANCES
Identity and Mimetic Conflict in
Melanesia and the West
Simon Harrison

6. SKILLED VISIONS
Between Apprenticeship and Standards
Edited by Cristina Grasseni

7. GOING FIRST CLASS?
New Approaches to Privileged Travel and
Movement
Edited by Vered Amit

8. EXPLORING REGIMES OF
DISCIPLINE
The Dynamics of Restraint
Edited by Noel Dyck

9. KNOWING HOW TO KNOW
Fieldwork and the Ethnographic Present
Edited by Narmala Halstead, Eric Hirsch
and Judith Okely

10. POSTSOCIALIST EUROPE
Anthropological Perspectives from Home
Edited by Laszlo Kurti and Peter Skalnik

11. ETHNOGRAPHIC PRACTICE
IN THE PRESENT
Edited by Marit Melhuus, Jon P. Mitchell
and Helena Wulff

12. CULTURE WARS
Context, Models and Anthropologists'
Accounts
Edited by Deborah James, Evelyn Plaice
and Christina Toren

13. POWER AND MAGIC IN ITALY
Thomas Hauschild

14. POLICY WORLDS
Anthropology and the Analysis of
Contemporary Power
Edited by Cris Shore, Susan Wright and
Davide Però

15. HEADLINES OF NATION,
SUBTEXTS OF CLASS
Working Class Populism and the Return
of the Repressed in Neoliberal Europe
Edited by Don Kalb and Gábor Halmai

16. ENCOUNTERS OF BODY
AND SOUL IN CONTEMPORARY
RELIGIOUS PRACTICES
Anthropological Reflections
Edited by Anna Fedele and Ruy Llera Blanes

POLICY WORLDS

Anthropology and the Analysis of Contemporary Power

Edited by

Cris Shore, Susan Wright and Davide Però

Berghahn Books
New York • Oxford

Published in 2011 by

Berghahn Books
www.berghahnbooks.com

©2011 Cris Shore, Susan Wright and Davide Però

Library of Congress Cataloging-in-Publication Data

Policy worlds : anthropology and the analysis of contemporary power / edited by
Cris Shore, Susan Wright and Davide Però.
    p. cm. -- (EASA series)
  Includes bibliographical references and index.
  ISBN 978-0-85745-116-3 (hardback : alk. paper) -- ISBN 978-0-85745-241-2
(pbk. : alk. paper) -- ISBN 978-0-85745-117-0 (ebook)
  1. Political anthropology. I. Shore, Cris, 1959- II. Wright, Susan, 1951- III. Però,
Davide.
  GN492.P48 2011 306.2--dc22

                        2011000956

British Library Cataloguing in Publication Data
A catalogue record for this book is available from the British Library
Printed in the United States on acid-free paper.

ISBN: 978-0-85745-116-3 (hardback)
ISBN: 978-0-85745-241-2 (paperback)
ISBN: 978-0-85745-117-0 (ebook)

Contents

Introduction

Chapter 1   Conceptualising Policy: Technologies
of Governance and the Politics of Visibility   1
Cris Shore and Susan Wright

SECTION I   **STUDYING POLICY: METHODS, PARADIGMS, PERSPECTIVES**
Introduction   27
Susan Wright

Chapter 2   Illuminating the Apparatus: Steps toward
a Nonlocal Ethnography of Global Governance   32
Gregory Feldman

Chapter 3   Politics and Ethics: Ethnographies of Expert
Knowledge and Professional Identities   50
David Mosse

Chapter 4   Peopling Policy: On Conflicting Subjectivities
of Fee-Paying Students   68
Gritt B. Nielsen

Chapter 5   'Studying Through': A Strategy for Studying Political
Transformation. Or Sex, Lies and British Politics   86
Susan Wright and Sue Reinhold

Chapter 6   What was Neoliberalism and What Comes Next?
The Transformation of Citizenship in the
Law-and-Order State   105
Susan Brin Hyatt

SECTION II   **STUDYING GOVERNANCE: POLICY AS A
WINDOW ONTO THE MODERN STATE**
Introduction   125
Cris Shore

Chapter 7   Intimate Knowledge and the Politics of Policy
Convergence: The World Bank and Social
Security Reform in Mexico   130
Tara Schwegler

Chapter 8   Shadow Governing: What the Neocon Core Reveals
               about Power and Influence in America   151
               Janine R. Wedel

Chapter 9   Espionage, Policy and the Art of Government:
               The British Secret Services and the War on Iraq   169
               Cris Shore

Chapter 10   The (Un)Making of Policy in the Shadow of the
               World Bank: Infrastructure Development,
               Urban Resettlement and the Cunning State in India   187
               Shalini Randeria and Ciara Grunder

Chapter 11   Sweden's National Pension System as a
               Political Technology   205
               Anette Nyqvist

**SECTION III SUBJECTS OF POLICY: CONSTRUCTION AND
               CONTESTATION**
               Introduction   223
               Davide Però

Chapter 12   The Case of Scanzano: *Raison d'État* and the
               Reasons for Rebellion   227
               Dorothy Louise Zinn

Chapter 13   Migrants' Practices of Citizenship and
               Policy Change   244
               Davide Però

Chapter 14   Integration Policy and Ethnic Minority
               Associations   264
               Clarissa Kugelberg

Chapter 15   The Elephant in the Room: Multistakeholder
               Dialogue on Agricultural Biotechnology in the
               Food and Agriculture Organization   282
               Birgit Müller

Afterword
Chapter 16   A Policy Ethnographer's Reading of
               Policy Anthropology   300
               Dvora Yanow

Notes on Contributors   315

Index   319

INTRODUCTION
Chapter 1

Conceptualising Policy: Technologies of Governance and the Politics of Visibility

Cris Shore and Susan Wright

A revolutionary moment in the world's history is a time for revolutions, not for patching ... Social insurance should be treated as one part only of a comprehensive policy of social progress. Social insurance fully developed may provide income security; it is an attack upon Want. But Want is one only of five giants on the road of reconstruction and in some ways the easiest to attack. The others are Disease, Ignorance, Squalor and Idleness ... [S]ocial security must be achieved by co-operation between the State and the individual ... in establishing a national minimum, [the State] should leave room and encouragement for voluntary action by each individual to provide more than that minimum for himself and his family. (Beveridge 1942: 1)

Why an 'Anthropology of Policy'?

This book is about how and why anthropology opens up new perspectives on the study of policy. As our authors demonstrate, the point of an anthropology of policy is not just to focus a new lens on particular fields of policy but, in doing so, to reveal larger processes of governance, power and social change that are shaping the world today. As the title suggests, policies belong to – and are embedded within – particular social and cultural worlds or 'domains of meaning'. But they create as well as reflect those worlds. From our perspective, policies are not simply external, generalised or constraining forces, nor are they confined to texts. Rather, they are productive, performative and continually contested. A policy finds expression through sequences of events; it creates new social and semantic spaces, new sets of relations, new political subjects and new webs of meaning. Identifying and analysing these policy worlds is the central aim of this volume. In stating this, we are adamant that the term 'policy worlds' does not imply essentialised or bounded entities; rather, we see policies as windows onto political processes in which actors, agents, concepts and technologies interact in different sites, creating or consolidating new rationalities of governance and regimes of knowledge and power.

A good case in point is the 1942 Beveridge Report, cited above, which provided an ambitious blueprint for the post-War welfare state in Britain and became a model for similar reforms in much of the developed world. Beveridge's proposals included a national network of hospitals and family doctors, a system of public health and support for elderly and disabled people, and children's allowances for food and clothing, all to be financed by a national system of comprehensive social insurance (Abel-Smith 1992). Like all major policy initiatives, it was deeply contested, being denounced by one former chairman of the British Medical Association as:

> the first step, and a big one, to national socialism as practised in Germany. The medical service there was early put under the dictatorship of a 'medical fuhrer' The Bill will establish the minister for health in that capacity. (BBC 1998)

Despite the initial hostility of doctors, who feared it would undermine their professional independence and threaten their incomes, the popularity of the new nationalised health system rapidly established a national political consensus that has survived to the present day and has made it impossible for neoliberal reformers to privatise it openly. Beveridge's plan for social insurance, in which the current workforce underwrote the security of the retired generation trusting that its own security would come from the future contributions of the next generation, produced a fundamentally new construction of the 'social', one that tied the welfare of every individual into membership of society. The Report conveyed an image of a new policy world, framing the space to be governed in a radically new way and recasting the roles of both the state and individuals.

The importance of policy as a subject of anthropological analysis arises from the fact that policies are major instruments through which governments, companies, non-governmental organisations (NGOs), public agencies and international bodies classify and regulate the spaces and subjects they seek to govern. Policy is a fundamental 'organising principle' of society which, like 'family', 'nation', 'class' or 'citizenship', provides a way of conceptualising and symbolising social relations, and around which people live their lives and structure their realities (Berger and Luckman 1966). Through the analysis of these policy processes we are able to observe the way fragments of culture and society are brought into new alignments with each other to create new social and semantic terrains. There are few, if any, populations today that are not in some way or another touched by the classificatory logics and regulatory powers of policy. Even societies that have no indigenous concept of policy find their lives and livelihoods subject to the policies of often remote governments, mining companies and other national and international agencies, as exemplified in Rumsey and Weiner's (2001) and Kirsch's (2006) studies of mining in Papua

New Guinea and Australia. Equally, in those countries where the idea of policy is not differentiated semantically from the term 'politics' (as in Denmark and Italy, where *'politik'* and *'politica'* are used respectively to cover both), policies nonetheless exist. In short, the reach of policy, understood in both a general as well as particular sense, is now truly global.

If part of the 'work of policy' is to classify and organise people and ideas in new ways, then it becomes easy to understand why policies can be such powerful vehicles for social change. Policies can serve as instruments for consolidating the legitimacy of an existing social order or they can provide the rationale for 'regime change' and the subversion of an established order. Like the architecture and internal organisation of an institution, policies reflect the rationality and assumptions prevalent at the time of their creation. However, this is not to suggest that the ideas (or ideologies) that create and sustain policy agendas are in any way static or monolithic. On the contrary, a key quality of policies is that, once created, they often migrate into new contexts and settings, and acquire a life of their own that has consequences that go beyond the original intentions.

This 'domaining effect' as we have called it is perhaps best illustrated in the rise of the 'audit culture' in the workplace of public and private sector organisations in Britain and beyond (Shore and Wright 1999; 2000; Strathern 2000). The introduction of the principles and techniques of New Public Management (NPM) into local authorities, government ministries, hospitals, schools and universities has profoundly modified the behaviour and self-understandings of these organisations and their staff. The new systems of 'internal markets', 'performance measurement', 'self-appraisal', 'external benchmarking', 'competitive ranking' and 'payment by results' may have boosted productivity and performance, but these forms of surveillance and disciplinary 'techniques of the self' individualise and isolate people, forging new types of flexible, self-managed and responsibilised subjects and increasing insecurity, stress and fear in the workplace (Rose 1989; Cruikshank 1999; Martin 1997; Strathern 2000; Larner and Le Heron 2005).

The creation and rapid spread of auditing technologies exemplifies how policies often have a 'runaway effect', actively reshaping the environments into which they have been introduced (Power 1997). Theoretically, we see policies as having complex 'social lives' as people interact with them and as they in turn enter into relations with institutions and other artifacts (Appadurai 1986). An even better way to theorise policies is to think of them as exemplars of what Bruno Latour (1996) terms 'actants' – that is, policies have agency; they shift action; and, like machines, they perform tasks and are endowed with certain competencies. Importantly, actants typically interact with other social agents in processes that are dynamic and contingent, and therefore have unpredictable effects.

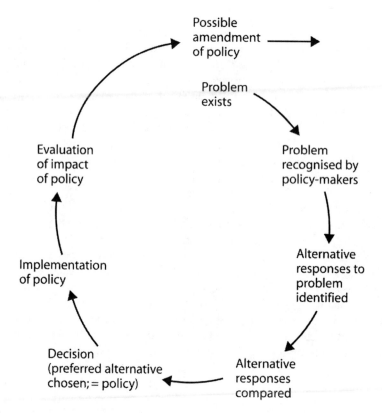

Figure 1. 'A realisation of the linear model: "the policy cycle"'
(Clay and Schaffer 1984: 4)

Anthropology and Interpretive Policy Analysis

To see policy as something that is processual and has agency is a very different approach from the one that has traditionally dominated policy studies. Anthropology shares with the interpretive turn in political science an aim to deconstruct policy in order to reveal patterns and processes in the organisation of power and governance in society. Both anthropologists of policy and interpretive policy analysts take a critical stance towards a dominant account of policy which is still regarded as 'common sense' by many policy professionals. This 'practitioner perspective' typically casts policy in terms of 'authoritative instrumentalism' – that is, it assumes that there are 'objective entities' out there called 'policies' that are the result of decisions made by some rational authority (e.g., a government, committee, management board or chief executive) and which reorganise bureaucratic action to solve particular 'problems' and produce a 'known' (or desired) outcome. In this conventional account, the work of policy consists of *analysing* the problem and appraising the range of possible responses, *selecting* a response on sound

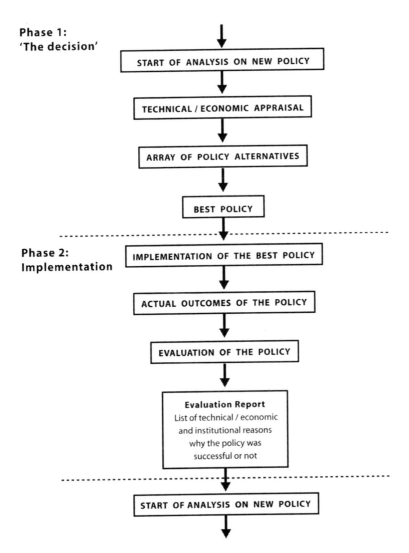

Figure 2. 'The "stage" or "cycle" model of the policy process'
(Colebatch 2000: 50)

and rational grounds, *implementing* the chosen course of action, *evaluating* whether the action produced the desired outcome and, in the light of that, *revising* the policy to be more effective in future. This is widely depicted as a linear process (Figure 1) or, recursively, is turned into a policy circle (Figure 2). Even though Clay and Schaffer warn that their linear model is a 'misleading conceptualization of policy practice' (1984: 3), such normative, ideal-typical flowcharts portray a mechanical model of policy as something 'out there' to be managed clinically and instrumentally. Despite some notable exceptions (Fischer 2003; Peters and Pierre 2006; Yanow 2000; Yanow and

Schwartz-Shea 2006), this practitioner approach also dominates academic ways of conceptualising policy.

In April 2007, we both attended an international conference on interpretative policy analysis (IPA) in Amsterdam.[1] Most participants were either academics or students of politics and policy studies; a few were also policy practitioners. What was striking from the papers and presentations was the repeated complaint about the positivistic assumptions and narrow outlook that continue to dominate teaching and research in policy studies and the limited way in which policy work is conceptualised. Moran, Rein and Goodin's *Oxford Handbook of Public Policy* (2006) was cited as an exemplar of this approach, with its continuing tendency to define policy work as a domain of activity confined to government elites and to questions about how rulers rule. This was a fairly accurate depiction of the book. While the editors aim to be broad and inclusive and to give voice to the whole spectrum of different perspectives on public policy, the way the book is framed echoes much of the 'high modernism' they themselves criticise. The legacy of positivism is evident from the first page, where the authors define policies as programmes 'by which officers of the state attempt to rule'. Public policies, they declare:

> are instruments of this assertive ambition, and policy studies in the mode that emerged from operations research during the Second World War were originally envisaged as handmaidens in that ambition. (Moran, Rein and Goodin 2006: 3)

The book ends 906 pages later with two appendices containing a précis of the 2004 Queen's Speech outlining the British government's legislative programme and a summary of President George Bush's 2004 'State of the Union Address'. These magisterial statements seem to exemplify the authors' idea of what public policy is all about. We do not deny that 'policy' works as an instrument of rule, which it clearly does; our point, instead, is that this narrow, instrumental vision of policy should not define the object of analysis or agenda of those who study policy. Despite talk of 'postpositivism' in the policy sciences (DeLeon and Martell 2006: 39), much of the literature continues to be framed within rational choice theories and positivistic models of perfect or bounded rationality in which economic actors pursue purposeful goals, decision makers make fully informed strategic choices and analysts measure policy effects in terms of calculable costs and benefits.[2]

Similar approaches are echoed in debates within political science over how policies travel internationally. Four main approaches can be distinguished in this literature. First, the 'diffusionist' perspective (Berry and Berry 1999) suggests that policies have a common point of origin and spread from there to one place after another across the globe. They focus on which states copy from each other, and the resulting patterns of adoption recall the diffusionist approach to the spread of cultural artifacts employed in nineteenth-century anthropology. The emphasis is on the similarity of policies appearing in different places rather than on the *meanings* they acquire as they shift into new contexts. Second, Dolowitz and Marsh (2000: 5) define 'policy transfer' as:

> knowledge about policies, administrative arrangements, institutions and ideas in one political setting (past or present) [being] used in the development of policies, administrative arrangements, institutions and ideas in another political setting.

While this approach gives some cognisance to context, it effectively treats political systems as separate entities. James and Lodge (2003) criticise its attempts to establish a continuum of policy transfer stretching from voluntary 'lesson drawing' at one extreme to 'coercive transfer' at the other. They argue that this continuum conflates a rational choice paradigm about which strategies to pursue to achieve particular goals, with a power dimension spanning from voluntary action to IMF and World Bank-imposed sanctions. 'New Institutionalism' offers a third approach, 'convergence'. This emphasises the structural forces – industrialisation, globalisation and regionalisation – which drive institutions towards 'isomorphism' or similar economic, social and political forms of organisation. While this avoids the pitfalls of rational choice theories and tries to give some agency to actors, the overwhelming focus is 'entrenched path dependencies' and agentless structural forces. A fourth approach, by Rizvi (2004: 28), moves closer to an interpretive analysis and argues for more attention to be given to the discursive and material practices through which people create the regularised patterns that both enable and constrain them.

The studies by Wedel, Randeria and Grunder, Müller and Schwegler (this volume) reveal the myriad interactions and alliances involved as actors move between local, national and international institutions in pursuit of their interests: they show that it is through these negotiations and political struggles that policies travel across scales and sites. Schwegler's study of Mexico's pension reform highlights how what was originally a policy pioneered and promoted by the World Bank gets taken up when national policy makers and politicians appropriate it as their own. In Randeria and Grunder's case, the World Bank failed to get the governments of India and Maharashtra state to adopt its protocols surrounding resettlement of people displaced by development projects. Here, it is local citizens who, by pursuing their rights through the World Bank's complaints procedures, make the World Bank's policy jump scale. NGOs operate in a similar way across local and international scales in Müller's study of their attempts to mobilise within the Food and Agricultural Organization (FAO) against policies to promote genetically modified crops.

Despite some policy scholars recognising the importance of language, rhetoric and persuasion as keys to understanding policy processes (Fischer 2003; Gottweis 2006, Yanow and Schwartz-Shea 2006), others continue to view policy analysis as a quasi-scientific activity that requires a clinical approach. Geva-May epitomises this perspective (2005: 2–5) when she equates learning to 'think like a policy analyst' with learning to 'think like a doctor' or other 'clinical disciplines': they should not be let loose on clients, she opines, without proper professional training, mastery of the appropriate 'tricks of the trade' and the diagnostic skills of a practising clinician. Policy analysis, she declares, is far too important to be left to untrained amateurs. Anthropologists and critical social scientists would argue to the contrary – learning to 'think and talk like a policy maker' on their terms alone is part of the problem. What gives anthropology its analytical edge is precisely its capacity to understand the meanings and subjective understandings of policy makers and, at the same time, to challenge received wisdom and think outside of the conventional policy box. As policy makers often depend on making their unstable social products appear apolitical and self-evident, anthropology can pose epistemological challenges to their professionalism, as Mosse's chapter in this book shows. Sustaining a tension between 'insider' and 'outsider' perspectives (or 'emic' and 'etic' accounts) is the hallmark of social anthropology. Social anthropologists are particularly experienced at tracking the genealogies and flows of policies and their impact on people's lives and everyday behaviour. But they are equally good at examining the meanings that those policies hold for those actors whose lives they touch and the cultural logics that structure those 'policy worlds'. To paraphrase Clifford Geertz (1973: 5), we take the analysis of policy to be 'not an experimental science in search of a law but an interpretive one is search of meaning'.

An interpretive approach also challenges the implicitly authoritarian concept of policy as a process that is not only linear and logical but also hierarchical. In the authoritarian view, policy formulation begins with a text (or vision statement) and its passage into legislation, then moves down a chain of command through various levels of administration, from national (and supranational) civil servants to local officers and finally the 'street level bureaucrats' who, Lipsky argues (1979), finally 'make' policy in their interactions with people on the ground. By contrast, anthropologists focus on how people make sense of things, i.e., what policy means to them. They are interested in the 'natives' point of view', i.e., the 'folk-model', or the actors' frame of reference. What makes the State of the Union Address (or Queen's Speech) anthropologically interesting is not simply its content or use of language, but what people say and think about it and how it affects their everyday lives. This book takes such an approach even further by asking not 'How does a policy affect people?' but 'How do people engage with policy and what do *they* make of it?' As elaborated below, anthropology's more open and democratic approach emphasises not only the messiness and complexity of policy processes, but particularly the ambiguous and often contested manner in which policies are simultaneously enacted by different people in diverse situations. Anthropology does not treat policy as an unproblematic given but rather as something to be problematised. It asks: what does policy mean in this context? What work does it do? Whose interests does it promote? What are its social effects? And how does the concept of policy relate to other concepts, norms or institutions within a particular society?

Locating the Agent in the Policy Process: A Case Study

These problems of conceptualising policy are exemplified in Barbara Cruikshank's book *The Will to Empower: Democratic Citizens and Other Subjects.* In her study of postwelfare-state governance in the U.S., Cruikshank illustrates how the most effective forms of domination are often those that go undetected; where power is hidden from view and presents no visible targets to oppose or resist. Her argument is that 'democratic modes of governance and social scientific ways of knowing (re)produce citizens who are capable of governing themselves, of acting in their own interests' (Cruikshank 1999: 3). Her analysis illustrates how anthropology can shed light on the emergence of new forms of governmentality (Shore and Wright 1997; Greenhalgh 2008). In the U.S. today, 'participation' and 'self-government' are often seen as solutions to something that is deemed to be lacking in the population. This idea is consistent with the goal of the early U.S. philanthropy movement of 'helping people to help themselves'. As Cruikshank notes, 'this is a manner of governing that relies not on institutions, organized violence or state power but on securing the voluntary compliance of citizens' (Cruikshank 1999: 4). To do this, as Hyatt (this volume) also shows, various 'technologies of citizenship' are mobilised in order to enlist the autonomy, interests and wills of citizens. These technologies are simultaneously 'voluntary and coercive … the actions of citizens are regulated, but only after the capacity to act as a certain kind of citizen with certain aims is instilled'. Democratic citizens are thus 'both the effects and the instruments of liberal governance' (Cruikshank 1999: 4).

To illustrate her argument, Cruikshank gives a vivid ethnographic vignette. Around 1989 she started to notice that most of the garbage bins in her neighbourhood of Minneapolis had new locks. A key consequence of this was that homeless people and recyclers who relied on 'dumpster diving' (i.e., scavenging food from the large dumpster bins placed outside supermarkets or close to shopping malls) were now much less free to live on their own terms. In short, those struggling to stay outside the arms of the 'poverty industry' now either had to steal or submit themselves to social service charity. Padlocking the dumpsters meant a whole means of subsistence was foreclosed.

As a civil rights activist, Cruikshank set out to find what authority, interests, officials or reasons lay behind this dumpster lockup policy in order to protest and reverse the decision. She asked cashiers at the local convenience store why the dumpster in the parking lot has been locked. They said it was because the store would be legally liable if anyone were to injure themselves while dumpster diving. Next, she asked a neighbourhood activist, who explained that it was because local residents had complained about noisy drunks congregating by the dumpsters; it was an issue of children's safety. Then she discovered that local college students in Minneapolis had been making maps of the local bins with timetables for when fresh spoils could be raided. In response to this fad, many local bagel and pizza shops had stopped putting out trash at night. Local shopkeepers, by contrast, explained to her that people were dumping household garbage (such as old washing machines and furniture) in the dumpsters; therefore, locking them was a good cost-saving measure. Similarly, local people involved in charities and healthcare told her that the lockups were a good thing, as this was really a public health matter and not a question of curtailing individual freedom.

Puzzled by this diversity of explanations and still no nearer to a plausible reason, Cruikshank next turned to ask the company that owned and emptied the dumpsters who had instituted the lockup policy and whether there was a law they were complying with. Nobody was able to give her an answer. She also called their insurance company and the city administration, but in each case failed to find anyone able to give an authoritative account. Despite her efforts, Cruikshank was unable to say where this policy originated or who its authors were. Finally, she asked some of the down-and-outs and homeless people of Minneapolis. They told her that the policy of locking up the city's dumpsters was a way for 'them' or 'the system' to get street dwellers off the streets and under the control of institutions.

Stepping back from this story, Cruickshank draws several interesting conclusions that are relevant to our discussion. The case study illustrates the messiness and ambiguity of the policy process. It challenges us to think about where a policy begins and ends – and what happens in a situation where one cannot identify an authority or agent behind an apparent policy initiative. The lack (or invisibility) of a policy author has major implications for democracy. If one cannot identify an actual cause, an individual or an institution that is responsible for a policy reform, how is effective resistance possible? As she puts it, '[t]he task for democratic theory, when faced with the facelessness of power, could be understood as the effort to give power a face or a name, to make it visible or accountable' (Cruikshank 1999: 15). This somewhat Kafkaesque case study illustrates problems that social scientists face in locating and identifying 'policy actors' in an age of advanced neoliberalism where so many of the functions of the state have been decentralised, outsourced and privatised, and where the idea of 'multi-level governance' has come to be an accepted idiom for describing the modern regulatory state.

The dumpster lockup example also highlights the hegemony of the practitioner perspective approach to policy. According to the logic of 'authoritative instrumentalism', when there was a change in regular practice, the common assumption – shared by all the actors in this policy drama – was that some higher authority must have made a decision, having determined that there was a 'problem' that needed to be 'solved'. Everyone constructed a story within this account, although no one had any actual evidence to support their assumptions, and when Cruickshank went looking, she was unable to find a decision or decision maker. This echoes what Elmore (1979) termed 'backward mapping', i.e., since there was an observed regularity, there must have been an authoritative choice which must have been made in order to achieve some rational outcome.

Similar kinds of teleological assumptions also structure most academic writing on policy. Edward Page has observed that some policies become established without ever having been consciously deliberated on, i.e., a category of policy that arises more from 'non-decision' and inaction (Page 2006: 220). Yet, while we may recognise that systematic regularities in government do not necessarily stem from the authoritative will of a decision maker (that is, not all policies have a sovereign 'author'), the assumption that they do nonetheless continues to frame academic discussion. This recalls Foucault's criticism of academic approaches to power and the state, and his observation that we have not yet succeeded in 'cutting off the king's head' in political analysis. By contrast, anthropologists seldom make these assumptions or look upon policy as a problem-solving device; instead, they ask how these ways of talking about governing influence the things that people do and say.

Studying Policy: Reflections on Methodology

Any strategy for knowledge starts from questions about how to conceptualise the object of study and define the field of research. With our approach to policy as a lens through which to study processes of political transformation, the field of research becomes not a particular people or organisation – far less a reified policy itself – but a 'social and political space articulated through relations of power and systems of governance' (Shore and Wright 1997: 14). This is not just a rhetorical but a contested political space. This conception of policy articulates closely with Foucault's (1980) concept of *dispositif* which both Feldman and Müller draw on to analyse the apparatus of power that is used to define populations and manage the subjects of policy. As Dreyfus and Rabinow (1983: 121) define it, *dispositif* refers to the 'ensemble' of practices, institutions, architectural arrangements, regulations, laws, administrative measures, scientific statements, philosophical propositions and morality that frame a disciplinary space. While *dispositif* refers to how ways of being and doing are framed, Bourdieu's (1977) concept of habitus is useful here for understanding the processes by which actors then come to internalise, embody and become habituated to those structuring frameworks. However, neither of these accounts make clear precisely how the elements that constitute a *dispositif* or habitus are brought together in an 'assemblage' or 'apparatus'. From our perspective, it is precisely the way that policy creates links between agents, institutions, technologies and discourses and brings all these diverse elements into alignment that makes it analytically productive.

In mapping the topography of a field, the key question is what is the range of organisations and categories of people that could become involved in any process of contestation over the policy in question? Traditionally, policy studies focused on the 'policy community' (Rhodes and Marsh 1992) understood narrowly as the 'relatively stable aggregation' of institutional actors, politicians, interested parties and pressure groups who find themselves 'camped permanently around each source of problems' (Colebatch 2002 [1997]: 33, quoting Davies 1964: 3). Interpretive policy studies and anthropology take a broader conception of the people involved in policy making to include the governed as well as the governors, in what Yanow terms a policy's 'interpretive community'. In Wright et al.'s current study of Danish higher education reform,[3] the field spanned international and national governmental agencies, industrial and other pressure groups, professional organisations, universities and their managers, academic and support staff and students, as well as the media, all of whom had an interest in shaping the universities of the future. In other words, an anthropology of policy includes not only those who govern but also conceives an active role for the governed, as well as the technologies that mediate between them.

Such a field is obviously too enormous to study ethnographically in its entirety. Whereas, in the Malinowskian model of fieldwork (epitomised by the small island or self-contained village), the field of research and the site of study were coterminous, now they are differentiated. The challenge is to select small sites that open windows onto larger processes of political transformation. In Strathern's (1992) terms, when working on a canvas as big as a process or a system, the problem is how to derive the 'figure' from the 'ground' and, once parts of the picture have been studied in ethnographic detail, then reintegrate the foreground into the background. Hugh Gusterson (2005) suggests 'tilting the field' so as to study a system from the perspective of a particular site in great detail and, from that, to trace out connections to and implications for the wider field. George Marcus proposed choosing multiple sites by following something as it moved across a field and in so doing revealed the workings of a system or a process of change. As he puts it: 'Strategies of quite literally following connections, associations, and putative relationships are thus at the very heart of designing multi-sited ethnographic research' (Marcus 1995: 97). He suggested six things one could follow: a 'thing', a conflict, a people, a biography, a story or a metaphor. We would add a seventh: follow a policy. Reinhold and Wright's approach to 'studying through' (this volume) takes that injunction further. In a historical ethnography of 1980s Britain, Reinhold (1994) showed how multiple conflicts over 'promoting positive images' of homosexuality occurred simultaneously in a range of local and national sites. By following the flow of events, she traced how the meanings of key words were altered and brought together in a new semantic cluster focused on the 'family'. This became a core ideological battleground out of which Prime Minister Margaret Thatcher's neoliberal ideology took shape. When studying through such processes of transformation, some of the elements within the field may rise to prominence and unanticipated new sites may appear, while others may shrink in importance or not feature at all as events unfold over time.

The idea of following a flow of events raises questions about how to conceptualise policy and its movement. While we criticise the top-down rationalist idea of a policy as an entity defined from on high by decision makers, which is then passed down a hierarchy of organisations until 'it' is implemented on people at the bottom, policies can have an objectified presence and very tangible effects. For example, when Eastern European countries such as Latvia and Lithuania were negotiating their accession to the European Union, they anticipated that conditions of membership to the EU's Economic and Monetary Union club would require them to adopt neoliberal, business-friendly and anti-trade union policies far more stringent than those operating within existing Member States. The result, as Woolfson (2007: 200) observes, was a '"race to the bottom" in labour standards' and employment rights in the new Europe as these postcommunist societies, eager to demonstrate their transition to free market economics, rushed to embrace the neoliberal doctrines they imagined the EU stood for. In short, these Baltic states went far beyond the EU's policy prescriptions and downgraded their national employment standards in ways that have eroded stable employment relations and fuelled the problem of 'social dumping'. The EU's *acquis communautaire,* or accumulated legislation, directives and regulations, appears to have had an objectified presence in their deliberations and actions even before it had been translated into national law.

A crucial dimension of policy is therefore the way it is imagined, and such imaginaries can be thought of as moving through time and space. In this sense, policies can be studied as contested narratives which define the problems of the present in such a way as to either condemn or condone the past, and project only one viable pathway to its resolution (Shore and Wright 1997: 3). Susan Greenhalgh's (2008) study of China's 'One-Child Law' provides an exemplary illustration of this, showing how cybernetic missile control engineers competed with other experts and specialists for 'epistemic ascendancy' as purveyors of the one 'true' science that could resolve China's population crisis in the period between 1979 - 1980. As Greenhalgh (2008: 10–14) observes, their successful domination of the policy-formation process derived from their unique cultural capital as defence specialists, which enabled them to define authoritatively both the policy problem itself and the correct action (or 'policy assemblage') for its solution.

The passage of law is one moment in a process of appropriation and contestation when a political coalition succeeds in silencing others, making their version authoritative and embedding it in the precepts and procedures of the state. But the dominant version can be immediately contested as it is translated into concrete situations. In tracing such a process of contestation, the key questions are: what are the different perspectives on an issue? Whose views prevail? How do these ways of seeing become hegemonic? However naturalised or taken for granted such policy narratives appear, there can still be attempts to disrupt their certainty, expose their ideological foundations and particularistic interests, and assert an alternative 'moral economy' (Scott 1998; Vike 1997; Zinn, this volume).

The way bureaucratic documents embed a particular vision of normative 'ruling relations' between decision makers and clients has been closely analysed by Dorothy Smith (2005). Norman Fairclough (1989) adopts a more diachronic perspective, analysing how a policy narrative 'moves' into new political and social spaces and how it is translated into new genres at each move. Sometimes, this movement is initiated from the top, with a narrative translated from a political speech to newspaper articles, to a law text, to guidance notes intended to reform bureaucratic action, to technical procedures to follow or forms to fill in on paper or on the computer. At other times, this movement starts among user groups or professionals who provide a service. Each move necessarily entails a *re-translation* from one genre to another, opening up space for further contestation. At every moment of translation, new voices enter with new ways of seeing the problem, reinforcing or contesting the concepts and assumptions written into the policy texts. Fairclough (2004) gives an example of a conversation among shop-floor workers, who were used to hierarchical management and suddenly received instructions to 'facilitate' themselves in self-managed teams. They discussed the management's document to unravel shifts in the concepts that described their workplace relations and tried to assert their own meanings by working the new words into classifications they already knew.

But if a policy is a narrative in a continual process of translation and contestation, we might ask when can a policy be said to exist? Bruno Latour's study of a project to build a new transport system in Paris offers an interesting way to conceptualise this. Tracing all the phases of research and development, he found that at each stage the project had to be re-created with a new range of experts, new financial and institutional backers, and new political supporters. For example, when they had overcome serious engineering problems and had prototype yellow cars running round a field, they thought they had a viable project. But to translate this into a logistical scheme that could operate on the roads and rails of Paris required bringing in new professions with new criteria and ways of seeing the problem. Suddenly the viability of the project had to be proved once again. Latour asks at what point was it possible to say that the project actually existed? In a similar vein, Schwegler (this volume) asks at what point can Mexico's pension reform be said to have come into existence? Why are there so many conflicting stories and claims about its authorship? Or in Shore's study of the British government's spying on the United Nations, why is such a policy officially denied when it is widely known to exist? The answer is that 'policy', even more than Latour's 'project', is a political process involving many actors all proposing how people should relate to each other, conduct themselves and be governed.

How do anthropologists and interpretive policy analysts decide where to locate themselves in this field? The trick is to find a vantage point from which to observe how the elements of the *dispositif* articulate with each other. For example, Feldman's 'nonlocal ethnography' entailed locating himself in an office concerned with EU migration management policy not to study its day-to-day organisational culture but to follow the processes by which four policy domains (security, development, employment and human rights) are brought into alignment through various intergovernmental meetings.

Finding a location from which to gain a sympathetic 'insider's' understanding of the actors' policy worlds and to appreciate their beliefs, values and ritualised practices is essential for an anthropologist. But it is equally important not to become inured to their normalities, to maintain sufficient critical distance to be able to keep asking fundamental questions about how they conceptualise their worlds and what this means for theoretical debates. Central to anthropological research is this continual oscillation between insider and outsider perspectives, which makes critical reflexivity possible. Anthropology does not offer a ready-made tool kit of methods that can be picked up and used instrumentally; rather, it is about the acquisition of an ethnographic sensibility, that is, a critical and questioning disposition that treats the familiar as strange and one that generates what we might call the anthropologist's habitus. From this perspective, every experience, encounter, conversation, document or public event provides ethnographic material. As the chapters by Shore, Wedel, Zinn, Feldman, and Wright and Reinhold demonstrate, political speeches, records of parliamentary debates, official reports, newspapers, television and radio broadcasts, websites and blogs, published interviews and autobiographies can all be read as significant cultural texts that shed light on the way policy problems are framed and contested. For all of the authors in this book, choosing sites for participation and 'being there' is important, but for none is this enough. All bring a critical reading to these texts, using insights borne of first-hand experience to question the cultural constructedness of 'common sense' and to continually analyse the taken-for-grantedness of policy processes. Sustaining an awareness of the contingency and the contested and inherently political nature of policies enables anthropologists and interpretive policy analysts to develop a more inclusive and democratic conception of policy.

Policies as Instruments of Governance

In our previous book (Shore and Wright 1997), we used a governmentality approach in order to explore the shift from welfare state to neoliberal regimes of government. This book develops from our previous study in several ways. First, the context in which we write has shifted. *Anthropology of Policy* was written at a point at which neoliberal forms of governance were still in a relatively early phase. Their key features (including competitive outsourcing, privatisation, deregulation, internal markets, output funding, performance indicators and payment-by-results) were in place, but the way they worked together as technologies of governance was only just becoming discernable. Today, those established forms of governance have become more sophisticated and seemingly more contradictory. If neoliberalisation entailed the fragmentation or 'agencification' of the state (Pollitt et al. 2001) and 'governing at a distance' (Rose and Miller 1992), these changes have often worked to increase centralised control. The post-9/11 environment, which has brought about an intensification of policing, anti-terrorism measures and a global obsession with security and risk management, highlights this. While much of this apparatus has been outsourced and subcontracted to private agencies, the overall effect has been to enhance governmental discipline and control. 'Steering' rather than 'rowing' the state (Osborne and Gaebler 1992) involves a new kind of 'biopolitics'; one that entails new ways of controlling populations, managing migrants and governing the conduct of individuals – as the chapters by Feldman, Müller and Però illustrate.

The paradox that the modern state appears to be shrinking yet is ever-more present in people's lives (Trouillot 2001) is evident in policies that promote NPM. As a technique of governance, NPM works by deflecting attention from the system itself onto the individual. It puts the spotlight on the proactive, 'self-managed' worker, the accountable, 'calculative self' and the 'responsibilised citizen'. The political technologies that are designed to produce these subjects remain in the shadows, their operations proving hard to discern. Revealing the mechanisms by which power operates remains a key objective both for anthropologists and critical policy analysts.

Governmentality approaches have been useful in capturing the complex operations of modern forms of state power (Burchell 1991; Rose 1999). Schwegler and Nyquist (this volume) explore how policy elites were able to bring about major pension reforms in Mexico and Sweden, respectively. Both reveal how such major changes to the conception of society – from a Beveridge-style collectivist idea to an individualised one – were cast in technical and politically neutral terms. Several other authors examine events and networks of actors and their political rhetoric in order to discern the deeper structural processes of change with which they are engaged. If, on the surface, terms like 'accountability', 'transparency', 'devolution' and 'empowerment' feature prominently, the chapters by Shore and Wedel in particular reveal cracks in the rhetorical façade behind which lie not only older and cruder power plays, but ones which undermine the core principles of democratic government. Governmentality creates spaces in which populations are classified and managed, sometimes in contexts where it is difficult to identify an author. Conversely, new forms of governance create spaces where particular individuals can appropriate and manipulate the resources of government behind the scenes to more personal political ends. For example, Shore's chapter shows how Tony Blair subverted the norms of parliamentary democracy and cabinet government, and imposed decisions borne of his own personal convictions. Similarly, Wedel's chapter illustrates how adeptly the Neocons in the U.S. moved between public and private roles within the ambiguous spaces of governance, exemplifying another facet of the adaptable and 'flexible self'. These power elites effectively captured the state and, in a manner reminiscent of nineteenth-century imperialists, used its formidable resources to advance private as well as political agendas. Whether it is neoliberalisation that has opened up the space in which these new political elites can operate or whether it is these elites themselves who bring neoliberal reforms into effect remains unclear. Whatever the answer, these studies reveal that there are traditional forms of realpolitik working in tandem with the so-called 'soft power' often associated with neoliberal governance.

Most of the chapters in this volume deal with policy and governance in self-professed democratic systems and all but two (on India and Mexico) deal with policy regimes in Europe and the U.S. This choice of geographical focus is deliberate. Most anthropological texts have conventionally focused attention on Asia, Africa, Latin America or parts of the Third (and Fourth) World, which tends to reinforce the misplaced assumption among policy professionals (including some political scientists) that anthropology has little to contribute to the study of 'advanced' Western societies and institutions. The case studies by Schwegeler, Müller, Randeria and Grunder, Wedel and Shore also illustrate how, in an increasingly interconnected world, policy processes observed in a U.S. or European context can profoundly influence non-Western societies and, indeed, the global order itself. Moreover, the tactics of power and governance identified in this book are not confined to the West either. Even non-democratic regimes in Asia and Africa typically mobilise their populations through state-sanctioned policies that seek to transform the spaces and subjects of governance (Scott 1998; Greenhalgh 2008). As noted earlier, there are many different forms of 'governmentality'.

Engaging with Policy: Actors, Agency and Contestation

A further way in which this book advances on our previous study (Shore and Wright 1997) is to respond to the criticism that governmentality approaches are somehow 'too Foucauldian' and allow too little space for individual agency. This book goes beyond the idea that political subjects are passive 'docile bodies' produced through the micro-physics of disciplinary power. In our previous book, we used Foucault's distinction between subjection and subjectification to propose that external constructions of the subject are not adopted unquestioningly by people in the formation of their own identities. Governments may try to use policy as an instrument to impose their ordering principles upon those they seek to govern, but 'reflexive subjects', to use Giddens's (1991) term, sometimes 'answer back'. Indeed, sceptical subjects tend to question the way they are being constructed, how they relate to institutions and how those institutions should respond to their needs and desires (Clarke et al. 2007: 139, 140). As John Clark et al. illustrate, in Britain, the 'Third Way' ideology of Tony Blair's New Labour government drew on multiple political and economic constructions of the public as 'citizens' and 'consumers'. These different interpellations of the subject as 'citizen-and-consumer' created ambiguous spaces in which individuals were able to engage in complex and creative reflections on the kinds of relationships they wanted to have with public services and the state. One of their informants expressed it like this: 'I know "consumer" and "customer" imply choice and that is what we are supposed to want.' As Clarke et al. (2007: 142) observe, here is 'a person who *hears* the process of subjection … recognizes its political-cultural character, and goes on to offer an alternative account of "what we want": as a "matter of right"'. In short, 'sceptical subjects' are able to:

> reflect upon the dominant discourse, its interpellations and the subject positions it offers. They reason about different sorts of identifications and the relationships they imply. They make choices about what terms evoke their desired personal and political subject positions. They suggest that the practice of scepticism is a popular – rather than academic – commonplace. (Clarke et al. 2007: 142)

Several case studies in this volume accord with Clarke et al.'s thesis concerning the reflexive capacities of political subjects. Hyatt, Però, Zinn and Müller demonstrate how people do understand the way policies seek to interpellate them as subjects and actively contest these constructions to project their own visions of their role in society. However, Kugelberg's study of African women in Sweden indicates that subjects are not always able to engage successfully with a regime of power. Believing they had to form an 'association' in order to access international development funding to support their families back home in Africa, they discovered too late that the Swedish government's policy on 'associations' was designed to support only ethnic minority communities within Sweden. The women's notion of transnationalism was incompatible with the boundaries imposed by Swedish official multiculturalism.

The crucial question is when does a policy lose its authoritative and hegemonic power to define a people or problem? Given that most policies do not provoke public unrest or mass protest, what happens to make a particular policy a focus of concerted opposition? These studies suggest that there are three phases in the process of puncturing the aura of government policy. First, those who are its intended subjects come to realise the processes of subjection involved. Second, they refuse to accept this image of their subject position or take on its norms and priorities as their own. Third, they become aware that their critiques and aspirations are shared, and mobilise to contest it collectively. The first phase, gaining critical purchase on the terms through which one is governed, tends to occur when events destabilise the taken-for-grantedness of established orders. As Burchell (1991: 119) notes, this process is often provoked when governments require people 'to alter how they see themselves as governed subjects'. This is one instance when people may begin to question the prevailing order of things. As Rose (1999: 20) puts it, such instances may introduce an 'awkwardness' into what is normally experienced as 'timeless, natural, unquestionable … interrupting the fluency of the narratives that encode that experience and making them stutter'.

When and why this 'creative stutter' results in individuals coming together for collective action is context-specific. In Però's three-country comparison, different government policies threatened to close the small spaces that immigrants had found for living and working in Bologna, Barcelona and London. The migrants were able to connect to different networks – the church, local politics and trade unions – to mobilise themselves collectively. In Zinn's study of southern Italy, Berlusconi's government expected its plan to site a nuclear waste disposal plant in a sparsely populated area with high unemployment to be uncontroversial. However, local people united en masse against the plan. What made their protest so effective was their success in demonstrating that, contrary to its moral claims of reasoned impartiality, the government's decision had been anything but impartial or in the national interest. The protesters turned the tables on the government's construction of themselves as 'irrational', 'emotional' and 'particularistic', and successfully contested the government's definition of the 'common good'. Zinn's account presents an unusual story of popular revolt: rarely are local actors able both to subvert a dominant policy discourse and recast it in their own terms.

The strategies and tactics involved in acts of resistance are well theorised in Michel de Certeau's *Practice of Everyday Life*. In one of his examples, indigenous Indians were unable to overturn the classifying order imposed on them by the Spanish colonisers, but they nevertheless did subvert it. Through apparent acts of voluntary submission, they 'made of' the laws imposed on them 'something quite different from what their conquerors had in mind' (de Certeau 1984: xiv). In highlighting the fact that very often people cannot overturn the regimes of power that dominate them, de Certeau provides a useful antidote to those inclined to romanticise resistance. As he says of the colonised Indians:

> they subverted the rituals, representations and laws not by rejecting or altering them, but by using them with respect to ends and references foreign to the system they had no choice but to accept. They were *other* within the very colonization that outwardly assimilated them; their use of the dominant social order deflected its power, which they lacked the means to challenge; they escaped it without leaving it. (de Certeau 1984: xiv)

Taking up de Certeau's distinction between 'strategy' and 'tactics', Müller (this volume) explores the dilemma of how NGOs interact with international agencies. NGOs campaigning for farmers' rights and seeking strategic alliances within the FAO walked a tightrope between maintaining a position outside of the FAO to influence its strategy whilst seeking tactical influence and creating alliances inside the organisation without being co-opted. Their tactic rested on a recognition that the FAO is not a monolithic entity and that its staff have different ideological agendas. The NGOs sought to strengthen those elements they agreed with, modify the FAO's biotechnology policy and even create an alternative *dispositif* more consistent with the interests they represented. As this case study shows, policy worlds open up ambiguous spaces in which actors and agents compete for influence. Even if they cannot overturn a particular policy, they use tactics and strategies to make of that policy something quite different from what its authors intended.

Policy Worlds beyond Neoliberalism?

Anthropology's contribution to policy studies goes far beyond its capacity to produce 'thick' ethnographic descriptions. It lies above all in its sensitivity towards the way in which policies work as instruments of governance, and its concern to explore how policies are understood by differently situated actors. Anthropology joins interpretive policy studies in posing the question '*how* does a policy mean?' (Yanow 1996), that is, what do policies mean to different audiences and how are those meanings conveyed? We suggest two further contributions. First, an anthropological approach recognises that policies are not simply instrumental governmental tools – they are actants that have agency and that change as they enter into relations with actors, objects and institutions in new domains. The challenge is to study policies as they develop and as they are enacted in everyday practice. That, in turn, requires a concept of policy very different from that of conventional policy science; to use the terminology of Science and Technology Studies, it calls for an idea of policies as 'assemblages' rather than as discrete 'things'.

Policies are not simply 'transferred', they are reinterpreted as they travel across cultural boundaries. This is rarely a neatly rational or coherent process and the effects are unpredictable, as policies tend to have 'social lives' that outlive their authors. The Beveridge Report, for example, reshaped post-War Britain and made a 'major contribution to world thinking about social security by setting a bold, comprehensive and integrated strategy … which perhaps influenced events more outside than inside Britain' (Abel-Smith 1992: 16).

Second, policy offers a useful diagnostic for understanding how systems of governance come into existence and how they construct subjects as objects of power. If national pension policies epitomised the idea of the social embedded in the Beveridge-style welfare state, Nyquist and Schwegler document the dismantling of that way of thinking and the construction of new pension arrangements based on the figure of the calculating, self-reliant and responsibilised individual. Such policies, which were designed to work through the capacities of self-motivated and free agents, symbolised and effected the transition to systems of neoliberal governmentality, governing 'through freedom', 'at a distance' or sometimes, as Cruikshank's 'dumpster lockup' policy illustrates, with no identifiable source of power.

The question this provokes is what happens next? The regimes of audit and accountability that have accompanied the spread of neoliberalism exhibit many of the tensions described above. These include incompatible managerial demands and expectations. For example, the new 'audited subjects' of schools, hospitals, police and fire services, local governments and universities are expected to meet increasingly unrealistic output targets and performance indicators that are often at odds with their professional self-understandings. Recent developments in management theory that expect individuals' motivations to align with the performance requirements of their institutions may add to these tensions. Institutions and managers must either establish systems that re-orientate their organisation to meet the performance indicators on which funding is calculated (and cease areas of service which no longer officially 'count') or they must encourage cynical reporting that bears scant resemblance to what people actually do in their everyday practice. As Amann (2003) has demonstrated, there is a growing disparity between bureaucratic reporting and actual practice that bears uncanny similarities to that which heralded the collapse of the centralised planning system of the Soviet Union. Whether this will result in new spaces for 'sceptical subjects' to reflect on, contest and unite to propose alternatives to the neoliberal construction of the individual and the social embedded in the concepts and policies of this 'audit society' (Power 1997) remains to be seen.

The 'democratic' notion of policy that we propose in this book, which is very different from the 'authoritative instrumentalism' of conventional approaches, entails opening up and sustaining a space for reflection by critical and reasoning subjects. They may be unequally positioned, but they can still exercise their creativity in shaping the kind of institutions and policy worlds that they would wish to inhabit.

Notes

1. Interpretation in Policy Analysis: Research and Practice', held in Amsterdam, the Netherlands, 31 May–2 June 2007.
2. For example, the 'rationality' model used by Jones, Boushey and Workman (2006: 49) is supposedly based upon the 'scientific analysis of the cognitive architecture of humans', which is allegedly based on an analysis of 'how people actually behave in experimental and observational situations where comprehensive rationality makes precise predictions about outcomes'.
3. 'New management – new identities?', retrieved 25 October 2010 from http://www. dpu.dk/site.aspx?p=5441.

References

Abel-Smith, Brian. 1992. 'The Beveridge Report: Its Origins and Outcomes', *International Social Security Review* 45(1–2): 5–16.
Amann, Ron. 2003. 'A Sovietological View of Modern Britain', *Political Quarterly* 74(4): 468–80.
Appadurai, Arjun. (ed.). 1986. *The Social Life of Things: Commodities in Cultural Perspective*. Cambridge and New York: Cambridge University Press.
BBC. 1998. 'Making Britain Better', 1 July 1998. Retrieved 13 October 2010 from http://news.bbc.co.uk/1/hi/events/nhs_at_50/special_report/119803.stm.
Berger, Peter and Luckman, Thomas. 1966. *The Social Construction of Reality*. London: Penguin.

Berry, Francis S. and William D. Berry. 1999. 'Innovation and Diffusion Models in Policy Research', in Paul Sabatier (ed.), *Theories of the Policy Process*. Boulder, CO: Westview Press.

Beveridge, William. 1942. *Social Insurance and Allied Services (The Beveridge Report)*. Presented to Parliament by Command of His Majesty, November 1942 HMSO: Cmnd 6404. Retrieved 13 October 2010 from http://www.fordham.edu/halsall/mod/1942beveridge.html.

Bourdieu, Pierre. 1977. *Outline of a Theory of Practice*. Cambridge: Cambridge University Press.

Burchell, Graham. 1991. 'Peculiar Interests: Civil Society and Governing "The System of Natural Liberty"', in Graham Burchell, Colin Gordon and Peter Miller (eds), *The Foucault Effect*. Hemel Hempstead: Harvester Wheatsheaf.

Clarke, John, Janet Newman, Nick Smith, Elizabeth Vidler and Louise Westmarland. 2007. *Creating Citizen-Consumers*. London: Sage.

Clay, Edward and Bernard Schaffer (eds). 1984. *Room for Manoeuvre: An Exploration of Public Policy in Agriculture and Rural Development*. London: Heinemann.

Colebatch, Hal K. 2002 [1997]. *Policy*. Buckingham: Open University Press.

Cruikshank, Barbara. 1999. *The Will to Empower: Democratic Citizens and Other Subjects*. Ithaca, NY: Cornell University Press.

Davies, A.E. 1964. *Australian Democracy*, Melbourne: Cheshire.

De Certeau, Michel. 1984. *The Practice of Everyday Life*, trans. S. Rendall. Berkeley and London: University of California Press.

DeLeon, Peter and Christine Martell. 2006. 'The Policy Sciences: Past, Present, and Future', in B. Guy Peters and Jon Pierre (eds), *Handbook of Public Policy*. London and New Delhi: Sage.

Dolowitz, David and David Marsh. 2000. 'Learning from Abroad: The Role of Policy Transfer in Contemporary Policy-Making', *Governance: An International Journal of Policy, Administration, and Institutions* 13(1): 5–24.

Dreyfus, Hubert and Paul Rabinow. 1983. *Michel Foucault: Beyond Structuralism and Hermeneutics*. Chicago: University of Chicago Press.

Elmore, R.F. 1979. 'Backward Mapping: Implementation Research and Policy Decisions', *Political Science Quarterly* 94(4): 601–16.

Evans, Mark and Jonathan Davies. 1999. 'Understanding Policy Transfer: A Multi-level, Multi-disciplinary Perspective', *Public Administration* 77(2): 361–85.

Fairclough, Norman. 1989. *Language and Power*. Harlow: Longman.

———. 2004. 'New Developments in Critical Discourse Analysis', paper given at Ph.D. course, DPU, 29 November–1 December 2004. Copenhagen: Danish School of Education.

Ferguson, James. 2006 [1990]. 'The Anti-Politics Machine', in Aradhana Sharma and Akhil Gupta (eds), *The Anthropology of the State. A Reader*. Oxford: Blackwell.

Fischer, Frank. 2003. *Reframing Public Policy: Discursive Politics and Deliberative Practices*. Oxford: Oxford University Press.

Foucault, Michel. 1980. *Power/Knowledge: Selected Interviews and Other Writings 1972–1977*. Hemel Hempstead: Harvester Wheatsheaf.

Geva-May, Iris. (ed.). 2005. *Thinking Like a Policy Analyst*. New York and Basingstoke: Palgrave Macmillan.

Geertz, Clifford. 1973. *The Interpretation of Cultures*. New York: Basic Books.

———. 1983. *Local Knowledge: Further Essays in Interpretive Anthropology*. New York: Basic Books.

Giddens, Anthony. 1991. *Modernity and Self-Identity. Self and Society in the Late Modern Age*. Cambridge: Polity.

Goodin, Robert E., Martin Rein and Michael Moran. 2006. 'The Public and its Policies', in Michael Moran, Martin Rein and Robert E. Goodin (eds), *The Oxford Handbook of Public Policy*. Oxford: Oxford University Press.

Gottweis, H. 2006. 'Argumentative Policy Analysis', in B. Guy Peters and Jon Pierre (eds), *Handbook of Public Policy*. London and New Delhi: Sage.

Greenhalgh, Susan. 2008. *Just One Child: Science and Policy in Deng's China*. Berkeley: University of California Press.

Gusterson, Hugh. 2005. 'Anthropology and Public Policy' IGAPP Panel on Reconceptualising the Field, *American Anthropologists Association, Chicago, December 2005*.

James, Oliver and Martin Lodge. 2003. 'The Limitations of "Policy Transfer" and "Lesson Drawing" for Public Policy Research', *Political Studies Review* 1: 179–93.

Jones, Bryan, Graeme Boushey and Samuel Workman. 2006. 'Behavioural Rationality and the Policy Process: Toward a New Model of Organizational Information Processing', in B. Guy Peters and Jon Pierre (eds), *Handbook of Public Policy*. London and New Delhi: Sage.

Kirsch, Stuart. 2006. *Reverse Anthropology: Indigenous Analysis of Social and Environmental Relations in New Guinea*. Stanford, CA: Stanford University Press.

Klein, Rudolf and Theodor Marmor. 2006. 'Reflections on Policy Analysis: Putting it Together Again', in Michael Moran, Martin Rein and Robert E. Goodin (eds), *The Oxford Handbook of Public Policy*. Oxford: Oxford University Press.

Larner, Wendy and Richard Le Heron. 2005. 'Neo-liberalizing Spaces and Subjectivities: Reinventing New Zealand Universities', *Organization* 12(6): 843–62.

Latour, Bruno. 1996. *Aramis or the Love of Technology*, trans. Catherine Porter. Cambridge, MA: Harvard University Press.

Lipsky, Michael. 1979. *Street-Level Bureaucracy*. New York: Russell Sage.

Majone, Giandomenico. 1989. *Evidence, Argument and Persuasion in the Policy Process*. New Haven, CT: Yale University Press.

Malinowski, Bronislaw. 1926. *Myth in Primitive Psychology*. London: Kegan Paul.

Marcus, George. 1995. 'Ethnography in/of the World System: The Emergence of Multi-Sited Ethnography', *Annual Review of Anthropology* 24: 95–117.

Martin, Emily. 1997. 'Managing Americans: Policy and Changes in the Meanings of Work and the Self', in Cris Shore and Susan Wright (eds), *Anthropology of Policy. Critical Perspectives on Governance and Power*. London: Routledge.

Moran, Michael, Martin Rein and Robert E. Goodin (eds). 2006. *The Oxford Handbook of Public Policy*. Oxford: Oxford University Press.

Noordegraaf, Mirko. 2000. 'Professional Sense-Makers: Managerial Competencies Amidst Ambiguity', *The International Journal of Public Sector Management* 13(4): 219–332.

Osborne, David and Ted Gaebler. 1992. *Reinventing Government: How the Entrepreneurial Spirit is Transforming the Public Sector*. New York: Plume.

Page, Edward. 2006. 'The Origins of Policy', in Michael Moran, Martin Rein and Robert E. Goodin (eds), *The Oxford Handbook of Public Policy*. Oxford: Oxford University Press.

Peters, B. Guy and Jon Pierre. 2006. 'Introduction', in B. Guy Peters and Jon Pierre (eds), *Handbook of Public Policy*. London and New Delhi: Sage.

Pollitt, Christopher, Karen Bathgate, Janice Caulfield, Amanda Smullen and Colin Talbot. 2001. 'Agency Fever? Analysis of an International Policy Fashion', *Journal of Comparative Policy Analysis: Research and Practice* 3: 271–90.

Power, Michael. 1997. *The Audit Society. Rituals of Verification.* Oxford: Oxford University Press.

Reinhold, Susan. 1994. 'Local Conflict and Ideological Struggle: "Positive Images" and Section 28', Ph.D. thesis. Brighton: University of Sussex.

Rhodes, R.A.W. and David Marsh. 1992. 'New Directions in the Study of Policy Networks', *European Journal of Political Research* 21(1–2): 181–205.

Rizvi, Fazal. 2004. 'Theorizing the Global Convergence of Educational Restructuring', in S. Lindblad and T. Popkewitz (eds), *Educational Restructuring. International Perspectives on Traveling Policies.* Greenwich, CT: Information Age Publishing.

Rose, Nikolas. 1989. *Governing the Soul. The Shaping of the Private Self.* London: Free Association Books.

———. 1999. *Powers of Freedom. Reframing Political Thought.* Cambridge: Cambridge University Press.

Rose, N. and P. Miller. 1992. 'Political Power Beyond the State: Problematics of Government', *British Journal of Sociology* 43(2): 173–205.

Rumsey, A. and J.F. Weiner. 2001. *Mining and Indigenous Lifeworlds in Australia and Papua New Guinea.* Adelaide: Crawford House Publishing.

Scott, James C. 1998. *Seeing like a State: How Certain Schemes to Improve the Human Condition Have Failed.* New Haven, CT: Yale University Press.

Shore, Cris and Susan Wright (eds). 1997. *Anthropology of Policy. Critical Perspectives on Governance and Power.* EASA Series, London: Routledge.

Shore, Cris and Wright, Susan 1999. 'Audit Culture and Anthropology: Neo-Liberalism in British Higher Education', *Journal of the Royal Anthropological Institute,* 5, (4): 557-75.

Shore, Cris and Susan Wright. 2000. 'Coercive Accountability: The Rise of Audit Culture in Higher Education', in Marilyn Strathern (ed.), *Audit Cultures. Anthropological Studies in Accountability, Ethics and the Academy.* EASA Series, London: Routledge.

Smith, Dorothy. 2005. *Institutional Ethnography. A Sociology for People.* New York: Altamira Press.

Stone, Diane. 2004. 'Transfer Agents and Global Networks in the "Transnationalization" of Policy', *Journal of European Public Policy* 11(3): 545–66.

Strathern, Marilyn. 1992. 'Ubiquities', *Annals of Scholarship* 9: 199–208.

———. (ed.). 2000. *Audit Cultures. Anthropological Studies in Accountability, Ethics and the Academy.* EASA Series, London: Routledge.

Taylor, Sandra, Miriam Henry, Bob Lingard and Fazal Rizvi. 1997. *Educational Policy and the Politics of Change.* London: Routledge.

Trouillot, M.R. 2001. 'The Anthropology of the State in the Age of Globalization', *Current Anthropology* 1(1): 125–38.

Turner, Victor. 1967. *The Forest of Symbols: Aspects of Ndembu Ritual.* London: Cornell University Press.

Vike, Halvard. 1997. 'Reform and Resistance: A Norwegian Illustration', in Cris Shore and Susan Wright (eds), *Anthropology of Policy. Critical Perspectives on Governance and Power.* EASA Series, London: Routledge.

Wedel, Janine, Cris Shore, Gregory Feldman and Stacy Lathrop. 2005. 'Towards an Anthropology of Public Policy', *Annals of the American Academy of Political and Social Sciences* 600: 30–51.

Woolfson, Charles. 2007. 'Labour Standards and Migration in the New Europe: Post-Communist Legacies and Perspectives', *European Journal of Industrial Relations* 13(2): 199–218.

Yanow, Dvora. 1996. *How Does Policy Mean? Interpreting Policy and Organisational Actions*. Washington DC: Georgetown University Press.

Yanow, Dvora. 2000. *Conducting Interpretive Policy Analysis*. Thousand Oaks, CA and London: Sage.

Yanow, Dvora and Peregrine Schwartz-Shea, (eds). 2006. *Interpretation and Method: Empirical Research Methods and the Interpretive Turn*. Armonk, NY: M.E. Sharpe.

SECTION I

STUDYING POLICY: METHODS, PARADIGMS, PERSPECTIVES

Introduction

Susan Wright

One problem faced by modern anthropology is to develop research strategies for investigating how the small details of social change that are observable in particular locations connect to wider processes of social, economic and political transformation. Some, following Gluckman and the Manchester School (Evens and Handelman 2006), say that this has always been a focal research issue; others trace it to the postcolonial crisis of community studies (Newby and Bell 1972). While it is still essential to engage in the ethnographic particularities and contingencies of 'what is going on' in specific places, that is not the end of the story. The challenge is to find ways of studying *through* the specificities of particular sites and their relationship to events in other sites to grasp large-scale processes of change and track the emergence of new systems of governing and formations of power. This calls for new ways of conceptualising and designing research – new strategies for knowledge or methodologies. The five chapters in this section all address this issue.

A major reason for focusing on policy is because it articulates social processes which span many locations. This provokes a re-examination of some taken-for-granted aspects of anthropological research, starting with the concept of 'field' itself, which refers both to the issue under study and the research location. In our chapters, such research issues include how policy professionals organise the ideas through which they operate (Feldman on migration management in the EU; Mosse on international development in India) and what impacts derive from reframing the state and its public services around ideas of 'the enemy within' (Wright and Reinhold on anti-gay legislation in the U.K.), the paying customer (Nielsen on fee-paying students in Denmark) or community development based on individuals' own assets

(Hyatt on the security state in the USA). When considering the locations relevant to a particular policy, the field can be very extensive, from everyday activities, through local institutions, to national and international agencies and governing bodies. Even if a field is delineated carefully at the start of a study, it is unlikely to be a static map. As the study progresses, the field can expand or contract as some institutions that were expected to be relevant to the issue become less so, and others assume an unexpectedly important role in events.

As noted in our introduction, 'field' and 'site' can no longer be treated as coterminous. If the field is the full range of people, activities and institutions potentially relevant for the study of the chosen issue, one of the arts of fieldwork is to choose sites within this field and design methods for their ethnographic study so that they shed light on the operations of political processes and their change over time. The anthropologists in this book have made strategic decisions about where to position themselves within their field. Each has considered how their chosen site(s) open a window onto the process of change with which they are concerned. Some, like Mosse, focused on how development professionals operate, and to do so, he studied their work both in the World Bank and in a site in India. Others follow a policy across different sites within a field. For example, Wright and Reinhold's chapter follows a conflict as it ranged back and forth between various local groups, a local authority, local and national media, national political groups and the Houses of Parliament. Feldman, in his study of the emergence of EU migration policy, makes a specific call for 'nonlocal ethnography'. His issue was the creation of an apparatus (in Foucault's terms, a *dispositif*) for conceptualising the EU's multifarious migrants as a population and object of regulation. His strategy was to choose an agency in which to locate himself, not to generate place-bound descriptions of the officials' daily work, but to catch a glimpse of the process of aligning the hitherto separate policy domains of security, employment, human rights and international development. From his vantage point in one agency, and using classic attributes of participant observation, he analyses how, without a central author or coordinating agency, a 'shared optic' began to inform a plethora of 'bits and pieces' of policy making in multiple locations – in political speeches, the creation of documents, the design of information systems, and mechanisms for inter-agency collaboration. The only way officials could represent this emerging 'anonymous constellation of control' to themselves was through a teddy bear mascot that they passed with great ceremony from one office to another. Feldman's 'nonlocal ethnography' captures the processes through which an apparatus emerges from the 'spaces in between' agencies and which is so difficult to grasp even for those intimately involved.

Our authors' research strategies also involve an expanded notion of what constitutes data. At the core is usually some form of participant observation or intensive interviewing, through which the anthropologist becomes aware of the active concerns, everyday concepts and political understanding of at least some of the sets of people involved in the issue under study.

The insights acquired from such day-to-day interaction then equip the anthropologist with the 'fieldwork eyes' (and ears) to scrutinise a wide range of materials emanating from other locations in the field. These can include documents from international agencies, governments and non-governmental organisations (NGOs), television, radio, newspaper articles, reports of meetings and verbatim records of parliamentary debates. Such sources are not just background material; they are analysed, alongside all other 'field' data, for key concepts, embedded assumptions and nuances of meaning, as well as for social, economic and political relationships, organisational dynamics and the operations of power.

One feature of anthropological research generally is that a research 'problem' often only emerges late on in the study. Even if the issue is clear at the start and the chosen site(s) provide a good vantage point to describe what is going on in the field, it is only when the existing empirical and theoretical literature about the issue fails to provide explanations for what is happening empirically that the anthropologist finds the 'problem' on which to focus the rest of the fieldwork and analysis. For example, Wright and Reinhold's chapter is based on a study that traced moment by moment through two years of political conflict how an attempt to 'promote' positive images of gay people in schools was turned into legislation against 'promoting' 'pretended family relations'. But why? What was at stake? This 'problem' prompted Reinhold to develop a strategy for 'studying through': she connected detailed utterances to five historical discourses about homosexuality and showed how, in a sequence of events across sites and over time, these historical discourses were reformulated to project a narrow definition of the 'normal family' and decry alternatives as subversive of the nation. She revealed the unpredictable but understandable process of political and ideological transformation under Thatcherism, which few grasped at the time.

'Transformation' is an analytical concept central to several other authors' strategies to connect small details to larger processes of change. If Feldman analyses the emergence of a discourse as part of a wider apparatus, or *dispositif*, for governing a population, Hyatt, in studying changes in the ways in which 'the poor' have been conceptualised and managed in the USA, traces the transformation from one *dispositif* to another – from Keynesianism to neoliberalism and then to an emerging security state. She argues (*pace* Sassen 2006) that history is not a unilinear shift from one form of the state to another; nor does any state formation emerge fully clothed and complete. Rather, new 'isms' wear and adapt some of the clothes of older ones. She focuses on the transmogrification of the 'figure' of the Welfare Queen to identify the emerging organising logic at the heart of a new formation and to see how it displaces the primacy of older logics. Used to dismantle welfare 'dependency' in the 1970s, this figure is reworked in the 2000s to argue that, however 'deficient', she contained all the capacities needed to make a success of her life. Hyatt asks how such an organising logic manifests itself in encounters between actual individuals and bureaucracies to produce effects on the ground. Her example of 'assets-based development' shows how people caring for young, sick or elderly families in poverty are to focus on developing their own individual fortitude and resiliency. In the security state, 'community' becomes a territory for patrolling and pacification, not for identification of systematic disadvantage and mobilisation for structural change, just as 'the state' becomes discredited as a source of redress for hardship. Hyatt reveals the micro-processes of transformation, showing how a new organising logic emerges by reworking some of the tropes of neoliberalism, while others recede.

Nielsen draws on Latour's (2005) ideas of transformation to consider how policy itself is conceptualised and deployed. The policy makers in her study shared the assumption (often made in the literature on governmentality) that policy conveys a rationality of governing which is converted into technologies of government, which then reframes the subjectivities of the target population. She questions this three-step progression – 'rationality-technology-subjectivity'. Both those who see policy as something 'implemented' and those who give subjects more agency and the ability to 'appropriate' policy treat policy as a thing with a sufficiently objectified and stable existence to travel through space and time. Her study of the actors involved in a conflict over the introduction of university fees for foreign students in Denmark found nothing to hold stable. Each incident involved a new constellation of interacting elements – fees, evaluations, meetings and written complaints, keywords and discourses, feelings and experiences – in which the meaning of each was informed by its relation to the others. Using Latour's notion of assemblage, Nielsen argues that what was assembled was not predetermined parts, but elements co-produced through their relations to each other in each incident. From this perspective, people were not just reacting to policy as an objectified, external force entering into a pre-existing context. Nor were the students' subjectivities just formed by implementation of the policy or technology of fee charging. Policy, in these terms, is a continually emerging effect of elements that are assembled and re-assembled in successive incidents. Each moment is a 'translation' where some similarities persist but differences also emerge. As in Feldman and Hyatt's studies, subjectivity and agency emerge from the 'in betweens' or relationships between elements in assemblages.

Between them, these chapters provide material for thinking about how to frame the key elements of any anthropological research strategy – the issue, the field, sites, what counts as data, the problem, the analytical concepts – and not least the implications of different ways of conceptualising policy itself. They show that a policy perspective offers a particular methodological tool for focusing on connections between actors, agents, discourses and sites and for exploring how small details of everyday life are part of larger processes of social and political transformation. Many other chapters in this book can also be read for methodological insights, just as the case studies in these chapters also contribute to the debates in the two later sections about changing forms of governance and the construction and contestation of policy subjects.

References

Evens, T.M.S. and Don Handelman (eds). 2006. *The Manchester School. Practice and Ethnographic Praxis in Anthropology*. Oxford: Berghahn Books.

Latour, Bruno. 2005. *Reassembling the Social. An Introduction to Actor-Network Theory*. Oxford: Oxford University Press.

Newby, Howard and Colin Bell (eds). 1972. *Community Studies*. New York: Praeger.

Sassen, Saskia. 2006. *Territory, Authority, Rights*. Princeton: Princeton University Press.

Chapter 2

Illuminating the Apparatus: Steps toward a Nonlocal Ethnography of Global Governance

Gregory Feldman

Studying the Apparatus

This chapter offers a methodological strategy for studying amorphous and decentralised policy regimes that function to regulate large populations. It approaches this task through Foucault's concept of the apparatus (*dispositif*), which Rabinow (2003: 50–51) explains as a device of population control and economic management composed of disparate elements that coalesce in particular historical conjunctures, usually moments identified as 'crises'. Its various technologies work by 'first specifying (and to that extent creating) those targets [i.e. populations] and then controlling (distributing and regulating) them' (2003: 50–51). Crucially, its elements are 'resolutely heterogeneous', incorporating 'discourses, institutions, architectural arrangements, policy decisions, laws, administrative measures, scientific statements, moral and philosophic propositions' (Foucault, cited in Rabinow 2003: 51).

The apparatus itself is a crucial object of ethnographic study in a globalised world, given its role in converting masses of people into quantifiable and manageable objects. However, it makes participant-observation rather difficult as it reaches through many disparate policy domains and locations. Indeed, when viewed through the lens of Foucault's dual notion of biopower – that is, both the disciplining of the individual and the regulation of the population – one can understand why anthropologists have shied away from studying such a social construction. As Greenhalgh (2003: 210) argues, anthropologists overwhelmingly focus on the disciplining of the individual while the other side of biopower, the regulation of the population, 'has languished in disciplinary obscurity'. The latter does not lend itself to participant-observation, in contrast to disciplining the individual, which involves more localised social processes.

European Union (EU) efforts to harmonise migration management exemplify an apparatus at work due to its amorphous character and the interweaving of different policy domains such as security policy, labour policy and demographic policy. The apparatus exemplifies the well-known challenge to ethnography in a global world: how to account for empirical processes that cannot be fully apprehended through participant-observation (Feldman 2008: 315–18; Shore 2006). Indeed, Jean and John Comaroff (2003: 154–5) argue that anthropology's response to globalisation and the power regimes it engenders 'has been conservative' and dogged by a 'hidebound empiricism'. Trouillot (2001: 135), likewise, cautions that reducing 'the object of study to the object of observation … reduces matters of methodology to matters of research techniques and mistakenly assumes all empirical studies to be necessarily empiricist in one form or another'. To avoid this pitfall, we should construct an anthropological methodology that equally includes participant-observation along with other research methods, lest we neglect what cannot be educed in the ethnographic moment per se. While this point is not new, more discussion is needed on what such a methodology would actually look like (cf. Gupta and Ferguson 1997).

This chapter introduces 'nonlocal ethnography' as a methodology that can highlight an apparatus and explain its historical emergence even if it evades the participant-observer. However, nonlocal ethnography does not dismiss participant-observation; rather, it shifts the primary object of study from location-specific practices to discourses that enable, organise and effectively integrate so many disparate policy practices beyond the locality. 'Nonlocal' thus describes discourses that are present in multiple locations but are not of any particular location. The challenge of nonlocal ethnography is not simply the logistical one of connecting ethnographic dots separated in space-time that compose a regime of population regulation; rather, it is to uncover how discourses give an emerging regime its shape and direction, i.e. that which gives the dots a particular configuration. To do so, nonlocal ethnography must retain two particular advantages of participant-observation tailored to location-specific fieldwork, but use them in a methodology that is not fixed too tightly to deep immersion in few places. Those advantages are displacement – or the alternative insights the ethnographer gains through removal from familiar cultural logics – and contingency – or the importance of particular, situated events in altering or sustaining the status quo. Nonlocal ethnography thus recognises the equal validity of any particular method that delivers those two advantages. It does not seek representations of daily practice per se, which participant-observation uniquely provides, but rather the decoding of a historically particular apparatus.

This chapter's next section shows how actors fuse together disparate policy domains into a broader *problematique* with the example of a speech given at the European Parliament. It then presents policy practices occurring at an important migration policy site in Geneva, Switzerland. These practices show one venue in which policy officials from different European and

North African nation-states discuss a common approach to 'regularising' illegal migration flows northward across the Mediterranean Sea. The section examines what participant-observation does and does not reveal about the larger apparatus at work. The third section sketches out how disparate migration policy domains nevertheless fit together in Europe in a piecemeal fashion, thereby forming a decentralised regime of migration management. It specifically shows how discourses of security and economy connect the work of the European Commission (EC), the EU and the Organization for Security and Cooperation in Europe (OSCE) to such issues as border management, biometric data, labour migration and demography. The chapter's fourth and final section takes initials steps towards formulating nonlocal ethnography as a methodology that can illuminate the apparatus. It offers a deeper construal of displacement and contingency as ethnographic cornerstones so as to retain the comparative advantage of participant-observation as a method without reducing the methodology to place-bound descriptions.

Weaving Policy Domains Together

A speech by Graham Watson, MEP and group leader for the Alliance of Liberals and Democrats for Europe (ALDE), illustrates how different policy domains get fused into Europe's migration 'problem'. Though clearly speaking from a liberal standpoint, he hits the key themes that compose the broader debate such as security, humanitarianism and development. The fusion does not indicate that a unified bureaucracy or singular policy exists (or will exist), but rather a shared optic for identifying migration problems that works across policy domains.

From the floor of the European Parliament in Strasbourg, Watson gravely recalled the 2007 case of Tunisian fishermen arrested for human smuggling when, in fact, they had rescued drowning migrants from the Mediterranean Sea as required by international maritime law. Watson (2007) began the speech by asking: 'Mr President, what could better illustrate the need for a common European immigration policy than the case of the Tunisian fishermen?' He then explained that 'Everything about that tragic event – from the migrants on a rubber boat on the high seas, to the people smugglers who put them there and the authorities who jailed their rescuers – is testament to the failure of Europe's approach to migration.' Pumping a clenched fist in the air, Watson continued:

> With every human tragedy, during a desperate do-nothing decade, Liberals and Democrats have asked one simple question: how many people must perish before governments see that lifting the drawbridge of Fortress Europe serves nobody's interests? Managing migration is as much in our interests as in the interests of those seeking our shores or prepared to die trying. While populism has propelled a policy forged in the furnace of fear, let us face the facts.

Seeking to globalise the migration problem, he framed the EC as Eurocentric: 'Let us make no mistake: the Commission's cozy calculation that we can take the best and leave the rest will not work. Pushed by poverty, hunger, squalor and war, people will keep crossing the Mediterranean whether they fit our criteria or not. Why? Because our agricultural and fisheries policies are out-pricing their products and raiding their natural resources.' Watson also appealed for continuing support to Frontex (the EU border control agency), which conservatives value more highly than liberals. With shrugged shoulders he conceded that: 'Of course we must patrol Europe's borders. The Moreno Sánchez report is right to demand that Frontex be given the budget, the staff and the equipment needed to do its job ... Longer term, however, only a comprehensive EU policy that punishes the people smugglers, provides legal routes in and creates hope where there is despair can counter prevailing trends.'

Watson highlighted many key themes driving the migration management issue and condensed them into a single speech: protecting people who risk their lives trying to enter Europe (humanitarianism); economic opportunities for self-enhancement for Europe and the migrants (liberalism); tighter border control to prevent illegal entries (security); fighting human smuggling networks (legality); and Europe's responsibilities to the south (development). Politicians, policy makers, business leaders and various sectors of the general public might disagree as to which themes should carry how much weight. Nevertheless, to fit them snugly into a single speech at the European Parliament requires the fusion of separate policy domains into a common problem. The sense of crisis surrounding the issue facilitates this fusion, which is integral to the formation of an apparatus.

The following sections show how these themes are acted upon and how these actions normalise a framework to understand the migration 'problem' and to construct the 'migrant' as an object of regulation. Again, the question here is not how migrants react to the policies that target them, but rather how policy processes enable the apparatus that identifies and regulates them.

The Daily Grind and Security as an Organising Metaphor

The work of the Mediterranean Managed Migration Project (3MP) illustrates how a framework of understanding emerges to both define and solve migration as a policy problem. The 3MP is collectively managed by the European Migration Policy Organization (EMPO), Europol (the EU's criminal law enforcement agency) and Frontex (the EU border control agency). This project reveals the organising role of security discourse in the daily work of EMPO staff, which acts as the secretariat for the project. However, the social significance of policy makers' daily routines is not found in their own mundane practices *per se*, which largely amount to drafting documents at computer terminals, communicating through email and attending meetings. Rather, it lay in their representation in policy texts of the migration situation 'on the ground', which reinforces a standard framework of understanding for policy purposes. Ethnography in this context reveals how EMPO staff 'see' migration as professionals more than what they 'do'. The operative question is how such representations function. It involves learning how notions of 'public order' delimit the range of acceptable interpretations of social reality as a particular policy problem: e.g. what is the risk posed by the EU's ageing workforce; what is threatening about uncontrolled migration; and what are the causes of illegal migratory flows? These representations, in turn, delimit the range of acceptable policy options for such questions as, who is allowed to enter a country and on what conditions; what measures should be deployed to thwart illegal migratory flows; and how can the migrant's potential be channelled into productive economic activity.

The 3MP develops non-binding common migration management guidelines between officials from participating North African countries or Arab partner states, and from participating European countries or European partner states. Fieldwork among the project's participants reveals the standardisation of policy practices among different actors as well as the project's aims and scope. The 3MP began as a trust-building exercise in 2002 among the two sets of partner states to help identify common priorities for migration management. One European 3MP official explained:

> You need to show you are reliable, that you are listening to their concerns ... With Arabs, they need to know where you are from. The personal side is important. They need to trust you. EMPO was not known in the Mediterranean. Communication is now set.

Nevertheless, the Arab partner states were concerned with equality as much as trust. Their list of areas of cooperation included in the conclusion of a May 2004 meeting began by asserting that:

> The suffering of the countries on the southern and eastern shores of the Mediterranean from the illegal migration as transit countries and as countries of temporary illegal residence represents the same suffering as that of the European States as countries of destination.

The two priorities that emerged in the project's early stages were the strengthening of measures to fight illegal migration and longer term efforts to tackle the migration problem at its roots through economic development. To the chagrin of Arab partner states (APS) delegates, the project would end up privileging matters of security and legality over development. Animosity filled early meetings, with APS charges of colonialism against the European partner states (EPS). One APS official was rumoured to have been demoted for baldly asserting at a 2007 meeting that: 'The position of European countries is to forget why people migrate: economic ... It is a form of colonialism and looting of Africa's richness.' Other APS delegates argued that: 'We are simply solving Europe's migration problem for them.' Nevertheless, a retired, veteran official for the United Nations High Commission for Refugees from

Lebanon played an instrumental role in convincing many APS delegates to stick with the project and to make their contributions where they could. From that point on, APS officials began bringing initiatives for cooperation to the meetings. EPS delegates described these particular officials as 'pragmatic'. The project could now focus on its four priority areas: reception and detention; return and readmission; anti-trafficking and anti-smuggling; and border management. In short, a potentially undermining position fell away, allowing the 3MP to continue on common (but not necessarily equal) security-conscious ground.

The EMPO secretariat's main priority is harmonising the preferences and priorities of participating states as these pertain to the 3MP's four priority areas. This involves much electronic communication with representatives in roughly twenty-seven participating states in the project. The 3MP staff, in consultation with their Frontex and Europol liaisons, devise discussion points and guiding questions to format the project's two- or three-day meetings. The Project Officer handles the laborious task of assembling the varied input from participating states into written form. The Program Manager strategises with the liaisons on how to create converging positions between the APS and EPS. An ordinary working day stretches from 9:00 A.M. to 6:30 P.M. Several staff talked of staying until 10:00 P.M. during peak times, while a few even worked past the midnight hour.

The EMPO staff's work routines are not the stuff of exciting or exotic ethnography: revise this draft of a concluding statement; contact that official to clarify his comment on 'x'; see what direction a more senior staff member wants to take a particular item of discussion, etc. Much of this occurs in front of a computer terminal. Yet the written word is vital in defining migration issues so as to require certain forms of inter-state cooperation. For example, the questions for one EMPO meeting were: 'What national, regional and/or international legislations best address smuggling and trafficking and in which way?'; 'Have previous investigation [sic] failed or yielded fewer results because of the lack of joint initiatives?'; 'How did your country learn from these failures?'; 'How do you efficiently organize different migrant groups into different centres?'; 'How would you describe the efficiency of "minimum standards" in the actual "on the ground" management of detention centres?'; or 'How do you implement social care for vulnerable groups in (a) reception centres and (b) detention centres?' While described by participants at the meeting as simply technical questions (i.e. non-political), they limit the range of discussion and standardise the type of knowledge produced.

The 3MP meetings, each dedicated to one of the four priority areas, offer more for ethnographic purchase. Their locations rotate according to the conference theme, for example, the meeting on combating human trafficking and smuggling took place at the Europol Headquarters in The Hague. Each meeting is co-chaired by delegates from one EPS and one APS. The hosts and the co-chairs give routinised introductory statements. The co-chairs routinely thank the hosts 'for making it possible for bringing us together here in ... [insert city name]'. Particular sessions feature a pre-selected delegate to give a presentation on how his/her own government deals with, for example, the reception and detention of illegal immigrants. The subsequent discussion period occasionally drew questions from other delegates interested in the comparison with their own government's practices. Hosts, chairs and delegates thank each other for stimulating interventions.

At each meeting, the 3MP Program Manager, a rising policy star with a postgraduate education in law and business crime, presents the secure website featuring the Interactive Map (or IMAP). With Africa and Europe shaded in subdued green tones, the map visually shows the known land, sea, and air routes of illegal migration from West, East and North Africa and the Middle East to Europe. The restricted version of the IMAP also functions as a clearing house on particular modes of immigrant transport, on the smuggling and trafficking networks, and on the migration-related laws and policies of the countries involved. Officials from authorised states and international organisations can access the most up-to-date information on migration flows from Africa to the EU. The Program Manager explained that: 'If countries use the IMAP for policy positions, then this helps create agreements between countries. It will probably bring the positions of the countries much closer.' Indeed, establishing a common frame for policy discussions – for the IMAP or other policy questions – achieves convergence and possibly standardisation.

During the 3MP meetings, EMPO's Project Officer (a Ph.D. in social science) endures at least two gruelling days of taking notes and preparing the concluding statement for the meeting's draft concluding statement. Much of this work occurs in the dead of night. I arrived one morning for breakfast at the meeting hotel at 6:30 A.M. only to find the Project Officer exiting the dining room to catch two hours of sleep before things began. At the intense last session, the co-chairs proceed through the typically three-page draft one line at a time while the delegates announce their suggestions for alternative phrasing. The Project Officer inputs many of the changes on the spot: one delegate requests the deletion of the word 'official' as an adjective describing the meeting's summary points; two others debate whether 'informal' should used to describe the project; another delegate requests that 'fighting human trafficking' be included. The point of this session is to produce a set of conclusions that officials from some thirty Arab and European governments find mutually agreeable.

At the end of the meeting, the current hosts handed over a brown teddy bear wearing a Europol T-shirt to the hosts of the next meeting. The Europol liaison explained to the new delegates that ever since an April 2006 meeting, the teddy bear has been kept by the delegates preparing for the next meeting and passed on again when that meeting finishes. The host and co-chairs of the next meeting will likely announce that they are 'looking forward to working with our partners from [enter country name] and to having a productive meeting'. The next several weeks will find the EMPO team busily finalising the meeting's conclusions, then emailing or faxing them back to the participating states for approval. The delegates are likely to have to show them to their superiors, each inundated with a myriad of tasks, so the process goes slowly. To solicit further feedback, the team has also created a secure website on which it posts questionnaires about the meetings' substantive discussions, technical format and logistical arrangements. The meeting's final recommendations are translated into English, French and Arabic. After all, as an informal project, there is still no legal requirement to adopt the migration management guidelines that all partners approved.

The rituals of these informal meetings ossify into a set communication pattern. The numerous discussions, the production of draft guidelines and the subsequent meetings replete with their routinised opening and closing statements have the effect of framing key migration issues. A reduced vocabulary and a stock-in-trade phraseology of 'problem' and 'solution' normalises power-knowledge practices commanded by an array of technocrats from governments and international organisations. Immersion in the office routine teaches the ethnographer how migration policy discourse is reproduced, a discourse that is heavily invested with notions of security and legality. Nevertheless, there is much that these meetings do not show about the emerging migration apparatus to which the 3MP is linked inextricably, even if informally. Its meetings are only possible and intelligible in relation to an array of other policy processes, all of which work through similar discourses of security and economy and galvanise around the identification of crisis.

The 'Anonymous Constellation of Control'

EU Member States and affiliated organisations construct the migration management apparatus in bits and pieces, sometimes through EC channels, other times bilaterally or multilaterally among themselves, and also through numerous initiatives led by other international organisations such as EMPO. The fusion of diverse policy domains and issues illustrated in the chapter so far are prerequisites for aligning a plethora of policy responses and actions, all of which constitute a regime of population regulation. The policy measures described below reflect a common concern with the 'threat' of 'illegal' flows (goods as well as people) and with the need to expedite 'legal' labour circulation. A major policy response to the tension between legal and illegal migration flows is to 'regularise' them, which involves the increased use of biometric data to monitor the population. The use of methods other than participant-observation illuminates crucial aspects of the EU's emerging migration management regime that are vital to contemporary modes of population regulation.

The emergence of a common approach to migration management in Europe is tightly linked to the liberalisation of the EU market including the free movement of goods, capital, services and labour across the EU's national borders. The 1985 Schengen Agreement created a visa-free zone among signatory states to facilitate cross-border flows of peoples and goods.[1] From the start, policy and public discussions were filled with worries that the relaxation of internal borders would encourage the circulation of unwanted commodities and illegal migrants along with the commodities they did desire (including labour). It thus seemed prudent for Schengen-area countries collectively to strengthen their common external border and airport entry points. Along with the spectre of uncontrolled migration, the high number of refugees from the Yugoslavian wars and the fear of labour immigration from eastern Europe gave political currency to neo-nationalist arguments that migration constituted a 'threat'.

Within this trajectory, the EC has laid out comprehensive plans to do nothing less than transform the EU's territorial space into an 'Area of Freedom, Justice, and Security' (European Commission 2004). It effectively raised the migration issue to the level of a security problem requiring careful management. EU leaders met in Tampere, Finland in 1999 to establish a framework for crafting a common immigration and asylum policy. The framework addressed the prevention of cross-border flows of illegal goods and persons, and the strengthening of police and judicial cooperation to combat international terrorist and criminal networks. The elements of a common immigration policy were spelled out in a five-year plan called the Tampere Programme (1999–2004). These included, in the EC's own terms, 'a comprehensive approach to the management of migratory flows'; 'fair treatment for third country nationals, partnerships with countries of [immigrant] origin'; and 'a common policy for asylum' (European Commission 2005a). More specific measures called on Member States to take into account the EU's economic and demographic situation, its capacity to manage immigrant reception, immigrants' historical and cultural links with countries of origin, the problem of brain drain and the need for specific integration policies. The Tampere Programme successfully enshrined these objectives in pan-European policy debates and developments.

The next EU policy step blended both internal and external security measures (i.e. policing and border patrolling respectively) into a single comprehensive programme for migration management. Invoking the notion of 'crisis' in the form of terrorist attacks in the United States on 11 September 2001 and in Madrid on 11 March 2004, the European Council argued that 'the security of the European Union and its Member States [had] acquired new urgency' (Council of the European Union 2004: 3). The EC and the European Council finalised the Hague Programme to advance and further specify the goals of the Tampere Programme. It emphasised cooperation on fighting and preventing illegal migration, human trafficking and smuggling, terrorism and organised crime. Its five-year action plan (2004–9) specified ten priorities built around these issues for 'a partnership for European renewal' (European Commission 2005b). These ten points convey the Tampere Programme's broad scope and bold ambition: 1) fundamental rights and citizenship; 2) fighting terrorism; 3) migration management; 4) internal borders, external borders and visas; 5) a common asylum area; 6) maximising the positive impact of migration; 7) privacy and security in information sharing; 8) fighting organised crime; 9) guaranteeing an effective European area of justice for all; and 10) sharing of responsibilities for these policy objectives.

The EC established the agency Frontex in 2005 to forge cooperation between Member States on border control, to assist in returning 'illegal' migrants and to coordinate joint operations guarding the EU's external border from illegal crossings. Some migration policy insiders find it a daunting agency, with one suggesting that 'it's already in their name: Frontex, like frontier. It's a military term. I think of the joint operations in the Aegean Sea with their patrol boats'. Frontex is also planning a network of national coastguards in the Mediterranean Sea that would coordinate Member States' surveillance systems including sea patrols, air patrols and information exchanges. This network will be partly modelled on the Nord-Balt integrated defence system established in the late 1990s by the Nordic and Baltic states against the Russian Federation. Director Ilkka Laitinen explained that 'We do not have to reinvent the wheel [as we try] to adapt these systems to the Mediterranean area' (United Kingdom Parliament 2006: Q610). From July to December 2006, Frontex ran Operation Hera to protect Spain's Canary Islands. In its first phase, 'experts' from France, Germany, Italy, Portugal, the Netherlands, and the U.K. helped Spanish officials to identify the countries of origin of 19,000 migrants and to return over 6,000 of them. In its second phase, Spain, Italy, Portugal, and Finland provided navy vessels and military aircraft to patrol the coasts of Senegal, Mauritania and Guinea. This mission pushed boats carrying over 3,500 migrants back to the shores of West Africa (Frontex 2006). Amazon I and II were similar projects based in eight European airports to target illegal South American immigrants (Frontex 2007).

The EU's strategies to 'regularise' migration management now extend beyond its own Member States and into sending and transit countries in Africa and the Middle East. This move should be seen in the context of the apparatus as a tool of economic management as well as an enforcer of public order. In 2005, the European Council passed the 'Global Approach to Migration'. It includes an ostensible commitment to 'cutting off the need for migration' through a development policy coordinated with EU immigration policy. EC officials proudly link these two issues as a sign of European distinction. A high official from the EC's Directorate for Immigration, Asylum, and Borders noted that:

> At the moment, Europe is the only immigration 'country' linking immigration and development ... not the US, Canada, Australia, and certainly not the Asian countries. China and India are not going to be worrying about this ...

Economic pragmatism is never far behind, however, as the same official added that 'In the long term, we may be desperate to get the people we need'. Thus, in a completely different project, the EU is developing European Job Mobility Portals to inform potential migrants about the opportunities and conditions for working in the EU. The first of these was set up in Mali in

2007. Immigration Liaison Officers are now being posted to EU embassies in sending and transit countries as well. Not all Member States are happy with the Portals, as they complicate their efforts to control their own labour markets. However, the EC maintains that these are necessary to reduce illegal flows and take pressure off the Member States on the EU's southern maritime border. These security measures are aimed at 'regularising' migration, i.e. stopping illegal flows, while designating specified labour migration as legal and desirable. Legal migration is to be encouraged and this is increasingly defined according to specific labour needs, as asylum claims are increasingly rejected and family reunification rules are increasingly tightened.

A major OSCE conference captured how separate policy concerns spoken about under the rubric of 'crisis' fuse together to create an apparatus across many different policy domains. The name of its 2005 capstone conference on international migration is suggestive: 'Demographic Trends, Migration and Integrating Persons Belonging to National Minorities: Ensuring Security and Sustainable Development in the OSCE Area'. Vladimir Špidla (OSCE 2005a), the European Commissioner for Employment, Social Affairs and Equal Opportunities, started the discussion by linking security to demography and labour in a speech entitled 'The Demographic Crisis: Required Reforms and New Policies':

> Europe today faces a considerable challenge: the challenge of demographic decline … Assuming that the Union accepted no further immigrants, its population would [fall] by more than 3% by the year 2030. And according to the Commission's latest projections … with zero immigration the Union could [lose] more than 60 million inhabitants by the year 2050. The trend in the working-age population shows even more sharply what awaits us, with a projected drop of approximately 21 million persons by the year 2030.

Brigita Schmögnerova (OSCE 2005b), of the UN's Economic Commission for Europe, similarly argued that: 'Europe is in the midst of a situation without parallel in demographic history … [these] population trends could pose serious challenges for the security and economic stability in [Europe].' The migration issue thus imbricates the fabric of EU society and demands 'regularisation', at least from the perspective of Europe's top bureaucrats.

The International Organization for Migration (IOM) leads many efforts to facilitate global labour circulation, as exemplified by the 2006 *Handbook on Establishing Effective Labour Migration Policies in Countries of Origin and Destination*. The *Handbook* (co-published with the OSCE and the International Labour Office) advocates measures to enhance 'circular migration' between sending and receiving countries in order to boost the economies of both. Many European countries, such as Italy and Spain, structure their quotas on labour migration intake to match the migrant supply with the particular labour demands. Other countries, such as Austria, determine their quotas as a percentage of their total labour force, which has been about nine per cent for the last few years (OSCE/IOM/ILO 2006: 101). Labour migrants in most

European countries must pass a labour market or resident worker test, which ensures that they are not taking jobs from domestic workers. The same applies to labour migrants who wish to change jobs if they have not met the minimal time necessary for free access to employment (OSCE/IOM/ILO 2006: 103). EU Member States adhere to the 'EU preference principle', which means that:

> Member States will consider requests for admission to their territories for the purpose of employment only where vacancies in a Member State cannot be filled by national and Community manpower or by non-Community manpower lawfully resident on a permanent basis in that Member State and already forming part of the Member State's regular labour market. (Cited in OSCE/IOM/ILO 2006: 104)

Labour migrants thus face a stiff filtering system designed to attract the most specific profile desired. Nevertheless, the UN's Global Commission on International Migration (2005: 5), authorised by Kofi Annan, explains that the international community needs 'to capitalize on the resourcefulness of people who seek to improve their lives by moving from one country to the other'.

However, opposed to the construction of the legal migrant as economic resource is that of the threatening and unregulated migrant. The EU has witnessed a proliferation of surveillance techniques to monitor migrants. International cooperation on the standardisation and upgrading of travel documents regularly occurs. Electronic passports have the ability to hold large amounts of biometric data and can be easily read at border checkpoints. The Visa Information System, the Schengen Information System and EURODAC ensure the rapid transfer of migrant data between EU Member States, thus facilitating the capture of 'illegal' migrants and 'false' asylum claims. Furthermore, technological advancements in document production (polymeric coated security paper, laser engraved data, micro-perforated photographs, colour-changing imagery, etc.) make forgery more difficult. Hence, European officials hope it will help to thwart illegal migration and expedite border crossing. Jan de Ceuster, who heads the EC's Border and Visas Unit, explained the rationale as follows:

> On the one hand, there are security considerations. It will be a means of permitting us to improve the fight against illegal immigration and threats to public order. But on the other – and this must not be forgotten – it will be a means of assisting the free movement of foreign nationals who need a visa, who travel in good faith. (Radio Free Europe 2005)

The European Parliament first rejected the introduction of biometric passports for technical and legal reasons. However, the European Council outmanoeuvred the Parliament by using an ambiguity in EU law that forced its approval (Statewatch 2004). Digitalised facial photographs and fingerprints are now required for visas in most EU countries. If the persistent efforts of private industry are any indicator, then advanced uses of biometric data will likely be found in iris scans, vein pattern recognition and facial recognition.

This sketch of international cooperation on migration management highlights the piecemeal formation of a comprehensive web of migration surveillance, an apparatus organised around a diffuse idea of 'crisis' that incorporates many migration issues. 'Illegal' migrants – those without the desired skills and accused of 'abusing the system' – are regulated through a range of negative measures. Frontex's joint border management ventures amount to 'a first line of defence' in preventing illegal migration. Migration routes are detected and analysed to inform strategies to combat illegal migration. Biometric data enables a near-perfect match between traveller and travel document, which facilitates the apprehension of migrants and transmission of data to police authorities across the EU. Member States attract particular categories of labour migrants – the main legal migration channel – to plug identified holes in their respective labour markets vacated by an ageing domestic workforce. To help guarantee that only potential immigrants with the desired skills apply, the EU is experimenting with placing job mobility portals in immigrant-sending countries. These disparate policy domains are collectively forming a migration management apparatus or what Ferguson (1994: 24) might describe as an 'anonymous constellations of control'. It is 'anonymous' as no particular actor drives it or bears responsibility for it. It is a 'constellation' insofar as the policy processes at play interlock (intentionally or not) while they remain decentralised. It is an agent of control for the simple fact that a migrant must negotiate it one way or another even if he or she manages to subvert it.

Population regulation requires a panoramic, though decentralised, gaze on the individual, as Foucauldian scholars have well demonstrated. What is more, objectification of the individual occurs (implicitly or explicitly) in a vast field of documents and writing (Dreyfus and Rabinow 1983: 159), which renders the matter particularly important for an anthropology of policy. Information about the individual is recorded, documented, duplicated, transmitted and shared by an array of authorities administering the state's (or group of cooperating states') territory. The multitude of processes whereby migrants are transmuted from three-dimensional human subjects into two-dimensional policy objects occurs through textual practices of policy representation, policy making and policy implementation. As such, teasing out the discourses that enable the EU's efforts to harmonise migration management demands careful attention to the innumerable policy documents pertaining to this endeavour. These documents encode the logic through which migrants are simultaneously objects of fear, exploitation and commodification. These examples constitute much more than the background of a localised ethnographic study. Instead, they form the very fabric of a broader de facto migration apparatus in which the 3MP materialised. The next section takes initial steps toward a nonlocal ethnography as a methodological approach that might help illuminate such a construct.

From Methods to Methodology:
Steps toward a Nonlocal Ethnography

What would a methodology look like that is not built on the 'local' as such but on the indirect relations among locales (cf. Gupta and Ferguson 1997)? We have seen in the case of migration management in Europe how an apparatus absorbs many different and disparate policy actors into its purview as it regulates large numbers of people. Even though the vast majority of these actors' policy work does not happen in face-to-face settings, one still observes among them a great conversation taking place indirectly, in dispersed sites and in many venues (policy statements, public statements, government brochures, national legislations, international conferences, etc.) We must ask how this conversation limits the possible policy constructions of the 'migrant' (for example) as a problem to be solved (DeGenova 2002). The ethnographic challenge is to illuminate how an apparatus historically emerges, logically functions and fabricates what it presents as an objective target of regulation. To do so, nonlocal ethnography does not call for the ethnographer's immersion in 'place' in order to represent daily practice *per se*. Rather, it investigates the discourses that enable the emergence of such a construct as the apparatus.

Many anthropologists see the problem of 'place' as basically a problem of methods. Thirty-five years ago, Nader (1972: 306–7) vigorously argued that if we are to address the most important contemporary problems, then we might have to 'study up' and 'shuffle around the value placed on participant-observation that leads us to forget that there are other methods more useful' for the problems we need to investigate. To deal with restricted access, Gusterson suggests 'polymorphous engagement', which involves meeting with informants 'across a number of dispersed sites, not just in local communities, and sometimes in a virtual form; and it means collecting data eclectically from a disparate array of sources in many different ways' (1997: 116). Shore (2006) argues that social anthropology should not be equated with ethnography to bypass the constraints of empiricism and to capture wider social processes. Gupta and Ferguson (1997: 37) suggest demoting 'the field' to just 'one element in a multistranded methodology for the construction of what Donna Haraway (1988) has called "situated knowledges"'. This move softens the division between ethnographic knowledge and other useful methods and genres such as archival work, statistical analysis, media analysis and interviews, which themselves can provide useful insights as "Genres seem destined to continue to blur."(Gupta and Ferguson 1997: 38).

However, this pragmatic use of varied methods would benefit from a clear epistemological justification lest we ignore the question of what isn't ethnography. In thinking further about the possibilities of a nonlocal ethnography, it is important to stress that it does not involve the abandonment of participant-observation. Rather, it calls for a deep assessment of the kind of knowledge that participant-observation delivers in order to create a flexible methodology that is not too fixed to a few places. Participant-observation serves the dual purposes: 1) of displacing the ethnographer in order to lessen internal biases for the better reception of alternative ideas, values, practices, etc.; and 2) of showing the importance of historical contingency in either reproducing or altering the status quo. A brief review of these features shows how we can retain the assets of participant-observation in order to create a nonlocal ethnography that is not overly tied to place as such.

First, Clifford (1997: 218) sees ethnography as one manifestation of a long tradition of Western travel practices. Ethnography as travel (or displacement) is the 'more or less voluntary practice of leaving familiar ground in search of difference, wisdom, power, adventure, an altered perspective'. On the one hand, his point reveals participant-observation's empiricist assumptions: learning through direct personal experience and immersion in cultural difference. On the other hand, and more broadly, displacement shows the importance of developing critical perspectives on one's social reality through the removal from it. However, Clifford also argues that 'Travel needs to be rethought in different traditions and historical predicaments' (1997: 218). As such, must the desired displacement be achieved solely through entry into an ostensibly alien cultural setting? Nonlocal ethnography would interpret 'displacement' to describe any inquiry that problematises what the researcher would otherwise take for granted. Displacement – the removal from familiarity – need not be reduced to matters of physical location, but rather deepened to include any experience in which discourse – the taken-for-granted assumptions that establish norms and deviation – is interrogated, problematised or, in a word, 'situated'. Ironically, to displace is to situate.

Secondly, participant-observation foregrounds the importance of historical contingency in human affairs, because 'being there' shows the ethnographer what is actually happening in contested moments. It reveals that social relations appearing in static form (e.g. the state) are only achieved through ongoing struggle, conflict and violence. This perspective renders ethnography a genealogical methodology, which sees history as the 'story of petty malice, of violently imposed interpretations, of vicious intentions, of high sounding stories masking the lowest motives' (Dreyfus and Rabinow 1983: 108). It shows how moments of rupture, conflict and discord result in power inequalities concealed through different political technologies. However, ethnography need not be reduced to participant-observation to achieve this desired insight. Many methods can account for change through time at local, national or global levels. In fact, deep immersion might occlude views of other domains and modes in which conflict is performed, revealed or concealed.

In sum, nonlocal ethnography reveals how a nonlocalisable apparatus emerges as a device of population management. It is quintessentially an ethnographic methodology because, like participant-observation, it critiques the hegemony of 'common knowledge' and traces the role of contingency in human affairs. However, nonlocal ethnography is not constrained by the limits of participant-observation because it does not assume that the principal form of knowledge is attained through direct sensory contact. It is not an empiricist methodology. As a methodology defined by the twin pillars of displacement and contingency, it can prioritise any method that suits the particular research design. In the case of migration management in Europe, these methods were archival research, analyses of political speeches and participant-observation in offices and international meetings, among others.

Despite arguments from the Comaroffs (2003), Trouillot (2001) and others, anthropologists have not fully questioned the limits of empiricism – and thus the centrality of participant-observation – in debates about global ethnography. While multi-sited ethnography helps us account for the increasing imbrication of the global and local in our research designs, it still assumes that actors are suspended in traceable, point-to-point relations even if these now span around the world. In contrast, the convergence of an EU migration management apparatus exemplifies how disparate policy processes still work together to regulate large-scale populations, an effect that cannot be apprehended through participant-observation alone and by mapping direct connections between actors. Moreover, today's globalised world should be recognised as more than networks and flows moving at hyper-speed. There is some method to the madness, which Agamben (1998) seeks in his basic question: how is it possible that modern society can reduce entire demographic groups to *homo sacer*, or 'sacred man', i.e. one who may be killed without consequence and is not worthy of sacrifice? Not only do migrants qualify as *homo sacer*, but so does everyone in mass society because all are reduced to quantifiable objects to simplify administrative and economic planning. Nonlocal ethnography helps us illuminate how an apparatus functions, which is a necessary step towards resisting it.

Acknowledgements

I am grateful for the time, attention and interest from the people involved in the 3MP, particularly those based at EMPO. This chapter also benefited from helpful comments from Pablo Mendez and Susan Wright, and also from questions and comments during presentations at the Södertörns University College, Stockholm; the Population Studies and Training Center, Brown University; the Graduate Student Methodology Seminar Series, Department of Geography and the Interdisciplinary Studies Graduate Program at the University of British Columbia. Special thanks are reserved for the collective input of the students in Susan Greenhalgh's graduate course on the anthropology of public policy at the University of California, Irvine, particularly Adonia Lugo, Connie McGuire and Shaozeng Zhang. Luna Vives provided excellent research assistance.

Notes

1. France, Germany, Luxembourg, Belgium and the Netherlands signed the Agreement in 1985. Implementation began in 1995 with Portugal and Spain joining the Schengen area that year. As of May 2008, twenty-seven EU Member States, not including the U.K., have signed the agreement. New Member States are set to implement its terms except Cyprus. Bulgaria and Romania have signed but are not yet implementing the agreement.

References

Agamben, G. 1998. *Homo Sacer: Sovereign Power and Bare Life*. Stanford: Stanford University Press.

Clifford, J. 1997. 'Spatial Practices: Fieldwork, Travel, and the Disciplining of Anthropology', in A. Gupta and J. Ferguson (eds), *Anthropological Locations: Boundaries and Grounds of a Field Science*. Berkeley: University of California Press, pp. 185–222.

Comaroff, Jean and John Comaroff. 2003. 'Ethnography on an Awkward Scale: Postcolonial Anthropology and the Violence of Abstraction', *Ethnography* 4(2): 147–79.

Council of the European Union. 2004. 'The Hague Programme: Strengthening Freedom, Security and Justice in the European Union #16054/04'. Retrieved 2 November 2010 from http://ec.europa.eu/justice_home/doc_centre/doc/hague_programme_en.pdf.

DeGenova, N. 2002. 'Migrant "Illegality" and Deportability in Everyday Life', *Annual Review of Anthropology* 31: 419–47.

Dreyfus, H. and P. Rabinow. 1983. *Michel Foucault: Beyond Structuralism and Hermeneutics*. Chicago: University of Chicago Press.

European Commission. 2004. 'Communication from the Commission to the Council and the European Parliament' COM (2004) 4002 final'. Retrieved 12 September 2007 from. http://ec.europa.eu/home-affairs/doc_centre/intro/docs/bilan_tampere_en.pdf. Retrieved 14 December 2010.

———. 2005a. 'Toward a Common European Union Immigration Policy'. Retrieved 20 July 2007 from http://europa.eu.int/comm/justice_home/fsj/immigration/fsj_immigration_intro_en.htm.

———. 2005b. 'The Hague Programme: Ten Priorities for the Next Five Years'. Retrieved 19 July 2007 from http://ec.europa.eu/justice_home/news/information_dossiers/the_hague_priorities/index_en.htm.

Feldman, G. 2008. 'The Trap of Abstract Space: Recomposing Russian-Speaking Immigrants in Post-Soviet Estonia', *Anthropological Quarterly* 81(2): 311–42.

Ferguson, J. 1994. *The Anti-Politics Machine: 'Development,' Depoliticization, and Bureaucratic Power in Lesotho*. Minneapolis: University of Minnesota Press.

Frontex. 2006. 'Longest Frontex Coordinated Operation – HERA, the Canary Islands'. Retrieved 2 November 2010 from http://www.frontex.europa.eu/newsroom/news_releases/art8.html.

———. 2007. 'South American Illegal Migration Tackled by Frontex'. Retrieved 2 November 2010 from http://www.frontex.europa.eu/newsroom/news_releases/art15.html.

Global Commission on International Migration. 2005. *Migration in an Interconnected World: New Directions for Action*. Retrieved 2 November 2010 from http://www.gcim.org/attachements/gcim-complete-report-2005.pdf.

Greenhalgh, S. 2003. 'Planned Births, Unplanned Persons: "Population" in the Making of Chinese Modernity', *American Ethnologist* 30(2): 196–215.

Gupta, A. and J. Ferguson. 1997. 'Discipline and Practice: "The Field" as Site, Method, and Location in Anthropology', in A. Gupta and J. Ferguson (eds), *Anthropological Locations: Boundaries and Grounds of a Field Science*. Berkeley: University of California Press, pp. 1–46.

Gusterson, H. 1997. 'Studying Up Revisited', *Political and Legal Anthropology Review* 20(1): 114–19.

Nader, L. 1972. 'Up the Anthropologist: Perspectives Gained from Studying Up', in D. Hymes (ed.), *Reinventing Anthropology*. New York: Pantheon Press, pp. 285–311.

OSCE (Organization for Security and Cooperation in Europe). 2005a. '"The Demographic Crisis: Required Reforms and New Policies", Speech delivered at the OSCE 13th Economic Forum, Prague, 23–27 May 2005'. Retrieved 2 November 2010 from http://www.osce.org/documents/eea/2005/05/14521_en.pdf.

———. 2005b. 'Opening Remarks by Ms. Brigita Schmögnerova. Demographic Trends, Migration and Integrating Persons Belonging to National Minorities: Ensuring Security and Sustainable Development in the OSCE Area'. Retrieved 2 November 2010 from http://www.osce.org/documents/eea/2005/05/14542_en.pdf.

OSCE (Organization for Security and Cooperation in Europe)/IOM (International Organization for Migration)/ILO (International Labour Office). 2006. *Handbook on Establishing Effective Labour Migration in Countries of Origin and Destination*. Geneva and Vienna: OSCE, IOM and ILO.

Rabinow, P. 2003. *Anthropos Today: Reflections on Modern Equipment*. Princeton and Oxford: Princeton University Press.

Radio Free Europe. 2005. 'EU: Brussels to Introduce Fingerprinting for Many Schengen Visitors by 2007' by Ahto Lobjakas. Retrieved 2 November 2010 from http://www.rferl.org/content/article/1056744.html.

Shore, C. 2006. 'The Limits of Ethnography versus the Poverty of Theory: Patron-Client Relations in Europe Re-Visited'. In special issue 'Beyond Ethnography', *Sites: Journal of Social Anthropology and Cultural Studies* 3(2): 40–59.

Statewatch. 2004. 'EU Governments Blackmail European Parliament into Quick Adoption of its Report on Biometric Passports'. Retrieved 2 November 2010 from http://www.statewatch.org/news/2004/nov/12biometric-passports-blackmail.htm.

Trouillot, M. 2001. 'The Anthropology of the State in the Age of Globalization: Close Encounters of the Deceptive Kind', *Current Anthropology* 42(1): 125–38.

United Kingdom Parliament. 2006. 'Memorandum by the European Commission, Directorate General, Justice, Freedom and Security'. House of Lords Select Committee on European Union, Minutes of Evidence, Session 2005–06. 2 March 2006.

Watson, Graham. 2007. 'Graham Watson on Immigration.' Speech posted on YouTube. Retrieved 2 November 2010 from http://www.youtube.com/watch?v=EgNjQ-l8psY.

Chapter 3

Politics and Ethics: Ethnographies of Expert Knowledge and Professional Identities[1]

David Mosse

As an ethnographer of policy, in 2004 I faced an unexpected problem. I had just completed an anthropological account of aid policy and practice based on over ten years' involvement in a British-funded (Department for International Development [DFID]) rural development project concerned with improving the livelihoods of a marginalised 'tribal' population in a poor region of western India (see Mosse 2005). When I returned my draft account of the project – my record of its achievements and its contradictions, its formal policy and informal processes, its expertise and its unscripted roles all now framed within a broader theoretical argument – to my project colleagues and counterparts, some raised objections. They made official complaints to my university, the publisher and my professional association, and tried to stall the publication process. They insisted that the account was inaccurate, disrespectful and, most significantly, damaging to their professional reputations. They claimed that it would harm their organisations and destroy the programme and its route to funding.

Only some, mostly programme managers and my international technical consultant colleagues, raised such objections. Many others, especially fieldworkers, strongly endorsed my account. And of course I vigorously defended the soundness of my research methods, the accuracy of my data and the validity of my interpretations. For the purposes of this discussion, it is also important to point out that this ethnography was carefully crafted so as to avoid controversy. It anonymised all individuals, reported only on actions taken in people's professional capacity, documented the genuine difficulties and dilemmas involved in addressing chronic poverty, and – while emphatically not an evaluation study – maintained that this was a worthwhile project with important benefits for thousands of very poor people. No independent reader considered the book damaging to any reputation or quite understood how it had generated such controversy. But the objections were real enough and forceful. Without going into the specifics of the case, this chapter is concerned with a more general tension between anthropological research and development expertise which it manifests, and that may occur more widely in the course of the ethnography of policy and practice.

I have discussed events surrounding the publication of my book *Cultivating Development* and their implications elsewhere (Mosse 2006a). I argued that while all anthropologists have some obligation to return their writing to the subjects of their research, anthropologist of public policy face the additional problem that their texts circulate within the same public space as, and compete with, the representations of their informants. I further suggested that the way in which professional informants respond to ethnographic description itself generates important research insights. Maximising the capacity of actors to object to what is said about them, as Latour (2000) puts it, is a methodology. But this does not mean that such 'objection' is a form of scientific triangulation. Indeed, objections rarely concern simple matters of fact, but reveal divergent epistemologies and frames of reference, perhaps those of managerial and interpretive viewpoints or of policy professionals and ethnographers.

The issues raised for the anthropology of policy by such cases are not just epistemological; they are also ethical. Some of my informants believed or claimed that they had been harmed by an anthropological account which, for this reason, was in contravention of disciplinary ethical guidelines (Sridhar 2005; Mosse 2006b). Powerful actors in the realm of international development presented themselves as human subjects of research in need of protection. Reacting to an anonymised account of their work with which they disagreed, they appealed to codes of research ethics, or implicitly to defamation law, on the grounds of a threat of harm to professional reputations. Ethical dilemmas abound here, especially around the question of consent. This research involved an extended negotiation of consent at the outset, but then raised the further question of what happens if policy professionals (civil servants, non-governmental organisation [NGO] managers or activists) attempt to withdraw consent later on in research or insist on their consent to research findings or publications? Does an agreement to collaborate and share results imply an obligation to be subject to editorial influence or control? How is consent separated from the demand for interpretive consensus? The debate on informed consent – already complicated enough in anthropology (see *American Ethnologist* 2006) – has scarcely considered the problems of negotiating interpretive difference in the later stages of research. Yet the very possibility of research on public policy and professionals is affected by the way in which powerful subjects of research can use ethical rules and procedures, Review Boards and the like – already instruments for the state regulation of social science – to evade social science scrutiny, resist critical analysis, gain control over research and protect reputations and public images of success.

'Insider' research in organisations poses additional difficulties, where ethnographers analysing their own and their colleagues' roles find that writing requires a re-negotiation of relationships or tension, even the rupture of professional and personal relations. The epistemological, ethical and emotional dilemmas of exit into ethnographic writing are every bit as complex as the negotiation of access to policy worlds (see Mosse 2006a). These have to be added to the conventional ethical concerns of consent, confidentiality, privileged access or data protection.

In this chapter I want to examine reasons for a more general tension between ethnography and professional life so as to throw light on what may underlie the kinds of interpretive conflicts and accusations of harm and damage to reputations that I, along with others, have encountered. The key question is why is ethnographic description experienced as threatening to professionals; not always, but commonly enough. I begin with the suggestion that, in part, the problem lies in the very nature of professional identity formation on the one hand and of ethnographic enquiry on the other. Having set up the problem, I then take a wider look at the world of professionals and expert knowledge (in international development) before returning to a core methodological dilemma posed by ethnographies of professionals and experts

The Ethnography of Development Experts and Professionals

It is clear that researching professional lives, 'studying up' (Nader 2002) or 'through' (Reinhold in Shore and Wright 1997:14; Wedel et al. 2005), and writing ethnographic accounts of those expert communities opens up important methodological and ethical issues, quite apart from the matter of techniques for describing networks or 'following the policy' (Shore and Wright 1997). In this section I want to suggest that some of these arise from fundamental incompatibilities between ethnographic and professional projects. But, first, in what ways is the ethnographic description of professionals difficult, contested or even impossible?

For those close to, or members of, professional communities, it may be impossible to provide accounts of social relations or politics because ethnographic subjects refuse to be objectified in these terms (Riles 2006: 63; 2001: 18). Miyazaki and Riles (2005) go further by pointing to the 'ethnographic failure' associated with attempts at research on/with expert subjects whose parallel theorising already incorporates sociological analysis. This descriptive failure results from the inability to 'objectify' or to 'localise' expert subjects and to maintain a 'defining distance' between ethnographer and subject.

Holmes and Marcus (2005) suggest that this 'end point' can be averted and ethnography 're-functioned', in part, by recourse to experts' own sceptical or self-critical moves. Writing of professionals in the financial world, these authors refer to the existence among experts of a 'self-conscious critical faculty that operates ... as a way of dealing with contradictions, exception, facts that are fugitive, and that suggest a social realm not in alignment with the representations generated by the application of the reigning statistical mode of analysis' (2005: 237). Making use of this 'para-ethnographic' dimension of expert domains, Holmes and Marcus invite anthropologists to find a 'collaborative' mode of research among those expert subjects who are neither natives nor colleagues, but stand as counterparts (2005: 248). As outsiders or insiders, ethnographers may then draw on the 'kind of illicit, marginal social thought', anecdotal or intuitive, that is deployed 'counterculturally and critically' among managers, international experts, fieldstaff, scientists or consultants (my colleagues and myself), and make of this a bridge 'to further the production of fundamental *anthropological* knowledge' (Holmes and Marcus 2005: 246).

This, indeed, was my own strategy in producing the ethnography of an international development intervention (Mosse 2005). But, as I indicated above, 'collaborative ethnography' – even 'self-ethnography' – founded on the para-ethnographic may not be so easy to pull off in practice. Holmes and Marcus themselves indicate the core of the problem when they refer to the 'implication for these [technocratic/managerial] regimes of the return of ethnography derived from the subversive para-ethnography ... back to the project's originating milieu' (2005: 241). In my case, the implications of the return of my ethnographic (or para-ethnographic) account to my expert and professional subjects (and colleagues) were objections and claims of harm to professional reputations. If this was an ethnographic 'end point', it was not so on account of epistemological sameness, but rather the difference between ethnographic and professional expectations.

At the very centre of this particular controversy was the question of 'professionalism'. What exactly was it that was damaging professional identities? The parts of the ethnography that my colleagues regarded as especially 'defamatory and potentially damaging to professional reputations'[2] were those that mentioned informal and unscripted roles, relationships, events and interests, or which provided unofficial interpretations. One colleague, for example, wrote that he took exception to the idea that we (international consultants) were motivated by seeking to secure an enduring relationship with the donor or project/area as a site for research and future consultancy income, insisting that 'we were a *professional* team'. By describing the wider financial, social and research context of consultancy work, my critics saw me as questioning their professionalism. Comment on the informal ways that lethargic bureaucratic processes of approval and budget release had to be 'facilitated' – the many courtesy calls, foreigner visits, cards, gifts or overseas training opportunities – was taken in the same way. Similarly, reference to the chameleon character of 'unscripted brokerage roles' and the manipulation of insider/outsider roles or the out-of-sight economy of favours and obligations existing on the margins of legitimacy were seen as unprofessional.

While my colleagues could, of course, themselves describe such roles, relationships and local constraints, they were professionally committed to their denial. Any notion of self-interest undermined professionalism, not least the observations that, proportionately, we – expatriate experts – were far greater beneficiaries than tribal villagers of the aid gifts we were honoured for bringing, or that some thirty-seven per cent of project costs went to Technical Cooperation, or that U.K. institutions, universities and consultants expected to profit from the flow of aid into projects. Such comments in my text were challenged as 'unnecessary' on the grounds that professionals' work in development is charitable. '"Profit,"' my colleague wrote to me, 'is the wrong word ... we all could have earned more doing something else. We chose not to because we believed in what we were doing.' Description of the contradiction between actual actions/events and authorised models was also regarded as damaging to professionalism. My crop scientist colleagues read the suggestion that the scientifically demonstrated benefits of improved seed varieties could disappear when re-embedded in the complex constraints of local livelihoods – networks of obligation, relationships of debt, input supply and migration – as doubting their science (Mosse 2005). My expert colleagues took exception to references to relationships as prior to knowledge, to investments directed at maintaining them as part of programme execution and to the idea that 'advice' crosses a boundary into 'control'. Such accounts of the real-life connections of consultant work were seen as disparaging, 'questioning our professionalism' and threatening to damage professional reputations.

If these ethnographic observations questioned professionalism, they did so by definition. That is to say, the self-representation of professional identity requires the erasure of discrepancies of practice, disjuncture or individual compromise. Professionals necessarily deny context and contingency, and suppress the relational, or even their own agency. Professionalism refuses significance to the event or individual action in favour of rules, principles, instrumental ideas and expert models. My 'para-ethnographic' work encountered a professional habitus that automatically transfers the actuality of events into the pre-given categories of acceptable and legitimate fictions (e.g., 'decisions taken by committee', relationships denuded of interest, power-free information) and idealised process (with no mention of pressure on staff to meet targets or threats of transfers). This habitus screens out extraneous factors and analyses problems in relation to solutions, producing a proper project history of design, implementation, learning and improvement.

The dilemma is that ethnographic description is composed precisely of those things that are professionally discounted and of meanings unruled by authorised policy interpretations. My ethnography refused to explain outcomes in terms of design; it unravelled the science of improved crop varieties into social relations, complicating stories of crop science and community action with irrelevant details of events or diverse interests. As my colleagues objected, this was not just unacceptable but professionally disempowering; at least for some, since other front-line workers found the description of the project's contradictions, with which they dealt daily, validating and empowering.

The broad point stands. Ethnographic description can be experienced as threatening to a professional (or epistemic) community formed around shared representations. The upset and anger reveals an antipathy between professional identity and the ethnographic project. Ethnography draws attention to the irrelevant, the routine, the ordinary; it examines the instability of meaning rather than defining successful outcomes of expert design; and when it turns its attention to the unnoticed effects of analytical forms (documentary artefacts, networks, matrices, annual reports, etc., as in Riles 2001), it detracts from the substance of official narratives.

There is one further specific reason why ethnographic description is threatening. Its field of inquiry – events, context, informal relations and divergent views – links it to narratives of programme failure. Whilst stories of success bury individual actions or events and emphasise policy, expert ideas, the system and the professional, so as to make an intervention appear a unified source of intention and power, directing attention to the transcendent agency of policy ideas, expert design or technology (and hence replicability), stories of failure search out the individual person and point to the contingent, the arbitrary, the accidental, the unintended and the exceptional. Development narratives of success are theory-rich; those of failure are inherently event-rich. Failure, then, is not simply the plan unrealised; it has the potential to unravel professional identities. By releasing the anecdotal, failure can undo the work of expertise and professionalism. It may license expression of suppressed and scattered doubts, drawing attention to the informal processes underlying official actions (Latour 1996). Failure is the eruption of precisely those things that professionalism suppresses – events, contingency, relationships – and that ethnography assembles. And this has the potential to disrupt the networks and interpretive communities built around success (Mosse 2005).

The professional worry about ethnographic accounts is compounded by the tendency of organisations in development to regard any description as an evaluation. My project colleagues felt judged; they read ethnography as negative evaluation. Moreover, they thought the judgment unfair, not so much because of what was written but rather because of how knowledge was produced. Of course, the ethnographic genre ignored the etiquette of praise and indirect comment, and did not judge professional action in its own terms, introducing what they considered to be diversions and irrelevant details. But, most particularly, ethnography is unfair or bad evaluation because it does not involve the usual negotiation of an acceptable story that mediates interpretative differences. Ethnography draws attention to different points of view and does not involve, or require, a drive to consensus. Indeed, it was the different approach to the construction of authoritative knowledge – an epistemological divide – and the refusal to subject description to the social processes of consensus under authorised frameworks that, in my particular case, was the immediate cause of dispute (see Mosse 2006a).

These observations about the interaction of the ethnographic and the professional can, I think, be taken further by a broader look at the world of international aid and the life of professionals, as well as at the nature of expert knowledge within it.

The World of Professionals

Strangely late and reluctantly, anthropologists have turned to the study of the social and cultural lives of global professionals, a mobile yet highly visible group in the capital cities of the developing world. Here, far from instantiating a cosmopolitan outlook that 'encompass[es] the world's [cultural] variety and its subsequent mixtures', they occupy cultural enclaves with shared consumption, lifestyle and values 'as restricted as any other strong ethnic identity' (Friedman 1997: 74). Friedman has a narrower elite conception of professionals than mine, but I do suggest an interconnection between the structural position and restricted sociality of international experts and the nature of their policy 'thought work'. The point is made by Eyben (2011), who as an insider ethnographer explores how the convergent and de-contextualised policy models of international development have their social basis. That is to say, policy models are 'travelling rationalities' (Craig and Porter 2006) framed and transported by locally transient but internationally permanent and close-knit groups of experts whose reach, intensity and centralisation is increased by electronic information and communication technologies (Eyben 2011). The further point is that the consolidation of aid models and the separation of the social and thought worlds of international professionals from local contexts is not a given, but requires constant work. Medical anthropologist Ian Harper provides a useful metaphor. Working in Nepal, he shows how the universalising knowledge of global experts (development consultants and advisers) is 'closed off' from other epistemologies and other health systems, dramatised in the 'walling off' of fortress hospitals from 'the cacophony of the street' (Harper 2011). This contrasts with the Nepali health workers who migrate to countries like the U.K. or the U.S.A. and cross boundaries between health systems and languages. They cannot isolate themselves from the demands of the poorly paid, low status or socially insecure in the countries to which they migrate. It is these migrant workers who are cosmopolitan in Hannerz's (1996) sense of displaying a 'reflexive distance from one's own culture', they who are 'open to new ways of knowing and being'.

Social and intellectual closure may be a weapon against the unmanageability of the immediately local, of uncertainty and the risk of failure, but the real dilemma is that aid professionals do have to engage in the messy, emotion-laden practical work of dealing with relationships and contingency: negotiating presence within national bureaucracies, NGOs or consultancy teams, compromise, rule bending, meeting targets and spending budgets. They have to negotiate identity, gender, age, race or nationality, not to mention personal security, loneliness, family relations and stress – issues hardly attended to in the literature – while shoring up their motivations within moral-ethical or religious frameworks that remain private. And yet, as experts and professionals, they have to make themselves bearers of context-free 'travelling rationalities' and transferable skills – whether in the realms of health sector reform, plant science or people's empowerment. From this come cosmopolitan and technocratic claims. Again, professionalism (career-building) requires recovering the universal from the particular, technocratic knowledge from the illicit relationships upon which it is actually based (Riles 2004). For different reasons, both the World Bank's investors and borrowers, and the charitable donors to Oxfam require the 'illusion of certainty' from their experts.

The participatory turn in international development makes the constitution of expert identities even more difficult. Professionals of participatory projects have to deny or conceal their own expertise and agency in order to preserve an authorised view of themselves as facilitators of community action or local knowledge, as 'catalysts' hastening but not partaking in the reaction. 'No, my contribution is nothing', proclaims one Indian community worker, 'because I am only [a] facilitator and mobilise the community who have the main power' (Mosse 2005: 154). So, to the professionals who face the problem of stabilising universals of expert knowledge, we must add those NGO employees, missionaries, charity workers or other 'professional altruists' whose commitment is to moral rather than purely technical universals, and whose professional subjectivity is framed by stories of altruism, heroic commitment and sacrifice, which involve processes of 'moral selving' (Arvidson 2008: 6, drawing on Allahyari 2000).

The constant demand to turn the political into the technical, to represent the mess of practice in ordered expert or moral categories is not easily handled. Professional identities are fragile. The reflexivity this generates among people well aware of their dilemma is evident in the ubiquitous backstage scepticism, the escape into irony, self-criticism, spoof and humour that is part of professional groups, whose members may self-marginalise from their own power, distancing themselves from the naïvety of the zealous 'true believers', as Annelise Riles (2006) points out, referring to human rights lawyers. The true professional is a bit cynical, but also resigned to the immovable dominance of official knowledge which ensures that scepticism is closeted and concealed (Riles 2006). Only occasionally do development professionals offer fuller first-person accounts of the real micro-politics of their expertise, revealing to the general reader the chaotic, arbitrary underbelly of 'objective' economic data or the rough politics of loan negotiation in developing countries, tellingly published decades after the events they describe (e.g., the confessional accounts of Griffiths 2003 or Perkins 2003). Anthropologists now join development economists, relief workers, NGO staff or diplomats who choose a position of reflective marginality. For professional altruists (or missionaries), the escape into irony or sceptical expressions of doubt may be more difficult, and the experience of contradiction more personally devastating, which may play some part in high levels of stress and its emotional consequences reported in psychological studies of aid workers and missionaries.

The vulnerability of these expert identities has a wider context in the nexus that interlinks institutions, policy ideas and professionals' lives. I turn to this now to see how the networks of knowledge workers who serve the development industry both organise and are organised by its ideas. The broad question is: how does international development produce 'expertise' and how does such knowledge 'work' within this global system?

Organising Ideas: Neoliberal Institutionalism

This is an important moment at which to reflect more broadly on knowledge processes and professional cultures in international development. Never before has so much been made of the power of ideas, or right theory, or good policy in solving the problems of global poverty. Extraordinary power is invested in context-free 'global' models and frameworks that travel and are expected to effect economic, social and (within a 'governance agenda') political transformation across the globe. Regarding the framing of international development policy, I want to make four broad points.

First, there is today unprecedented global expert consensus on how poverty is to be eliminated and how the poor are to be governed. While, on the one hand, the ideological conditions for aid are set by an emphasis on partnership, consultation, local ownership, transparency or publicity (such that aid agencies claim to repudiate intervention in poor countries in favour of supporting the conditions within which development can happen), on the other hand, new processes of aid 'harmonisation' align internationalised policy and its technical instruments.

Secondly, this consensus involves, crudely speaking, a marrying of orthodox neoliberalism and a new institutionalism – the latter being the notion that poverty (and violence) is the result of bad governance and what is needed are stronger institutions, for instance, for the delivery of services accountable to the poor. This is no return to state provision, but, as Craig and Porter put it, there is a disaggregating and marketising of the state, breaking up existing forms of (corrupt, patrimonial) rule and then 'using markets to replace and reconstruct the institutions of governance' (2006: 9, 100) and at the same time re-embedding markets in regulatory and constitutional frameworks.

Thirdly, development policy models are formalistic, framed by the universal logic of new institutional economics and of law (accountability, transparency, etc.). These are the generally applicable 'travelling rationalities' that orchestrate professional thought work and assert the technical over the political, the formal over the substantive, and the categorical over the relational, while concealing the regional, institutional or sector specificity of the development process (Craig and Porter 2006: 120).

Finally, as Craig and Porter (2006) argue, international policy making is vertically disaggregated. The processes of knowledge formation involve both the delegation upwards of rule making and policy framing to the international stage, to international agencies, private organisations, NGOs and networks of experts; and the delegation downwards to 'responsibilised' communities (2006).

Ethnographic studies have examined the nature of such expert knowledge 'upwards' and 'downwards'. The first of these focuses on practices at the organisational centre. It is not difficult to see how a combination of formalism and internationalisation (delegation upwards) allows a technicalisation of policy and the centralisation of expertise, enhancing the status of a certain transnational class of experts entrenched at national level in ways that involve unprecedented convergence (Woods 2006: 66, 67, 68). Development policy trends, especially of the 1980s, demanded high levels of expertise and produced economic models that were rapidly internationalised, often in the context of crisis or uncertainty (Woods 2006). The 'delegation downwards' extends formalist models from national economies to the intimate spaces of communities, encouraging the local self-reengineering of institutions and state-citizen relations through new incentive structures, modified rules, new forums for accountability or conflict resolution, or local competitive bidding for resources (Li 2007); in short, 'getting social relations right', as Woolcock (1998) has put it. This demands new forms of expertise and the deployment of social science (including ethnography) 'to render society technical' (Li 2007), conceived in terms of calculative rationality, neoliberal ideas of self-organisation or the deficits/surpluses of social capital so as to allow designed interventions.

Whether at the national or the community level, neoliberal policy ideas expect to provide effective levers of social change. But the ethnographic point is that ultimately local or national institutions fashioned by expert knowledge come to be re-embedded in relations of power that alter their functioning; development's travelling rationalities get translated (back) into local social and political arrangements – perhaps through the interests of local collaborators, official counterparts or brokers – with unanticipated and maybe perverse effects. Craig and Porter (2006) show how local power easily colonises the spaces created by national Poverty Reduction Strategy programmes, turning rules to different ends. Their careful case studies from Vietnam, Uganda, Pakistan and New Zealand show that donor-established liberal frameworks of governance are incapable of disciplining existing power. Instead, they have the effect of pulling 'a thin institutionalist veil over fundamental (often territorial) aspects of poverty, and making frail compromises with territorial governance around community, local partnership and some kinds of decentralization' (2006: 27).

Ethnography of aid contributes to disabusing the formalist 'delusion that agency can be incentivized to operate independently of political economy' (Craig and Porter 2006: 11, 120) or that political orders can be reorganised by international policy or aid flows. In all these cases, as Timothy Mitchell argues, the effects of policy and expertise do not arise from pre-formed designs imposed from outside, but are wrought through the rupture and contradictions they effect in existing social, political and ecological systems (Mitchell 2002: 77).

Development professionals are not, of course, ignorant of these facts. Many understand all too well that formal models are slippery in application, finding 'fraught accommodation with the political economy of place, history, production and territorial government' (Craig and Porter 2006: 120). But the fact is that development policy is resolutely optimistic about the power of its favoured approaches and institutional solutions, overplaying impact and blurring the normative and the actual. Such optimism is premised on a denial of history as well as politics. This is the practice, as Pritchett and Woodcock (2004) put it, of 'skipping straight to Weber', that is, transferring principles of bureaucratic rationality from place to place, which involves institutional mythologies that conceal the fact that in reality, institutional solutions 'emerge from an internal historical process of trial and error and [of] political struggle' and that part of 'the solution' is to hide this fact (2004: 201).

Development's travelling orthodoxies ought to be fragile in the face of historical reality, local politics and the reality of incentives, but they are not. In fact, they are remarkably resilient and sustain over-optimism about the possibilities of their application (Craig and Porter 2006). Asking how this is so takes us from the characteristics of policy ideas to the institutional processes within which professionals produce them. It involves turning from the way formal models are unravelled by politics in the places where they are applied to the way that policy ideas are shaped by the politics of the institutions in which they are conceived.

Institutional Processes of Knowledge Production

There are a number of ethnographic approaches to the study of expert policy making. First, there is the study of expert knowledge in relation to institutional power – the political economy of knowledge and its governmental effects – including how expert knowledge is critical to maintaining legitimacy and defining organisational cultures. Such studies focus on the World Bank's economic knowledge (St Clair 2006), its environmental knowledge (Goldman 2005) and its social development expertise (Li 2007). Secondly, there is the ethnographic attention to extra-institutional or transnational networks of experts through which policy is shaped. For example, Janine Wedel's (2000) work on the U.S.A.'s economic aid programme to Russia generated a striking account of crony relationships between expert players from Harvard and their Russian partners in the so-called Chubais Clan.

Thirdly, there are ethnographies concerned with the transmission mechanisms of expert knowledge, especially those operating internally within institutions. Such work focuses on the everyday practices of professionalisation, ideological control through structures of incentives or internal career-building, and the self-disciplining of aid bureaucrats that give resilience to expert ideas at the centre in the face of contradictory evidence (cf. Schmidt 2000). Here we find not only the high-level blindness of orthodox neoliberals to the social effects of market liberalisation in Russia (underpinned by the relationships between IMF economists and Wall Street) so starkly portrayed by Joseph Stiglitz (2002), but equally the many technical fads and fashions such as the 'Training and Visit' approach to agricultural extension that the World Bank continued to up-scale, internationalise and package into multi-million dollar loans, long after the approach had lost credibility outside (Anderson et al. 2006). This is the corollary of aid's individualising narratives of failure, namely 'group think', censorship and reliance on templates, which minimise individual risk by dispersing accountability and blame (in case of failure) to the institution as a whole (Woods 2006), and now more widely through interlocked orthodoxies of different international aid organisations (Eyben 2011).

Failure itself, or accounting for it, may provide an important means to affirm the salience of ruling policy ideas, expertise or technology, precisely by assigning the causes of failure to contingent factors, individual error and a variety of residual elements including 'cultural factors'. By distributing events cleanly either side of a divide between the intended and the contingent, failure helps protect professionals and instantiate frameworks of proper interpretation.

A fourth type of research shifts attention away from the rationality of power, whether disciplinary or governmentalising, towards knowledge production as a micro-political field, to actor worlds and the social life of ideas. One aspect is the importance of actor relationships in the shaping and salience of policy ideas. Decision-making knowledge – even apparently hard economic facts and statistics – is produced out of complex relationships, contests over status, across different disciplinary points of view, through team leadership struggles, conflict management or compliance with client frameworks that define what counts as knowledge, as shown by Peter Griffiths's (2003) engaging story of a World Bank-funded consultancy on the economic analysis of food policy in Sierra Leone in the mid 1980s.

The other aspect is the importance of policy ideas themselves in mediating social and professional relationships. In this sense, strategically shaped and deployed expert ideas (and their artefacts, files and documents) are a means of agency and have social effects at their point of formulation. Policy ideas gain currency because they are socially appropriate, perhaps because (as I have argued for the idea of 'participation') they can submerge ideological differences, mediate diverging understandings of development and so win supporters. In actor network terms, they are good translators. Ideas are cutting edge and able to legitimise financial flows because they have social efficacy as well as intellectual merit (or even in its absence) or because they function as 'boundary objects' and allow dialogue but preserve a certain structure of institutional power (St Clair n.d.).

My own study of social development 'thought work' in the World Bank is a case in point (Mosse 2011b). Participating in the world of non-economist social scientists at the World Bank in 2003–4, it became clear to me that these professionals defined policy concepts so as to manage their structural vulnerability in an 'economics fortress' (Cernea 1995: 4). Essentially, their conceptual work helped manage their relationship with the dominant disciplines and power holders in the World Bank (task managers, vice-presidents and regional budget holders) in order to attend to their own 'system goal' of protecting professional space. Tactical concessions pushed the collective analytical work towards instrumental formulations of the social and to social analysis that could be 'sold' to World Bank staff and other donors as 'products' – business lines, models, best practices, tools, how-to-do manuals, etc. These were high-profile corporate knowledge products (social capital, 'integrated country social analysis', etc.) useful for the internal negotiation of loans and projects but of limited influence either on operations or in development research.

Expert knowledge that is in this way strategic or 'anticipatory' – that is, shaped in ways that anticipate the reaction of others (Schwegler 2008) – is often conceptually incoherent. This is also quite normal. Examples can be multiplied to show how expert consensus is in response to policy makers' exigencies, how 'politics drove the technocrats and not vice versa' or how 'Ideas prevail not because they are the "best" ideas in technical or professional sense but because they best meet the social, organizational, and political needs of key actors' (Woods 2006: 69). But such knowledge or expert consensuses are also fragile and unstable. Policy notions that are political in conception are vulnerable to shifts in institutional politics, even while being robust in face of contractions of practice. Oriented towards the changing demand for 'corporate products', the World Bank's social development professionals (including anthropologists) demonstrated this vulnerability as well as the progressive loss of a capacity for ethnographic reflection on the contradictions of development practice – and in consequence contributed to a wider knowledge system that perpetuated the separation of the world of policy rationality from the contingencies of practice.

It is not then the failure of globalised development policy to execute planned social transformation around the world that has to be explained, but rather the success of institutions in sustaining prevailing neoliberal institutionalist models as an accepted interpretation of what is going on and what can be accomplished. What needs to be explained is the striking expert capacity to represent complex events in formalistic terms, which allows social change to be understood as subject to policy levers acting directly on the behaviour of economic agents through manipulable structures of incentives so as to produce global accountability, efficiency and equity (the World Bank's social development goals).

Timothy Mitchell's insight in his *Rule of Experts* is exactly this. The pervasive 'gaps' between policy and practice, the ideal and the actual, representation and reality are not a disappointment, but are actively maintained by the operations of expertise precisely in order to preserve policy as a structure of representation that allows actual practice to be seen as the outcome of the policy ideal; this is in order to reproduce a sphere of rational intention that can appear external to and generative of events or to 'rearrange power over people as power over ideas' (Mitchell 2002: 90). The ethnographic task, then, is to examine the social mechanisms through which the aid industry creates and sustains the expertise that governs it (and the ethnographically encountered 'professionalism') as well as the relationships, events and politics that this expertise conceals (cf. Mosse 2005).

The Failure of Ethnography

This glancing review reveals expertise or professionalism in international development as a complex and unstable social product, born of institutional politics that are subject to shifts and ruptures. There is homology (not determinism) between the processes of knowledge production in international institutions, the life worlds of aid professionals and the tensions of social science encounters with which I began. Development professionals are drawn into sustaining frameworks of interpretation and the suppression of threatening ethnographic reality, although this itself is a deeply 'un-professional' view of things. Perhaps now it is easier to see how fraught the relationship between development professionals and ethnographers can be. The analysis through which an anthropologist generates fresh knowledge and fulfils his or her professional identity is exactly that which is seen to undermine the professionalism of development experts and managers. But there is also an irony. In objecting to my ethnographic account, my development professional colleagues were in fact endorsing one of its key points, namely 'that authoritative actors work hardest to defend projects as "systems of representations", not only against the destabilizing contingencies of practice, but also now against competing (ethnographic) representations existing potentially within the same public space' (Mosse 2006a: 942). The more they objected, the more evidence they supplied for this argument.

From another point of view, however, the claims of ethnographers to understand and represent others' professional lives are arrogant. In effect, anthropologists make themselves cosmopolitan by rendering other experts 'local', whether they be World Bank officials, aid consultants or international health experts. Ethnography denies to others their cosmopolitan claims by contextualising, localising and placing them in relationships. Our ethnographic localising strategies are damaging to the work of professional identity formation and to cosmopolitan claims that are always fragile. Failing to take professionals on their terms, ethnography can invoke rage. Claims of damage to professional reputations may follow; defamation cases may be threatened.

But matters do not end with objections raised against illicit accounts that subvert official technocratic/managerial views or intercept the rule of experts. In defending themselves, anthropologists' professional interlocutors may themselves work to localise our own cosmopolitan claims – and to unravel our professional anthropological knowledge – by placing it back in relationships. The way in which expert informants raise objections – refusing ethnographic exit from fieldwork relations (see Mosse 2006a) – may actually challenge the basis of ethnographic description.

In my case, objectors did not dispute the factuality of the research so much as its social basis. The problem was that I did not share their premises that the social can and should only be analysed socially, and that the truth about the project had to be consensual, public and accountable. Indeed, the way that it analyses the play of power and interests in the public realm means that anthropology rarely concedes to a democratic process of knowledge production. Ever since Malinowski set out its basic method, ethnography has been premised on some separation of the work of writing from the relations of fieldwork; and from the tension between 'field' and 'desk', identification and distanciation, comes the potential for critique. What my objectors sought, above all, was to collapse this separation by a refusal to engage with the text and to insist on the re-incorporation of me, its author, into the moral relations of a professional group, thus disallowing ethnographic exit. Given the essentially relational nature of ethnographic knowledge – in the sense both that knowledge is collaborative, dialogical, gained by way of relations, and that (in consequence) the relationship between researcher and the object of enquiry becomes a property of the object itself (Hastrup 2004: 457) – ethnographic representations have the potential to unravel when our informants (as did mine) attempt to unpack our 'evidence' back into our relationships with them (see Mosse 2006a).

In other words, expert informants offer an epistemological threat by localising or parochialising our ethnographic cosmopolitanism, by re-embedding our professional (academic) knowledge in social relations (just as we did theirs), denying the worth of our 'evidence' or social research, and especially by resisting the anthropological boundary between ethnographic writing and the relations of fieldwork that is the pretext for description. This traces another route to Miyazaki and Riles' ethnographic 'end point', where expert subjects make a 'radical disjuncture between the moment of ethnography [the ethnographic encounter] and the moment of writing [the description and analysis] untenable' and when there is a failure 'to assert analytical control over the material' (2005: 326–28) .

Sometimes, anthropologists will find it impossible to mark a boundary and 'objectify' cosmopolitan colleagues as social actors; they may fail to exit from professional communities so as to allow description (or the analysis may have to side-step into mimicry or parallel modes, as in Riles 2001, 2006). At other times, such boundary making may be contested through objections, as I have described. Finally, a descriptive account of the 'culture of development' may itself (as Riles argues in the case of the culture of human rights) be drawn into and become instrumentalised by the existing institutional discourse. The critique of professional knowledge is absorbed as anthropologists, for example, in the World Bank, instrumentalise their own analysis.

Today anthropologists are caught between twin demands, on the one hand, of entering the public realm and contributing to public policy and, on the other, of generating a critical anthropology of those same knowledge processes, including the 'non-public' aspects of public knowledge. Dilemmas arise particularly where the users of research are also the subjects of research (and vice versa), and where research generates information on non-public institutional relations that, when published, circulates within these same systems competing with their own knowledge. Clearly, the right to academic knowledge can no longer be taken for granted and has to be negotiated alongside other forms of knowledge. Through a mode of interaction that solicits objections to ethnographic representations without requiring resolution, anthropologists can engage with professional interlocutors and public knowledge regimes beyond consensus while acknowledging the genuine underlying tensions of epistemology and purpose.

Notes

1. This chapter draws on the introductory essay of an edited volume on the anthropology of expertise and professionalism in international development (Mosse 2011b) and extracts some passages from the text of a public lecture given in November 2007 at the Universities of Guelph and Simon Fraser, Vancouver (the 2007 Hopper Lecture supported by the Canadian International Development Research Centre [IDRC]) and in revised form as an inaugural lecture at SOAS, London on 18 January 2008. Some passages first appeared in a Forum article in *Focaal* Volume 52 (2008). I am grateful to Sue Wright for her editorial suggestions.

2. Quotes from correspondence with my critics which I refrain from attributing.

References

Allahyari, R. 2000. *Visions of Charity: Volunteer Workers and Moral Community.* Berkeley and London: University of California Press.

American Ethnologist. 2006. 'AE Forum: IRBs, Bureaucratic Regulation, and Academic Freedom', *American Ethnologist* 33(4): 477–548.

Anderson, Jock R., Gershon Feder and Sushma Ganguly. 2006. 'The Rise and Fall of Training and Visit Extension: An Asian Mini-Drama with an African Epilogue', *World Bank Policy Research Working Paper* 3928, May.

Arvidson, Malin. 2008. 'Contradictions and Confusions in Development Work: Exploring the Realities of Bangladeshi NGOs', *Journal of South Asian Development* 3(1): 109–34.

Cernea, Michael. 1995. 'Social Organisation and Development Anthropology', *Environmentally Sustainable Development Studies and Monograph Series*, No. 6. Washington DC: The World Bank.

Craig, David and Doug Porter. 2006. *Development Beyond Neoliberalism: Governance, Poverty Reduction and Political Economy.* London and New York: Routledge.

Eyben, Rosalind. 2011. 'The Sociality of International Aid and Policy Convergence', in D. Mosse (ed.), *Adventures in Aidland: The Anthropology of Professionals in International Development.* Oxford: Berghahn Books.

Friedman J. 1997. 'Global Crisis, the Struggle for Cultural Identity and Intellectual Pork-barrelling: Cosmopolitans versus Locals, Ethnics and Nationals in an Era of Dehegemonisation', in P. Werbner and T. Modood (eds), *Debating Cultural Hybridity: Multi-Cultural Identities and the Politics of Anti-Racism*. London: Zed Books, pp. 70–89.

Goldman, M. 2005. *Imperial Nature: The World Bank and Struggles for Social Justice in the Age of Globalisation*. New Haven and London: Yale University Press.

Griffiths, Peter. 2003. *The Economists' Tale: A Consultant Encounters Hunger and the World Bank*. London: Zed Press.

Hannerz Ulf. 1996. *Transnational Connections*. New York: Routledge.

Harper, Ian. 2011. 'World Health and Nepal: Producing Internationals, Healthy Citizenship and the Cosmopolitan', in David Mosse (ed.), *Adventures in Aidland: The Anthropology of Professionals in International Development*. Oxford: Berghahn Books.

Hastrup, Kirsten. 2004. 'Getting it Right: Knowledge and Evidence in Anthropology', *Anthropological Theory* 4(4): 455–72.

Holmes, Douglas, R. and George E. Marcus. 2005. 'Cultures of Expertise and the Management of Globalisation: Towards a Re-Functioning of Ethnography', in Aihwa Ong and Stephen Collier (eds), *Global Assemblages: Technology, Politics and Ethics as Anthropological Problems*. Oxford/New York: Blackwell, pp. 235–52.

Latour, Bruno. 1996. *Aramis, or the Love of Technology*, trans. Catherine Porter. Cambridge, MA and London: Harvard University Press.

———. 2000. 'When Things Strike Back: A Possible Contribution of Science Studies', *British Journal of Sociology* 51(1): 107–23.

Li, Tania Murray. 2007. *The Will to Improve: Governmentality, Development, and the Practice of Politics*. Durham, NC: Duke University Press.

Mitchell, Timothy. 2002. *Rule of Experts: Egypt, Techno-politics, Modernity*. Berkeley: University of California Press.

Miyazaki, Hirokazu and Annelise Riles. 2005. 'Failure as an Endpoint', in Aihwa Ong and Stephen Collier (eds), *Global Assemblages: Technology, Politics and Ethics as Anthropological Problems*. Oxford and New York: Blackwell, pp. 320–31.

Mosse, David. 2005. *Cultivating Development: Ethnography of Aid Policy and Practice*. London and Ann Arbor, MI: Pluto Press.

———. 2006a. 'Anti-Social Anthropology? Objectivity, Objection and the Ethnography of Public Policy and Professional Communities', *Journal of the Royal Anthropological Institute* 12(4): 935–56.

———. 2006b. 'Ethics and Development Ethnography', *Anthropology Today* 22(3): 23–24.

———. 2011a. 'Social Analysis as Corporate Product: Non-Economists/ Anthropologists at Work at the World Bank in Washington DC', in D. Mosse (ed.), *Adventures in Aidland: The Anthropology of Professionals in International Development*. Oxford: Berghahn Books.

———. (ed.) 2011b. *Adventures in Aidland: The Anthropology of Professionals in International Development*. Oxford: Berghahn Books.

Nader, Laura. 2002 [1969]. 'Up the Anthropologist. Perspectives Gained from Studying Up', in D. Hymes (ed.), *Reinventing Anthropology*. Ann Arbor: University of Michigan Press, pp. 284–311.

Perkins, John. 2003. *Confessions of an Economic Hitman*. London: Plume.

Pritchett, Lant and Michael Woolcock. 2004. 'Solutions when the Solution is the Problem: Arraying the Disarray in Development', *World Development* 32(2): 191–212.

Riles, Annelise. 2001. *The Network Inside Out*. Ann Arbor: Michigan University Press.

———. 2004. 'Real Time: Unwinding Technocratic and Anthropological Knowledge', *American Ethnologist* 31(3): 392–405.

———. 2006. 'Anthropology, Human Rights, and Legal Knowledge: Culture in the Iron Cage, *American Anthropologist* 108(1): 52–65.

St Clair, Asunción Lera. 2006a. 'The World Bank as a Transnational Expertised Institution', *Global Governance* 12(1): 77–95.

———. n.d. 'Ideas in Action: Human Development and Capability as Boundary Objects', unpublished manuscript.

Schmidt Jeff. 2000. *Disciplined Minds: A Critical Look at Salaried Professionals*. Lanham (Maryland), Boulder, New York and Oxford: Rowman & Littlefield.

Schwegler, Tara. 2008. 'Take it from the Top (Down)? Rethinking Neoliberalism and Political Hierarchy in Mexico', *American Ethnologist* 38(4): 682–700.

Shore, Cris and Susan Wright (eds). 1997. *Anthropology of Policy: Critical Perspectives on Governance and Power*. London and New York: Routledge.

Sridhar, Devi. 2005. 'Ethics and Development: Some Concerns with David Mosse's *Cultivating Development*', *Anthropology Today* 21(6): 17–19.

Stiglitz, Joseph. 2002. *Globalization and its Discontents*. New York: W.W. Norton & Co.

Wedel, Janine. 2000. *Collision and Collusion: The Strange Case of Western Aid to Eastern Europe*. New York: Palgrave.

Wedel, Janine, Cris Shore, Greg Feldman and Stacy Lathrop. 2005. 'Toward an Anthropology of Public Policy', *Annals of the American Academy of Political and Social Science* 600, July: 30–51.

Woods, Ngaire. 2006. *The Globalizers: the IMF, the World Bank and their Borrowers*. Ithaca and London: Cornell University Press.

Woolcock, Michael. 1998. 'Social Capital and Economic Development: Towards a Theoretical Synthesis and Policy Framework', *Theory and Society* 27: 151–208.

Chapter 4

Peopling Policy: On Conflicting Subjectivities of Fee-Paying Students

Gritt B. Nielsen

Introduction

In spring 2005, an Amendment was passed by the Danish Parliament to internationalise Danish universities by encouraging Danish students to study abroad and foreign students to come to Denmark. The Amendment required Danish universities to charge tuition fees from certain non-European students who previously had studied for free. Half a year after the passing of the Amendment, a group of Chinese students taking a master's degree at a Danish university wrote a complaint directly to the Minister of Science about the 'low quality' of their programme. The students had been charged fees and their complaint, amongst other things, was that the university had lowered its standards so as to accept unqualified students and make more money. This incident can be seen as the first test of the legal and moral aspects of the government-initiated policy. In terms of legality, an investigation was called for because the university had charged the fees before the Amendment took effect. In terms of morality, the students felt that the programme did not live up to the description they had been given when in China. Teachers and university officials, on the other hand, saw the students' tactic of writing a complaint directly to the Minister, and the Ministry's subsequent request for an account from the university, as immoral and illegitimate. They embraced a notion of the student as a 'co-owner' or 'partner' of the university and perceived the students' behaviour as typical of 'customers' and as such undesirable.

By taking as its point of departure the Chinese students' complaint, this chapter discusses the relations between the Parliamentary Amendment and the conduct of a group of fee-paying students. It questions the relationship between policy and subjectivity, and seeks to explore how different ways of 'peopling' policy, as Stephen Ball (1997) has phrased it, lead to different understandings of the workings of policy and its relations to the production of subjectivity. Inspired by Foucault and parts of the Anglo-Saxon governmentality literature (Rose and Miller 1992; Dean 1999; Rose 1999), I conceptualise policy as a relation between, first, political programmes and justifications for particular ways of exercising power ('political rationalities'); second, everyday practices and methods introduced to govern particular people in particular ways ('governmental technologies'); and, third, the perceptions, experiences and conduct ('subjectivities') of the people towards whom these rationalities and technologies are directed.

Despite the fact that Dean, Rose and Miller all advocate a focus on the interplay between 'political rationalities' and 'governmental technologies' (see, e.g., Rose and Miller 1992: 175), they and other 'governmentality studies' have been criticised for overemphasising political discourses and programmes at the expense of the everyday practices, strife and negotiations through which policy is constantly enacted and re-enacted. As O'Malley, Weir and Shearing argue, these studies are at risk of generating 'ideal typifications which often are in danger of being little more than the systematized self-representation of rule' (O'Malley, Weir and Shearing 1997: 504; see also Clarke et al. 2007: 20f.). In other words, if politics and policies are reduced to a mentality of rule or a practice of thinking (cf. governmentality), the 'peopling' of policy tends to become implicit and one-dimensional: the persons towards whom a policy directs its efforts are construed in the image of, and as mere effects of, a political rationality. The relation of rationality-technology-subjectivity becomes a neat three-step progression. In contrast, ethnographic explorations into people's everyday lives often show that their subjectivities and their use of technologies are rarely as clear-cut and neat as is presented in a political rationality. The challenge, therefore, is to explore the connections between larger programmes or rationalities and locally negotiated practices without ending up either with an idealised reproduction of general political rationalities in a one-dimensional or implicit peopling of policy, or with descriptions of myriads of complex local practices with no connection to larger structures and policy processes in society (a criticism raised against some micro-ethnographic studies).

I will start by exploring how the publicly known story-line of the Amendment and the Chinese students' complaint turns policy into an objectified item and brings into focus an almost causal relationship between the three policy elements (rationality-technology-subjectivity). I then draw on a wider ethnographic enquiry into the students' accounts of their complaint in the context of their everyday lives. Their accounts not only complexify the picture; they destabilise the otherwise relatively neat relationship between rationality, technology and subjectivity, and call for new ways of theorising policy processes. The chapter shows that ethnographic enquiry has the potential to make an important contribution to policy studies by 'peopling' policy with multi-dimensional actors whose subjectivities are created in the intersections or assemblages of different rationalities, technologies, norms and values.

A Case of Illegal Fees and the Chinese Students' Complaint

In order to explore different notions of policy, I shall briefly outline the publicly known storyline of the Amendment, the fees and the Chinese students' complaint. The Danish Parliament passed the Amendment to the 2003 Danish University Act in spring 2005 (Folketinget 2005). The official aim of the Amendment was to promote the internationalisation of Danish study programmes – as had also been suggested by the OECD (2004). A scheme to offer free places and grants was set up to attract the best-qualified students from around the world. To finance this scheme, the Danish government argued that, instead of all students, regardless of place of origin, studying for free in Denmark, it was necessary to introduce full fees for certain non-European students.[1] An important argument for the Amendment was that Danish taxpayers should no longer pay for the increased number of foreigners and especially Chinese students studying in Denmark. So, when a major Danish newspaper in the summer of 2005 made public the news that a particular Danish university had increased its intake of Chinese students by eighty per cent in the preceding year, certain politicians accused the university of strategic money making and an abuse of state subsidies (Svanholm 2005d; Aarslund and Svanholm 2005).[2] The reason for the accusation was that 2005 was the last year before the Amendment took effect and was thus the last year that universities would get state funding for these kinds of students.

The university denied the accusations and explained that they had accepted the Chinese students as part of a long-term internationalisation strategy prepared before the Amendment was passed. However, a few days later, the same newspaper revealed that the Chinese students had in fact paid a fee equivalent to about 13,500 Euros, even though the university at the same time received state funding for the students (Svanholm 2005c). The university's rector explained that the fees were charged for extra services which were not covered by the state funding and that such fees were made legal by the University Act 2003. Furthermore, he argued that, before approving the fees, he had asked the Ministry of Science for permission. In his words, the Ministry in a phone conversation had accepted that the university could charge fees. The Ministry denied having approved the fees. Instead, the Minister asked the State Attorney to investigate the legal aspects of the university's charging fees.

Three months later, a group of Chinese students from the same university heard about the still ongoing investigation and as 'students directly involved in the affair', as they put it, they found it important to provide the Minister with what they saw as 'related information'. Therefore, eight of the students wrote an official complaint about their study programme directly to the Minister of Science and made the headlines in a national newspaper (Svanholm

2005a and 2005b). Claiming to speak for more than 100 Chinese students on the particular master's programme, they complained that the programme was of low quality:

> We feel totally disappointed by the quality of the education provided ... it [is] not worth the amount we paid ... We have evidence showing [that] the charging of tuition [fees] has directly resulted in the poor educational quality. (Chinese students' complaint to Minister of Science, 6 November 2005)

They felt they had ended up in a 'Chinese ghetto' and that 'the programme was purposely established only [to collect fees from] Chinese students' (ibid.: 3). The students complained that the university department had lowered its admission standards in order to recruit students and make more money. In addition, they complained about cancelled lectures and inexperienced teachers with poor English language skills. They said that the programme did not contain the courses and the internship in a business enterprise that they had expected, and that the title of the degree had also been changed after they had enrolled (due to an order from the Ministry). By providing the Minister with this 'related information' and arguing that the education programme was not worth the money they had paid, they hoped to be reimbursed.

When confronted by the press with the students' complaint, the Minister announced that he would look into the situation because, as he said, 'we should be able to deliver a commodity with which also Chinese students are satisfied'.[3] The 'we' here is obviously not the 'we' of the university or the department responsible for the international programme. It is a 'we' alluding to a more national unit or identity. The Minister therefore announced that he wanted the university to give him an account of the whole process concerning the quality of the programme. Two days after the publication of the students' complaint, the State Attorney issued his decision concerning the legality of the fees. He ruled that the university had charged the fees illegally. Fees could be charged for extra services but only if these were voluntary, which had not been the case with the Chinese students. Furthermore, some of the expenditure for which the university had charged fees was covered by the normal state subsidies. Therefore, the university was to partly reimburse the students.

Objectified Policy – Implemented or Appropriated

In the story of the Amendment and the students' complaint, there are two important and intersecting strands. One concerns the negotiation of the legal aspects of the student fees, as outlined above. The other strand revolves around notions of morality: who or what should have a say in the process of defining and assuring quality, and what are the acceptable modes of conduct? How can these strands of the policy process be understood and conceptualised? And how do different kinds of 'peopling' of policy entail different analytical notions of 'policy' and the rationality-technology-subjectivity triad? I will start this section by outlining two central analytical approaches to studying policy and explore what policy notions are actualised, and how and when in our story. In the following section, I turn to the moral strand of the story to further discuss the relation between policy and subjectivity.

One common way of perceiving policy processes is as a linear movement running from problem identification and policy formation to policy implementation and evaluation – an approach that rather simplistically can be described under the canopy of 'implementation studies' (Shore and Wright 1997; Ball 1997). By endorsing a linear logic, implementation studies perceive the policy process as starting with an idea, rationality or programme that is then turned into a technology and is implemented in different settings so that the people at whom these rationalities and technologies are directed find their perceptions, experiences and conduct (subjectivities) adjusting accordingly. This logic not only posits the policy as a movable object, and one that can be 'identically' articulated in the different elements of the 'rationality-technology-subjectivity' triad; it also assumes a certain temporal linearity, so that in our case the Ministry or Parliament would be treated as the source of origin, the university as the site or context of implementation and the students as the target whose subjectivity is to change.

In the story of the Amendment, the system of law reinforced the logic of linear implementation. In a sense, the university embraced the government's overall internationalisation strategies that were encapsulated in the Amendment, but had acted prematurely by introducing obligatory tuition fees for the non-European students before the Amendment officially came into effect. Because the university had not followed the expected linearity of legal policy processes, an investigation was required to invoke the proper order of implementation. However, this process and the university's premature conduct is a good example of the problems that the logic of linear implementation often faces. Policy processes are rarely actualised in a neat and linear movement from a source of origin to its sites of implementation – they tend to be messier and far more contingent than this logic assumes. This is the reason why, within the field of anthropology, it has been suggested that processes of 'appropriation' rather than 'implementation' should be studied (Sutton and Levinson 2001).

To Sutton and Levinson (2001), the term 'appropriation' is meant to assign agency and creativity to the people towards whom a policy is directed. In this way of thinking, people are not puppets of policy but 'take in' elements of the policy according to their own situated interests and values: 'appropriation is a kind of taking of policy and making it one's own' (2001: 3). In other words, the 'appropriation' approach is an attempt to more thoroughly 'people' policy with the voices and bodies that negotiate, accept and resist policy elements in their everyday lives. From this perspective, the university could be seen as appropriating a certain set of ideas and transforming them into (illegal) action. The Amendment articulated a particular 'rationality' that linked the internationalisation of higher education to global competition and marketisation and introduced the 'technology' of student fees for certain foreign students. But the fees that the university charged were not, in a linear and legal sense, introduced as an implementation of the Amendment. The Rector from 2002 to 2006 was the chair of the international committee of the Danish Rector's Conference, which was not negative about introducing fees for foreign students (Rektorkollegiet 2004a: Ad4; 2004b: 19). He participated in various different national and international seminars on the internationalisation of universities and had a good knowledge of the political arena and trends towards internationalisation. In this vein, the university seemed to appropriate – or be appropriated by – a kind of international policyscape (Ball 2006), i.e., a general set of ideas about marketisation and internationalisation that were emerging in Denmark and were already manifested in other countries where fees had been introduced (e.g., the U.K. and New Zealand).

The difference between 'implementation' and 'appropriation' to a large extent seems to concern questions of agency, ownership and origin. In both perspectives, policy becomes objectified as a force or identifiable phenomenon which people can appropriate to fit their own life situation (the logic of appropriation) or are appropriated by (the logic of implementation). 'Implementation' stresses the 'sameness' of the policy throughout its different elements of rationality-technology-subjectivity and thereby resembles what Bruno Latour calls 'diffusion' and 'transportation' (Latour 1986; 1999: 15; 2005: 106; 37f.). In the diffusion/implementation perspective, a phenomenon, like an order or claim, is seen as being disseminated, transported and complied with because it has an inherent logic and force attributed to it from its initial source. In contrast, 'appropriation' seems to point to policy as a series of 'translations' or 'transformations' where no idea or technology can ever be 'transported' as completely the 'same' (Callon 1986: 224; Law 2003; Latour 2005: 108). The notion of translation has been taken up by some organisation studies to show how ideas are transformed into different actions in diverse institutional contexts (Modell 2005: 538–39).

The two logics of implementation and appropriation each locate agency in a different dimension of the triad. Whereas 'implementation' alludes to a process where 'the policy' becomes objectified and imbued with an agency that attempts to (successfully or otherwise) subjugate persons, the notion of 'appropriation' alludes to the opposite process whereby persons or organisations as actors are able to translate the 'policy', a more inert and transformable object, in their own image. This is similar to the idea of appropriation in the art world, which refers to a practice whereby a creative actor copies, incorporates or 'steals' other artists' images, gives them new meaning by putting them in a new context and signs them as his or her own (Schneider 2003). Accordingly, notions of ownership and origin become essential when the policy analysis takes as its point of departure either the 'implementation' or the 'appropriation' of an objectified policy or particular policy elements. Invocation of ownership and origin provide the owner with a certain (moral or legal) power and legitimacy to act in particular ways. In our story, the university claimed that recruiting Chinese students and charging them fees had nothing to do with the particular Amendment. It was part of their own long-term internationalisation policy, they said, while claiming that the charging of fees had been made legal by the University Act 2003, not its Amendment. The reference to the (presumed) phone conversation between the Rector and the Ministry about the legality of the fees discloses another attempt to locate responsibility and make the origin of the fees legitimate. But the stringent textual demands of legal matters made the transient words of a phone conversation irrelevant. The Chinese students also tried to invoke a certain ownership over the programme in order to influence or appropriate the policy process of legal assessment. However, their notion of ownership, as I will now reveal, drew on ideas of 'customer rights' and conflicted with the university's ideal of democratic 'co-ownership' over the institution, the programme and their own course of study.

Appropriating Policy Subjectivities? The Student as Customer and Co-owner

The moral strand of the story highlights the relation between policy and subjectivity, and allows us to explore the production of subjectivity in a more nuanced way. As political tools of government and power, policies aim at regulating and adjusting a certain sociality by attempting to govern the field of action of particular people. Consequently, their influence on the conduct and perception of individuals depends on the degree to which individuals accept or internalise the norms and codes of conduct endorsed through a policy – an interplay that Rabinow (1984) has phrased as one between external 'subjection' and internal 'subjectification'. The former, with its external construction of the subject, echoes 'implementation', while 'appropriation' resembles the process by which the subject makes the external construction her or his own.

In the story, the most prominent keyword describing the Chinese students' subjectivity was the notion of 'customer'. This concept was not promoted directly in the Amendment (as has been the case for example in the U.K.'s 2003 White Paper, *The Future of Higher Education* [see Tlili and Wright 2005]) but was essential to the leaders' and teacher's explanations of the students' behaviour and modes of participation. In their complaint to the Minister, the students enclosed a former complaint to the Head of Department in which they evoked the notion of 'customer':

> If the lectures are not interesting and don't meet our requirement, we believe it reasonable not to attend especially (if) there is no improvement after complaints. As customers, we believe we have rights to reject low quality products! (Chinese students' complaint to the Head of Department, February 2005)

The Chinese students attempted to get back their fees by using the language of the law: they talked of themselves as customers with certain 'rights' and of the programme as a 'product' with 'low quality' which was 'not worth the amount they had paid'. If the university had evoked arguments of ownership over the international programme and the introduction of fees in order to claim, if not a legal, then at least a moral integrity, the students tried to appropriate the policy process by linking the issue of 'legality' to a question of 'quality'. By referring to 'rights', they claimed ownership over the programme (construed as a commodity) and hence attempted to influence or 'appropriate' the policy process in their image.

The students' argument about 'low quality' did not fit the legal logic and therefore officially was not used directly in the legal investigation into the fees. However, the students did succeed in actualising the link between 'fees' and 'quality' in a manner that made the Minister respond, contrary to normal procedures, by demanding an account from the university. The Minister endorsed a market logic and customer discourse similar to that of the students when he argued that it was necessary to look into the case because 'we' as a nation should be able to deliver a satisfactory commodity to foreign students. The behaviour of the students and the Ministry were in no way illegal but, morally, from the Rector's, the Head of Department's and the teacher's perspectives, both the students and the Ministry had acted in an illegitimate way:

> The complaint should have gone to us in the first place and the Ministry should have sent it back to us as soon as they had received it – indicating that it is the university's job to deal with this. (Rector, December 2005)

> In public administration, custom would prompt this case to be returned and treated locally … It's not normal to say: we will take this case, and deal with it because someone has managed to get the newspapers to write about it. (Head of Department, November 2005)

With the students' complaint and the Minister's response, power relations were reshuffled between students, the university leaders and the Ministry, and an unprecedented room of manoeuvre for students in Denmark opened up. But to the university leaders, the process had undermined the university traditions of autonomy and local management: first, the students should have exhausted the options available to them within the university's internal systems before going public and complaining to the Minister. Second, and this the leaders perceived as even worse, the Ministry had interfered with university traditions of local management by requesting an account.

In terms of the Minister's conduct, the leaders felt that the right-wing government had used the opportunity to put the university – which had been criticised as being left-wing – in a bad light. In terms of the Chinese students' (immoral) conduct, the charging of fees was to a considerable extent construed as the motivation for their behaviour:

> With foreign paying students, new relations arise between them and the university. They act as customers or clients, while we want to turn them into … ehm … to be a part of the university and … to have a certain ownership of it. This university is to a very large extent based on students and student participation. (Rector, December 2005)

Founded in the wake of the 1968 student revolts, this university explicitly encouraged their students to be 'co-owners' of the university. In brochures and the diverse interviews I conducted with Danish students, teachers and leaders, a 'co-owner' was described as one who takes responsibility for his or her own learning and participates actively in the governing bodies in order to influence the development of the education and the university as a whole. He or she enters into dialogue with other parties of the organisation and sees himself or herself as an integrated and co-responsible part of the university. The teacher stated that a relaxed democratic atmosphere prevails at the university where students and teachers most often find solutions through dialogue and consensus. If the students want to complain, 'that's fine', he said, 'it's part of the democratic culture … and then we follow the rules'. That is, the students should use the instruments of complaint available within the system. To this teacher, the Chinese students had dismantled the ideal of dialogue and internal quality assurance, and the fee charging was to a great extent construed as the cause of their conduct:

> It's a kind of poison, money, in this relationship because you don't have this student-teacher exchange [of relaxed dialogue] … when you start to have money involved, then things change. The professors and the institution are under a different pressure. (Teacher, December 2005)

The university managers and the teacher were well aware that other issues like cultural differences and traditions had also played a part in the process of the complaint, but they all evoked the fees as the first and foremost explanation of the students' conduct. The rationale was that when students pay for their education, their behaviour, thoughts and desires are bound to change. Money, as a powerful 'poison' infused in an otherwise democratic and participatory sociality, is here believed to transform students into 'customers' – that is, persons who rely on complaint systems, vote with their feet and do not necessarily get involved in the governing bodies and democratic dialogue with teachers and fellow students, as the Head of Department phrased it. In this perspective, co-owners are seen as 'active', while customers are 'passive' students.

In this line of the story, policy is enacted as a phenomenon that establishes new spaces of power and new subject positions. One particular 'governmental technology' (the student fees) with an attached 'political rationality' (marketisation) is promoted as the source of origin of these new spaces of power and manoeuvring. The fees are construed as having an almost inherent rationality or intentionality which the students are bound to internalise and embody. Here, the linear logic of implementation seems to prevail. A consistent student identity is assumed in a linear movement of causality between the policy's rationality, technology and subjectivity, i.e., between marketisation, money and (im)moral customer behaviour.

Eventalising Policy and Questioning the Power of Money

The causal reductionism promoted within this strand of emic statements seems to be strategic. By attributing a 'poisonous' power to money, other governmental technologies, traditions and codes of conduct are deemed secondary to the production of certain kinds of student subjectivities. As is the case in some governmentality and implementation studies, a thin 'peopling' of policy is here conjured up – the policy process is peopled with what Ball calls 'cardboard cut-out people, one-dimensional caricatures who fail to display the complexities, contradictions and paradoxes that you and I demonstrate' (Ball 1997: 270). One way of exploring these complexities and of moving beyond the one-dimensional peopling produced with the implementation logic (whether emic or etic) is to follow Foucault and 'eventalise' the process. By 'eventalisation', Foucault refers to the process of questioning the invocation of historical constants and of working towards a pluralisation of causes by 'rediscovering the connections, encounters, supports, blockages, plays of forces, strategies, and so on, that at a given moment establish what subsequently counts as being self-evident, universal, and necessary' (Foucault 1994: 226–27). I argue that an 'eventalisation' of the Chinese student case shows that a series of smaller incidents leading up to the ministerial complaint engaged the students in what I will later call different assemblages of language, practices and rationalities. It is in the in-betweens of these shifting assemblages rather than in some inherent power and agency of either 'the policy programme', 'the technology' or 'the students' that the story developed in certain but contingent directions.

By talking about 'customer rights', 'products' and 'value for money' and by filing the complaint to the Minister, the Chinese students indeed seemed to confirm the university managers' analysis of customers as persons who seek influence through complaints, who walk out on classes and who claim value for money as a 'right'. Likewise, a statement from one of the complaining students shows that her emotional debt to her parents who had paid for her studies had encouraged her to speak up about her dissatisfaction: 'I do it [complain to the Minister] for my parents' sake', she said to the newspaper. 'They have worked very hard. It would be a lack of respect to them if I just accepted these conditions' (Svanholm 2005b). Here, the money indeed seemed to be an initiating force of the complaint process, but we can only speculate whether the money was the only element that made this particular student feel dissatisfied and made her speak up.

However, once we start exploring the use of particular keywords and technologies, the clear-cut link between marketisation, fees and student-customers becomes blurred and even dismantled. Two of the Chinese students I interviewed, Jung,[4] a woman in her thirties, and Wang, a man in his late twenties, had been among the main driving forces behind the complaint to the Minister. When I asked them about the notion of 'customer' which they had used in their complaint, they explained that in their view, all students are customers – not only fee-paying foreign students but also non-paying Danish students since, in the latter case, the state pays the university for each student. Accordingly, Jung and Wang said that they did not expect their position or rights to be any different or better than those of the non fee-paying Danish or foreign students. On the contrary, it was because they felt they had been granted fewer rights and poorer information and services than non-paying students that they had spoken up and complained. The word 'customer', taken as a signifier of a particular subject position within a larger discursive frame, no longer seemed to relate neatly with the technology of 'fees' and a rationality of 'marketisation'. Fees were not the relevant marker for being a customer in the eyes of the Chinese students. They compared their own situation with other foreign and Danish students, and found themselves worse off, with less knowledge about the Danish university system, their rights and opportunities. They told me they had had no introduction to the university's governance system and traditions for dealing with complaints.

The programme had been set up with no direct connection to a study board (in which half of the members by law are students) but with a steering group consisting of the Head of Department and the teachers in charge. However, the teacher I interviewed stated that he had tried to encourage the students to elect some representatives to participate in the meetings of the programme's steering group, but that none of the students had wanted to volunteer. Jung and Wang had not heard of such an offer, they said, but agreed that in general the Chinese students had not been good enough at communicating with the teachers and university managers. This was because, as Jung said, to raise criticism towards 'the authorities' is seen as 'aggressive' and inappropriate behaviour in China:

> I just think, we students also have some responsibility on this case, because we didn't … Chinese students just are not good at raising hands and saying 'Stop'. Or 'You should not do that, you should …' We just come to accept what you give us. Actually, during many lectures I was so dissatisfied and just left. Okay, I took the first hour, then I just left, because it was a waste of my time. I think, maybe, I should have raised my hand and then said it. [pause] But I *did* raise [it] many times … Because I think I'm more experienced and my English is much better. But it's like always me, so, okay, I don't do it … We are not so aggressive to say no. (Jung, December 2005)

In her choice of vocabulary, critical participation mainly becomes a question of rejecting something or commanding a change – it is not something taking place in a respectful and equal dialogue. Criticising the teaching is quite extraordinary for Chinese students and Jung and Wang, like the teacher, described the Chinese students as inherently 'passive' in terms of getting involved in developing and influencing the structure and content of courses. The university's self-perception as a 'democratic' university was not only foreign to but also unrealisable for most of these Chinese students.

Jung and Wang were older and more experienced, they said, and therefore they had been capable of taking different initiatives to communicate the dissatisfaction of the class – the complaint to the Minister was only the last in a series of attempts, they stated. Previously, they had expressed their complaints through talking to teachers, filling out course evaluations, writing a letter to the Head of Department and attending a meeting with the Head of Department and the teachers. None of this had led to a satisfactory outcome, they felt. Rather, the different governmental technologies of 'informal dialogue' (often used by the Danish students and teachers and promoted as essential to 'co-ownership'), 'written course evaluations', 'meetings' and 'written complaints' were all attributed different rationalities and intentions by the different participants – and as such caused a great deal of misunderstanding and increased dissatisfaction.

To Jung and Wang, the criticisms they voiced in the course evaluations had not led to the expected changes and as such had not proved to be a means of student participation or co-ownership. The teacher explained to me that at best only around fifty per cent of the students had responded and since these were positive overall, they had not changed any major aspects of the course. Jung and Wang felt ignored and, on behalf of the whole class, they and a handful of other students therefore decided to write a complaint to the Head of Department, which was followed up by a meeting with the Head of Department and a teacher. The latter two told me they had complied with some of the wishes of the students and tried to explain why the rest of their requests were not feasible. But, once again, the expectations about the meaning and power of a technology conflicted. When the Head of Department and the teacher did not receive any further complaints from the students, they thought things had improved and the students were satisfied with the explanations and changes put forward at the meeting. But the students were not satisfied. Apparently the meeting did not have the same status for them as for the Head of Department and the teacher: "It was only a meeting', Wang said to me and explained that they had expected a written reply to their complaint as a follow-up on the meeting. This never came, but at that point they no longer felt up to confronting the Head of Department or the teachers about it. Only when they heard about the legal investigation into the fees did they decide – helped, and maybe also encouraged, by a Danish politician of Taiwanese origin running for the government party in an upcoming local election – to write directly to the Minister to provide him with 'related information'. They hoped this would enhance their chances of reimbursement for a programme they felt they had tried to change for a long time.

Assembling Policy and Student Subjectivities

The eventalisation of the (one-dimensional) relation between market rationality, the technology of fees and the student–customer subjectivity promotes new understandings of policy and of agency than were evoked when the focus was on implementation or appropriation. Maybe the fees did give some of the students an extra incentive to go as far as to write a complaint to the Minister about the quality of the programme. However, fees do not simply turn students into 'passive customers'. As Bloch and Perry (1989) have convincingly argued, money cannot be said to have an inherent power to introduce a certain kind of transformation or revolution in society. Money exchange systems will always relate to existing exchange systems and it is at the intersections of these systems that certain values or moralities emerge. In this view, the rationality or intentionality of the technology of fees is not inherent or internal to it; rather, the technology takes on its meaning when intersecting with other practices, technologies and rationalities – when relating to other elements in transient assemblages[5] that again are associated in larger clusters or assemblies of assemblages (Latour 2005: 260; Deleuze 2006).

Assemblage – like context – means a composition or collection of elements. But what is assembled is not a set of predetermined parts – e.g., a singular object entering into a pre-existing and fixed whole or context – rather, the parts or elements are co-produced through relations. This is Latour's point when stating that 'we are not to follow a given statement through a *context*. We are to follow the *simultaneous* production of a "text" and a "context"' (Latour 1991: 106). In contrast to Modell (see above) in organisation studies, who used 'translation' to describe how ideas are transformed and objectified into actions in certain institutional contexts, Latour here uses 'translation' to refer to a co-production of text and context, i.e., a process of enacting or performing a given phenomenon or reality, not a transformation of either the text (i.e., appropriation) or the context (i.e., implementation).

The focus on constantly emerging assemblages puts in question the human subject or consciousness as 'the universal operator of all transformations' as Foucault has phrased it (1991: 70). It questions the power of human individuals' strategies for gaining ownership, as is highlighted in implementation and appropriation studies:

> The understanding and definition of the human agent as essentially purposeful and self-directive now takes second place to agency as the general collection and dispersion of parts and fragments which co-define each other in a mutable and transient assemblage of possibilities and relations. (Cooper, in Spoelstra 2005: 111)

Agency and subjectivity here emerge in the 'inbetweens' of 'mutable and transient assemblages of possibilities' or networks in which the elements can be anything from objects, technologies and practices to feelings, desires, discourses, keywords and other non-corporeal relations: 'subjectivity is not a property of human souls but of the gathering itself' (Latour 2005: 218). In a certain time and space, the technology of 'fees' was linked up with other governmental technologies like 'informal dialogue', 'evaluations', 'meetings' and 'written complaints' to constitute an overall assembly of assemblages. In the process of forming this overall assembly, previous linkages between certain technologies (like 'evaluations' and 'meetings') and the rationality and subjectivity associated with 'co-ownership' were disassembled. To Jung and Wang, these technologies did not give them influence, and to the teacher and the Head of Department, these technologies now seemed to actualise the notion of 'passive customer' rather than 'active co-owner'. It was in these mutable assemblages – which were partially connected to and co-produced a particular policy – that certain possibilities of student conduct and subjectivity emerged.

Conclusion

For anthropologists, a focus on policy processes has the advantage that it spans government, local administration and everyday life, and therefore cuts across what are often conceived of as different societal scales or levels (Moore 1994). But how should these different scales and their relations to each other be conceptualised in our policy analysis? How should policy be 'peopled' in order to explore the relations between policy and particular subjectivities? I have sought to discuss these questions by unfolding the story of the Amendment, the fees and the Chinese students. As a starting point, I conceptualised policy as a triad of rationality-technology-subjectivity. In order to analyse the intersecting legal and moral strands of the story, I then explored three different notions of policy – as a process of 'implementation', a process of 'appropriation' and a process of 'assembling assemblages' – and discussed how they each people policy differently and highlight certain (causal) links within the triad.

Where some 'implementation studies' and 'governmentality studies' can be criticised for over-emphasising the political rationality and producing a one-dimensional and implicit peopling of policy, the notion of 'appropriation' attempts to recognise the complex and messy processes of negotiation, translation and redefinition of certain policy elements in a given situation or context.

In our story, attempts at appropriating the policy and influencing the legal assessment of the students' fees included actors such as the Ministry, the university leaders and the Chinese students. The students' conduct in complaining to the Minister was conceived of by the university staff as immoral and to a significant degree was seen as a direct consequence of the fact that the students had paid fees. Money was conceived as the very 'poison' that had generated undesirable student–customer subjectivity.

If the focus is on the diverse appropriations of policy elements in particular sites – i.e., how people make policy their 'own' – the task of the researcher becomes one of exploring the claims of origin and ownership of the policy, how it travels, what is accepted or rejected and who has the power to decide and define it. Accordingly, the notions of both 'implementation' and 'appropriation' presuppose policy as a somehow objectified essence that can be followed as it moves in different settings. A dichotomy is assumed between 'policy force' and 'local responses' in that 'the policy' (objectified as, for example, words or technologies) is defined as a substance, entity or 'text' that meets a 'context' which it appropriates (i.e., a process of 'implementation') or in which it is appropriated by particular intentional people (i.e., a process of 'appropriation').

This objectified notion of policy is prevalent among many interlocutors engaging in policy negotiations. However, as in the present case, there is no easy way of knowing from where a rationality or a technology stems; often, there is no single point of origin and therefore no easy way to determine who or what is 'implementing' or 'appropriating' which logics, keywords or technologies from whom, how and where. By focusing on origin and ownership, this kind of enquiry seems to direct the analysis towards explicit negotiations of intentional (and maximising) human beings. Ethnographic enquiries of processes of policy 'appropriation' therefore often focus on the conduct of the charmed circles of policy negotiators. Like the public version of the Chinese students' case with which this chapter began, the focus is on the statements of the 'usual suspects' of politicians, university leaders, politically engaged teachers and students. This is of course just one particular (and indeed politically important) way of peopling policy. However, a focus on the explicit negotiation of an objectified policy pays less attention to how links between policy and subjectivity are enacted and re-enacted in the mundane practices and situations of ordinary people who are not directly and intentionally involved in strategic manoeuvres, and attempts to redefine and obtain ownership of a particular policy.

To the Chinese students, all students were customers – not just the fee-paying students. They dismantled the self-evident link between 'customer' and 'student fees' promoted by the university staff and replaced this with a link between customer and certain general standards of treatment. I have suggested that an eventalisation of 'self-evident' and 'natural' knowledge established in the explicit negotiation of a particular policy shows how no actor is clearly situated within one rationality, one technology or one subjectivity. This approach allows us to 'people' policy with multi-dimensional and interconnected actors – or rather with mutable assemblages of keywords, technologies, things, actions and passions that create potentialities for action. Here, policy is neither a singular unity nor an all-encompassing totality providing an explanatory frame for the social. The student subjectivities are not just appropriated from the policy or technology of fee-charging but are constantly re-enacted through the different assemblages of the story-line as it unfolded and as defined in my analysis. Explorations of these assemblages, in which subjectivity constantly emerges, provide us with insights into the space of resonance in which the debate over the objectified policy takes form.

Subjectivity becomes a question of connections or associations rather than a property of human souls. There is no single force or source of origin, no third dimension to which we can ascribe causality. Rather, a multiplicity of agencies populates the policy world.

Notes

1. More precisely, tuition should be charged for students from outside the European Union and the European Economic Area (EEA) who are not enrolled on an exchange programme or allocated free places and grants. To attract the exceptionally gifted non-European students a number of scholarships were established (seventy-five in the first year). Hitherto all students, whether Danish or international, had received free full-time university education, and the state paid the university so-called taximeter subsidies (i.e., output payments given to the university each time a student passed an exam).
2. Tv2 Lorry, 28 July 2005, 7.30 PM.
3. TV Avisen, 7 November 2005, DR1, 6.30 PM.
4. The names 'Jung' and 'Wang' are pseudonyms.
5. Deleuze and Guattari (1987: 85f.) name two overall kinds of assemblage elements: the discursive forms of expression (system of signs, language, non-corporeal effects) and the non-discursive forms of content (material practices and systems of things, actions and passions). Deleuze (2006 [1977]: 52) uses man–horse–stirrup as an example of an assemblage in which the elements co-define each other. The invention and use of the stirrup made possible new military techniques because man gained lateral stability and could hold tight a lance under his arm – 'the stirrup replaced the energy of man by the power of the animal' (ibid.).

References

Ball, Stephen J. 1997. 'Policy Sociology and Critical Social Research: A Personal Review of Recent Education Policy and Policy Research', *British Educational Research Journal* 23 (3): 257–74.

——. 2006. *Education Policy and Social Class: The Selected Works of Stephen J. Ball.* New York: Routledge.

Bloch, M. and J. Parry. 1989. 'Money and the Morality of Exchange', in T.H. Eriksen (ed.), *Socialantropologiske Grunntekster (1996).* Oslo: Ad Notam Gyldendal.

Callon, Michel. 1986. 'Some Elements of a Sociology of Translation: Domestication of the Scallops and the Fishermen of St Brieuc Bay', in J. Law (ed.), *Power, Action and Belief. A New Sociology of Knowledge?* London, Boston and Henley: Routledge & Kegan Paul.

Clarke, John, Janet Newman, Nick Smith, Elizabeth Vidler and Louise Westmarland. 2007. *Creating Citizen-Consumers. Changing Publics and Changing Public Services.* London, Thousand Oaks and New Delhi: Sage.

Dean, Mitchell. 1999. *Governmentality. Power and Rule in Modern Society.* London: Sage.

Deleuze, G. 2006 [1977]. *Dialogues II*. Translated by H. Tomlinson and B. Habberjam. London and New York: Continuum.

Deleuze, G. and F. Guattari. 1987. *A Thousand Plateaus. Capitalism and Schizophrenia.* Minneapolis and London: University of Minnesota Press.

Folketinget. 2005. *Lov om ændring af lov om universiteter (Lov nr L114)*, 28 April. Retrieved 1 November 2010 from http://www.folketinget.dk/doc.aspx?/ Samling/20042/lovforslag/L114/index.htm.

Foucault, Michel. 1991. 'Politics and the Study of Discourse', in G. Burchell and P. Miller (eds), *The Foucault Effect: Studies in Governmentality*. London: Harvester Wheatsheaf.

———. 1994 [1978]. 'Questions of Method', in J. Faubion (ed.), *Essential Works of Michel Foucault 1954–1984*. London: Penguin.

Latour, Bruno. 1986. 'The Powers of Association', in J. Law (ed.), *Power, Action and Belief: A New Sociology of Knowledge*. London: Routledge & Kegan Paul.

———. 1991. 'Technology is Society Made Durable', in J. Law (ed.), *A Sociology of Monsters. Essays on Power, Technology and Domination*. London and New York: Routledge.

———. 1999. 'On Recalling ANT', in J. Law and J. Hassard (eds), *Actor Network Theory and After*. Oxford: Blackwell.

———. 2005. *Reassembling the Social. An Introduction to Actor-Network-Theory*. Oxford: Oxford University Press.

Law, John. 2003. 'Traduction/Trahison: Notes on ANT', Centre for Science Studies, Lancaster University, Lancaster LA1 4YN,10 August. Retrieved 1 November 2010 from http://www.lancs.ac.uk/fass/sociology/papers/law-traduction-trahison.pdf.

Modell, Sven. 2005. 'Students as Consumers? An Institutional Field-Level Analysis of the Construction of Performance Measurement Practices', *Accounting, Auditing & Accountability Journal* 18(4): 537–63.

Moore, Sally Falk. 1994. 'The Ethnography of the Present and the Analysis of Process', in R. Borofsky (ed.), *Assessing Cultural Anthropology*. New York: McGraw-Hill.

O'Malley, Pat, Lorna Weir and Clifford Shearing. 1997. 'Governmentality, Criticism, Politics', *Economy and Society* 26(4): 501–17.

OECD. 2004. Reviews of National Policies for Education: University Education in Denmark – Examiners' Report. Pre-publication version. 6 January 2004.

Rabinow, Paul. 1984. *The Foucault Reader*. London: Penguin.

Rektorkollegiet (The Danish Rectors' Conference). 2004a. *Høring over udkast til Forslag til lov om ændring af lov om universiteter*. 8 October. Copenhagen: Rektorkollegiet.

———. 2004b. *Internationalisering af de danske universiteter. Vilkår og virkemidler.* Debatoplæg fra Rektorkollegiet. February. Copenhagen: Rektorkollegiet.

Rose, Nikolas. 1999. *Powers of Freedom. Reframing Political Thought*. Cambridge: Cambridge University Press.

Rose, Nikolas and Peter Miller. 1992. 'Political Power Beyond the State: Problematics of Government', *British Journal of Sociology* 43(2): 173–205.

Schneider, Arnd. 2003. 'On "Appropriation". A Critical Reappraisal of the Concept and its Application in Global Art Practices', *Social Anthropology* 11(2): 215–29.

Shore, Cris and Susan Wright. 1997. 'Policy. A New Field of Anthropology', in Cris Shore and Susan Wright (eds), *Anthropology of Policy. Critical Perspectives on Governance and Power*. London and New York: Routledge.

Spoelstra, Sverre. 2005. 'Robert Cooper: Beyond Organization', in C. Jones and R. Munro (eds), *Contemporary Organization Theory*. London: Routledge.

Sutton, Margaret and Bradley Levinson. 2001. 'Introduction: Policy as/in Practice – A Sociocultural Approach to the Study of Educational Policy', in M. Sutton and B. Levinson (eds), *Policy as Practice – Toward a Comparative Sociocultural Analysis of Educational Policy*. Westport, CT and London: Ablex Publishing.

Svanholm, Gitte. 2005a. 'Kinesiske studerende klager over RUC [Chinese Students Complain About RUC]', *Politiken.dk*, 6 November.

———. 2005b. 'Kinesiske studerende: RUC er en fuser. [Chinese Students: RUC is a Flop]', *Politiken*, 7 November.

———. 2005c. 'RUC opkræver 100.000 kroner i gebyr af udlændinge [RUC Demands a Fee of 100.000 Dkr from Foreigners]', *Politiken*, 29 July.

———. 2005d. 'Studerende taler "cirkusengelsk" på universitetet [Students Talk "Circus English" at University]', *Politiken*, 24 July.

Tlili, Anwar and Susan Wright. 2005. 'Learn to Consume, Teach to Account?', *Anthropology in Action* 12(1): 64–77.

Aarslund, L. and G. Svanholm. 2005. 'Udlændinge overtager danske studier [Foreigners Take Over Danish Programmes]', *Politiken*, 28 July.

Chapter 5

'Studying Through': A Strategy for Studying Political Transformation. Or Sex, Lies and British Politics

Susan Wright and Sue Reinhold

The 'anthropology of policy' emerged, partly, out of work in the 1980s and 1990s which sought to analyse the major political transformations occurring in Britain under Margaret Thatcher's governments and beyond. Reinhold's study (1994a) of an ideological struggle over 'positive images' of gay people was an important contribution to this project. The story started with a dispute in Haringey Council, London, over attempts to counter negative stereotypes of gay people in schools. This conflict fed into national debates, which resulted in legislation, transformed the political definition of 'the family' and contributed to the emergence of a new discourse of governance. This study sharply posed a question with which anthropologists had been dealing since the postcolonial critique of community studies: how to analyse what was happening in particular ethnographic locations not as a self-contained entity called a people, village or tribe, but as part of large-scale systems of power and processes of change, in which multiple actors and distant institutions could have great influence on people's lives (Mitchell 1966: 56 quoted in Nader 1972; Abu-Lughod 1990: 42). Shore and Wright (1997) proposed that one way of doing this was to focus on policy as a continuous process of contestation across a political space that could extend from local residents to interest groups, local institutions and authorities, the media, national government and, in some cases, international agencies. No linearity was presupposed in this idea of policy: neither a linear movement down a hierarchy, from policy makers at the top to policy recipients at the bottom, nor a linear sequence of activities through time, from formulation through decision making to implementation. A policy could as well emerge from a local dispute as from a national political party's think tank. Hegemony and contestation are central to this idea of policy: political conflicts defend or unsettle established discourses and advance particular ways of conceptualising the role of the individual, social institutions and even of government itself. In such contests, people are trying to make their version not only dominant but authoritative, especially by drawing on the power of the state (Wright 1998).

The 1980s and 1990s saw several attempts to reframe anthropological 'strategies for knowledge' so as to grasp the contribution of local sites to large-scale processes of transformation. Several anthropologists pointed to the tendency for even well-meaning (progressive) researchers to 'study down'. This is when anthropologists investigated a problem as framed by (but not including) those in power, whether they were colonial administrators concerned about methods of maintaining order (Asad 1973: 18), business managers interested in workers' control over levels of production (Wright 1994: 3, 8) or local authorities puzzled by categories of people who did not respond to policies as intended (Wright 1992). Gough's (1969) work on the role of anthropology in emerging new forms of imperialism did much to frame this debate. In short, why, if anthropologists are still interested in domination, do they tend to focus their attention on the dominated, the 'other', rather than making the processes of domination the subject of anthropological inquiry? Such questions prompt an investigation which includes the perspectives of those who dominate and an analysis of the ways in which they sustain their dominance.

It was Nader (1972, 1980) who turned this debate into a well-formulated strategy for 'studying up' via a 'vertical slice'. For example, she and her students took a problem, like people trying to complain about their children's injuries from non-flammable clothing catching fire. They mapped all the public policies, government agencies and commissions, public professions, courts, insurance firms, industrial corporations, manufacturers, retailers, and their trade associations and lobby organisations that had some bearing on or responsibility for the continuing sale of these dangerous clothes (Nader 1980: 38–39). This resulted in a 'vertical slice' cut out of the economic, administrative and political systems that play a role in child rearing and the lives of families. Parents whose children were affected might be unaware of the existence of such hidden or distant hierarchies. Nader's students studied up the hierarchy to find how networks of power, which might not exist on paper, worked to disguise their operations and forestall citizens from taking action (Nader 1972: 293–94). This was a major advance in anthropological methodology, but it still had two problems. First, it retained the notion of the vertical organisation of government and power. True, instead of those at the top being given the power to define or frame an anthropological problem, Nader's approach took a perspective from below. But this approach did not allow for the possibility of competing definitions being simultaneously contested from many different positions – up, down and across – a policy field or their contingent effects on each other. Second, the vertical slice also tended to be a slice in time. The issue under research was treated as static. Instead, an anthropology of policy must ideally follow how an issue is framed and reframed over time. Reinhold's concept of 'studying through' offers a strategy which enables researchers to follow a process of contestation as it tracks back and forth across different sites in a policy field and over time, so as to reveal how a new governing discourse emerges and becomes institutionalised.

This chapter sets out a repertoire of analytical concepts necessary for studying such processes of political transformation. Drawing on Reinhold's study of contestation over 'positive [gay] images' in Britain from 1986 to 1988, it considers how to conceptualise a 'history of the present' and the meanings of 'events', 'keywords' and, not least, 'studying through'. The object of this study was not gay people themselves, or the 'gay community' in the context of policies that affected them; rather, the point was to show how 'gay' came to prominence, how its meanings were negotiated and how it worked as a symbol in political struggles in 1980s Britain. A comparison can be made with Metcalfe's (1990) study of British and Australian coal miners, which points to the meaning of 'miners' in the larger world within which they live. Metcalfe is not concerned with the way of life of coal miners in marginal 'communities'; he explores how the vilification of coal miners is central to the political rituals of Britain and Australia, and to the mainstream process of constructing class identity and bourgeois morality as 'miners have been at once morally marginal and symbolically central' to the larger society (Metcalfe 1990: 50). Paraphrasing Metcalfe, Reinhold (1994a: 17) asked why British society has insisted on talking about lesbians and gay men 'instead of simply averting its embarrassed eyes?' (Metcalfe 1990: 49). How did gay marginality become central to cultural contestation and political transformation in Britain in the late 1980s? Reinhold's study tracked how 'gay' became one of Thatcher's 'enemies within', signalling a threat to the nation, to its bedrock in 'the family' and to its morality and security. The aim of this chapter is to set out the research strategy and analytical concepts developed by Reinhold to show the process by which a new political ideology emerged and became dominant in 1980s Britain.

Political Transformations under Thatcher

Our story starts in 1983 when a national tabloid, the *Daily Mail*, reported that a book called *Jenny Lives with Eric and Martin* was available in the library of a school run by the left-wing Haringey Council in London. In fact, the book was in a teacher's resource centre and was not available to children. A translation of a Danish publication, this was among the first children's book to depict ordinary episodes in the life of a family with gay parents. The *Daily Mail*'s story was the first of many attempts by the tabloids to create alarm about what they called homosexual propaganda. It was not until 1986 that a further conflict broke out in Haringey, and within weeks it had ranged over local and national political terrain in an uproar that lasted two years and ended in legislation. In 1985, in its election manifesto, the Haringey Labour Party had extended its approach to equal opportunities to include a call for positive images of homosexuality in local schools. Rank-and-file Labour

Party members voted their approval for the manifesto and treated this issue as obvious and uncontentious. Conservatives claimed that teaching children that homosexuality is normal was 'turning the world upside down' and in an election leaflet they attacked the council for wishing to turn 'abnormal into normal and normal abnormal'.[1] A 'Committee for a Free Britain' claimed that mothers in Haringey were scared to send their children to school, where such teaching would corrupt children, spread AIDS, destroy the family and lead to social revolution. After Labour won the election in Haringey, 'promoting positive images' was adopted as education policy (but was never implemented). This policy sparked press coverage and demonstrations, and provoked a moral panic about homosexuals' and left-wing councils' trying to indoctrinate young children and undermine the family. At a Haringey Council meeting, there was a fight in the council chamber between those promoting and opposing positive images, in which coffee and cushions were thrown and eggs used to pelt opponents. A local newspaper's report of the event was repeated verbatim in Parliament and treated as authoritative. Meanwhile, two groups formed in Haringey: Positive Images, which supported the council's policy; and the Parents' Rights Group, which lobbied against it. The Parents' Rights Group found its local actions foiled and defeated, but it built up links with a number of Conservative MPs and members of the House of Lords. The policy in Haringey was used as a prime piece of 'evidence' by those arguing for the need for legislation against 'promoting' homosexuality.

In 1986, a member of the House of Lords tabled a Private Member's Bill entitled 'An act to refrain local authorities from promoting homosexuality'. This Bill was passed in the Lords and was adopted by a Conservative MP in the House of Commons, but the 1987 General Election intervened. Following their election victory, the Conservative government proposed a Local Government Act, which was designed to put school services out to competitive tender. As this legislation was going through Parliament, at a late stage Conservative MPs suddenly introduced the following highly incongruous amendment as Section 28 of the Act:

> The following section shall be inserted after section 2 of the Local Government Act 1986 (prohibition of political publicity)
>
> **Prohibition on promoting homosexuality by teaching or by publishing material**
> (1) A local authority shall not—
> (a) intentionally promote homosexuality or publish material with the intention of promoting homosexuality;
> (b) promote the teaching in any maintained school of the acceptability of homosexuality as a pretended family relationship.
> (2) Nothing in subsection (1) above shall be taken to prohibit the doing of anything for the purpose of treating or preventing the spread of disease.[2]

Whereas previous laws had made certain sexual acts illegal, this was the first legislation directed against a sexual identity in Britain. Although there had been no warning and little time to mobilise, there were strong protests against

Section 28. A thousand people lobbied Parliament and big demonstrations were held in London and Manchester. The day before it became law on 24 May 1988, some lesbians abseiled from the public gallery of the House of Lords down into the chamber where the lords were in session. Later, the same women got into the BBC studio while the national six o'clock news was on air – 'We've been rather invaded' said one of the news presenters, whilst the other sat on a protester who had chained herself to a chair.

Section 28 increased the visibility of gays: two national groups, Stonewall and Outrage, were formed and campaigned actively for many years. But Section 28 also created fear. Its wording was very unclear. The government circular that informed local authorities how to implement the law drew the teeth out of Clause 28, but for fear that supporters of Section 28 would take test cases to court, many local councils still interpreted its vague formulation as a prohibition against providing or funding services for gay people, or publishing literature which represented gay people as 'normal'. In the only court case to arise from Section 28, in 2000, the Christian Institute unsuccessfully took Glasgow City Council to court for funding an AIDS support charity, which it claimed promoted homosexuality. Reports circulated about schools being unclear as to whether or how to deal with homophobic bullying and about teachers scared to discuss gay issues with children. If fear and uncertainty helped to bring Section 28 into effect, the Conservatives also had to work hard to keep campaigning against positive images of homosexuality. Brian Souter, a Scottish capitalist, used his personal wealth to set up a 'Keep the Clause' campaign. This continual effort to sustain the discourse against 'promoting' homosexuality made politicians fearful of attempting to unsettle it. It was a full five years after Tony Blair's Labour government had come to power, with substantial electoral support from gay people, that Section 28 was finally repealed in November 2003.

This story unfolded in the context of wider changes in the 1980s and Mrs Thatcher's declared intention to turn Britain into a market economy of enterprising individuals. The government had 'modernised' the economy by removing foreign exchange controls to build up the financial sector, had closed many of the nationalised heavy industries and privatised others, and was attempting to 'roll back' the 'nanny [welfare] state', and especially reduce the activities of local councils. The Thatcher government had won a year-long (1984–85) conflict with striking miners, thus breaking the last stand of unionised workers against the widespread closure of heavy industry in Britain. During this strike, the miners had suffered much violence, both physically from the police and morally and politically at the hands of the government. Miners, hitherto industrial heroes, were now labelled by the government as 'the enemy within'. The government proceeded to apply this phrase to black people who rioted in many inner city areas, including Haringey, in 1985,[3] and to a succession of other opponents, including gay people. After breaking the power of the strongest working-class trade union, the Thatcher government turned its attention to reducing the power of the professionals associated with the post-war welfare state. The government saw teachers, social workers and doctors as standing in the way of a shift from producer-defined to consumer-led and market-based services. For example, parents and tenants were 'empowered' to take responsibility for their own schools and social housing estates (Hyatt 1997), thereby 'releasing' them from the control of local authorities. Where local authorities responded with reforms and experiments intended to revive their constituents' involvement in and commitment to public services, the government ridiculed them and labelled them 'the loony left' (Finlayson 2003: 19). The government included in this 'loony' category those local councils that defended teachers' desires to present students with positive images of the wide variety of family forms then found in Britain, including gay families.

The transformation underway was as much ideological as economic. Mrs Thatcher famously declared:

> There is no such thing as society. There are individual men and women, and there are families. And no government can do anything except through people, and people must look after themselves first. (Thatcher 1987)

'Society', the keyword of the welfare state, and the cluster of other keywords associated with it – public, community, collective – were repudiated. In their place, 'the individual' took centre stage, surrounded by a new supporting cast of words – enterprise, competition, market – and of other words whose meanings were re-worked in this new context – notably, family, nation and freedom. The struggle against 'promoting' images of gay people in Haringey was taken up by New Right politicians nationally in their quest to give 'family' a narrow definition and to marginalise and demonise alternatives. Through these struggles over language, a new semantic cluster emerged which conveyed an image of Britain as made up of enterprising individuals who would look out for their own family by competing against everyone else in markets for employment and housing, and in pseudo-markets for health, education and other services. According to this new conception, individuals were expected to relate to each other competitively (not collectively) and to govern themselves in accordance with the government's idea of a moral order centred on the nuclear family. Any alternative, such as 'promoting' 'pretend' families, was subverting 'the family' and thus the very fabric of the nation.

Histories of the Present and Fields of Contestation

With hindsight, we can see the formation of a new ideology of governance and the new technologies and forms of power through which it operated. Many of us involved in trying to study it at the time could not understand the strange shifts taking place in the meanings of once-familiar words, or see the picture that was gradually emerging, as much through conflicts within the cabinet as between central government and local councils, or in local actions.

Reinhold had the advantage of being slightly removed from the immediate action. An American who arrived in Britain on an elite scholarship, she started research very soon after Section 28 had been legislated, when emotions had not yet died down and memories were still raw. She could see an end point to her historical ethnography before she started. Given the social and political complexity of urban London and the existence of substantial written records relating to this conflict, she was able to combine the methods of an ethnographer, political scientist and historian. Her identity as a foreigner and as an academic made her own self-presentation inchoate and she was able to interview and interact with both right- and left-wing participants with equal ease. Her status, enhanced by a highly prestigious scholarship, gave her access to the upper echelons of Parliament and both Conservative and Labour Party headquarters, and she gained introductions to local politicians and activists both on the left and the right. While she used the classic methods of participant observation and interviews, just as important were primary and secondary texts, and the study of newspaper and document archives at the local authority, the public library and party headquarters. It was still an enormous puzzle to work out how and why the words 'promote' and 'pretend' had entered the law text, how events had taken particular turns, what definition of the family the legislation had eventually authorised, and to answer the following question: why was this so crucial for the survival of the nation?

Geertz warns against 'doing history backward' (1968: 59 quoted in Fox 2002: 178): starting from a known outcome and focusing on how a present situation was produced or was even bound to arise. Fox provides a counter-argument, that doing history backwards is necessary because we know that something happened, but that it did not have to happen only in that way:

> historical transformation is always contingent; in other words, the historical processes surrounding a core set of relationships are complex and can potentially lead to may different manifestations. Only by tracing the processes that create a particular manifestation is it possible to answer the question of why one outcome prevails over others. (Fox 2002: 180)

A history of the present aims to catch the emerging contours of new ideological formations and emerging systems of governance, knowing that every moment has several potential meanings which point to different possible futures. This unpredictability and contingency has to be the dominant perspective, while also aiming to understand what is emerging. As Moore (1987: 727) puts it, where the focus of anthropology is change-in-the-making, the core questions are not just 'how was the present produced?' but 'what is the present producing?' What is needed is a methodology that recognises that events consist of multiple happenings which radiate out in different directions and involve a multiplicity of competing claims and contestations (Hastrup 1992: Moore 1987). As we will see below, these themes are highlighted in the way discourses on homosexuality were contested and transformed with the emergence of the new Thatcherite ideology.

If the object of anthropological inquiry becomes tracing a process of political transformation through a 'hodge podge' of events (Kapferer 2005: 92), this raises questions about how to conceptualise the field and sites of research. For an anthropology focused on processes of change, the field cannot always be delimited in advance. Often, the potential constituents of a field can be predicted with some accuracy, but as events unfold, the field might grow or reshape and new sites that were not originally predicted might become relevant. In a way that prefigured Marcus' (1995) injunction to 'follow something' that moves across a field, Reinhold followed the emergence of a policy via a conflict that tracked back and forth between different sites that included a local council, local teachers, parents' groups, the local and national press, particular MPs and members of the House of Lords, and the chambers of both Houses of Parliament.

One of the characteristics of such a field is that people inhabit different worlds – while some may be members of the kinds of face-to-face communities anthropologists have long studied, many of the people involved may not know each other, or even know of each other, let alone share a moral universe. Yet their actions in one place may have consequences far beyond this. This is particularly the case when actors have power that is backed by institutions. How can one follow a conflict, understand its impact or delineate the relationships it creates without face-to-face contact? As Marcus put it, any cultural activity is constructed by multiple agents in varying places and ethnography must be strategically conceived to apprehend and represent the 'chunks, cross-sections, [and] bits' of interaction between different locales, their multiplicity and their unintended consequences (Marcus 1989: 25, viii, 9, 15).

Reinhold does this by delineating five different ways that ideas about homosexuality were communicated:

1. Contextualised and face-to-face (statements or actions made by local actors in a specific political location).
2. Broadcast across different contexts (statements or actions made by national actors which, because of their expanded range, were less contextualised).
3. Direct interactions between local and national actors.
4. Mediated interactions between local and national actors (e.g., a local newspaper's account of an event is picked up by a national tabloid and is quoted in Parliament as an authoritative version of events).
5. Communication of shared images (unconnected speakers in different places drawing on a common and increasingly dominant discourse about gay people as political extremists, child seducers, disease-spreaders and anti-family demons).

While this schema helps to systematise the complex interactions between events occurring across the field, Reinhold stresses the importance of focusing on the 'agentive power' involved in each interaction. She argues that it is not possible to assess the general outcome of a conflict in Haringey Council Chamber or in the House of Lords on the consciousness of people as they read the *Hornsey Journal* over breakfast (1994a: 20). But it is possible to focus in detail on how people and public actions challenge the historical construction of a dominant ideology and how they assert new meanings of keywords or re-assert older associations. In this way, it is possible to trace a process of transformation. According to this approach, a discourse or ideology, however dominant it may appear, is never stable. In Britain, many meanings of homosexuality are always 'in play': 'if an ideology remains dominant it is a result of concerted agentive effort and transformation on eternally shifting ground' (Reinhold 1994a: 276). Making an ideology dominant is not a 'trick' that a single agent (e.g., 'Thatcher') pulls off. Rather, many people with different agendas are involved in a continual process of creating, negotiating and contesting an ideology (Wright 1998).

Following Processes of Contestation over 'Positive Images'

Reinhold followed how this process of contestation had unfolded. A starting point was when Haringey Council's Equality Committee proposed extending their approach to race equality to cover the promotion of positive images of homosexuality in schools. When the rank-and-file Labour members agreed to include this in their local election manifesto, and when the Conservatives responded by attacking them as the 'loony left', the meaning of homosexuality was up for discussion. The dominant ideology of homosexuality as deviant and dangerous could no longer pass as an unremarked or taken-for-granted public truth; these actions dislodged that ideology from its hegemonic status. In the heated contestation over the meanings and images of homosexuality that followed, different groups clearly had differential capacity to make their meanings 'stick' (Thompson 1984: 132). But those working with the dominant terms of a discourse had the advantage, because it was their definition that was being negotiated and they could set the terms of the debate, to which others had to respond (Hall 1988: 62). Those asserting an alternative ideology would have to be sophisticated political strategists and would have to have a clear and attractive discourse. The 'positive images' protagonists failed on both counts. They had inserted positive images into the manifesto with only a vague idea of what that meant or how it could be achieved.

The local Labour Party was divided on its stance towards homosexuality and equality, so that the idea of 'positive images' was not underpinned by a clear political philosophy. Some advanced a feminist argument that heterosexism, with its very narrow ideology of marriage and the family, was equivalent to racism, which councillors widely accepted was a heinous system of governmental classification for constructing and ruling people. Some, who saw the difference between race and racism, still mistakenly conflated heterosexuality with heterosexism. Other Labour politicians took an essentialist stance, arguing that people were born into homosexuality, which was the immutable identity category of a minority. Homosexuals deserved a fair deal, but were a lower priority than oppressed racial minorities. This essentialised discourse was not effective against the Conservative's constructivist argument that homosexuality was a lifestyle choice adopted by men who wanted to prey on children and seduce and corrupt them, and as such should be resisted and rejected. The Conservatives seized the initiative, arguing that the Labour council wanted 'gay lessons' in schools to 'promote' homosexuality among children. Council officers only wanted children to respect others' different lifestyles and to end anti-gay name-calling, but they began to put their arguments over in the terms set by the Conservatives, referring to 'gay lessons' and 'abnormal sex education' (Reinhold 1994a: 90–92). The Conservative's response to 'positive images' clearly caught the Labour party without a clear intellectual position from which to argue for their alternative to the dominant discourses about homosexuality.

The Haringey Labour Party also lacked a political strategy for mobilising support for 'positive images' among head teachers and the public. Embarrassed by their badly prepared campaign, the council's political leadership remained silent for months whilst the idea of 'positive images' was attacked by the Conservatives (Reinhold 1994a: 86, 100). This silence invited the Conservatives to intensify their attack. Worse, the extreme left (the Socialist Workers' Party and the Revolutionary Communist Party) tried to step into the political lacuna and take over the 'positive images' campaign. This made it more difficult to win local public support for the campaign. When the officers did regain control of the campaign, their effort went into negotiating inside the council over the meaning of 'positive images' rather than mobilising political support locally or nationally.

In contrast, certain members of the Conservative Party mobilised locally and in Parliament. They took the process of contestation further by ridiculing the Labour Party's position and trying to make it 'unsayable'. They inverted the council's language on equality and lambasted its actions to counter social or racial discrimination. The Conservatives highlighted Haringey as the vanguard of the loony left, with the Home Secretary calling Haringey's leader (of Afro-Caribbean origin) 'the high priest of race hatred' and 'Barmy Bernie' (Reinhold 1994a: 49). In response, the national Labour Party tried to distance itself from such Labour-controlled local authorities and their strategies to counter the 'divide and rule' divisive discourses and strategies of the Thatcher government. The Conservatives' language became more extreme, with a Campaign for Normal Family Life and a claim by a Conservative councillor that council officers were 'a bigger threat to normal family life than even the bombers and the guns of Adolf Hitler' (Reinhold 1994a: 68). The Parents' Rights Group became involved with MI5's former head of domestic subversion who, during the miners' strike, helped set up a rival union and advised the Prime Minister. During the 1987 General Election, he chaired a Committee for a Free Britain, in whose leaflet the vice-chair of the Parents' Rights Group declared herself 'scared' of council policies on gays (Reinhold 1994a: 151, 185–86). The MI5's 'enemy within' was now extended to the Labour Party which, it was claimed, was trying to change the British way of life irrevocably (Reinhold 1994a: 190). These actions split the extreme right and the moderate wings of the local Conservative Party.

Contact between those vilifying the council's 'positive images' and Conservative MPs and members of the House of Lords intensified. Reinhold's analysis of all *Hansard* records of Parliamentary debates in 1986–88 concerning local government, education and Haringey show the Conservative Party taking a progressively more extreme position and the Labour Party backing off into silence. A Conservative MP quoted Haringey when arguing for measures to protect children from aggressive gay proselytising; the Haringey Labour MP did not defend the council and the Labour front bench tried to distance itself from its local left wing.[4] In the next debate, a member of the Conservative front bench reversed the government's previous position and espoused the view that equal opportunities initiatives for homosexuals were a threat to the family as the normal unit of society.[5] When a backbencher's Bill against the promotion of homosexuality failed because it was inquorate, Mrs Thatcher declared she would support its reintroduction.[6] In 1987, the Labour Party Conference refused all motions on gay rights. Soon after, the Ministry of Education issued a circular to local authorities that parent governors were to control sex education, provide a clear moral framework about stable family life and proscribe teaching about homosexuality as a norm.[7] A month later, Section 28 against 'the promotion of homosexuality' was slipped into the last stages of the Local Government Act.[8]

Does anyone ever win discursive battles? Although the Parents' Rights Group could not find a wide audience in Haringey Council or on the streets for its discourse about fear of gays, its parliamentary lobbying succeeded in making its discourse not only dominant but, in Asad's (1979: 623) terms, authoritative when it was inscribed in legislation. This opened the way for people to draw on the agentive power of the state, the police and the courts to endorse their dominant construction of gays as a threat to the family. When Section 28 became law, it looked like specific Conservative MPs and members of the House of Lords, in alliance with local groups like the Parents' Rights Groups, had successfully pushed their party and their leader to an extreme position against homosexuality, and had outmanoeuvred both the national and local Labour Party. In the ascendant, the former head of MI5 offered to fund a test case and the government said it would support anyone taking legal action against Haringey council (Reinhold 1994a: 217–18). Just at the moment when it appeared that this discourse had unassailable dominance, moderate Conservatives reasserted themselves, fearing that the party was acquiring an image of intolerance and vilification. Hence the subsequent guidance from the Ministry about how local authorities should interpret Section 28 moderated the tone and made the meaning very vague.

In sum, once the Conservatives agreed to open the issue of 'positive images' up for discussion, a formerly dominant discourse about gays as unnatural and dangerous lost its hegemonic foothold. It became debateable. The previous discourse could never be returned to its former dominant position. Conservative activists were intent on creating an authoritative discourse which would pre-empt and prevent radically opposed utterances (Asad 1979: 285–86), and they were spectacularly successful in silencing the Labour Party both locally and nationally. The weakness of the Conservatives' position was evident in their attempts to contest 'positive images', with repeated and ever more extreme statements about the threat to normality, morality, the family and the nation. As a result, Mrs Thatcher was accused of giving such high-profile public attention to the existence and lifestyles of gay people that she herself was promoting homosexuality. Conservative activists were reined in by moderate Conservatives concerned about the party's growing reputation for intolerance, vilification and lack of compassion. Hall's (1988: 51) ultimate test of a dominant discourse is that it operates through discursive regularity — through establishing its own repertoire of concepts which are used with regularity to formulate its objects of knowledge and constantly to interrupt, displace and rearrange other discourses. The next section shows how opponents appropriated and inverted the meanings of 'positive' and 'promote' such that Haringey council stopped using them, and how a new discursive regularity about a narrow definition of the family as the core unit of the nation was established. But this discourse was always known as 'Conservative' or 'Thatcherite': it never acquired such dominance that its proponents could pass it off as unmarked, neutral and objective. Its internal logic never acquired the hegemonic status of an order grounded in nature or common sense. The opponents of Section 28 in the late 1980s may have lost the battle, but by the turn of the century, they had won the war.

Keywords and Historical Trajectories

Through these events and interactions between unbounded sites, we see how the meanings of keywords – 'positive', 'promote', 'pretend' and 'family' – were contested and changed. Reinhold traces how these words connected to five historical discourses about homosexuality in Britain. She shows how, as the meanings of central words in the conflict changed, these five discourses were re-worked and brought into a new ideological formation. To do this, she made a detailed discourse analysis of the official records of debates in the Houses of Parliament, speeches of politicians, reports of meetings in the local council, political parties and pressure groups, ephemera like leaflets and flyers, and coverage in national and local media.

These five historical discourses appear in the text of Section 28 itself. The first, the introductory sentence which links homosexuality with 'political publicity', draws on an historical association between homosexuality and subversion and treachery in Britain. Most notoriously, Burgess and McClean, two homosexual Cambridge graduates, were communists and spies for the Soviet Union during the Cold War. Now, instead of working for the KGB, homosexual subversives were claimed to be even more dangerous because they worked inside Haringey Council and within the rule of law to undermine the institutions of local government.

This 'homosexuals as threat-to-the-nation' discourse demonised 'positive images' by claiming that it posed the same threat as anti-racism to a supposedly peaceful and unified community. A formative moment was when a black woman, who immigration officers had trussed up to take into detention, died in a housing estate in Haringey and a white policeman died in the ensuing riot. In a reversal of oppressions, ordinary white families were referred to as prisoners in their own homes, surrounded by a black lawless mob that was the product of anti-racist zeal. Opponents of Haringey's equal opportunities polices forged a link between anti-racism and black insurrection, and claimed positive images subverted national safety. The subversive homosexual was joined at the hip to the lawless black, and the government claimed to give voice to the tolerant majority overborne by myriad enemies within.

The second discourse concerns 'promoting'. This word occurs twice in Section 28 as 'promoting homosexuality' (Clause 1(a)) and once as 'promoting in teaching' (Clause 1(b)), but is never defined in the legislation, by the government or by backbenchers. 'Promoting' was first used in Haringey by proponents of 'positive images' of lesbian and gay people, but the meaning was completely changed during the conflicts, and the opponents of the local policy succeeded in making 'promotion' mean 'teaching your children to be gay'. This drew on historical discourses about homosexuals as predators of innocent children who entice and seduce their prey. Opponents made a new association between that discourse and education by accusing Haringey council of using its schools to proselytise homosexuality. Conservatives in Parliament took up this new use of 'promote' to conjoin two hitherto separate acts – education and seduction or corruption. As one MP put it:

> If [a council] has a policy ... of appointing teachers regardless of sexual orientation how can the House be surprised at the parents' fears that their children will be put into the hands of perverts, practicing homosexuals, who are interested in children, lesbians and so on. Of course they are frightened, concerned and feeling violent because they will not allow that to happen to their children.[9]

Parliamentary debates about sexual education emphasised the need to ensure teachers promulgated 'heterosexual loving relationships' as the norm and prevented the spread of knowledge about homosexuality. By associating 'promotion' with education, the latter also became a negative noun that fed into the government's attacks on 'loony left' local councils and on welfare state professions, especially teachers.

The third discourse not only highlighted dangers to innocent children but emphasised the importance of keeping gay experiences to a phase in growing up and avoiding it becoming a lifestyle. This was presumably the stance of MPs who had experienced homosexuality at their public schools. There was an established discourse in Parliament and the media that associated homosexuals with disgust, as the contemptible and sad victims of seducers. The parliamentary debates on Section 28 contained a series of spectacular Conservative assertions from the House of Lords – a place of absolute privilege, where politicians, whilst scrutinising legislation, were unusually liberated with their points of view, to the benefit of the ethnographer. As one Lord put it, homosexuality:

> is a phase. If it is encouraged, if it is taught to be a way of life, there are some – and I say only some – who will not pass out of that stage, but will remain homosexuals and follow the homosexual way of life to their lasting unhappiness.[10]

The danger posed by 'positive images' was that of a happy homosexual. The Lord who introduced the Bill that acted as a model for Section 28 said in his opening remarks

> we have for several decades past been emancipating minorities who claimed that they were disadvantaged. Are they grateful? Not a bit. We emancipated races and got inverted racism. We emancipate homosexuals and they condemn heterosexism as chauvinist sexism, male oppression and so on. They will push us off the pavement if we give them a chance.[11]

Such speakers feared that, once emancipated, the positive image of a happy homosexual life would spread like a contagion and the privileged position of heterosexuals would be threatened.

A fourth discourse associated homosexuality with 'the spread of disease'. Clause 2 resulted from a lobby against Section 28 undermining health education programmes, which were aimed at promoting safe sex among homosexuals and stemming the AIDS epidemic. Long after the Wolfendon Report (1957) and the British Medical Association (1972) had denied that homosexuality was a disease, homosexuality was called a plague, and both 'positive images' and AIDS were called epidemics. When linked to the seduction discourse (above), homosexuals became associated not just with bringing moral corruption on their victims but with promoting death.

The fifth discourse concerns Clause 1(b), which prohibits local authorities from promoting the teaching of the acceptability of homosexuality as a 'pretended family relationship'. Why put so much effort into excluding homosexual partnerships as a family form? During parliamentary debates on sex education and homosexuality between 1986 and 1988, 'family' was mentioned 230 times but was only defined twice – as the 'natural' and 'normal' unit of husband, wife and children (Reinhold 1994a: 389). Rising numbers of unmarried mothers and rates of divorce since the 1960s showed that British family forms were much more varied than the 'normal' unit described in the Lords (Reinhold 1994a: 391). This variety was reflected in the government's own definition of families in the 1980 Housing Act:

A person is a member of another's family ... if he is his spouse, parent, grandparent, child, grandchild, brother, sister, uncle, aunt, nephew or niece, treating –
(a) any relationship by marriage as a relationship by blood, any relationship of the half blood as a relationship of the whole blood and the stepchild of any person as his child; and
(b) an illegitimate person as the legitimate child of his mother and reputed father; or if they live together as husband and wife.

An MP who opposed Clause 28 pointed out that this broad definition of the family embraced remarriage, illegitimacy and common-law households:

[it] includes everyone but the goldfish and the budgie. Do the Government mean that two people of the same sex who live together cannot be classed as family?[12]

In the course of the parliamentary debates, the Conservatives' condemnation of single-parent families diminished considerably, whilst gay partnerships raising children became the focus of special censure. These shifts drew a new boundary not so much between 'normal' and 'abnormal' family forms, but between the ideologically correct and 'real' as opposed to incorrect or 'pretend' family forms. By default, a wider variety of family forms came to be included on the correct side of the boundary, while lesbian and gay couples were 'exiled from kinship' (Reinhold 1994a: 402, 410, citing Weston 1991). The idea that homosexual partnerships could be loving or lasting, or that gays could produce children or be good parents, provoked outrage. If they tried to pass as a 'genuine family relationship',[13] they made 'our proper established family institutions look odd or queer'.[14] Hence the special focus on boundary marking: the real danger was from gay people engaging in 'pretended' family relationships that looked like the genuine article.

Conservatives promoted the husband, wife and children unit as the building block of the nation, on which the state and indeed civilisation depended. As Mrs Thatcher put it, 'the family is the first place where we learn those habits of mutual love, tolerance and service on which every healthy nation depends for survival'.[15] She declared that a nation is an extended family and 'a nation of free people will only continue to be great if family life continues and the structure of that nation is a family one' (Thatcher 1987). Commenting on such logic, Caplan (1983: 124) explained that 'the family figures as the true and natural unit of freedom ... Attack the family and freedom itself bleeds'. This is why positive connections between 'gay' and 'family' must be forced into retreat (Reinhold 1994b: 77).

Conclusion: Studying Through

Reinhold shows how homosexuals became an 'other' of choice in the Conservatives' politics of revilement (1994a: 469) and how 'gay', whilst being marginalised, became symbolically central to the emerging

Thatcherite ideology in Britain. In the process of outlawing the 'promotion of homosexuality' as a 'pretended family relationship', the Conservative government redefined 'the family' much more narrowly. This was one strand of their reform of the welfare state, in which they tried to defeat all the 'enemies within' who could subvert the achievement of a nation made up of enterprising individuals, each using their freedom to compete in markets and pursue their own, their family's and hence the nation's interests and prosperity. But this ideology developed incrementally and, at the time, even many Conservatives struggled to find out what was happening.

Reinhold termed the methodological strategy devised to analyse this process of political and cultural transformation 'studying through'. This approach does not simply invert anthropology's traditional stance of 'studying down' and follow Nader's advice of 'studying up'. 'Studying through' avoids presuming a hierarchical relation between policy makers determining policy and implementing it on the governed. It also avoids the presumption that policy making follows a linear sequence of events from problem definition to policy formulation to implementation (as also discussed in the Introduction to this volume). Instead, 'studying through' follows a discussion or a conflict as it ranges back and forth and back again between protagonists, and up and down and up again between a range of local and national sites. The aim is to follow a flow of events and their contingent effects, and especially to notice struggles over language, in order to analyse how the meaning of keywords are contested and change, how new semantic clusters form and how a new governing discourse emerges, is made authoritative and becomes institutionalised. What is studied is a process of political transformation through space and time.

In sum, 'studying through' has three main elements. First, it entails a multi-sited ethnography with a wide conception of the field. There is a constant tracking back and forth, up and down and back again to trace connections between events in different local and national sites. Wedel (2004: 169), adopting the term for her aid ethnography, talked of 'studying through – and through again'. Second, 'studying through' involves a history of the present, with an awareness that each event has multiple potential effects with unpredictable significances for the future. Moore (1987: 735) calls this treating each event as a starburst, with effects radiating in all directions, across sites and scales. Of course, some actors on the starburst have more power than others. Reinhold traces different people's actions and responses, showing how they tried or failed to capture and use the potential of, or the fallout from, each event. Reinhold conveyed this sense of the indeterminacy of events even though her study started soon after Section 28 was passed. Ethnographers who live through a flow of events and record them as they happen are even better placed to capture the recurrent feeling of future unpredictability. Yet such ethnographers widely use Reinhold's methods too: interviewing soon after the event to capture people's memories, emotions, reflections and analyses; and using written records as close as possible to the moment – verbatim as in *Hansard* or mediated as in the press. Such a perspective on the history of the present conveys the unpredictability and contingency of policy outcomes whilst highlighting the 'agentive power' behind particular actions and interpretations. It shows how political events actually unfolded, but is sensitive to the fact that each moment represents only one of many possible and situationally defined outcomes.

Third, 'studying through' involves political and epistemological reflexivity, that is, an awareness of the wider historical and political context in which actors and events are framed, and an analytical openness not only to the conditions that have produced the present but to what the present is producing. One way of connecting the detailed analysis of a flow of events to wider political and historical processes of change is to focus on keywords. If, by following a flow of events, Reinhold showed how, in just two years, 'promoting' positive images was contorted into 'promoting homosexuality' and the strange concept of 'pretended family relations' emerged, a discourse analysis of contemporary and parliamentary records revealed the fuller significance of these highly emotionally charged fights. Reinhold analysed how speakers, each time they used these terms, made associations to ideas of sexuality, family and nation. These references connected contemporary utterances to five historical discourses about homosexuality. Her analysis of how these discourses were being reworked and brought into a new relationship enabled her to identify the emerging contours of a wider ideological transformation to which the contest over Section 28 contributed.

In Geertz's (1968) terms, this approach to what the present is producing treats life as lived forwards but understood backwards; however, it does not treat the present as if it was bound to arise. It avoids the Whig view of history, which takes its stance in the current *status quo* and traces how one thing led to another to create the inevitability, and immutability, of the present. Reinhold connects a long view of ideological change to detailed studies of the unpredictability of the contests at any moment. This fulfils Fox's (2002: 178, 180) ideal of showing that 'something happened' and how one outcome came to prevail over others, but that it did not have to happen only in that way. This policy ethnography therefore involves a strategy of studying through a sequence of events across sites and through time, and through the reformulation of historical discourses, to reveal an unpredictable but understandable process of political and ideological transformation.

Notes

1. Tottenham Conservative local election leaflet, 'Fight Back' No. 27, 1986.
2. Retrieved 25 January 2008 from the Office of Public Sector Information: http://www.opsi.gov.uk/acts/acts1988/Ukpga_19880009_en_5.htm.
3. The first urban riots under Thatcher took place in 1981 in Brixton, Handsworth, Southall, Toxteth and Moss Side. The second round in 1985 started in

Handsworth, Birmingham (9–11 September), followed by Brixton, South London (28 September) and Broadwater Farm Estate, Haringey (6 October).
4. Education Bill, House of Commons, 21 October 1986, coll. 1055–98.
5. Rhodes Boyson, Local Government debate, House of Commons, 5 December 1986, col. 1250.
6. Margaret Thatcher, House of Commons, 14 May 1987, col. 413.
7. DES Circular 11/87 November 1987, paragraph 22.
8. House of Commons, 8 December 1987, Standing Committee A, coll. 1199–231.
9. Harry Greenaway, MP for Ealing North (where the council had a policy similar to Haringey's), House of Commons, 21 October 1986. col. 1091.
10. Baroness Faithfull, House of Lords, 18 December 1986, col. 329.
11. Earl of Halsbury, House of Lords, 11 February 1987, col. 709, 18 December 1986, col. 310.
12. Cited by Allan Roberts MP, House of Commons, 8 December 1987, col. 1217.
13. Lord Monson, House of Lords, 16 February 1988, col. 630.
14. Lord Mason of Barnsley, House of Lords, 2 February 1988
15. Thatcher to Blackpool Party Conference, 9 October 1987, Conservative Party News Service Ref 644/87.

References

Abu-Lughod, Lila. 1990. 'The Romance of Resistance: Tracing the Transformations of Power through Bedouin Women', *American Ethnologist* 17(1): 41–55.

Asad, Talal. 1973. 'Introduction' in Talal Asad (ed.), *Anthropology and the Colonial Encounter*. London: Ithaca Press, pp.9–19.

———. 1979. 'Anthropology and the Analysis of Ideology', *Man* 14(4): 607–27.

Caplan, Jane. 1983. 'Conservatism and the Family' *History Workshop Journal* 16: 123–28.

Finlayson, A. 2003. *Making Sense of New Labour*. London: Lawrence and Wishart.

Fox, Richard. 2002. 'The Study of Historical Transformation in American Anthropology', in A. Gingrich and R. Fox (eds), *Anthropology by Comparison*. London: Routledge, pp.167–84.

Geertz, Gifford. 1968. *Islam observed*. Chicago: University of Chicago Press.

Gough, K. 1969. 'New Proposals for Anthropologists', *Current Anthropology* 9: 403–7.

Hall, Stuart. 1988. 'The Toad in the Garden: Thatcherism among the Theorists' in C. Nelson and L. Grossberg (eds), *Marxism and the Interpretation of Culture*. Chicago: University of Illinois Press.

Hastrup, Kirsten. 1992. 'Out of Anthropology: The Anthropologist as an Object of Dramatic Representation', *Cultural Anthropology* 7(3): 327–45.

Hyatt, Susan B. 1997. 'Poverty in a "Post-welfare" Landscape: Tenant Management Policies, Self-governance and the Democratisation of Knowledge in Great Britain', in Cris Shore and Susan Wright (eds), *Anthropology of Policy: Critical Perspectives on Governance and Power*. London: Routledge, pp. 217–38.

Kapferer, Bruce. 2005. 'Situations, Crisis, and the Anthropology of the Concrete. The Contribution of Max Gluckman', *Social Analysis* 49(3): 85–122.

Marcus, George. 1989. 'Imagining the Whole. Ethnography's Contemporary Efforts to Situate Itself', *Critique of Anthropology* 9(3): 7–30.

Marcus, George. 1995. 'Ethnography in/of the World System: The Emergence of Multi-sited Ethnography', *Annual Review of Anthropology* 24: 95–117.

Metcalfe, A.W. 1990. 'The Demonology of Class. The Iconography of the Coalminer and the Symbolic Construction of Political Boundaries', *Critique of Anthropology* 10(1): 39–63.

Moore, Sally Falk. 1987. 'Explaining the Present: Theoretical Dilemmas in Processual Ethnography', *American Ethnologist* 14(4): 727–36.

Nader, Laura. 1972. 'Up the Anthropologist – Perspectives Gained from Studying Up', in Del Hymes (ed.), *Reinventing Anthropology*. New York: Random House.

——. 1980. 'The Vertical Slice: Hierarchies and Children', in G.M. Brittan and R. Cohen (eds), *Hierarchy and Society*. Philadelphia: Institute for the Study of Human Issues.

Reinhold, Susan. 1994a. 'Local Conflict and Ideological Struggle: "Positive Images" and Section 28', unpublished D.Phil. thesis in Social Anthropology, University of Sussex.

——. 1994b. 'Through the Parliamentary Looking Glass: "real" and "pretend" families in contemporary British politics', *Feminist Review* 48: 61–79.

Shore, Cris and Susan Wright (eds). 1997. *Anthropology of Policy: Critical Perspectives on Governance and Power*. EASA Series, London: Routledge.

Thatcher, M. 1987. 'AIDS, Education and the Year', *Woman's Own*, 31 October.

Thompson, J. 1984. *Studies in the Theory of Ideology*. Oxford: Polity.

Wedel, Janine. 2004. '"Studying Through" a Globalizing World: Building Method through Aidnographies', in Jeremy Gould and Henrik Secher Marcussen (eds), *Ethnographies of Aid: Exploring Development Texts and Encounters*. Roskilde: Roskilde University Centre, International Development Studies, Occasional Paper 24, pp. 149–73.

Weston, Kath. 1991. *Families We Choose: Lesbians, Gays, Kinship*. New York: Columbia University Press.

Wright, Susan. 1992. 'Community Development: What Sort of Social Change?', *Journal of Rural Studies* 8: 15–28.

——. 1994. '"Culture" in Anthropology and Organizational Studies' in Susan Wright (ed.), *Anthropology of Organizations*. London: Routledge.

——. 1998. 'Politicisation of Culture', *Anthropology Today* 14(1): 7–15.

Chapter 6

What was Neoliberalism and What Comes Next? The Transformation of Citizenship in the Law-and-Order State

Susan Brin Hyatt

Understanding Transformation

In 1996, Katherine Verdery published her well-known book *What Was Socialism, and What Comes Next?*, in which she ruminated on the nature of the changes that swept the Soviet bloc countries following the fall of the Berlin Wall in 1989. In that work, Verdery questioned the way in which 'the transition' away from socialism was reified by scholars into a unitary 'thing', a clearly focused and delineated object of study, as though 'socialism' was (and is) any more stable and unitary a category than is (or was) 'capitalism' or 'democracy'. As she wrote in her introduction (1996: 15):

> I have used the word 'transition' several times and should say a word about my views of it. In my opinion, to assume that we are witnessing a transition from socialism to capitalism, democracy, or market economies is mistaken…

She argued for seeing the 1990s as a period of, as she writes:

> transformation in the countries that have emerged from socialism; these transformations will produce a variety of forms, some of them perhaps approximating Western capitalist market economies and many of them not.

Following her example, my intention in this chapter is to mark the present as, similarly, a period of transformation away from the kinds of policies and programmatic innovations that characterised what we might call 'neoliberalism's high noon' and towards an emergent configuration that people have already begun to describe as the 'law-and-order' or 'security' state. As have others, I suggest that we are living in a moment where the liberatory rhetoric associated with neoliberal policy, with its celebration of such values as free markets, consumer choice and 'freedom', appears to be in retreat, giving way to a darker vision of society harnessed to the valorisation of policing as the primary mechanism for governance. Giroux (2006: 6) captures this transition brilliantly in a quotation he attributes to two influential American neoconservatives, David Frum and Richard Perle (the latter was also one of the key architects of the invasion of Iraq). They confidently asserted that '[a] free society is not an un-policed society. A free society is a self-policed society'.

But what exactly is entailed in this project of self-policing and how are we policed at all levels of society, ranging from the overarching international and national measures associated with the 'Global War on Terror' down to the quotidian aspects of everyday life? How can we understand the micro-processes of self-policing as sites where expressions of contradiction, contestation, resistance and acquiescence might allow us to glimpse and analyse this particular moment of transformation?

Although much recent work on neoliberalism has acknowledged the persistence of its authoritarian underbelly (see, for example, Giroux 2006, 2008; Harvey 2005), rather less attention has been paid to how the Keynesianism that proceeded it also set the stage for the gradual unfurling of those practices that characterise neoliberalism. The result has been, as John Clarke (2004: 14) has put it, to see history as:

> a unilinear shift from one thing to another. In the process, both the past and present/ future tend to be oversimplified – and sometimes grotesquely oversimplified ... The temptation in telling definitive stories is to treat each persistence, or other troubling deviations, as merely 'residual,' doomed to wither away.

In theorising this moment of transformation, the primary question then becomes not what is neoliberalism (or Keynesianism or authoritarianism for that matter) but what effects do these social-political-economic systems produce on the ground? Following Sassen (2006), my goal in this chapter is to historicise the 'assemblages' of practices that constitute each of these ideologies and that provide the connective tissue that links them to one another.

In the U.S. A. in particular, the turning point when neoliberalism mutated decisively into authoritarianism is conveniently marked by the events of 11 September 2001. Of course, no particular date, 9/11 included, can ever be asked to represent a definitive end point for any era (or a beginning point for any other); however, 9/11 marks the moment where the public discourse in the U.S.A. and elsewhere moved decisively away from the free market-oriented mantras of neoliberalism and towards the increased invocation of such alternative values as 'safety', 'security', 'control', 'containment' and 'protection'. As Giroux (2005) has written:

> As politics is separated from economic power, the state surrenders its obligation to contain the power of corporations and financial capital, reducing its role to matters of surveillance, disciplinary control, and order.

The idealised subject of neoliberal policy was the citizen-consumer who was 'responsibilised' to make wise and prudent choices in the 'free market' of utilities and services, ranging from healthcare to schooling. In contrast, the idealised subject of the law-and-order state is now the citizen who both polices and agrees to be policed. In the U.S.A., this shift in emphasis is captured most vividly by the frequent invocation of an anti-crime policy initiative, popularly glossed by the phrase 'broken windows'. This label derives from a 1982 article published in the *Atlantic Monthly* magazine and written by two scholars then at Harvard University. Their primary claims, as put forth in that article, were as follows:

> Consider a building with a few broken windows. If the windows are not repaired, the tendency is for vandals to break a few more windows. Eventually, they may even break into the building, and if it's unoccupied, perhaps become squatters or light fires inside.

> Or consider a sidewalk. Some litter accumulates. Soon, more litter accumulates. Eventually, people even start leaving bags of trash from take-out restaurants there or breaking into cars. (Kelling and Wilson 1982)

The image of 'broken windows' came to symbolise the early 'warning signs' of a neighbourhood's impending downward spiral into deterioration and crime. In order to prevent that outcome, citizens were urged to be ever-vigilant for signs of danger in their midst (see Cattalino 2004; Chesluk 2004). This kind of local-level policing echoed the national security measures associated with the post-9/11 period. Just as 'homeland security' promised to create a zone of safety within a *cordon sanitaire* drawn around national borders, so should neighbourhood residents now be similarly prepared to safeguard the well-being of their communities by patrolling its perimeter for any sign of 'suspicious' people who might seem to constitute, as Mary Douglas might have put it, 'matter out of place'.

'Broken windows', as both a metaphor and a programmatic motif, was popularised by Rudy Giuliani (Mayor of New York from 1994 to 2001), who enacted zero-tolerance policing strategies that targeted the behaviours of such individuals as 'homeless people, panhandlers, prostitutes, squeegee cleaners, squatters, graffiti artists, "reckless bicyclists", and unruly youth' (Smith 1998: 3), all of whom were blamed for visiting excessive crime on the law-abiding and tax-paying citizens of New York. This focus on individual behaviours served to mask the degree to which it was actually contemporary urban policy that explained the symptom of neighbourhood decline often bemoaned by community residents. The shredding of the social safety net, which thrust more people into poverty and homelessness, is but one expression of the evisceration of public sector services; another is that the signs of physical decay deplored by community activists at local meetings – the poor street lighting, inadequate trash collection, pot-holes and shabby neighbourhood commercial strips – are more likely to be consequences of structural disinvestment than the handiwork of badly behaved individuals.

It is not only 'good citizens' who are drawn into this project of policing; as Loic Wacquant argues, in European social democracies, in contrast to the mass incarceration policies now prevalent in the U.S.A., it is rather those social service agencies, once intended to ameliorate the effects of social disadvantage, that are:

> also called to take an active part in it since they possess the informational and human means to exercise a close surveillance of 'problem populations' – this is what I call *social panopticism*. (Wacquant 2001: 407, emphasis in original)

It is the extent to which all of the social institutions of everyday life have now been converted into sites for policing that suggests we have moved into a very different period with a new 'organizing logic' at its heart, to borrow Sassen's (2006: 7) term.

Sassen (2006: 8) also provides some useful guidance for developing a methodology with which to track such transformations. As she explains:

> some of the old capabilities are critical in the constituting of the new order, but that does not mean that their valence is the same; the relational systems or organizing logics within which they come to function may be radically different. The critical issue is the intermediation that capabilities produce between the old and the new orders: as they jump tracks they are in part constitutive and at the same time can veil the switch by wearing some of the same old clothes.

To be sure, policing – and punishment – have always been part of liberal democratic societies, as Foucault (1979) so memorably noted; it is a matter of the degree to which they are now privileged as key to the exercise of governance that suggests we have moved onto new terrain. In order to track these transformations and to suggest some methodological tools we might use in the service of understanding the process of transformation itself, the questions I have posed are: how does this new law-and-order state manifest itself at the level of the grassroots? Through what mechanisms, everyday practices and capabilities – again to borrow from Sassen (2006: 12) – does it continue to proliferate and replicate itself, thereby achieving new levels of penetration that act to displace the primacy of older logics? To this end, I suggest that it is the careful examination of local-level programmes that allows us to make visible what Davis (2008) has called 'the intimacies' of social policy. 'Intimacies' are, in this context, those encounters among individuals and between citizens and the bureaucracies that monitor their everyday lives; documenting them can reveal to us the underlying 'common sense' that determines what operative ground rules are in play and allow us to see moments of conflict and tension.

The ubiquity of crime-watch programmes and of community meetings organised around the concept of 'broken windows' is one space in which to observe these interactions; another is in the popularity of a new model for community action, known as Asset-Based Community Development (ABCD). Both crime-watch and ABCD (and a host of other programmes) play a role in producing and reproducing the phenomenon I am calling 'grassroots authoritarianism', and both have gained traction on the global stage as well as within the U.S.A. (see, for example, Bratton et al. 1998 on zero tolerance policing in the U.K.; and O'Leary n.d. on ABCD and rural development programmes). I suggest that, in order to historicise the emergence of these processes, we begin by examining how Keynesian policies in the U.S.A. and the U.K. ended up 'jumping tracks' and metamorphosing into the constellation of policies we eventually came to know as neoliberalism.

From the Welfare State to Neoliberalism

The well-deserved critique of neoliberal policy that has dominated the literature over the past ten years has, on the one hand, rendered the Keynesian period that preceded it invisible and, on the other hand, has also led to an overly optimistic retrospective view of that epoch. In looking back at the welfare state, the question we might ask is: what capabilities were always inherent in Keynesianism that set the stage for the eventual emergence first of neoliberalism and later of the law-and-order state?

To understand the continuities between Keynesianism and neoliberalism, we need only look back at the rationales that were used in the service of dismantling its provisions. A key moment in this process in the U.S.A. was the passage of the Personal Responsibility and Work Opportunity Reconciliation Act of 1996 (PRWORA), otherwise known as 'welfare reform'. The legislation, signed into law by President Clinton and supported by the then Republican-dominated Congress, mandated that single mothers must be engaged in 'work-related activity' in order to maintain their eligibility for cash benefits; it also limited receipt of such benefits to five years over the lifetime of an individual. The draconian character of this legislation cannot be overstated. At the same time, we should keep in mind that the old welfare state was also structured by those same racialised and gendered hierarchies of inequality that made up the larger capitalist economy within which it was situated. As such, many scholars have acknowledged that the function of welfare states was not so much to eliminate poverty as it was to ameliorate its potentially socially disruptive effects (see, for example, Piven and Cloward 1971).

In looking back at Keynesianism and its links to neoliberalism, it is worth remembering that welfare policies in the U.S.A., the U.K. and elsewhere did not emerge in their entirety as an outcome of a single set of honourable intentions aimed at addressing the predations of poverty; rather, they emanated gradually out of a roiling brew made up of very contradictory interests. Concern over improving the health and welfare of mothers and infants, for example, was also linked with rather less savoury agendas associated with eugenics and with the perceived need to guarantee the future robustness of 'national stocks', particularly in the context of two world wars. Rates of infant mortality were considered to be evidence of maternal neglect, motivating local governments and charitable organisations to establish classes in 'mothercraft' aimed at reforming the supposedly inadequate habits and behaviours of poor and working-class mothers (see Hyatt 1999: 103).

The government programme most closely associated with the notion of the welfare state in the U.S.A. was (before its eradication in 1996) known as Aid to Families with Dependent Children (AFDC). But, as Morgen and Maskovsky (2003: 325) note, the dismantling of AFDC was only made possible by 'the centrality of a racialized, demonizing, dependency discourse'. In contrast to the assault on cash benefits in other Western welfare states (see Kingfisher 2002), welfare restructuring in the U.S.A. was enabled by a long history of conflating race with poverty, which stigmatised African American women in particular (Goode 2002). I will argue later in this chapter that the 'organising logic' of Asset-Based Community Development reproduces this same conflation of race and poverty (though it is less overt). In doing so, it moves towards the parallel goals of withholding forms of investment from particular communities and of discrediting the role that government might play in redressing social and economic inequalities.

The dismantling of welfare in the U.S.A. was facilitated by the materialisation in the late 1970s of the figure of the so-called 'welfare queen', whose lurid representations in the media were used as a rationale for the eventual dismantling of AFDC. The 'welfare queen' was both implicitly and explicitly understood to be African American. As a result of her alleged sexual profligacy, she was the mother of several illegitimate children presumably fathered by different – now absent and irresponsible – men, and she and her children were supported only through the beneficent generosity of hard-working and tax-paying citizens (Davis 2004: 275–76).

Although there was never any evidence that any such person ever existed (Davis 2004: 275–76; Cruikshank 1999: 105), the figure of the 'welfare queen' became the public face of a social programme that was alleged to have become inefficient and bloated, and that had created unhealthy dependencies in the poor (particularly the Black poor), depriving them of the capacity to live up to the obligations of citizenship (see Hyatt 2001). In addition, there was another important but less recognised role played by the welfare queen: she became the transitional figure who made possible the move away from Keynesianism and towards the forms of accountability that later became associated with the logic of the 'audit culture', a key tenet of neoliberal management. It is Cruikshank who makes this connection explicit. As she writes:

the welfare queen was accountable in a very strange way ... that is, she was the subject of numbers and the innovations in auditing techniques applied to welfare case data in the 1970s. (Cruikshank 1999: 104)

Cruikshank goes on to describe the new systems for assessing the accountability of welfare recipients that were initiated during the 1970s. She outlines how, in an effort to prove to the public that relatively few women on welfare were, in fact, 'cheats' and that subsidies were being well utilised, administrative mechanisms for verifying the eligibility of recipients were ramped up:

> new verification requirements for AFCD eligibility could include photo identification, sometimes fingerprints, two proofs of residency, verification of social security numbers ... birth certificates, proof of school attendance, and so forth. (Cruikshank 1999: 112)

This embrace of the value of such auditing techniques and accountability now stretches across the political spectrum and has formed something of a consensus over the past thirty years; in addition, these strategies for certifying the eligibility of welfare recipients are now being extended across populations as a means of verifying the legitimacy and identity of all citizens.

Cruikshank's work reveals how the scaffolding that ultimately served as the jumping off point for dismantling welfare provision was already embedded in policies adopted during the waning years of Keynesianism. Again, as she notes:

> Indeed, these strategies of welfare-fraud prevention – strategies that changed the terms of welfare – made Reagan's attack possible, made the welfare cheat 'real'. (Cruikshank 1999: 112)

I do not mean to suggest that critics of neoliberalism are not aware of the many other forms of policing that accompanied welfare; indeed, the stories are legion of how women on welfare were subject to constant surveillance from welfare workers for any signs of male support or 'under the counter' earnings (although everyone knew that it was impossible to support children on welfare payments alone). Cruikshank, however, has called our attention to somewhat less well-known mechanisms of accountability that are now being deployed in the interest of monitoring other 'suspicious' populations, including immigrants, political dissidents and suspected terrorists.

Another well-established critique of neoliberalism is that, in its embrace of strategies for fostering self-help and 'empowerment', the burden of rectifying deleterious conditions is removed from the purview of public agencies and is deposited on the shoulders of the poor and disadvantaged themselves. However, it is worth remembering that the 'empowerment moment' also had its roots in the welfare state in the U.S.A. and the U.K. In the 1970s, for example, influenced by the U.S.A.'s War on Poverty programmes, with their emphasis on the 'maximum participation of the poor', the British Home Office established the short-lived experiment known as the Community

Development Project (CDP). The professional organisers hired to staff the twelve projects, all of them located in poor communities in England and Wales, ultimately became a radicalising force and produced several trenchant critiques of British poverty policy. One such booklet, published in 1977 and written by CDP workers, summarised three of the government's assumptions that under-girded the logic of the programme:

> Firstly, that it was the 'deprived' themselves who were the cause of 'urban deprivation'. Secondly, the problem could best be solved by overcoming people's apathy and promoting self-help. Thirdly, locally-based research into the problems would serve to bring about changes in local and central government policy. (CDP 1977: 4)

The scepticism embodied in those sentiments seems quite contemporary and it anticipates Cruikshank's later analysis of similar flaws in the U.S.A.'s War on Poverty (Cruikshank 1999: Chapter 3). Even back in the 1970s, it was clear to many British activists that the rationale behind the CDPs was not to address directly the conditions of poverty that obtained in poor communities; rather, their goal was to provide those communities with professional community development workers, who would 'help' the poor by – and I am borrowing from Cruikshank's language here – 'empowering [them] to become self-governing' (Cruikshank 1999: 68).

Spelling out these historical connections between Keynesianism and neoliberalism helps us to see 'the intermediation that capabilities produce between the old and the new orders' (Sassen 2006: 8). It is worth remembering that the positive aspects of the welfare state have also persisted into the present. Bush's efforts to privatise social security, for example, were ultimately unsuccessful and were resisted across the political spectrum (see Morgen, Yasmin and Fridell 2005). In order to understand, then, how we have moved from neoliberalism to the law-and-order state, I outline below the fundamental nature of citizenship under the regimes of neoliberal social policy.

Neoliberalism and Citizenship

I have been arguing here that in our analyses of neoliberal social policies, we should place more emphasis on its continuities with the past rather than seeing such policies as representative of a decisive break from the welfare state. Competition and individualism, after all, are values broadly associated with Western democracies and capitalism in general and they have a long historical trajectory in social policy. But distinctive changes have taken place as well. In looking back at the debates from the mid 1990s on 'ending welfare as we know it', as former President Clinton put it, it is astonishing to see how divorced these discussions were from concurrent political debates and social science research on the consequences of outsourcing and deindustrialisation for urban economies. This research also mapped the transformation in many locales from an economy based on manufacturing to one based on services, noting the resultant drastic polarisation between salaries and benefits at each end of the service economy spectrum that such shifts instigate. One explanation for this disconnect is the racialisation of poverty discourse in the U.S.A.: 'poverty talk' continues to be about African Americans and about the particular inadequacies of their 'street' culture (see Wilson 1997 and Anderson 1999 for two such examples). The problem of deindustrialisation has mostly been linked to the falling fortunes of the white working class, even though in many locales, it has, in fact, been African Americans and particularly African-American men who, as the last ones hired, have been the first ones fired. In addition, the post-Keynesian shrinking of the public sector has also contributed to the downward mobility of Blacks as those bureaucracies often hired African Americans – and particularly African-American women – since the gendered and racially stratified nature of the labour market blocked other routes into the working and middle classes.

There is much more work to be done on how the racialised and gendered hierarchies of inequality that were intrinsic to the era of the welfare state have continued into the neoliberal period. In a brilliant article on the consequences of a welfare-to-work programme in New York State, Dana-Ain Davis shows how Black and white women in the area she calls River Valley County who were forced into workfare jobs were also 'tracked' according to race. That is, white women were offered training in white-collar occupations like computer programming or were encouraged to pursue further education, whereas Black women were almost uniformly 'coerced into low-paying service work, mostly as day care workers, home health aides, and cashiers – positions historically held by Black women' (Davis 2004: 278).

What is particularly alarming at present are the ways in which the parameters of what constitutes a 'good citizen' are rapidly contracting. The astronomical increase in rates of incarceration over the last decade, along with the proliferation of reformist institutions such as boot camps for the young and charter and private schools that promise new levels of discipline for inner-city children, speak of the extent to which this new period we have entered might be described as what Nikolas Rose has called 'the penal-welfare complex' (2000: 335). Similarly, Loïc Wacquant refers to:

> [the] *penalisation of poverty* designed to manage the effects of neoliberal policies at the lower end of the social structure of advanced societies. (Wacquant 2001: 401, emphasis in original)

The dramatic increase in rates of incarceration has been well documented, especially in the U.S.A. (Rose 2000: 336). These rates of incarceration in the U.S.A. are not spread evenly across the population, but are most concentrated for low-income African-American males (though women are now emerging as the fastest growing population in prisons). According to a 2003 report presented to the U.S. Commission on Civil Rights, disparities based on race, ethnicity and gender in sentencing and incarceration are not only characteristic of the U.S.A. but can be seen in other Anglophone democracies as well (Mauer 2003: 11). If the welfare queen was the transitional figure who moved American policy from Keynesianism to neoliberalism, it is at present both 'illegal' immigrants and young Black males whose visages haunt the shift from neoliberalism to the law-and-order state.

I have already mentioned the ways in which community-based activism increasingly revolves around participation in neighbourhood crime-watch programmes. Chesluk has described this phenomenon as:

> order-maintenance policing' whereby people must be persistently vigilant against 'criminal outsiders who threaten stable, homogeneous communities, creeping into the structures of society through neglected cracks in the orderly facades of everyday urban life. (Chesluk 2004: 251).

While both Chesluk (2004) and Cattelino (2004) analyse citizen policing as evidence of neoliberalism with its economically polarising policies and emphasis on the tensions of displacement created by gentrification, an alternative reading of their work might suggest that they are also documenting the emergence of the citizen crime-fighter, soon to become the privileged subject of the law-and-order state. What is significant at the present moment is that just as the move to 'empower' citizens diminished the value of those trained experts and professionals who were once the trusted executors of the welfare state, strategies of citizen policing have taken this initiative one step further. These strategies devolve responsibility for maintaining public 'law-and-order' onto neighbourhood residents, thereby weakening the boundary that separates community-based organisations from penal-juridical institutions. As Loic Wacquant (2001: 404) puts it: 'After a long eclipse, the prison thus returns to the frontline of institutions entrusted with maintaining social order'.

In order to make visible the far reach of the law-and-order state, I now turn to a discussion of a community-based organisation that is not ostensibly concerned with crime, but that, I argue, is also a site where the local-level reproduction of the assumptions that constitute the phenomenon that I am calling 'grassroots authoritarianism' can be seen.

Asset-Based Community Development and Grassroots Authoritarianism

Many people who have written incisive analyses of the effects of neoliberal social policies have remarked upon the ways in which the logic of the market militates against the ability to create a sense of collectivity. As Bourdieu has noted, the monetarist economic policies associated with neoliberalism are 'aimed at *putting into question all of the collective structures* capable of obstructing the logic of the pure market' (1998: 96 original emphasis).

Much of the new language associated with both neoliberalism and the law-and-order state purports to celebrate 'community' while at the same time actually working to undermine those values. The use of the term 'stakeholder', for example, has become popular language to suggest the importance of cooperation and collaboration. But are all 'stakeholders' really equal to one another? Furthermore, the term 'stakeholder' is clearly meant to echo 'shareholder', but is the notion of stock market 'shareholding' really a model for civic cooperation and community engagement? After all, large institutional shareholders brandish quite a bit more influence than do individual shareholders. In his discussion of how new modes of governance associated with the Third Way seek to give citizens a stake in something, Nikolas Rose observes that:

> The stake has to be generated in a different way, in the ethic that shapes the values that guide individuals, their sense of duty, obligation, honour – at a level that is deeply rooted in the mores of persons and their relations with one another. (Rose 1999: 475)

As Rose goes on to note, these rituals of inclusion are also rituals of exclusion. Similarly, community crime-fighting measures are predicated on the assumption that everyday citizens will be able accurately to assess who belongs in their community and who does not, whose intentions are good and whose are malign.

And here we come to my discussion of Asset-Based Community Development (ABCD). According to the authors of the foundational text for this movement, *Building Communities from the Inside Out*, there are two approaches to rebuilding what they call 'devastated' communities. Here is the critique that the authors offer of what they call 'the traditional approach':

> For most Americans, the names 'South Bronx' or 'South Central Los Angeles' or even 'Public Housing' call forth a rush of images … They are images of needy and problematic and deficient neighborhoods populated by needy and problematic and deficient people … Once accepted as the whole truth about troubled neighborhoods, this 'needs' map determines how problems are to be addressed, through deficiency-oriented policies and programs. Public, private and nonprofit human service systems, often supported by university research and foundation funding, translate the problems into local activities that teach people the nature and extent of their problems and the value of services as the answer to their problems. As a result, many lower income urban neighborhoods are now environments of service where behaviors are affected because residents come to believe that their well-being depends on being a client. They begin to see themselves as people with special needs that can only be met by outsiders. They become consumers of services, with no incentive to be producers. (Kretzmann and McKnight 1993: 2)

Note that the names 'South Bronx', 'South Central Los Angeles' and 'Public Housing' all refer to predominantly African-American communities. Here, Kretzmann and McKnight are, in fact, echoing the rhetoric associated with the 'welfare queen' as a justification for dismantling public provision, except that now, it is not only welfare recipients who are accused of greedily devouring expensive services, but entire communities who are represented as feeding at the trough of public munificence.

Furthermore, one wonders just where Kretzmann and McKnight are finding these 'environments of service', given the fact that the communities they mention have, as they note later in their text, largely been abandoned by the state (Kretzmann and McKnight 1993: 5). Their charge – that the residents of such neighbourhoods have 'no incentive to be producers' – completely disregards a long and rich history of participation in unpaid activism and volunteerism, particularly among African-American women.

What vision do Kretzmann and McKnight offer as an alternative to this 'needs-based' model for community development? Their formulation, 'asset-based development', encourages neighbours and communities to look within in order to find that what they really needed was there all along. Their techniques for executing asset-based development include the following recommendations:

> Each community boasts a unique combination of assets upon which to build its future. A thorough map of those assets will begin with an inventory of the gifts, skills and capacities of the community's residents. Household by household, building by building, block by block, the capacity mapmakers will discover a vast and often surprising array of individual talents and productive skills. (Kretzmann and McKnight 1993: 6)

The diagram that appears on the page opposite these instructions shows a map that assumes the shared recognition of clear-cut and discrete neighborhood boundaries; moreover, like crime watch programmes, this model also creates images of neighbourhoods as bounded homogeneous spaces that stand in contradistinction to other such bounded spaces.

Another text generated by this movement, *The Community Building Workbook*, describes the many successes garnered from this model that is, as the author puts it, 'asset-based, internally-focused, and relationship-driven' (Rans 2005: 2). One of the narratives included in the *Workbook* recounts the work of an organisation called 'Beyond Welfare'. Beyond Welfare has a laudable goal: to eliminate poverty in Story County, Iowa by 2020. And here is how they propose to do this.

First of all, the founder of Beyond Welfare was once, herself, a welfare recipient; she describes the feelings of 'worthlessness and helplessness that were reinforced by public assistance and the injury of the negative attitudes projected by human service providers and the general public' (Rans 2005: 9). The degradation to which welfare recipients were subjected has been well documented. But what this statement takes for granted is that receiving public assistance necessarily has to be a source of deep humiliation. It is worth noting that other contemporary recipients of public subsidies, including such entities as corporations, gentrifying downtowns and sports stadiums, do not seem to find this a particularly mortifying experience.

ABCD advocates the implementation of such practices as 'Dream Paths', in which participants articulate their dreams and the group brainstorms to come up with a path to their realisation. There are 'Circles of Support' in which volunteers visit and support needy families and 'Listening Pairs', a period of focused, non-judgmental listening between two people. All of these activities derive much of their inspiration from 12-step programmes; people help one another with resources when possible, but there is no suggestion that once social ties have been created among people, they could perhaps be mobilised to work on issues that might actually lead to structural change.

One woman, Liz, who has a teenaged son and a mother with Alzheimer's, both of whom she cares for, describes how her participation in the organization makes her feel:

> My mom's medication costs $600 a month, so most of what I make goes to care for her. Some people ask me, 'Don't you get depressed? Don't you get down'? But I don't. I just keep going. My faith helps me and the Circle of Support is there. (2005: 15)

Frankly, Liz's life circumstances do sound rather grim; perhaps it would be more helpful for her Circle of Support to advocate for a guaranteed living wage in Story County or for an insurance programme to subsidise the cost of prescription drugs. But no, with government now discredited as a possible source of redress for such hardships and with success measured in terms of individual triumphs, people have only to look within and to depend only on their faith and each other for remedies to their predicaments.

Despite their invocations of community, participants in Beyond Welfare actually undermine communal values by emphasising examples of individual fortitude as the key to success. Lauren Silver (2008) makes a similar case in her analysis of the current use of the term 'resiliency' in much of the social service literature. In her study of young, single mothers, many of whom were African American, she writes:

> identifying 'odds-defying' has been core to the construct of resilience. This concept is problematic because if analysis of program success is focused upon individual responses, the institutional inequities that maintain oppression, based upon race, class, gender, and location, remain hidden. (Silver 2008: 8)

Silver recounts the story of a teenage single mother of two whose determination to stay in college, despite multiple obstacles, was publicly celebrated as evidence of the power of 'resiliency'. However, behind the scenes of this cheerful public narrative of apparent self-sufficiency, Silver supplies the rather more grim backstory: this particular young woman was, in fact, heavily supported in this endeavour by a number of social workers and agencies, and even with this 'hidden' assistance, she was ultimately overwhelmed by the challenges she faced and, out of the public eye, was forced to drop out of school (Silver 2008: 10). The point here is that the possibilities for creating institutionalised support systems aimed at helping single mothers attend school were devalued in favour of asserting that the key to success lay in the sincerity of one's individual motivations, no matter how daunting the challenges may be.

One suspects that the 'small victories' heralded by the members of Beyond Welfare are similarly ephemeral and that they may come at an extreme cost to its participants. As the epigraph to the *Hidden Treasure* workbook states: 'Our purpose is not to help people. Our purpose is to build a different kind of neighborhood for us all' (Rans 2005: 1). But why must 'helping people' and 'building' a neighbourhood necessarily be constructed in opposition to one another?

Despite the assertions that members of Beyond Welfare practise true compassion, one of the pastors involved with the group is described as follows:

> She is an ally on a Circle of Support Partner (*sic*) to an undocumented Guatemalan woman who has 'all the issues around being undocumented in this climate'. She admires her participant's resourcefulness even while she gets frustrated with recurring problems. (Rans 2005: 13)

Given the degree to which state terror is now regularly visited upon undocumented workers in the U.S.A., including regular deportations without due process, why not mobilise the Circle of Support to work on immigration reform? Getting 'frustrated' with 'recurring problems' is nothing in comparison to the indignities the Guatemalan woman and other undocumented workers face on a regular basis. And, again, this narrative suggests that 'problems' are attributed to individual deficiencies rather than to larger structural issues.

The language of ABCD is laced with a kind of Evangelical Christian rhetoric and like communitarianism, which appears to be its progenitor, it projects a muscle-bound sense of its own moral righteousness. Discussions of racism, homophobia, xenophobia and sexism do not appear in this literature, nor does poverty or inequality in any substantive way. Participants in these programmes are policed for any signs of backsliding or failure to live up to their obligations to the group. One Hmong immigrant woman 'credits her Circle of Support with helping her to leave "the mentality of poverty"' (Rans 2005: 17). But why not tackle poverty itself rather than 'the mentality of poverty'? We might also raise questions about the degree to which groups like Beyond Welfare are, in fact, heavily subsidised by such sources as foundation grants, church donations and other 'invisible' sources of income, while their rank-and-file participants are required to practise 'self-reliance'.

How do ABCD and its affiliated programmes illustrate the transformation of neoliberalism into the phenomenon I am calling 'grassroots authoritarianism'? First, there is the complete disengagement from politics and from the state. To be sure, these values were also associated with neoliberalism, but even in its purest form, neoliberal ideology still acknowledged that there was a very important role for the state to play. As Kingfisher and Maskovsky (2008: 117) have noted, rather than characterising neoliberalism as 'the retreat of the state', 'descriptions of neoliberalism should instead emphasize critical shifts in the ways that governments intervene in markets'.

More disturbingly, the arguments in favour of ABCD as presented in *Building Communities from the Inside Out* rely on racialised images of impoverished neighbourhoods as sinkholes that suck up whatever public resources they can get their hands on, implying that it is white taxpayers who are unfairly called upon to provide these subsidies. In place of the 'empowerment' discourse that once characterised neoliberalism, there is a strongly punitive undercurrent in ABCD's publications. Even the name 'Beyond Welfare' is suggestive: it is not post-welfare, as workfare is. It is beyond welfare because there is no longer any such thing as 'welfare' in the sense of the collective public good.

During neoliberalism's 'high noon', community-based organisations and 'faith-based' groups were charged with the task of socialising their participants to become 'wise consumers'; they were linked to the state through a range of funding streams and were enmeshed in local bureaucracies as service delivery was increasingly devolved from the public sector.

Community organisation are now vehicles not so much for service delivery as they are for that project that Wacquant called social panopticism. As Rose also writes:

> Community is not simply the territory within which crime is to be controlled; it is itself a *means* of government: its detailed knowledge about itself and the activities of its inhabitants are to be utilized, its ties, bonds, forces and affiliations are to be celebrated, its centres of authority and methods of dispute resolution are to be encouraged, nurtured, shaped and instrumentalized to enhance the security of each and of all. (Rose 2000: 329)

Under its guise of compassion and concern, Beyond Welfare actually functions as an extension of the security state; by denying the reality of the injustices its members are experiencing, it serves a means of social pacification. It argues for their individual 'resiliency' as the key to overcoming hardships and categorically rejects the possibility of social movements as a means of bringing about structural change. Most importantly, it establishes categories of belonging and exclusion that facilitate its patrolling of its members' behaviours but, in the end, that also compromise its potential to extend its reach (see also Hyatt 2008).

Understanding Policy in the Law-and-Order State

In theorising the transition from Keynesianism to neoliberalism to authoritarianism, it is not so much a question of defining moments of decisive rupture as of identifying how the 'organizing logics' of these ideologies 'jump tracks'. As Sassen writes:

> Rather than a model, I am after a finely graded lens that allows me to disassemble what we have come to see as necessary aggregations and to track the formation of capabilities that actually have ... jumped tracks, that is to say, gotten lodged in novel assemblages. (Sassen 2006: 11)

I have suggested that although the overarching tropes of consumerism and markets that characterised neo-liberalism have certainly not disappeared from the social landscape, they have now lodged themselves in a new assemblage that I (and others) have described as the law-and-order state.

The overarching focus of current social policies has shifted from the enactment of state-level measures intended to promote the operation of 'free markets' to appropriating a range of local-level and, in many case, community-based and voluntary sector mechanisms with the aim of safeguarding our safety and security. This concern opens the door to seeing the mechanisms of governance aimed at 'protecting us' as products of a state that is simultaneously less visible and more visible. It is less visible because the focus on individual achievement obscures the role of the state in creating and reproducing inequalities. It is more visible through its deployment of authoritarian modes of rule that are reproduced at the grassroots level. Following Sassen, I have attempted to use history as an 'analytic of change' in order to show how the transformations from Keynesianism to neoliberalism and from neoliberalism to authoritarianism are neither finished nor complete. I suggest that its 'newness' is inherent in the degree to which security has become the overarching preoccupation of contemporary governance. As Rose suggests:

> I would like to suggest that we are, indeed, witnessing some intelligible shifts in ways of thinking about and seeking to ensure control. However, to understand such shifts, it is necessary to de-centre analysis from the 'criminal justice system' ... and to relocate the problem of crime and its control within a broader field of rationalities and technologies for the conduct of conduct. (Rose 2000: 324)

Taking exception to one of Rose's formulations above, however, I would suggest that what we are looking at is not so much an effect of the 'conduct of conduct' that characterised neoliberal modes of governmentality as it is evidence of the heavy-handed actions of a state that patrols and polices its citizenry in the interests of promoting security. The contours of this new law-and-order state do not represent a decisive rupture with the rationalities of neoliberalism. The 'organizing logic' which is mobilising this political formation, however, is no longer premised on the model of the 'free market'. Instead, the law-and-order state takes as its primary purpose the goal of preventing crime and terrorism, even if this stance comes at the cost of compromising our liberty. This fixation with security reproduces itself at the level of neighbourhoods, community organisations and even families, generating new mechanisms for social panopticism and exclusion.

The project of policing was always an element of both Keynesianism and of neoliberalism. As Giroux (2005: 1) points out, 'Market fundamentalism and the militarization of public life mutually reinforce each other'. I am in agreement with that observation and suggest that we are witnessing the micro-processes of transformation as they move from one 'organising logic' to the next. As the preoccupation with security becomes more prominent, other allied concerns do not disappear; rather, they recede, perhaps only temporarily, into the background.

In the end, the law-and-order state is not yet a *fait accompli*. We are living in a world where all manner of activists still fight to restore and protect our everyday democracies. There are still grassroots organisations all over the world dedicated neither to crime-fighting nor to asset-counting but to bringing about structural changes intended to address inequality. These activists and organisations are located at the interstices of transformation, where new 'organizing logics' continually arise to displace older ones. The future, as always, remains up for grabs.

Acknowledgements

I am very grateful to Sue Wright for inviting me to contribute to this project and for her unyielding support and careful feedback. Cris Shore also provided encouragement and valuable insights. Don Nonini took the time to send me detailed comments, most of which I will also put to use in future work. My friend Dana-Ain Davis revived my flagging energies and confidence, and pointed me in new directions. As always, the shortcomings that remain are mine alone. This chapter began its life as a talk presented at the 'Policy and the Everyday' conference held at the University of Massachusetts-Amherst in May 2006. I thank the Graduate Association for the Anthropology of Europe for that invitation, Milena Marchesi, Flavia Stanley and Leyla Keough in particular.

References

Anderson, Elijah. 1999. *Code of the Street: Decency, Violence, and the Moral Life of the Inner City*. New York: W.W. Norton and Company.

Bourdieu, Pierre. 1998. *Acts of Resistance: Against the New Myths of Our Time*. New York: New Press.

Bratton, William J., Williams Griffiths, Ray Mallon, John Orr and Charles Pollard. 1998. *Zero Tolerance: Policing a Free Society*. London: IEA Health and Welfare Unit.

Cattelino, Jessica R. 2004. 'The Difference that Citizenship Makes: Civilian Crime Prevention on the Lower East Side', *PoLAR* 27(1): 114–37.

CDP Publications. 1977. *Gilding the Ghetto: The State and the Poverty Experiments*. London: CDP Inter-Project Editorial Team.

Chesluk, Benjamin. 2004. 'Visible Signs of a City Out of Control: Community Policing in New York City', *Cultural Anthropology* 19(2): 250–75.

Clarke John. 2004. *Changing Welfare, Changing States: New Directions in Social Policy*. London: Sage.

Cruikshank, Barbara. 1999. *The Will to Empower: Democratic Citizens and Other Subjects*. Ithaca: Cornell University Press.

Davis, Dana-Ain. 2004. 'Manufacturing Mammies: The Burdens of Service Work and Welfare Reform among Battered Black Women', *Anthropologica* 46(2): 273–88.

———. 2008. 'Feminist Ethnography and Activism and the Intersection of Neoliberal Policy in the US', unpublished paper.

Foucault, Michel. 1979. *Discipline and Punish: The Birth of the Prison*. New York: Vintage Books.

Giroux, Henry A. 2005. 'Cultural Studies in Dark Times: Public Pedagogy and the Challenge of Neoliberalism'. Retrieved 12 April 2008 from http://www.fastcapitalism.com.

———. 2006. 'Dirty Democracy and State Terrorism: The Politics of the New Authoritarianism in the United States', *Comparative Studies of South Asia, Africa and the Middle East* (26)2: 163–77.

———. 2008. 'Slouching Towards Bethlehem: The New Gilded Age and Neoliberalism's Theater of Cruelty', *Dissident Voice*. Retrieved 1 November 2010 from http://www.dissidentvoice.org/2008/03/slouching-towards-bethlehem.

Goode, Judith. 2002. 'From New Deal to Bad Deal: Racial and Political Implications of Welfare Reform', in Catherine Kingfisher (ed.), *Western Welfare in Decline: Globalization and Women's Poverty*. Philadelphia: Pennsylvania University Press, pp. 65–89.

Harvey, David. 2005. *A Brief History of Neoliberalism*. Oxford: Oxford University Press.

Hyatt, Susan B. 1999. 'Poverty and the Medicalisation of Motherhood', in Tessa Pollard and Susan Hyatt (eds), *Sex, Gender and Health*. Cambridge: Cambridge University Press, pp. 94–117.

———. 2001. 'From Citizen to Volunteer: Neoliberal Governance and the Erasure of Poverty', in Judith Goode and Jeff Maskovsky (eds), *New Poverty Studies: The Ethnography of Power, Politics and Impoverished People in the US*. New York: New York University Press, pp. 201–35.

———. 2008. 'The Obama Victory, Asset-Based Development and the Re-Politicization of Community Organizing', *North American Dialogue*, (12)1: 17–26. Retrieved 1 November 2010 from http://sananet.org/NAD/NADOct2008.pdf.

Kelling, George L. and James Q. Wilson. 1982. 'Broken Windows', *Atlantic Monthly*, March. Retrieved 1 November 2010 from http://www.theatlantic.com/doc/198203/broken-windows.

Kingfisher, Catherine. 2002. *Western Welfare in Decline: Globalization and Women's Poverty*. Philadelphia: Pennsylvania University Press.

Kingfisher, Catherine and Jeff Maskovsky. 2008. 'Introduction: The Limits of Neoliberalism', *Critique of Anthropology* (28)2: 115–26.

Kretzmann, John P. (Jody) and John McKnight. 1993. *Building Communities from the Inside Out: A Path Toward Finding and Mobilizing a Community's Assets*. Chicago: ACTA Publications.

Mauer, Marc. 2003. *Comparative International Rates of Incarceration: An Examination of Causes and Trends*. Retrieved 1 November 2010 from www.sentencingproject.org.

Morgen, Sandra and Jeff Maskovsky. 2003. 'The Anthropology of Welfare "Reform": New Perspectives on U.S. Urban Poverty in the Post-Welfare Era', *Annual Review of Anthropology* (32): 315–38.

Morgen, Sandra, Priscilla Yamin and Mara Fridell. 2005. 'Anti-tax Politics, Neoliberalism and "deKeynesianism": A Case Study from Oregon', unpublished paper, presented at the *104th Annual Meeting, American Anthropological Association, Washington DC.*

O'Leary, Tara. n.d. 'Asset Based Approaches to Rural Community Development, Association for Community Development for Carnegie UK Trust'. Retrieved from http://www.abcdinstitute.org/docs/ABCD-IACDGlobal.pdf.

Piven, Frances Fox and Richard Cloward. 1971. *Regulating the Poor: The Functions of Public Welfare.* New York: Vintage Books.

Rans, Susan A. 2005. *Hidden Treasures: A Community Building Workbook from the Asset Based Community Development Institute.* Retrieved 1 November 2010 from http://www.nationalserviceresources.org/files/legacy/filemanager/download/community_development/hiddentreasures.pdf.

Rose, Nikolas. 2000. 'Government and Control', *British Journal of Sociology* (40): 321–39.

Sassen, Saskia. 2006. *Territory, Authority, Rights.* Princeton: Princeton University Press.

Silver, Lauren. 2008. 'The Politics of Regulation: Adolescent Mothers and the Social Contest of Resiliency', *Voices* (8)1: 8–11. Retrieved from http://www.aaanet.org/sections/afa/Spring2008Voices.pdf.

Smith, Neil. 1998. 'Giuliani Time: The Revanchist 1990s', *Social Text* (57): 1–20.

Verdery, Katherine. 1996. *What Was Socialism, and What Comes Next?* Princeton: Princeton University Press.

Wacquant, Loic. 2001. 'The Penalisation of Poverty and the Rise of Neo-liberalism', *European Journal on Criminal Policy and Research* (9): 401–12.

Wilson, William Julius. 1997. *When Work Disappears: The World of the New Urban Poor,* New York: Vintage Books.

SECTION II
STUDYING GOVERNANCE: POLICY AS A WINDOW ONTO THE MODERN STATE

Introduction

Cris Shore

A key problem faced by anthropologists, particularly those interested in policy, is to understand how the pattern of events and social relations that we observe within a particular field relate to wider processes of globalization and change occurring in economies and societies. An anthropology of policy aims to track the way macro-level forces or events impact upon (and interact with) the local. However, it is also interested in what micro-level studies can reveal about the nature and trajectory of those broader historical and political processes themselves. While it is important to provide ethnographic accounts that explore how actors engage with these systemic forces, it is equally important to reflect on what ethnographic insights tell us about these broader structural processes of continuity and change that shape people's conditions of existence. If one challenge is to find new methodologies for studying the specificities of particular sites in order to grasp the complex ways in which policies construct relationships between actors, institutions and events, another is to find new ways to conceptualise and contextualise those connections. In their own way, each of the five chapters in this section address this issue and, in doing so, makes important observations about the shifting trajectories of different regimes of governance.

Since the 1980s, it has become fashionable among sociologists and political scientists to talk of 'neoliberal governmentality' as the defining economic and political order of our times. While there is undoubtedly merit in such an approach, it is important to remember that neoliberalism comes in many different guises and should not be treated as something uniform or monolithic. The same can be said for 'governmentality', Foucault's term for the rationality of modern government and the calculative practices and technologies through which subjects are governed (Foucault 1991). As the chapters in this section illustrate, there are many different forms of governmentality, different 'governmentalities' – social democratic, liberal, post-liberal, illiberal – which often operate at the same time. These range from the classic Swedish welfare state which is fast being dismantled, as Nyquist's chapter illustrates, to the rapid post-1980s lurch towards deregulation and privatisation epitomized by the so-called 'New Zealand model' (Dale 2001), variants of which occurred (and continue to develop and mutate) in the U.K., the U.S., Canada and Mexico.

What unites the chapters in this section is that they all use policy as a lens for analysing wider and more systemic aspects of the way state power operates. In so doing, they also shed new light on the changing nature of the modern state itself. Anette Nyquist's study of pension reform in Sweden shows how one of the last bastions of European social democracy was quietly dismantled by an alliance of technocrats and politicians who implemented neoliberal policies of privatisation and the 'responsibilisation' of citizens that echoed those of 1980s Thatcherism in Britain. Her ethnographic account explores the way this sea-change was engineered. She identifies the technologies that the government used to recast the once highly contested subject of national pensions policy into a seemingly apolitical matter to be decided upon by experts and technicians.

While the design of Sweden's new pension system provides a good example of 'policy transfer', the question of how policies migrate and where they originate are often far more problematic than they appear. This is exemplified in Tara Schwegler's study of pension reform in Mexico. Whereas Nyquist examined the processes by which a new national system was engineered, Schwegler focuses on the different stories that the World Bank and Mexican policy elites tell about who authored Mexico's pension reform. As in Sweden, the architects who devised the new system seemed more preoccupied with the architecture of the system itself than with its effects on ordinary citizens. Even the authors of policy, it seems, are not immune from the technologies and persuasive rhetoric they deploy in order to convince sceptical citizens that certain key areas of policy and politics must be removed from the political sphere. This recalls Mitchell Dean's observation that part of the liberal-democratic project of governing society 'is to make sure that the governed population does not interfere with the process of governing society itself' – which also means governing the governors, politicians and public servants (Dean 2007: 8). In both these studies, technocrats and politicians sought to claim responsibility for authoring a policy which, somewhat paradoxically, entailed creating market mechanisms that would absolve any individual or government of responsibility for setting pensions levels in future.

These chapters draw attention to another feature of government and policy making in an age of globalisation: the way in which nation-states are being decentred, downsized and 'hollowed out' as transnational and nongovernmental organisations take over many of their former functions

(Jessop 1999: Steinmetz 1999: 10). One effect of this shift towards 'multilevel governance', as it is sometimes optimistically termed, has been the creation of new spaces of government in which local, national and supranational actors can operate, but which are outside or beyond the sphere of democratic politics and public accountability. As Smouts observed in her review of the concept of 'governance' and its uses, 'governance' typically serves as 'an ideological tool for a minimum-state policy' and 'could well conceal under its idealist and consensual attire, the most devious type of economic liberalism' (Smouts 1998: 83, 88). These processes are exemplified in Shalini Randeria and Ciara Grunder's chapter, which explores the complex negotiations that took place between the World Bank and the regional government of Maharashtra, India's richest state, over a World Bank-funded urban resettlement project in Mumbai. Their study shows how the 'cunning state' government of Maharashtra tried to subvert the World Bank's attempts to impose greater accountability and redress the grievances of those displaced by this urban development project, rendering itself unaccountable for policies that it had jointly formulated with the World Bank. This study also shows how the increasing 'juridification' of national policy domains in India is blurring the distinction between hard and 'soft' law, weakening national sovereignty and accountability, and undermining citizenship rights. To whom do citizens turn for justice when neither local, national nor international bodies can be held responsible for the policies that govern their lives and livelihoods?

Loss of accountability arising from the 'hollowing out' of the nation-state is also exemplified in the chapters by Wedel and Shore. The same combination of economic and political forces that, after 1990, transformed the Soviet Union from a socialist command economy to an anarchic form of 'fast capitalism' and fuelled the rise of the oligarchs and the Russian Mafia were also evident in the U.S. under the Bush regime. 'Flex nets' is the term that Janine Wedel uses to describe these informal groups or covert cabals who, like the 'cunning state' actors described by Randerei and Grunder, became adept at 'jumping scales' and shifting between public and private roles. This shape-shifting enabled them to circumvent the codes of conduct pertaining to public office on the one hand and the norms and ethics of business on the other. The Washington-based 'Neocons', whose core members included Dick Cheney, Donald Rumsfeld and Paul Wolfowitz, exemplified the way such flex nets operated. It also illustrated a more profound sociological phenomenon that had been occurring under the Bush regime: a mutation within the structures of national and global governance that had generated a new form of governmentality, one that threatened to undermine many of the core features we have come to associate with liberal democracy and open government.

'What comes after neoliberalism' is a question specifically addressed by Hyatt (this volume), whose chapter is also germane to this section. Her conclusion, like that of other governmentality scholars, is that liberalism and authoritarianism are far from incompatible and that this combination of government rationalities is increasingly evident in a new type of 'law-and-order' state (Dean 2007),

Similar processes are identified in Cris Shore's study of the politics of state-sponsored spying in Britain. Shore's chapter tracks the sequence of events that unfolded following a former British Cabinet minister's disclosure on national radio that the U.K. government was secretly bugging the offices of the Secretary General of the United Nations, Kofi Annan, in order to put pressure on its wavering allies in a crucial vote on the U.S.-led war against Iraq. As in Wedel's account of the U.S., Shore asks whether the post-9/11 environment and the dictates of the 'war on terror' had created the conditions for a new type of state and governmentality, or whether revelations of state-sponsored spying simply reflected a more traditional, albeit usually hidden, face of government. What both studies illustrate is that the modern state is rarely a unified, coherent or homogeneous actor. However one might label this ever-more complex, fragmented and incoherent type of polity, Shore's study highlights a complaint frequently voiced by political pundits and constitutional experts during the Blair years; namely that key national and international policies – including the decision to take Britain to war – were increasingly being made in secret by small cliques of personal friends and advisers of the Prime Minister (Blair's 'sofa-government') without the involvement of ministers or elected parliamentarians and without formal minutes being taken. As in the U.S., the effect of such systems of governance by informal networks and covert cabals is to subvert democratic accountability. The rise of these groups is another reflection of the way that nonstate actors have taken control over policy areas such as welfare, education, punishment, law –and even war-making – as nation-states have progressively downsized or, as in the U.S., seemingly been captured by powerful interest groups with policy agendas of their own.

Each of the chapters in this section takes policy as a lens to reveal something unique about the changing relationship between governments and policy making in a world turned upside down by neoliberalism and the post-9/11 war on terror. Taken as a set, they provide a powerful analytical window onto the modern nation-state, the relocation of state power and the changing contours of contemporary forms of governance.

References

Dale, Roger 2001. 'Constructing a Long Spoon for Comparative Education: Charting the Career of the "New Zealand Model"', *Comparative Education* 37(4): 493–500.

Dean, Mitchell 2007. *Governing Societies: Political Perspectives on Domestic and International Rule*. Maidenhead: Open University Press.

Foucault, Michel. 1991. 'Governmentality', in Graham Burchell, Colin Gordon and Peter Miller (eds), *The Foucault Effect: Studies in Governmentality*. London: Harvester Wheatsheaf, pp. 87–104.

Jessop, Bob. 1999. 'Narrating the Future of the National Economy and the National State: Remarks on Remapping Regulation and Reinventing Governance', in G.

Steinmetz (ed.), *State/Culture: State-Formation After the Cultural Turn.* New York: Cornell University Press, pp. 378–406.

Steinmetz, George. 1999. 'Introduction', in G. Steinmezt (ed.), *State/Culture. State-Formation After the Cultural Turn.* Ithaca and London: Cornell University Press, pp. 1–50.

Smouts, M.-C. 1998. 'The Proper Use of Governance in International Relations', *International Social Science Journal* 50(155): 81–89.

Chapter 7

Intimate Knowledge and the Politics of Policy Convergence: The World Bank and Social Security Reform in Mexico

Tara Schwegler

Between 1993 and 2001, nine Latin American countries undertook significant structural reforms of their old-age insurance systems.[1] The scope, form and political context of these reforms varied widely; however, they all included an expanded role for the private sector in the provision of retirement pensions, prompting many scholars to declare that Latin American countries had privatised their public pension systems (Quiesser 1998; Orenstein 2008).[2] Latin America experienced multiple waves of market-oriented reform in the 1980s and 1990s, and for many observers, the pension reforms were the most recent manifestation of neoliberal policy convergence – the 'tendency of policies to grow more alike in the form of increasing similarity in structures, processes, and performance' – in the region (Drezner 2001: 53).

Explanations of neoliberal policy convergence attribute the strong resemblance among pension reforms to a host of factors, but they generally emphasise the heavy hand of external actors in orchestrating the reform effort. The fiscal position of most Latin American countries deteriorated dramatically during the 1982 debt crisis, and the consequent capital shortages that plagued their economies left their governments with little choice but to acquiesce to the demands of external agents in order to access much-needed cash (Stokes 2001; Schneider 1998). Although several accounts highlight the pivotal role of international investors in creating strong financial incentives for neoliberal reforms (Dion 2006; Kay 2000), nearly all of them assign a leading role to the World Bank in spearheading the reform movement across national contexts (Orenstein 2008; Teichman 2004; Madrid 2003).

The case for the increased leverage of the World Bank during this time period is strong, and it is an essential starting point for any discussion of the sources of policy convergence in the region. Nevertheless, as I conducted field research with Mexican policy makers and World Bank officials on the genesis and development of the New Law of Social Security – Mexico's version of pension reform – I encountered significant contestation between and within the two groups as to who was responsible for the reform and the conditions to which it responded. Whereas representatives of the World Bank presented a unified front in claiming that they had prompted the Mexican government to embark on pension reform, Mexican policy makers – technocrats and nontechnocrats alike – rejected this claim and instead asserted that the policy was an organic response to Mexico's unique political and economic circumstances. In light of the strong local opposition to the meddling of international financial institutions (many Mexicans blame them for the economic hardship of the 1980s and 1990s), it might be argued that policy makers downplayed the involvement of the World Bank for political reasons. However, the risk of political reprisals for the officials was minimal, since their views were expressed in confidential interviews long after the reform was passed. Why, then, do World Bank officials and Mexican policy makers maintain starkly different views of the reform's trajectory?

This chapter argues that this contestation reveals critical yet frequently overlooked dynamics in the space of negotiation between Mexican policy makers and World Bank officials. In what follows, I present both accounts of the reform process in order to ascertain their political effects in the domestic and international contexts. My aim is not to determine which perspective is correct, but rather to discover the political significance of their divergence. First, I outline the key components of the New Law of Social Security, followed by Mexican policy makers' interpretations of the origin of and impetus for the reform effort. Next, I assess the World Bank officials' countervailing view that it was they, not the Mexican policy makers, who first detected the flaws in the public pension system, paying particular attention to how each side justifies its perspective. Finally, I consider what the ongoing contestation reveals about the relationship between World Bank and Mexican officials and the role of the policy convergence debate within it. I contend that through their divergent accounts, Mexican policy makers and World Bank officials attempt to claim a privileged vantage point, or intimate knowledge, of the country's economic, political and social situation. Thus, at stake in the divergence is not who can claim credit for the reform – the World Bank officials openly express a willingness to let the Mexican officials do that – but, instead, who had the prescience to detect the flaws in the pension system in the first place. This leads me to conclude that the sources of policy convergence are not only hotly contested in academic forums but are actively negotiated between policy makers and representatives of international financial institutions.

What's New about the New Law of Social Security?

On 12 December 1995, Mexico's Congress approved the New Law of Social Security by the slimmest of margins after a highly public legislative struggle. The reform began as a response to the mounting budget deficit of the Mexican Social Security Institute (Instituteo Mexicano del Seguro Social [IMSS]), but it quickly mushroomed into a major overhaul of social welfare provision in Mexico. Unlike the Social Security Administration in the U.S., which covers only the provision of retirement pensions, the IMSS is not only 'the Mexican equivalent of Social Security, but also of Medicare, Medicaid, the National Endowment for the Arts and even Club Med and Wal-Mart' (DePalma 1995). Among the benefits it provides are: healthcare; retirement, death and accident pensions; nurseries for the children of working mothers; and social and cultural services such as self-service stores, theatres, sports complexes, funeral parlours and vacation centres (IMSS 1995). Access to IMSS services is limited to employees of the private sector and of the Institute, yet coverage has been selectively extended to specific groups over time. The number of IMSS affiliates now reaches nearly fifty million (roughly half of the population of Mexico).

Among the myriad changes mandated by the New Law, the one that received the most attention – nationally as well as internationally – was the change in the provision of retirement pensions. Since its inception in 1943, the pension branch of the IMSS had operated as a pay-as-you-go (PAYG) system, 'whereby current outlays on pension benefits are paid out of current revenues from an earmarked tax, often a payroll tax' (World Bank 1994: xxii). The revenues from payroll taxes reside in a collective fund managed by the government. The New Law replaced the PAYG system with a fully funded system of individual accounts, in which the money collected through payroll taxes is deposited directly into individual accounts administered by private fund managers called AFORES (Administradoras de Fondos Para el Retiro, or Retirement Fund Administrators). Under the new system, a worker makes a monthly contribution to an individual account managed by an investment management firm. AFORES may be established by the private sector, the IMSS or trade unions (Queisser 1998), and the worker chooses his or her own AFORE. Although there are many fine shades of distinction with respect to the privatisation of social security, the move from a PAYG system to a system of individual accounts is generally identified in the public discourse as privatisation, because it constitutes a move from a collective fund held by the government to a system of individual accounts administered by the private sector.

While Mexico's reform falls within a stream of similar reforms, just how similar is a matter of dispute. According to the World Bank, the fiscal deterioration of Latin American public pension systems (and PAYG systems more broadly) was an inevitable consequence of shifting demographics that revealed the underlying volatility of PAYG schemes (Holzmann 2000). This account highlights the structural inevitability of a shift from public to private sector schemes. In contrast, Mexican policy makers assert that the New Law represents an ideologically and historically distinct formation that is informed by other models but is not dictated by them. They offer the New Law's unprecedented transition financing mechanism, its microeconomic innovations and its melding of collective and individual well-being as evidence of a uniquely Mexican interpretation of the challenges faced by the IMSS. In order to counter the claim of the structural inevitability of pension reform as advanced by the World Bank, they underscore the temporal contingency of the reform, adducing the highly specific and unusual political and economic circumstances under which it was adopted as evidence of this.

Most scholarly accounts seek to document the veracity of the divergent accounts. While much can be gained from isolating the determinants of domestic policy, I argue that these divergences shed light on deeper political processes. Rather than trying to compare accounts to determine which is more likely, my objective is to examine the conditions of possibility for their coexistence to reflect on what they reveal about Mexican politics and relationships between Mexican policy makers and World Bank officials.

Narrating Progress in the Twentieth Century: The World Bank's Shifting Influence

Technically speaking, the World Bank is not actually a bank but a multilateral institution responsible for directing credit towards developing countries. The World Bank and the funds it administers – the International Bank for Reconstruction and Development (IBRD) and the International Development Association (IDA) – are owned by the 185 member countries and are charged with the task of delivering low-cost loans for the improvement of health, education and living standards in developing countries.

The liberal conception of representation is embedded in the multilateral design of the World Bank. 'Building a truly international organization in which all members had some stake and felt responsible for decision-making was a central objective of the World Bank's intellectual father, Harry Dexter White, from the very beginning' (Gavin and Rodrik 1995: 329). While its express purpose was to provide credit for projects that private credit markets would not, the World Bank found it necessary to take into consideration the broader policy context in order to assess individual country's creditworthiness and thereby defend its sterling rating. As early as 1954, the IBRD expressed the need to stipulate that a country maintain economic stability as a condition of a loan. From the outset, conditionality was not conceived as an indirect conduit through which to influence domestic policy, but rather as a reflection of standard lending practices.

The World Bank's mandate has undergone several significant changes during its sixty-four-year history. Initially charged with the reconstruction of

Europe's infrastructure at the close of the Second World War, the Bank then shifted its attention to the expansive needs of newly independent countries in the 1950s. Since the beginning, the Bank has relied on project-based lending, which entails raising funds for specific projects that are 'well-defined and financially viable', and has therefore managed to convince lenders of its creditworthiness (de Vries 1996: 225). The bulk of the Bank's projects by the middle of the twentieth century involved infrastructure development. Despite its current reputation as the voice of neoliberalism, domestic protectionism (under the banner of import-substituting industrialisation in the 1940s and 1950s), central planning and public enterprise were the centrepieces of its lending until the early 1980s. These projects reflected the post-war Keynesian consensus until it began to show signs of fatigue in the 1970s. The appointment of former Defence Secretary Robert McNamara to the head of the Bank in 1971 resulted in a reorganisation of the Bank's agenda, making antipoverty measures its number one priority (Sanford 1988).[3]

The most notorious adjustment in the Bank's practices came in the early 1980s under the Presidency of A.W. Clausen. During his tenure, 'poverty alleviation was demoted to priority zero' and the Bank became more actively involved in 'preventing economic collapse in borrower countries, helping heavily indebted countries cope with their international payments difficulties, and encouraging basic economic policy reform and structural adjustment in developing countries' (Berger and Beeson 1998: 45). In this revised role, the Bank has achieved a heightened visibility over the past twenty-five years, playing a more integral role in the elaboration of neoliberal programmes in developing countries.

This most recent shift in the Bank's directives has led many scholars to examine the extent of its role in neoliberal policy convergence in Latin America in the 1980s and 1990s. Scholarship on policy convergence tends to place the bulk of responsibility on external forces, be they structural (the international investment community) or institutional (the World Bank and other international organisations). The structural account holds that domestic policy makers must yield to the implicit (and sometimes explicit) demands of the capricious international investment community or risk devastating capital flight (Maxfield 1997; Madrid 2003). In contrast, agent-based accounts emphasise the role of institutions such as the World Bank (acting alone or in concert with reform-minded technocrats) in orchestrating policies across national boundaries (Teichman 2004; Woods 2007; Orenstein 2005). Within this genre, however, accounts vary widely as to the nature and strength of the World Bank's influence. Some scholars regard the Bank as unabashedly coercive, identifying conditionality as the mechanism by which it compels countries to adopt stringent economic measures (George and Sabelli 1994), while others point to the Bank's indirect role in promulgating institutional norms, producing policy briefs and facilitating contacts as the key to its influence (Goldman 2005; Barnett and Finnemore 1999).

The scholarship on the role of the World Bank in pension reform in Latin America echoes the typological distinction between structural forces and autonomous actors as the source of policy convergence. While several analysts point to Latin America's acute vulnerability to market forces in the wake of the debt crisis as a particularly potent engine of reform (Dion 2006; Kay 2000), most contend that the 'the financial leverage borne by IFIs … [was] a powerful catalyst of pension privatization in Latin America' (Brooks 2007: 48; see also Cruz-Saco and Mesa-Lago 1998; Madrid 2003). Especially prominent in the discussions of pension reform in Latin America is the notion of an elite consensus between 'transnational policy actors' housed in the World Bank and U.S.-educated technocrats (Orenstein 2008). Accordingly, 'transnational policy actors' were able to achieve greater influence because they espoused market-oriented views of reforms that resonated with politically powerful technocrats (Orenstein 2008; Teichman 2004). Fundamentally, whether they emphasise the World Bank as acting alone or in concert with technocrats, these accounts privilege the role of external factors in pension reform.

However, my ethnographic data suggests that the scholarly attention devoted to external factors may obscure important aspects of the domestic political context and the political space that domestic policy makers and World Bank officials jointly occupy. From these conflicting accounts, I contend that several deep-seated assumptions about the World Bank and host governments demand closer scrutiny.

First, although there are explicit institutional mechanisms through which the Bank can impose its views, its influence on national policy exhibits pronounced historical and regional variation. National governments are not as powerless as these assessments may lead one to believe (see Randeria and Grunder, this volume). With respect to the former, to regard the influence wielded by the World Bank in 1982, for example, as completely undiminished in 1992 is to seriously overestimate the invincibility of international institutions. In regards to the latter, Randeria (2007) has coined the term 'cunning state' to denote middle-income countries such as India, Russia and Mexico that have discovered 'space for manoeuvre' among the dicta of international financial institutions through the selective deployment of institutional strength and weakness. Thus, not only is the World Bank's influence subject to vicissitudes but, in addition, national policy makers can and do play an active role in contesting that influence.

Secondly, the relationship between World Bank officials and technocrats is more complex than their educational credentials alone would suggest. Relations between World Bank officials and Mexican technocrats were cordial, but collegiality does not necessarily translate into a political alliance. Technocrats and World Banks officials belong to the same 'epistemic community' in the sense that they share similar educational backgrounds (most frequently, Ph.D.s in economics from prestigious universities in the U.S. and Europe), participate in the same global policy networks and attend the same international conferences (Adler and Haas 1992). Nevertheless, despite the common perception that technocrats are blind adherents to technical models, they keep their political wits about them. Even though they may agree with their colleagues at the World Bank on certain ideological matters, they remain beholden to a broad constellation of domestic political interests that cannot be subordinated to technical and/or ideological considerations.

Together, these observations highlight the political stakes of claims about policy convergence. In the domestic political field, my data shows that the involvement of the World Bank became a discrete political variable in the definition and articulation of bureaucratic alliances. That is, in the initial phases of the reform process, allegations of proximity to the World Bank became a primary means of differentiation between political teams as they attempted to consolidate their ranks and establish the uniqueness of their reform proposals. Thus, rather than supplanting politics with technical discussion, a new form of political wrangling took place through the idiom of World Bank involvement.

In the international context, these observations suggest that the discourse of policy convergence potentially obscures the active negotiation of influence that occurs between officials from the World Bank and Mexico. Despite its willingness to step aside and allow national governments to take credit for its initiatives, the World Bank does not have a neutral stake in how the movement of policy ideas and expertise is interpreted. The World Bank's ability to secure credit and, most importantly, to portray itself as the leading mechanism of international policy change rides on how its actions and advice are apprehended and followed (or not). For their part, Mexican officials have a vested interest in asserting their autonomy from the World Bank. The Bank is frequently criticised for its one-size-fits-all approaches, and by differentiating themselves from the World Bank, Mexican policy makers can effectively demonstrate their awareness of and sensitivity to Mexico's unique political, social and economic needs. This pattern echoes the dispute between World Bank officials and the Japanese government over the role of state intervention in the East Asian miracle. Whereas the World Bank was quick to portray the East Asian miracle as part of the narrative of neoliberal progress through the reduction of state intervention, the Japanese government strenuously objected, claiming that state intervention had been a vital component of the East Asian miracle (Berger and Beeson 1998). Subjecting these negotiations to closer scrutiny reorients the scholarly debate over the scope of the World Bank's influence to a consideration of the ways in which that influence is actively negotiated – and to what ends.

Early Attempts at Reform: Technocrats in Action

The contemporary minimalism of the conference room belies its location: it could just as easily be the deliberate decorating scheme of an elite international corporation in Mexico City or the forced austerity of a university strapped for funds yet hoping to project an image of cosmopolitanism. Everything in the room is adequate, perhaps even elegant, but nothing is extravagant.

A stark, rectangular conference table dominates the room, encompassing most of the functional space. Twelve perfectly matched and well-maintained conference chairs are positioned equidistantly from one another around the table. Marker boards adorn two walls in the room; the other two walls are fairly nondescript and innocuous.

On this particular day, each of the chairs is occupied, and the occupants' attention is focused on a slew of paper charts randomly taped to the walls around the room, in sharp contrast to the otherwise orderly setting. Bright rays of sun stream into the room, lighting up what, if it were not for the infamous pollution-choked air in Mexico City, would be a crystalline sky. From the windows of the eighth-floor conference room, the occupants have a bird's eye view of one of the central commercial arteries in Mexico City, Avenida Insurgentes Sur – home to several Ministry of Finance offices and located approximately four miles southwest of the Zócalo and the National Palace.

The room is filled to capacity with men dressed in two-piece suits, ardently debating the contents of the charts pinned to the walls. Each chart contains the name of a different country and lots of illegible scrawl. Among the countries represented are Chile, Singapore and Argentina. Only the voices in the background hint as to the significance of the charts:

> 'Recognition bonds are not an option here in Mexico. If we change the system, we are going to have to think carefully about Article 123 of the Constitution. That is, assuming we get the go-ahead from the unions.'

> 'Yes, we have to exercise "cuidado laboral" (labor caution). That was something the reformers in Chile didn't have to worry about. But here it is a different political context, and we have to think about the unions' reaction, especially in light of NAFTA negotiations.'

> 'I think we can convince the unions if we sell it properly. If you look at Italy, Hungary, Germany and Switzerland, nearly 30% of each worker's wages supports a pensioner. We don't have that type of dependency ratio now, but we are moving in that direction. Right now we're at 16:1; but depending on the demographic figures, the rate of convergence to 2:1 could be quite fast. The unions are not going to be thrilled about seeing payroll taxes increase to pay the difference, and we will end up further crippling small business owners if we pass the tax to them. We have to make up for this difference somehow.'

> 'But where are we going to get the money? We have to think about fiscal cost. In countries like the United States and Germany, fiscal strength is not a limitation, but here in Mexico the fiscal limitations are an important consideration. We have to evaluate the functioning of our financial system to see what kind of financial system we need to have to accommodate a reform. If we don't have the proper financial instruments in place, the plan won't work.'

The participants in the discussion are clearly not dilettantes in economics; almost all of them hold Ph.D.s in economics from prestigious universities in the U.S., and those that do not have taken a rigorous five-year Licenciatura programme at the Autonomous Technological Institute of Mexico (ITAM).

The scene gives the appearance of an academic workshop in economics, but, in fact, we are looking in on a 1991 meeting of the Project on the Stabilization of Pensions, a joint project of the Bank of Mexico and the Ministry of Finance. Although the room was drenched in sunshine when the meeting started, the sun would have long since set before the meeting adjourned. Further, there would be many more meetings of this sort before any substantial recommendations would be put forth.

Several important aspects of this scene merit attention. First, the participants displayed a keen awareness of the reform initiatives in other countries long before the World Bank's watershed book on pension reform was released in 1994. Their familiarity with conditions in other countries suggested that there were alternative networks of knowledge transmission among policy makers in various countries unmediated by the World Bank. Secondly, the role of comparisons is somewhat counterintuitive: rather than attempting to build similarities between Mexico and other countries, the participants seemed to be invoking comparisons to establish the manifold ways in which Mexico's situation differs from that of other countries. Here, comparison fosters a growing sense of the need to develop a proposal that responds to Mexico's unique circumstances rather than to indiscriminately import a reform from another country.

The impetus for the Project was the deplorable state of the contingent liabilities of the IMSS. One of the Project members recalled that 'the financial part of the Ministry of Finance detects problems from the expenditure perspective that have important public policy implications, and they had an eye on pensions for some time, because they represented a hole in the public finances. That's why they initiated the reform' (personal interview, 28 January 2000). The Project found that the IMSS had a deficit equal to approximately eighty per cent of Mexico's GDP in 1990 when in fact it should have been running a surplus in the pension sector due to the favourable dependency ratio (e.g., a sizable working population supporting a small group of retirees) that the IMSS had enjoyed for many years (Sales-Sarrapy et al. 1998). Furthermore, it produced detailed actuarial estimates of the future solvency of the IMSS and came to the grim conclusion that, depending on the sets of economic assumptions used, the IMSS could go bankrupt as early as the year 2000.

Although these projections paint a bleak picture, many PAYG systems around the world run virtual deficits, in the sense that surplus funds collected when the dependency ratio is favourable are often used for other purposes or to mask other areas of the budget deficit. 'In spite of their financial problems, most Latin American pension systems were in better shape than their counterparts in industrialized countries, which have not been privatized. Public pension spending represented less than 2 per cent of gross domestic product in … Mexico … as opposed to more than 10 percent in most European countries' (Madrid 2003: 57). Of the pressing economic problems in Mexico, it might be argued that the pending financial shortfall of the social security system was less urgent, especially given the fact that previous shortfalls had been corrected by doing just that – raising the payroll tax (Bertranou 1995).

A preliminary draft of the Retirement Savings System (Sistema de Ahorro para el Retiro [SAR]) proposal was completed by the end of 1990:

> It was not made public and contained very imprecise elements about the reform ... The central elements of the proposal were three: (1) the immediate creation of a pensions system that was supplementary to the public one (IMSS) and privately administered (the type of administration was not clear); (2) the gradual incorporation of contributions to the IMSS and to the supplementary system: in five years, half the contribution to the SIVCM would go to the new system, the other half being incorporated in ten years (total transference); and (3) the global contributions to the system would grow until the final privatization. (Bertranou 1998: 90–91)

The preliminary proposal was informally passed on to IMSS officials and the Social Union of Mexican Businessmen (USEM) for review. Certain officials within the IMSS opposed the transfer of pension resources to the supplementary system after ten years (this plank was jettisoned almost immediately [Madrid 2003]), and although they applauded the greater role of the private sector in the SAR proposal, the businessmen expressed concern that they would bear the brunt of higher premiums (Bertranou 1998).

The Pension Project took the proposal back to the drawing board in light of the comments made by the IMSS and the USEM and backed away from the explicit timeframe for transferring resources to the private sector. In June 1991, the government presented a revised proposal to the Labor Congress (CT, Congreso de Trabajo) for review (Bertranou 1998). In the interim, a new issue was brought into the mix. The banking system, which had been nationalised in 1982, began a process of reprivatisation in 1991. 'The banks ... pressed [the Ministry of Finance] and the [Bank of Mexico] for the creation of financial investment instruments that would enable the restructuring of assets. The government understood the need to create financial mechanisms to stabilize the monetary supply ... which had been requested before by the stockbrokers and now by the banks' (Bertranou 1998: 92–93). The SAR reform was ideally positioned as a mechanism with which to inject fresh capital into the nascent private banking sector, and this rationale did not escape officials at the Ministry of Finance. Indeed, during negotiations for the subsequent New Law, IMSS officials would define their opposition to the economic logic of the Ministry of Finance by accusing Ministry of Finance officials of being more concerned with generating business for banks than with securing the goal of intergenerational equity enshrined at the IMSS.

This brief summary of the early technical discussions highlights several important features of the political context in which the New Law was initiated. First, it demonstrates that Mexican officials used the experiences of other countries to systematically build an understanding of the unique circumstances that Mexico faced, and they did so of their own accord – not at the insistence of the World Bank. Secondly, it supports the perception of Mexican policy makers that the reform was acutely vulnerable to local political pressures. Though there was a general sense among policy makers that the reform would be taken up again in the next presidential administration (1994–2000), pension reform was not a done deal by any stretch. It is against this backdrop that the World Bank asserted its role in the reform process.

Plausible Deniability and Informal Contacts: The World Bank's Timeline

A Director at the World Bank office in Mexico City looks out onto the commercial sprawl of Avenida Insurgentes Sur from his twenty-fourth-floor office. Impeccably appointed, his office bears all the trappings of a typical executive suite. He glances at his agenda for the day: meetings, meetings, meetings. He has approximately half an hour before the first one is scheduled to start, so he decides to look over a recently completed report by his staff on the Mexican government's contingent liabilities. The report identifies future retirement pension obligations, housed at the IMSS, as one of the largest contingent liabilities in the Mexican government. The World Bank would certainly be willing to offer loan assistance to fund a transition to a fully funded system of pension administration. He glances again at his watch – twenty minutes until his meeting. Maybe it is time to call one of his contacts at the Mexican Ministry of Finance. He asks his secretary to ring his Ministry of Finance contact and, by chance, she is able to catch him in his office (his day is full of meetings as well, so it is often difficult for them to touch base). Their conversation opens with a brief exchange of pleasantries about their families and then turns to the report. Much to the Director's surprise, after he raises the report's findings, his Ministry of Finance contact declares that several agencies in the Mexican government have been working on reform proposals. It is getting pretty political, and since the next election year (1994) is just around the corner, rival camarillas have been competing to assume leadership on the preliminary proposals that will be implemented in the next administration as a way to secure their positions in the bureaucracy. The contact goes on to explain that timing is the real issue; something has to be done, it is just a matter of whether it will be a sweeping or incremental reform. He assures the World Bank Director that the technocratic wing in the government (headquartered in the Ministry of Finance and the Central Bank) wants to see a full privatisation of the IMSS, but there are important considerations, such as the historical might of the IMSS union, which is the largest in the country. The Ministry of Finance contact suggests that, in the face of these obstacles, perhaps the World Bank would be willing to fund a study mission to Chile. The Director smiles to himself. It's a good start. 'Let me know when you think you'll have a team ready to go and we'll help you line things up and put you in contact with the right people.'

If we go simply by dates, then the World Bank would appear to be a latecomer to the Mexican party. It was not until 1994 that the World Bank published what has become known as the quintessential manual for pension reform, a policy research report entitled *Averting the Old Age Crisis: Policies to Protect the Old and Promote Growth* (Brooks 2007). The title faithfully captures the report's punchline, which is that the mounting inadequacy of traditional schemes of retirement security provides an opportunity for low-income and middle-income countries to adopt policies that will also stimulate capital accumulation and long-term growth. Using data compiled from around the world, the report predicts that PAYG systems of pension administration will confront new challenges as the number of young people paying into these systems declines in relation to the number of retirees drawing on benefits.

However, the fact that the World Bank had not set out in writing its position on old age security until 1994 does not eliminate the possibility of its prior influence on Mexican policy making. As a source of funds for study missions, the Bank always loomed in the background, even in the early 1990s. Economists who work at the Bank offices in Mexico City assert that the Bank was an equally important presence at least as early as 1993, if not earlier. A poverty economist reported that:

> The Bank has been doing fiscal sustainability studies since 6 or 7 years ago, and we knew that one big share of the government's contingent liabilities was IMSS. Everyone at the Bank knew it was a problem, but given the political sensibility at the time, no one wanted to broach the subject [with the government]. So the Bank started to establish contacts and talk on an informal basis with government officials. That is the way the Bank operates – they don't want to be in the newspapers, because then it will be, 'The Bank says this, the Bank says that'. (Personal interview, 21 January 2000)

Her comments suggest a more diffuse avenue of influence. The World Bank team charged with producing the 1994 report based its findings on data collected in the early 1990s and includes information exchanged within the Bank prior to the report's publication. The Bank exerts influence by establishing long-term relationships between its staff and government officials, thereby creating networks through which the Bank can circulate studies of interest. In the case of the New Law, the Bank employee asserts that Bank officials had been in dialogue with Mexican officials well before the 1995 Law was officially opened to public discourse. Furthermore, she gives a rationale for why there are no institutional footprints of these contacts: they are by nature informal and therefore eminently deniable.

In terms of the timeframe of the 1995 reform, the Bank official is unequivocal in her assertion of the Bank's omniscience. Later in the interview, she claims that the Bank directed the government's attention to the urgent need for reform of the IMSS, not vice versa:

> WB economist: The Bank feels satisfied with helping the government, working through established channels. Whatever the people in the government say, I have books and documents that show it was a partnership in designing the loan.

> The Bank doesn't want to show that it was involved. The ultimate goal is that the government undertakes the reform and the credit goes to the government.

TS: But a lot of officials in the government have told me that the World Bank wasn't involved at all. Why do you think that is?

WB economist: I hate to say it, but probably because of ego. That's the way the government is – they want to take all the credit. But it is ridiculous, because the Bank knew well ahead of the government that there was a problem [with the IMSS], but it was not possible to do anything because of the organisation. (Personal interview, 21 January 2000)

Her comments suggest that at issue is not who can take credit for the reform, but rather who detected the problem in the first place. She readily admits that the Bank wanted the Mexican government to get credit for the reform, yet she bristles at the suggestion that Mexican policy makers detected the problem first. This distinction is analytically significant because it shows that the struggle has far more to do with establishing who has a more intimate knowledge of Mexico's macroeconomic condition than with taking credit for the reform. The emphasis on diagnosis underscores the fact that the Bank is attempting to establish the primacy of its vantage point by situating Mexico's fiscal imbalances in a broader regional trajectory.

The Shifting Political Function of the World Bank: Bureaucratic Alliances and the Domestic Political Field

The effects of the divergent accounts could also be felt in the Mexican political field, where the involvement of the World Bank became a key term in the definition and articulation of bureaucratic alliances. As the reform process wore on, however, the rival teams closed ranks and pronounced that the final version of the New Law was uniquely Mexican, suggesting that Mexican policy makers, technocrats and nontechnocrats alike, ultimately regarded the New Law as bearing the unmistakable traces of domestic negotiations. This finding is provocative because it unsettles the view that pressure from international institutions undermines domestic politics (Ferguson 1994). Instead, the involvement of the World Bank generated novel forms of political affiliation.

Early on, divisions within the bureaucracy were articulated through the claim of ideological proximity to the Chilean reform, which was implicitly linked to the World Bank. Reflecting on the first reform proposal informally presented to the IMSS by the Ministry of Finance, a senior official at the IMSS sardonically quipped that:

> the World Bank people and many analysts had their eyes on Chile. The idea the Ministry of Finance had was to translate the Chilean law to Mexico – they wanted to copy the whole thing. If you look in the documents, it is an important issue – the people at the Ministry of Finance still believe that we have to copy the Chilean

system. They think that there might be deficiencies if we do not copy enough. (Personal interview, 4 February 2000)

Without mentioning a direct alliance, he cast the World Bank and the Ministry of Finance as de facto collaborators through their alleged mutual admiration of the Chilean reform. By repeatedly referring to the Ministry of Finance's desire to 'copy' the Chilean reform, he portrayed the Ministry of Finance as blindly pursuing the Chilean model, thereby suggesting that whether the model was appropriate for Mexico was of minor concern. Through the imputed ideological synergy between the World Bank and the Ministry of Finance, he effectively distinguished the Ministry of Finance's proposals from the initiatives being bandied about at the IMSS.

In response, officials at the Ministry of Finance refuted this charge by clarifying the nature of their interactions with the World Bank. The Coordinator of the interinstitutional working group unabashedly acknowledged the World Bank's assistance, but denied that it had a controlling stake in the policy-making process:

> Let me tell you first that I am a fan of the World Bank. I can tell you that the World Bank was involved and very interested in the Mexican reform ... They didn't provide too much advice, but they were very useful on trips. The World Bank was opening contacts for us in Chile and Argentina, and would invite us to seminars on pension reform in Washington. I did not ever feel that the Bank was ahead of us or that we were making a mistake. There was an informal group of participants at the World Bank, but it wasn't really the idea of the World Bank to do the reform. The idea came in Mexico. Our work with the World Bank was quite friendly – I never perceived that they were trying to make us do something we didn't want to do ... I don't remember them ever saying, 'You didn't perform this or that'. (Personal interview, 18 June 2003)

By painstakingly elaborating the role of the Bank, he confidently projected the idea that Mexican policy makers adeptly used the resources offered by the Bank without ceding control to it. According to his account, Mexican officials consulted with Chilean officials, but they adopted a reform that ultimately reflected Mexican interests. Embedded in this disagreement about the extent of World Bank involvement are multiple claims about the ideological tendencies of various officials and the originality of reform proposals, suggesting that the World Bank's (contested) participation was a crucial node in the definition and articulation of bureaucratic alliances.

Despite these differences, however, most Mexican policy makers regarded the final version of the New Law as a unique product of the Mexican context. When asked about the World Bank's involvement in the reform process, the senior IMSS official responded:

> In the actual process, I never talked to anyone from the Bank. Although there was the World Bank bible, or catechism, on pension reform, based on three pillars, public, private, and voluntary, it was an obsolete, ad hoc solution. The Mexican

system is not like that ... The World Bank produced a paper on pension reform in 1991–92, but it was not very good. (Personal interview, 4 February 2000)

The 'bible' to which he disparagingly refers is the aforementioned 1994 policy report, *Averting the Old Age Crisis: Policies to Protect the Old and Promote Growth*. By comparing the report to a religious text, he metaphorically reduced it to an ideological treatise, thereby calling into question its very scientificity. By indicting the technical merit of the World Bank documents on the subject, he challenged the World Bank's authority vis-à-vis the Mexican government. Although his previous comments expressed his concern that the Ministry of Finance team was too committed to the Chilean model, he ultimately concluded that the Mexican proposal was distinct from it.

When I posed the same question to his colleague from the Ministry of Finance, the response was strikingly similar:

> Yes, the World Bank was involved in 1995–96. But it is very important to point out that the reform wasn't done to follow their recommendations – it was done because of conviction. The reform was not guided by the World Bank, but we took advantage of the opportunity to get credit from the reform. It was like that. It is an important distinction between correlation and causation. (Personal interview, 26 January 2000)

His comments implicitly turned the tables on the relationship between the World Bank and the Mexican government by claiming that Mexican officials used the surface similarities between their reform and the World Bank model to obtain a loan to fund the transition to the new system. Furthermore, they underscored the way in which the World Bank became a shifting political signifier in the policy making process. At first, allegations of proximity to the World Bank were deployed to discredit specific reform proposals, but at the end of the process, the teams were nearly unanimous in their assessment that the World Bank played a minimal role. In terms of governance, this finding suggests that the World Bank does not have a single, uniform effect on local politics; rather, its political function shifts as the political process evolves.

The 1994 Peso Collapse, the National Savings Rate and the Political Resonance of Economic Ideas

By situating the Mexican reform in the broader trajectory of Latin American reforms, the World Bank implies that exogenous political events in Mexico played a minimal role in the reform's adoption. Not surprisingly, Mexican officials insist on the contrary, claiming that the unique political circumstances engendered by the 1994 peso collapse not only moved the reform up on President Zedillo's list of priorities but also generated broad-based public support for the reform.

President Ernesto Zedillo was sworn into office on 1 December 1994. The inauspicious circumstances of his nomination as the PRI's presidential candidate (he was one of the only eligible candidates after the previous nominee was assassinated in March 1994), as well as his apparent lack of personal charisma, had deprived him of the surge in political capital that candidates typically experience in the honeymoon phase of their administrations. Nevertheless, the high tide of support for outgoing President Salinas augmented Zedillo's political capital, putting him in a more favourable bargaining position vis-à-vis the labour movement and other powerful political actors. According to a close advisor, among Zedillo's political aspirations were the privatisation of the electricity sector and perhaps even the privatisation of PEMEX, the state-owned petroleum conglomerate (personal interview, 18 October 1999).

Just three weeks into his administration, those aspirations were permanently dashed. On 22 December 1994, the Central Bank of Mexico announced that it had exhausted its foreign currency reserves and could no longer defend the peso against devaluation. Near the end of the day, the peso was allowed to float, triggering a devaluation of forty per cent, one of the worst devaluations in Mexican history. Just as the Mexican peso collapse of 1994 robbed Mexicans of the precious little economic progress that had been made in the twilight years of the Salinas administration, it robbed Ernesto Zedillo of what little political credibility he had upon assuming the presidency. Instead of riding the crest of Salinas's popularity, Zedillo was consigned to pick up the pieces left by the outgoing administration.

However, there was a light at the end of the political tunnel. An unanticipated consequence of the peso collapse was the public's heightened awareness of Mexico's vulnerability to rapid outflows of foreign capital, most frequently attributed to Mexico's low national savings rate.[4] The logic is as follows: savings are necessary to support consumption, and if national savings are insufficient, the country will have to attract foreign capital to finance current consumption. Mexico had been running a sizable current account deficit in the early 1990s (approximately $13.5 billion) and, to finance this deficit, had become increasingly reliant on foreign investment. 'Domestic savings dropped from 22 per cent of gross domestic product in 1988 to 15.8 per cent in 1994, obliging Mexico to depend heavily on foreign capital for its investment needs' (Madrid 2003: 74).

With his approval rating at a paltry thirty per cent, Zedillo needed whatever support he could get, and he embraced the domestic savings rate as a nationalist project. Thus, 'boosting the country's savings rate became one of the Zedillo administration's main policy goals, featured prominently in the government's National Development Plan' (Madrid 2003: 75). The coordinator of the 1995 working team confirmed that the political resonance of increasing the national savings rate attracted Zedillo to the New Law:

> I remember preparing notes for President Zedillo, and he was very open to the idea [of moving from a PAYG system to a system of individual accounts] … He saw it

as a fiscal effort which could be presented as a noble purpose. He concurred with the view that it would be a means for increasing savings. Though we were aware that the literature claiming that a reform of this type does not support an increase in voluntary savings, we thought that at least it would increase compulsory savings. I think that was what interested Zedillo the most. (Personal interview, 18 June 2003)

This economist is clearly well versed in the scholarly literature and acknowledges from the outset that increasing the national savings rate is not an unambiguous consequence of the proposed reform in the pension system. His comments indicate that President Zedillo, himself an accomplished economist, was equally conscious of the inconclusive economic debate over the effects of fully funded systems on the national savings rate. Nevertheless, despite their technical reservations, Zedillo and his working team recognised the political expediency of making a higher national savings rate one of the central goals of the New Law.

The national savings debate took on greater momentum as the discussion of social security reform moved to the public stage in mid 1995, and it was a central factor in clinching public support. The 1995 working team member responsible for selling the reform to labour leaders explained the decisive effect that the savings rate argument had on public opinion:

If you recall the crisis of 94, one of the major causes was that foreign investment was supporting domestic borrowing, and the level of internal savings was very low. We had a high dependency on external financing, and that dependency was used to explain the crisis. Given the low levels of domestic saving, we were heavily dependent on foreign investment, so any internal or external shock could provoke a crisis. This was the explanation used to explain the suffering of the 94 crisis to politicians and to the general public. It was said to be a conviction that generated support for the reform. It is not so clear that the pension system will raise the domestic savings rate, but it is the understanding of many people, and it helped to sway public opinion towards the reform. (Personal interview, 21 January 2000)

In 1995, then, the Mexican public was more receptive to social security reform in a way that it had not been in 1991–92, and the Zedillo administration had a greater incentive to focus its energies on this particular piece of legislation, for it allayed the shared concern of Mexican citizens and international investors about Mexico's vulnerability to rapid capital movements. These factors also provided the context for policymakers to assert that the New Law was a homegrown response to a historically specific constellation of factors.

Conclusion: Intimate Knowledge and the Politics of Policy Convergence

This chapter has sought to trace the competing claims of World Bank officials and Mexican policy makers in order to examine how each group substantiates its interpretation of the origin of the New Law of Social Security in Mexico.

Whereas Mexican policy makers emphasise their independent evaluations of other reforms and the political contingency of the New Law, the World Bank stresses its pivotal role in alerting the government of the future insolvency of Mexico's public pension system. While most existing scholarship seeks to definitively establish whether domestic or external factors predominated, I argued that this ongoing divergence highlights significant political processes in the domestic political field and in the relationship between Mexican policy makers and World Bank officials.

The way in which the World Bank was invoked in struggles between Mexican policy makers suggests that it has neither a constant nor uniform effect on the Mexican political field. Instead, its function shifted during the policy-making process. Initially, allegations of proximity to the World Bank became an idiom through which political teams were consolidated and resistance to neoliberal models of pension reform was expressed. As the policy making process developed, rival political teams mutually rejected the World Bank's influence on the final version of the reform, thereby representing the New Law as a unique product of the Mexican political process. Domestic policy makers' differential engagement of the World Bank points to the multifaceted and evolving role of the World Bank in shaping the domestic political landscape.

More broadly, the coexistence of divergent accounts reveals the political valence of the discourse of policy convergence. The World Bank and Mexican policy makers both acknowledge one another's participation in the New Law, and neither is particularly focused on taking credit for the reform. What is at stake in their divergent accounts is who has an intimate knowledge of Mexico's situation and, by extension, who is in the best position to set the policy agenda. The World Bank asserts that its bird's-eye view of regional trends puts it in a privileged position to detect policy problems, whereas Mexican policy makers assert that their familiarity with the intricacies of Mexico's social, political and economic reality enable them to more adeptly interpret and define policy problems. Mexican policy makers accrue significant political capital by asserting their independence from the World Bank and claiming that the New Law is a unique historical product of local circumstances. This interpretation not only appeases Mexican citizens who worry about the excessive interference of international financial institutions, but also gives Mexican policy makers discursive traction in their struggle with the World Bank over who ultimately controls the domestic agenda. World Bank officials, in contrast, derive political capital by positioning the Bank as the pre-eminent mediator of global policy change at a time when new circuits of knowledge transmission and policy sharing are emerging that largely sidestep international institutions such as the World Bank (Woods and Martinez-Diaz 2009). The World Bank attempts to recoup the damage that these circuits do to its reputation by claiming that it brought the issue of social security reform to the attention of domestic policy makers. At the root of this ongoing contestation is how and to whom regional policy trends are attributed. Analyses that uncritically accept the

World Bank's influence on policy convergence inadvertently recapitulate this narrative and overlook the space of negotiation between World Bank policy makers and domestic policy makers.

An ethnographic approach to divergent accounts reveals a space of contention in contemporary governance, one that would otherwise be obscured by the discourse of policy convergence. This is not to deny that forms of policy coordination exist but, rather, to illustrate the political stakes involved in how that process is narrated. Consequently, it underscores the need for more sustained ethnographic attention to how the ideological links between policies are narrated so that anthropologists can broaden the horizon of their efforts to 'study up' by connecting the dynamics of domestic governance to the international political economy.

Notes

1. Peru reformed its system in 1993 followed by Colombia and Argentina in 1994, Mexico in 1995, Uruguay in 1996, Bolivia in 1997, El Salvador in 1998, Costa Rica in 2000 and the Dominican Republic in 2001 (Barrientos 2006). The first reform of this type was implemented in Chile in 1981 under the oppressive regime of Agustin Pinochet, and it remains the touchstone against which subsequent reforms are compared.
2. A similar wave of reforms occurred in Eastern Europe in the 1990s (Müller 2001).
3. While the humanitarian gesture of alleviating poverty is a noble one, it must be understood within the geopolitical context of the Cold War. As Secretary of Defence under Kennedy and Johnson, McNamara subscribed to the theory that the spread of global poverty made populations vulnerable to communist movements. Containing communism, then, entailed alleviating poverty.
4. Though foreign investment alone cannot bear the full blame for the peso devaluation, an argument can certainly be made that Mexico's excessive dependence on foreign capital exacerbated the severity of the collapse. See Weintraub 2000 for a detailed discussion.

References

Adler, Emanuel and Peter M. Haas. 1992. 'Conclusion: Epistemic Communities, World Order, and the Creation of a Reflective Research Program', *International Organization* 46(1): 367–90.

Barnett, Michael N. and Martha Finnemore. 1999. 'The Politics, Power, and Pathologies of International Organizations', *International Organization* 53(4): 699–732.

Barrientos, Armando. 2006. 'Poverty Reduction: The Missing Piece of Pension Reform in Latin America', *Social Policy and Administration* 40(4): 369–84.

Berger, Mark T. and Mark Beeson. 1998. 'Lineages of Liberalism and Miracles of Modernisation: The World Bank, the East Asian Trajectory and the International Development Debate', *Third World Quarterly* 19(3): 487–504.

Bertranou, Julian F. 1995. 'La política de la reforma a la seguridad social en México: analises de la formulación de sistema de ahorro para el retiro', *Estudios Sociológicos* 8: 3–24.

——. 1998. 'Mexico: The Politics of the System for Retirement Pensions', in María Amparo Cruz-Saco and Carmelo Mesa-Lago (eds), *Do Options Exist? The Reform of Pension and Health Care Systems in Latin America*. Pittsburgh: University of Pittsburgh Press, pp. 85–108.

Brooks, Sarah M. 2007. 'Globalization and Pension Reform in Latin America', *Latin American Politics and Society* 49(4): 31–62.

Centeno, Miguel Angel. 1994. *Democracy Within Reason: Technocratic Revolution in Mexico*. University Park, PA: Pennsylvania State University Press.

Cox, Robert. 1996. 'The Executive Head: An Essay on Leadership in International Organization', in Robert Cox (ed.), *Approaches to World Order*. New York: Cambridge University Press, pp. 317–48.

Cruz-Saco, Maria Amparo and Carmelo Mesa-Lago (eds). 1998. *Do Options Exist? The Reform of Pension and Health Care Systems in Latin America*. Pittsburgh: University of Pittsburgh Press.

De Vries, Barend A. 1996. 'The World Bank as an International Player in Economic Analysis', in A.W. Coats (ed.), *The Post-1945 Internationalization of Economics*. Durham, NC: Duke University Press, pp. 225–44.

DePalma, Anthony. 1995. 'After Bitter Legislative Battle, Mexico Revises Social Security', *New York Times*, 9 December: A4.

Dion, Michelle. 2006. 'Globalizacion, democratizacion y reform del sistema de seguridad social en Mexico, 1988–2005', *Foro Internacion* 183(1): 51–80.

——. 'Globalization and Policy Convergence,' *International Studies Review* 3(1): 53–78.

Drezner, Daniel. 2005. 'Globalization, Coercion, and Competition: The Different Pathways to Policy Convergence', *Journal of European Public Policy* 12: 841–59.

Ferguson, James. 1994. *The Anti-Politics Machine: "Development," Depoliticization, and Bureaucratic Power in LeSotho*. Minneapolis: University of Minnesota Press.

Gavin, Michael and Dani Rodrik. 1995. 'The World Bank in Historical Perspective', *American Economic Review* 85(2): 329–34.

George, Susan and Fabrizio Sabelli. 1994. *Faith and Credit: The World Bank's Secular Empire*. Boulder: Westview Press.

Goldman, Michael. 2005. *Imperial Nature: The World Bank and Struggles for Social Justice in the Age of Globalization*. New Haven: Yale University Press.

Holzmann, Robert. 2000. 'Pension Reform: Where Are We Now?', *International Social Security Review* 53(1): 3–10.

Instituto Mexicano de Seguridad Social (IMSS). 1995. *Diagnóstico IMSS*. Mexico: D.F.

Kay, Stephen. 2000. "Recent Changes in Latin American Welfare States: Is There Social Dumping?', *Journal of European Social Policy* 10(2): 185–203.

Madrid, Raul Lorca. 2003. *Retiring the State: The Politics of Pension Privatization*. Stanford: Stanford University Press.

Maxfield, Sylvia. 1997. *Gatekeepers of Growth: The International Political Economy of Central Banking in Developing Countries*. Princeton: Princeton University Press.

Mesa-Lago, Carmelo. 1997. 'Social Welfare Reform in the Context of Economic-Political Liberalization: Latin American Cases', *World Development* 25(1): 497–517.

Müller, Katharina. 2001. 'The Political Economy of Pension Reform in Eastern Europe', *International Social Security Review* 54(2–3): 57–79.

Orenstein, Mitchell A. 2008. *Privatizing Pensions: The Transnational Campaign for Social Security Reform*. Princeton: Princeton University Press.

———. 2005. 'The New Pension Reform as Global Policy', *Global Social Policy* 5(2): 175–202.

Quiesser, Monika. 1998. *The Second-Generation Pension Reforms in Latin America*. Paris: OECD Development Centre.

Randeria, Shalini. 2007. 'The State of Globalization: Legal Plurality, Overlapping Sovereignties and Ambiguous Alliances between Civil Society and the Cunning State in India', *Theory, Culture & Society* 24(1): 1–33.

Sales-Sarapy, Carlos, Fernando Solís Soberon, and Alejandro Villagómez Amezcua. 1998. 'Pension System Reform: The Case of Mexico', in M.S. Feldstein (ed.), *Privatizing Social Security*. Chicago: University of Chicago Press, pp. 135–76.

Sanford, Jonathan. 1988. 'The World Bank and Poverty: The Plight of the World's Poor is Still a Major Concern of the International Agency', *American Journal of Economics and Sociology* 47(3): 257–75.

Schneider, Ben Ross. 1998. 'The Material Bases of Technocracy: Investor Confidence and Neoliberalism in Latin America', in Migual A. Centeno and Patricio Silva (eds), *The Politics of Expertise in Latin* America. London: Macmillan.

Shore, Cris and Susan Wright (eds). 1997. *Anthropology of Policy: Critical Perspectives on Governance and Power*. New York: Routledge.

Stokes, Susan C. 2001. *Mandates and Democracy: Neoliberalism by Surprise in Latin America*. New York: Cambridge University Press.

Teichman, Judith. 2004. 'The World Bank and Policy Reform in Mexico and Argentina', *Latin American Politics and Society* 46(1): 39–74.

Weintraub, Sidney. 2000. *Financial Decision-Making in Mexico: To Bet a Nation*. Pittsburgh: University of Pittsburgh Press.

Woods, Ngaire. 2007. *The Globalizers: The IMF, the World Bank, and Their Borrowers*. Ithaca: Cornell University Press.

Woods, Ngaire and Leonardo Martinez-Diaz (eds). 2009. *Networks of Influence? Developing Countries in a Networked Global Order*. New York: Oxford University Press.

World Bank. 1994. *Averting the Old Age Crisis: Policies to Protect the Old and Promote Growth*. New York: Oxford University Press.

Chapter 8

Shadow Governing: What the Neocon Core Reveals about Power and Influence in America[1]

Janine R. Wedel

Since 2002, much debate in America has focused on the war in Iraq and the subsequent occupation. The 'neoconservatives' – working to pursue their goal of remaking the world in their image of America – have won mainstream media recognition as never before. Names like Richard Perle, Paul Wolfowitz and Douglas Feith – the chief architects of the war – have easily rolled off the tongues of television commentators. And although there is awareness that these architects played a role, how and why they prevailed in helping to shape the Bush administration's policies to take the U.S. to war has not been satisfactorily explained.

This chapter attempts to illuminate how and why this occurred by charting a social network phenomenon I call 'flex nets' (Wedel 2004b, 2009). The appearance of this phenomenon signals changes taking place in governing and society – in the U.S. and the wider world – that undermine the principles that have defined modern states, free markets and democracy itself. To illustrate this phenomenon, I highlight the workings and impact of a particular flex net. What I call the 'Neocon core' – a tiny subset of a dozen or so long-connected neoconservatives – is the most prominent identifiable flex net in the U.S. Understanding how such a group operates is critical to grasping the implications of the new phenomenon.

Flex nets evolved in the more networked ecosystem of the late twentieth and early twenty-first centuries. They are at the top of the food chain of influence wielding. They draw for membership on a limited circle of players who interact with each other in multiple roles, both inside and outside of government to achieve mutual and consistent goals over time. They resurface as a group in different incarnations and configurations to pursue those goals – which are ideological and may also be financial. Flex nets pool the positions of their members, many of whom assume overlapping and shifting roles in government, nongovernmental and business organisations. Their members conflate state and private interests. They are adept at relaxing both governments' rules of accountability and businesses' codes of competition, thereby challenging principles that have defined modern states, free markets and democracy itself.

Although this phenomenon has sweeping implications, it is not yet well charted and defies description in conventional terms. Traditional social science and public policy categories cannot account for the peripatetic machinations of flex nets, much less their innovations at the state-private nexus. Flex nets cannot be reduced to political elites or influential cliques. Although flex nets, like lobbies and interest groups, perform a crucial age-old function of the modern state – to mediate between state and private sector – and also incorporate aspects of these forms, flex nets also differ from them in crucial ways. As political scientist Simon Reich (2006) has noted, flex nets are a paradox in terms of political representation: They are more amorphous and less transparent than conventional political lobbies, yet, conversely, they are also more coherent and less accountable. Flex nets perplex prevailing thinking about corruption and conflicts of interest, and confound conventional means of holding players to account.

The Changing Ecosystem

Several transformational developments converged to create the conditions under which flex nets would thrive: the diffusion of authority spurred by several decades of government outsourcing and deregulation as neoliberalism was widely promulgated; the end of the Cold War – that is, of relations dominated by two competing alliances; and the advent of ever-more complex technologies. The neoliberal reorganisation of government occurred within countries, often under pressure from international financial institutions like the International Monetary Fund and the World Bank. Beginning in the early 1980s, the policies of governing administrations promoted outsourcing, privatisation, deregulation and free trade. As these prescriptions were being advanced around the world by the international financial institutions, the communist governments of Eastern Europe collapsed.

The subsequent end of the Cold War became the second driving development in the reconfiguring world. No longer did two great behemoths locked in decades-long conflict dictate the fates of Third World nations and regional conflicts. As the system of bipolar authority vanished, boundaries broadly became less distinct, more permeable and harder to regulate. Self-organising networks and entities surged. New playing fields without rules and referees – or sham ones – offered profitable targets for corporations and nongovernmental organisations (NGOs), as well as organised crime groups, which, naturally, thrive on ambiguous borders.

A third development, the advent of ever-more complex technologies, encouraged the processes already underway. The advance and use of complex technologies favour horizontal networks over hierarchy, flexible manoeuvring over bureaucratic process, and teams over individual actors (Rycroft and Kash 1999). Control of information and information technology (IT) is a key component of this third development. Not only does IT substantially elude state and international regulation, even IT employed in the name of the state can be largely under the control of private contractors, as in the U.S.

All three developments – the neoliberal reorganisation of government, the ending of the Cold War and increasingly complex technologies – unleash(ed) forces that opened the door to a proliferation of 'nonstate' actors who sometimes work for states and planted the seeds for the consolidation of power and influence. The increased delegation of authority to nonstate actors enabled them to become guardians of information that once rested in the hands of state and international authorities. While supposedly working on behalf of those authorities, these players could guard information and privatise it for their own purposes, all the while eluding detection.

I first became aware of the potential of unofficial information to sustain a subterranean system – and even to reshape formal institutions – some twenty-five years ago in Eastern Europe. In communist societies where official information was widely discredited, the most important asset was reliable information, the acquisition of which usually required trust. As a social anthropologist in Poland in the 1980s, I watched how people mobilised semiclosed networks in and outside of the formal bureaucracy and economy to obtain scarce information, resources and privileges. An environment of shortage and distrust of the state encouraged 'dirty togetherness', a Polish sociologist's reference to cliquishness and close-knit networks of family, friends and other trusted associates (Podgorecki 1987: 57–78). Groups that are 'dirty' together share an overall agenda and coordinate efforts to achieve it.

When the command structure of a centrally planned state that had owned virtually all the property, companies and wealth breaks down and no authoritarian stand-in is put in its place, a network-based mode of governing and business develops to replace it. As the communist governments of the region collapsed in 1989 and the Soviet Union broke apart in 1991, a dirtier togetherness took hold among well-placed operators – now not merely to survive but to thrive. After 1989 and 1991, the states of Eastern Europe and the former Soviet Union began privatising hitherto state-owned national resources – with the help of U.S. and U.K. models, sponsors and consultants. The introduction of the new policies, combined with the unraveling of state control, presented ideal conditions for long-standing informal groups, schooled in circumventing the overbearing communist state through dirty togetherness, to move in and both substitute for and transfigure official structures. Flex net-like groupings – known, for instance, as 'institutional nomads' in Poland and 'clans' in Russia and the Ukraine – positioned their members at the state-private nexus, rose to fill leadership vacuums and sometimes acquired state-owned wealth at firesale prices.

Governing by network is obviously much more intense in states moving rapidly away from communism than in stable democracies such as the U.S. But another variant of intertwining state-private power has been evolving in the U.S, albeit more gradually. There, the reconfiguring of the balance between state and private interests, combined with a hollowing out of the regulatory and monitoring functions of the state, has created new opportunities for coordinated groups of players, or flex nets, to take over public policy agendas in pursuit of their own interests.

How did this come about? The contracting out of government services and functions, which began in earnest with the Second World War, gained momentum with Ronald Reagan's 'small government' and Margaret Thatcher's deregulation in the 1980s. Today, gathering bipartisan support urging the accelerated outsourcing of government services combines with a proliferation of entities involved in governing, a diminution of monitoring and regulation, and a movement of policy-making legitimacy to the private sector. By the time the U.S. launched its current military campaign in Iraq (the most privatised war in U.S. history), two-thirds of those doing work for the federal government in any capacity were not on its payroll but, instead, received their paychecks from consulting firms, other companies, NGOs and think tanks (Light 2003). Not only are services subject to appropriation, so too are government functions, information and legitimacy. Contractors perform more than three-quarters of the federal government's information technology work (Government Executive 2003), control crucial databases (e.g., Reddy and Goo 2004), execute military and occupying operations (e.g., Hutton 2007), draft official documents (e.g., Department of the Army 2003; Guttman 2004; Verkuil 2007) and select other contractors (e.g., Makinson 2004). At the same time that private companies are acquiring government functions, the number of civil servants available to oversee them has declined (Light 1999: 207–9; 2003), thus decreasing the government's capacity to monitor the process (e.g., Government Accountability Office 2005).

Just as government information and authority have been fragmented through the contracting out of its functions, institutions such as the Foreign Service and other well-established modes of representation have weakened, while the use of special envoys and quasi-official consultative bodies has proliferated. State-private bodies and boards, such as Vice-President Dick Cheney's Energy Task Force and former First Lady Hillary Rodham Clinton's Health Task Force, have mushroomed. According to the Congressional Research Service, 'quasi-government' organisations – 'federally related entities that possess legal characteristics of both the governmental and private sectors' – 'have grown in number, size, and importance in recent decades' (Moe and Kosar 2005: D1). As I saw in Eastern Europe, state-private entities with ambiguous status can serve as vehicles through which private interests direct state resources and functions, thereby enlarging the unaccountable use of state power and resources. When such bodies proliferate (sometimes under the guise of 'privatisation'), an unaccountable state sphere expands (Kamiński 1996, 1997; Wedel 2004a: 221–29).

A similar process is at work in the U.S. with the growth of 'shadow government' (e.g., Guttman and Willner 1976; Wedel 2009). As spending increases for private contracts and state-private entities, government risks becoming less accountable while creating more opportunities for private players to pursue – and consolidate – their private interests. The intensification of executive power in the U.S. after the end of the Cold War (e.g., Howell 2007: 267–382; Pfiffner 2007a, 2008) provides yet another favourable condition for the consolidation of power. Flex nets position themselves for maximum efficiency – both to take advantage of a fragmented system and to benefit from centralised power.

Flex Net Features

The following features make flex nets effective and distinguish them from other influencers such as lobbyists, interest groups, conspiratorial groups, Mafias, cliques and elites. (These groupings have by no means disappeared; some are even nourished by the same transformational developments that feed flex nets.) First, flex nets form an exclusive informal network that serves as a multifaceted backbone. While their roles and the organisational and political environments in which they operate may change, the group provides continuity. Unlike lobbyists (who offer politicians support and resources in exchange for access and preference in policies) and interest groups (which defend the interests of a particular group or promote a political cause [Bogdanor 1987: 295; Grant 2003; Robertson 2004: 241]), flex nets are not formal or permanent entities and have no interest in becoming incorporated. Although members of flex nets are united by shared activities and interpersonal histories, the existence of the network is unannounced. Flex nets are also not conspiracies whose members must keep their activities – and often, the very existence of their group – secret. While some of the group's activities in support of its goals are publicly unrevealed, others are fully in the open, invite media attention and may even be crafted by public relations specialists.

Group cohesion is aided by the second feature of flex nets: shared conviction. Members of a flex net act as a continuous, self-propelling team to achieve goals that are grounded in their common world view. Flex nets thus differ from the powerful 'Wise Men' of the past, such as the influential advisers who refashioned American foreign policy at the end of the Second World War and John F. Kennedy's 'Best and Brightest' who executed the Vietnam War in the 1960s. These men were mainly instruments of the presidents whose policies they pursued, whereas flex nets are self-sustaining teams with their own agendas. There was little of the long-term constancy or independent pursuit of group goals that defines flex nets.

The third characteristic of flex nets is that they form a resource pool. The resource pool is the base from which players organise the interrelations between the state and private spheres and from which they blur boundaries and bend rules. Members pool their multiple roles and statuses as they place themselves in positions – government entities, companies, consulting firms, think tanks, NGOs and the media – relevant to achieving their goals. Working together extends the potential influence of the group. At least some members of a flex net perform overlapping and shifting roles and are skilled at manoeuvring among them – often leaving a dust trail of ambiguity in their wake. The elusiveness of flex nets helps to make them more difficult to hold to account than lobbyists, interest groups, and the like.

While flex nets, like Mafias, work at the interstices of state and private (Blok 2001: 9126), pursue common goals and share rules of behaviour, flex nets should not be confused with Mafias (which, in the classic usage, are a type of patronage system, run by family enterprises, that developed in Sicily and Calabria, Italy.) Unlike flex nets, whose numbers primarily seek to influence policy, Mafias pursue illegal transactions to gain power or wealth and employ violence to achieve their objectives (Varese 2003).

Finally, flex nets forge a (re)shaped habitat – their fourth feature. A flex net's strength lies in its coordinated ability to reorganise governing processes, authorities and bureaucracies to suit the group's purposes. Members of flex nets both use and supplant standard governing structures, often setting up alternative might-be-official, might-be-unofficial organisations or authorities.

For all these reasons, flex nets also cannot be reduced to cliques (a core group whose members contact one another for multiple purposes and advance their own interests [Boissevain 1974: 174; Seymour-Smith 1986: 40]). Although flex nets can be seen as a type of clique (Kurczewski 2007), cliques do not typically possess key features of the flex net *modus operandi* that define its operations.

Similarly, flex nets also are not merely political elites. While elites in many contexts exert power and control, as anthropologists (e.g., Shore and Nugent 2002; Dogan 2003) have shown, flex nets – small, mobile and with a certain *modus operandi* – are more than political elites. With regard to elites in the U.S., important historical work has been done to dissect the structure and function of influence groups, including the networks that propel them. Political scientist Phillip H. Burch's *Elites in American History* (1981), a study of American political power from the Civil War to the New Deal, depicts the web of ties among government officials and the threat that those connections pose to the notion of democratic government (Burch 1981). Most famously, a half-century ago, in his treatise *The Power Elite*, sociologist C. Wright Mills (1956) coined the term to describe the pyramid of power – the tiny, singular group of elites at the pinnacle of America's business, military and political establishments. This interlocking constellation of government officials, military leaders and corporate executives, he argued, effectively controlled major political and social decision making.

By contrast, members of flex nets inhabit a space that lies beyond traditional positions of authority. They flex power by pooling resources within their networks and juggling roles, often by passing and supplanting formal institutions and policy-making processes. Poised to work closely with executive authorities, flex nets eschew legislative and judicial branches of government that may interfere with their activities. They also cut through bureaucracy, connect entities doing government work and streamline decision making. Such resilient networks can seem an attractive antidote to sluggish governing.

The Neocon Core

In its mode of operating and extraordinary influence, the Neocon core bears a striking similarity to Eastern European groups and networks that I observed at the state-private nexus as the region transitioned away from communism. During the administration of George W. Bush, the most visible members of the Neocon core were Richard Perle, Defense Policy Board chairman and member during part of George W. Bush's first term; Paul Wolfowitz, Deputy Secretary of Defense in the first term of George W. Bush and later head of the World Bank; I. Lewis 'Scooter' Libby, the former chief of staff to Vice-President Dick Cheney, who was indicted in October 2005 (for charges including obstruction of justice and perjury in the Valerie Plame CIA 'outing' case); and Douglas Feith, Undersecretary of Defense until August 2005. Flex nets are not strictly bounded: Membership in the group is dynamic and all members are not equally important at all times. Moreover, a number of associates who, at times, have facilitated the group's agendas, in conjunction with group members, can also be identified.

For several decades, members of the Neocon core have pursued their foreign policy ideals, first primarily to bring down the Soviet Union and later to transform the Middle East – and the world – according to their own vision. The thinking of neoconservatives appears to have been significantly shaped by their experience of the Second World War and the age of American pre-eminence that followed. The heroic fight against fascism contributed to their sense that constant vigilance is necessary to avert the next Nazi-type threat and that it is America's right – even duty – to export organised violence in the service of U.S. interests. In addition, the fact that victory over fascism was achieved far from U.S. soil, without the trauma of war at home, bolstered the notion that America can triumph in war abroad without endangering security at home. The post-Second World War experience of American dominance, buoyed by notions of progress and democracy, further honed the neoconservative view that America can, and should, refashion the world (e.g., Wald 1987; Dorrien 1993; Blumenthal 1986: 122–65; Mann 2004: 21–36 and 90–94).

To propel the U.S. to war, the Neocon core built on its impressive track record of, among other means: bypassing government bureaucracy; creating and pushing alternative intelligence findings to supplant those of U.S. entities; and relying on personal relationships with trusted (by them) brokers who manage vital aspects of relationships between nations. And while key members of the core have been honing this *modus operandi* over several decades and its policy endeavours have not always met with success, its *modus operandi* has been one step ahead of the transformational global and American developments underway. The core may even have helped to advance some of these changes.

In 1998, core members Paul Wolfowitz and Elliott Abrams, an operative in the arms-for-hostages Iran-Contra affair who later served the George W. Bush administration as Deputy Assistant to the President and Deputy National Security Advisor for Global Democracy Strategy, respectively, were among the signatories of a letter to President Clinton calling for the removal of Saddam Hussein. Donald Rumsfeld, Secretary of Defense under George. W. Bush, also signed the letter (New American Century 1998). In a George W. Bush presidency and especially after 9/11, the group saw an opportunity to advance its vision. The core positioned its members to emerge as chief decision makers with broad influence in Middle Eastern affairs. Core members were so intimately involved in advocating, executing and justifying the war, from so many complementary and interconnected positions (as detailed below), that it is difficult to imagine the decision to invade Iraq independently of the group's influence. In addition to its goals for Iraq, the Neocon core also has had designs on Iran and has been pressing for American intervention there. Its stated aim in Iran was – and is – 'regime change'.

To study the operations of these players and how they help drive policy formation and implementation, I have pursued two primary foci: the players' roles, activities and sponsors; and their social networks, organizations and *modus operandi.*

Representational Juggling

Members of the Neocon flex net excel at a game I call 'representational juggling'. Foremost among them is the well-known Richard Perle, a former Assistant Secretary of Defense under President Ronald Reagan. Some of America's top investigative reporters and inspectors general of government agencies have tried to prove he is corrupt, yet he eludes prosecution because he is a master representational juggler. Perle surfaces at the epicentre of a head-spinning array of business deals, consulting and lobbying roles and ideological initiatives, consistently courting and yet skirting charges of conflicts of interest. He played a significant role in taking the U.S. to war in Iraq through, for instance, his efforts to organise the gathering and dissemination of 'information' – both inside and outside government – demonstrating that Iraq had weapons of mass destruction, and his sponsorship and promotion of Ahmed Chalabi, the Iraqi-born businessman, exile and founder of the Iraqi National Congress who was bent on the overthrow of Saddam Hussein.

Perle avoided congressional confirmation hearings by declining to take a fully fledged position in the first term of the George W. Bush administration. Instead, he accepted the chairmanship of the Defense Policy Board, a Pentagon advisory body with a mixed state-private character that provides its members with access to classified information and top-secret intelligence reports. During the run-up to the Iraq war, Perle used the Board as a policy platform from which to call for the overthrow of Saddam Hussein – a cause for which he had long been working. At the same time, Perle also represented the telecommunications firm Global Crossing Ltd. in its dealings with the U.S. government (which he does not deny) and for which he was investigated by the Pentagon (Labaton 2003; Silverstein and Neubauer 2003: 1). He also allegedly offered defence-related clients sensitive information gleaned through his position on the Board (Silverstein and Neubauer 2003) and angled for investment funds from a Saudi national who was endeavouring to influence U.S. policy towards Iraq (Hersh 2003).

One role (Chairman of the Defense Policy Board) thus enhanced Perle's usefulness in other roles (pundit, consultant) and hence his financial and influence opportunities. Perle could appear as an official or patron in one situation, a client to an official in another and a lobbyist in a third. He is larger than any of these roles – an institution unto himself – and has no necessarily fixed address. Although his influence may be aided by a particular role, it is not defined by or confined to any one of them. The Pentagon investigated some of his consultancy activities, but Perle wriggled his way out of trouble. The model that Perle exemplifies – the government adviser-business consultant-policy advocate – has become much more pervasive over roughly the past two decades. It is much more common today, with nongovernmental and hybrid bodies centrally involved in governing, often holding great sway and with much less clarity about where organisations begin and end.

Perle promoted a tanker deal in a coauthored *Wall Street Journal* op-ed piece (Donnelly and Perle 2003) from which he stood to profit, billing himself simply as a resident fellow at the American Enterprise Institute (Hilzenrath 2003: E01; Hartung 2003). An uninformed reader would not know that Perle had any financial interest in the deal or that he was both lobbying and advising the government. Framing his activities under the guise of his role as an AEI fellow gave him the appearance of a disinterested public intellectual and neutral observer. In this case, he cloaked his interests, which were ostensibly motivated by one role (making money or advocacy – i.e., lobbying for a policy) under the rubric of another (AEI fellow).

Perle's repertoire of roles – which can be kept separate, merged, combined and interplayed among themselves to reinforce each other – yields him not only flexibility but also deniability. His ability to skirt accountability in one instance by claiming he was operating in another confounds traditional means of accountability. The ambiguity that swirls around him is not just a byproduct of his activities; it can also enhance his influence. Operating above and beyond institutions, as well as within them, players like Perle sidestep, obfuscate and play on the boundaries of state and private. This is not to say that they erase the boundaries altogether. In fact, the players often need the distinction: they use the spheres of state and private selectively for what each can enable and mitigate the constraints of one sphere by switching to another. While tapping into the state sphere for specific resources, privileges and the trappings of state authority, they cannot operate effectively if they are fully accountable to it. Thus, they also operate in the private sphere, which additionally avails them of profits and opportunities that the state cannot realise, even when it is the sole source, for instance, of classified information or government contracts.

The Power of the Collective

Although Richard Perle is often in the news as an individual, he could not be where he is were it not for the flex net to which he belongs – a close-knit dozen or so neoconservatives. Members of the Neocon core have been interlinked for as long as three decades through government, think-tank, business and advocacy roles, as well as family ties. Like all flex nets, members of the core gained influence by quietly boosting one another, promoting one another for influential positions and coordinating their multipronged efforts inside and outside of government to achieve mutual goals. The Neocon players' propensity to work concertedly to achieve their goals over time – even to the point of skirting regulations that might keep them from doing so while still appearing to uphold the letter of the law – lies at the heart of their effectiveness.

The Neocon core provides a running example that spans several decades. Consider the relationships among Richard Perle, Paul Wolfowitz and Douglas Feith – three of its principal players. In 1973, as a senior staff member of the Senate Armed Services Committee, Perle helped Wolfowitz, then an assistant professor at Yale, find employment in the Arms Control and Disarmament Agency (ACDA). Five years later, Wolfowitz was investigated for passing a classified document to an Israeli government official through a go-between, according to Stephen Green, a retired journalist who has written for two decades about Israeli espionage in the U.S. and has been interviewed by the FBI in recent years about long-ago activities of these and other members of the Neocon core (Green 2004). (An inquiry was launched and dropped, and Wolfowitz continued to work at the ACDA until 1980.)

In 1978, while working as an aide to Senator Henry 'Scoop' Jackson on the Senate Armed Services Committee, Perle was caught in a security breach by CIA Director Stansfield Turner, who urged that Jackson fire him. Perle received a reprimand but was kept on staff, according to a report in the *Washington Post* by Sidney Blumenthal (1987: B1). In another instance, according to investigative reporter Seymour Hersh, Perle was questioned by the FBI after a wiretap picked him up discussing with an Israeli Embassy official classified information (which he said he obtained from a National Security Council staff member) (Hersh 1982).

In 1982, Perle, as Assistant Secretary for International Security Policy in President Reagan's Defense Department, hired and later promoted Feith after he had been fired from his post as a Middle East analyst at the NSC. Feith was fired, Green found, because he was the subject of an FBI inquiry into whether he had supplied classified material to an Israeli official (Green 2004). After leaving the Pentagon in 1987, Perle became a highly paid consultant for a lobbying firm, International Advisers Inc., which Feith established in 1989. By serving as a consultant only, Perle – who had supervised U.S. military assistance to Turkey while at the Defense Department – was able to bypass federal regulations prohibiting anyone from representing a foreign government right after leaving government (Shafer 2003).

The mutual assistance among these three men continued into the new millennium. In 2001, Perle and Wolfowitz championed Feith for the position of Undersecretary for Policy in the Pentagon. In that post, Feith in turn selected Perle as Chairman of the Defense Policy Board. (Perle resigned as Chairman in March 2003 amid allegations of conflicts of interest and from the Board altogether a year later.) Perle, Wolfowitz and Feith exemplify behaviour of a flex net and how its members' mutual assistance multiplies the group's effectiveness. What may have been at first serendipitous opportunities in career development, shared interests and friends helping one another evolved into a dynamic pursuit of joint goals. As evidenced by the mutual aid round robin in these examples, it is highly unlikely that these players could have continued to secure such important positions and wielded such influence merely as individuals on their own. Perle, Wolfowitz and Feith constitute a microcosm of the larger Neocon group of some dozen or so players, all of whom, like these three, are intertwined with other members many times over.

The *Modus Operandi* of a Flex Net

To have significance, these horizontal relations would have to influence policy while undermining standard governing and policy processes. Over the past decade and a half in particular, the Neocon core has embarked on that course in part by creating and empowering alternative structures, both within and outside of government, to realise its policy aims. The core's success in achieving those aims has been greatly facilitated by the aforementioned transformational developments, which created a hospitable environment for the reconfiguration of governing structures and the creation of alternative authorities. In the 1990s, the Neocon core worked largely through lobbying organisations that it set up and empowered. Post-9/11 insecurity and a presidency favourably disposed towards parts of the neoconservatives' agenda enabled the core to activate its long-time goal of toppling Saddam Hussein. Members of the core set out to meld relevant government units and processes to their purposes, or bypass them, and also exerted influence through quasi-government entities and might-be-official, might-not-be-official dealings.

Setting Up Organisations

An integral building block of the Neocon core's operations in the 1990s was its creation of a host of organisations to further its agenda in the Middle East. Variously pegged as think tanks, educational associations, policy conveyors and the like, members of the core were prime movers in – and started – a series of organisations of influence, including the Center for Security Policy and the Jewish Institute for National Security Affairs. They were also instigators and signatories of 'letterhead organisations', albeit influential and landmark ones such as the Project for the New American Century, as well as the Committee for Peace and Security in the Gulf, the Committee for the Liberation of Iraq and the U.S. Committee for a Free Lebanon. Although letterhead organisations may sound inconsequential, their significance is often in their founding and the buzz their founders create. The collection of players, appearing under different guises, can create the impression that their reach is ever widening.

Reorganising Government for Policy Results

Encouraged by a malleable political environment after 9/11, Neocon core members set out to overthrow Saddam Hussein. They exerted influence, in part, by bypassing or altering standard government units and workings, such as intelligence-gathering and decision processes, and supplanting them with their own. They marginalised officials who were not part of their group and operated through cross-agency cliques that enabled them to limit information and activities to their associates (Lobe 2003).

The key centers of decision making regarding national security and Iraq were the Pentagon and the office of Vice-President Dick Cheney, according to numerous accounts by previously well-placed officials. Lawrence B. Wilkerson, who served as Chief of Staff to Secretary of State Colin Powell from 2002 to 2005, speaks of a covert 'cabal' led by Vice President Cheney and Secretary of Defense Donald Rumsfeld. Wilkerson characterises its 'insular and secret workings' as 'efficient and swift – not unlike the decision making one would associate more with a dictatorship than a democracy' (Wilkerson 2005: B11).

Neocon core members played pivotal roles in both the Vice President's office and the Pentagon. In the latter, Paul Wolfowitz, Deputy Secretary of Defense, and Douglas Feith, Undersecretary of Defense for Policy, influenced and justified the decision to go to war, aided by alternative structures that they set up and controlled. They established their own duplicative governmental entities that sometimes served to bypass or override the input of otherwise relevant entities and processes. Two secretive units in the Pentagon that dealt with policy and intelligence after 9/11 – the Counterterrorism Evaluation Group and the Office of Special Plans – were created under Feith. These were staffed in part by people whom Richard Perle helped to recruit from Neocon-associated organisations such as the American Enterprise Institute. One alternative hub of decision making in the Pentagon set up and run by the Neocon core was characterised by the Vice-Chairman of the Senate Select Committee on Intelligence (2004) as an illegal 'private intelligence' operation. In 2007, the Pentagon's Inspector General, who looked into Feith's prewar intelligence activities, found Feith's operation to be 'inappropriate' but not illegal (Department of Defense 2007).

As in the Pentagon, in the Vice-President's office, Neocon core members exerted considerable influence. 'Scooter' Libby, who had worked with Paul Wolfowitz in the Reagan administration, was a principal player. Libby served simultaneously as Vice-President Cheney's chief of staff and his national security adviser, and he allegedly ran an informal national security operation (e.g., Prados 2004: 44–51). Wilkerson observed the process from his perch as Powell's Chief of Staff. He reports that Cheney's office operated an 'alternate national security staff' that undercut the actual National Security Council (*International Herald Tribune* 2005). Wilkerson contends that 'many of the most crucial decisions from 2001 to 2005 were not made within the traditional NSC process' (Wilkerson 2005: B11). A vice-president's office having such a substantial role in national security policy, let alone such a huge one as that of Cheney's shop, is unprecedented in U.S. history, according to some analysts (e.g., Phillips 2005: 59; Prados 2004: 44–51).

Working Through Might-be-official, Might-not-be-official Structures and Activities

The effectiveness of a flex net's efforts, even when some of its members are in an administration that is 'in power', depends partly on having key members outside of formal government. Being on the outside enables members to work through might-be-official, might-not-be-official structures and engage in ambiguous activities, as illustrated by Richard Perle's overlapping roles.

The same can be said for Neocon core member Michael Ledeen, an important former operative in the 1980s Iran-Contra affair. While holding the 'Freedom Chair' at the American Enterprise Institute (with which many members of the Neocon core are affiliated), Ledeen engaged in might-be-state, might-be private policy initiatives vis-à-vis Iran. Ledeen arranged two secret meetings with the expatriate Iranian arms dealer Manucher Ghorbanifar (Marshall et al. 2004), the goal of which, according to him, was to put U.S. officials in touch with Iranian dissidents (Strobel 2004). Also participating in the meetings was Lawrence A. Franklin, a Pentagon employee who worked in Feith's Undersecretary of Defense for Policy office, as well as in Feith's Office of Special Plans, and was later convicted of passing classified documents about Iran to Israel via AIPAC (the American Israel Public Affairs Committee), the pro-Israeli lobbying group (e.g., Markon 2006: A1). The Senate Intelligence Committee investigated these meetings and found, in the words of investigative journalist Laura Rozen, 'that the Pentagon meetings with Ghorbanifar were inappropriate but neither unauthorized nor illegal. It found that the meetings had been authorized by [deputy National Security Advisor] Stephen Hadley and then deputy defense secretary Paul Wolfowitz, among others' (e.g., Rozen 2008; Senate Select Committee on Intelligence 2008).

Conclusion

The existence and operations of flex nets illustrates a major shift taking place in the U.S. system of governing – and beyond. Compared with traditional influencers such as lobbyists and interest groups, flex nets pose a far greater threat to the principles of democracy and free markets that have defined modern liberal democratic states. Flex nets are at once more effective in wielding influence and yet less visible, transparent and accountable to the public. They pursue policies in their own interests while reorganising standard government processes, circumventing checks and balances, and reshaping institutions to concentrate and even expand unaccountable state power. Although some activities of flex nets may call to mind notions of conflicts of interest and corruption, their workings illustrate why these labels no longer suffice. As a Washington observer sympathetic to the neoconservatives' aims told me: 'There is no conflict of interest, because they define the interest.'

Not only does understanding lag behind, so too do monitoring and auditing practices. Today's 'audit culture' is ill-equipped to deal with complex systems (McIntyre 2002). Standard auditing practices tend to break things down into parts, but the potential influence and 'corruption' of members of flex nets is interrelated. To monitor flex nets effectively, it is crucial to consider all the components collectively and how they interact.

The complexity of governing today – and challenges to democracy – call for a disciplinary framework that can track the interactions between public policies and private interests that are increasingly prevalent around the globe. An anthropological approach is well suited to examine interactions among governmental, nongovernmental and supranational entities, as well as informal links within and around them. A focus on the roles of players and their social networks and sponsors can help elucidate these interactions. For instance, network analysis can illuminate patterns of influence and show how actors connect different levels (such as 'state' and 'private', 'macro' and 'micro', or 'local' or 'national' and 'global') as well as processes (such as 'top down' versus 'bottom up' or 'centralised' versus 'decentralised').

The complexity of governing also calls for employing multiple methods. Ethnographic and interview research alone will not suffice. Inquiry should also involve consulting relevant published and unpublished reports, internal memoranda and documents, and findings by government investigatory and auditing bodies and congressional or parliamentary committees. An anthropology of policy has invaluable contributions to make to understanding

– and indeed grappling with – today's complex governing processes and their implications for democracy. The new breed of players represented by flex nets is highly effective. They dazzle both governments and electorates in part because they serve a need; they connect a confusing, fragmented world. But there is a downside to a world run by such players, who are far removed from the input of voters and the oversight of governments. The reorganising world has yet to recognise the phenomenon of such players, let alone come up with a means of monitoring their activities. Anthropological analysis can, crucially, help turn this around.

Notes

1. The argument in this chapter is further detailed and documented in Wedel 2009. I would like to thank Cris Shore and Susan Wright for their helpful comments on this chapter.

References

Blok, A. 2001. 'Mafia', in *International Encyclopedia of the Social and Behavioral Sciences Vol. 13*. Amsterdam: Elsevier.

Blumenthal, S. 1986. *The Rise of the Counter-establishment: From Conservative Ideology to Political Power*. New York: Times Books.

———. 1987. 'Richard Perle, Disarmed but Undeterred', *Washington Post*, 23 November, B1.

Bogdanor, V. (ed.). 1987. *The Blackwell Encyclopedia of Political Institutions*. Oxford: Basil Blackwell.

Boissevain, J. 1974. *Friends of Friends: Networks, Manipulators and Coalitions*. Oxford: Basil Blackwell.

Bruce, S. and S. Yearley. 2006. *The Sage Dictionary of Sociology*. London: Sage.

Burch, P.H., Jr. 1981. *Elites in American History: The Civil War to the New Deal*. New York: Holmes & Meier Publishers, Inc.

Department of the Army. 2003. 'Contractors on the Battlefield', *Field Manual No. 3-100.21*. Washington DC: Department of the Army.

Department of Defense, Office of Inspector General. 2007. 'Review of Pre-Iraqi War Activities of the Office of the Under Secretary of Defense for Policy', Report No. 07-INTEL-04, 9 February.

Dogan, Mattei, ed. 2003. *Elite Configurations at the Apex of Power*. Leiden-Boston: Brill.

Donnelly, T. and R. Perle. 2003. 'Gas Stations in the Sky', *Wall Street Journal*, 14 August.

Dorrien, G. 1993. *The Neoconservative Mind: Politics, Culture and the War of Ideology*. Philadelphia: Temple University Press.

Government Accountability Office. 2005. *High Risk Series: An Update*. Washington DC: Government Accountability Office.

Government Executive. 2003. 'Experiences Give and Take', *Government Executive*, 1 July.

Grant, W. 2003. 'Interest Groups', in Iain McLean and Alistair McMillan (eds), *The Concise Oxford Dictionary of Politics*. Oxford: Oxford University Press.

Green, S. 2004. Interview, 30 August.

Guttman, D. 2004. 'The Shadow Pentagon: Private Contractors Play a Huge Role in Basic Government Work – Mostly Out of Public View', Washington DC: Center for Public Integrity. Retrieved 2 November 2010 from http://projects.publicintegrity.org/pns/report.aspx?aid=386.

Guttman, D. and B. Willner. 1976. *Shadow Government: The Government's Multi-Billion-Dollar Giveaway of Its Decision-Making Powers to Private Management Consultants, 'Experts' and Think Tanks*. New York: Pantheon Books.

Hartung, W.D. 2003. 'The Booming Defense Business', *Los Angeles Times*, 10 December.

Heclo, H. 1978. 'Issue Networks and the Executive Establishment', in A. King (ed.), *The New American Political System*. Washington DC: American Enterprise Institute.

Hersh, S.M. 1982. 'Kissinger and Nixon in the White House', *Atlantic Monthly*, May. Retrieved 2 November 2010 from http://www.theatlantic.com/issues/82may/hershwh2.htm.

Hersh, S.M. 2003. 'Lunch with the Chairman', *New Yorker*, 17 March.

Hilzenrath, D. 2003. 'Perle Article Didn't Disclose Boeing Tie', *Washington Post*, 5 December, E01.

Howell, W.G. 2007. 'Unilateral Powers: A Brief Overview', in James P. Pfiffner and Roger Davidson (eds), *Understanding the Presidency*, 4th ed. New York: Pearson-Longman.

Hutton, J.P. 2007. 'Testimony of John P. Hutton, Acting Director, Acquisition and Sourcing Management, Government Accountability Office'. Hearing of the Defense Subcommittee of the House Appropriations Committee; Subject: Defense Contracting; Witness Panel I, 10 May.

International Herald Tribune. 2005. 'Former Powell Aide Links Cheney's Office to Abuse Directives', *International Herald Tribune*, 3 November.

Jordan, G. 2004. 'Interest Groups,' in Adam Kuper and Jessica Kuper (eds), *The Social Science Encyclopedia*, 3rd ed. New York: Routledge.

Kamiński, A. 1996. 'The New Polish Regime and the Specter of Economic Corruption', Summary of paper presented at the *Woodrow Wilson International Center for Scholars, Princeton, 3 April*.

———. 1997. 'Corruption under the Post-Communist Transformation: The Case of Poland', *Polish Sociological Review* 2(118): 91–117.

Kurczewski, J. (ed.). 2007. *Lokalne Wzory Kultury Politycznej*. Warsaw: Wydawnictwo Trio.

Labaton, S. 2003. 'Pentagon Adviser Is Also Advising Global Crossing', *New York Times*, 21 March.

Ledeen, M.A. 2006. 'Do the Right Thing: Let's Avoid Making a Catastrophe Out of an Embarrassment', *National Review Online*. Retrieved 2 November 2010 from http://www.nationalreview.com/ledeen/ledeen200601180843.asp.

Light, P.C. 1999. *The True Size of Government*. Washington DC: The Brookings Institution Press.

——. 2003. 'Fact Sheet on the New True Size of Government', Washington DC: The Brookings Institution, Center for Public Service, http://www.brookings.edu/gs/cps/light20030905.pdf.

Lobe, J. 2003. 'U.S.: Ex-Pentagon Aide Hits "Deceit" and "Subversion" on Iraq', *Inter-Press Service*, 5 August.

——. 2004. 'U.S. Right Weaves Tangled But Effective Web', *IRC Right Web*, 12 January. Retrieved 2 November 2010 from http://rightweb.irc-online.org/rw/844.html.

Makinson, L. 2004. *Outsourcing the Pentagon: Who Benefits from the Politics and Economics of National Security?* Washington DC: Center for Public Integrity.

Mann, J. 2004. *Rise of the Vulcans: The History of Bush's War Cabinet*. New York: Viking.

Markon, J. 2006. 'Pentagon Analyst Given 12½ Years in Secrets Case', *Washington Post*, 21 January, A1.

Marshall, J.M., L. Rozen and P. Glastris. 2004. 'Iran-Contra II?', *Washington Monthly*, September.

Mattei, D. (ed.). 2003. *Elite Configurations at the Apex of Power*. Boston: Brill.

McIntyre, M.E. 2002. 'Audit, Education, and Goodhart's Law, Or, Taking Rigidity Seriously', 14 May. Retrieved 2 November 2010 from http://www.atm.damtp.cam.ac.uk/people/mem/papers/LHCE/dilnot-analysis.html.

Mills, C.W. 1956. *The Power Elite*. New York: Oxford University Press.

Mitchell, J.P. 1996. 'Patrons and Clients', in Alan Barnard and Jonathan Spencer (eds), *Encyclopedia of Social and Cultural Anthropology*. New York: Routledge.

Moe, R.C. and K.R. Kosar. 2005. *The Quasi Government: Hybrid Organizations with Both Government and Private Sector Legal Characteristics*. Washington DC: Congressional Research Service.

New American Century. 1998. 'Letter to the Honorable William J. Clinton', 26 January. Retrieved 2 November 2010 from http://www.newamericancentury.org/iraqclintonletter.htm.

Pfiffner, J. 2007a. *The Modern Presidency*, 5th ed. Belmont, CA: Thompson Wadsworth.

——. 2007b. 'The Institutionalist: A Conversation with Hugh Heclo', *Public Administration Review* 67(3): 418–23.

——. 2008. *Power Play: The Bush Administration and the Constitution*. Washington DC: The Brookings Institution.

Phillips, D.L. 2005. *Losing Iraq: Inside the Postwar Reconstruction Fiasco*. New York: Basic Books.

Podgorecki, A. 1987. 'Polish Society: A Sociological Analysis', *Praxis International* 7(1): 57–78.

Prados, J. 2004. 'The Pros from Dover', *Bulletin of the Atomic Scientists* 60(1): 44–51.

Reddy, A. and S. Kehaulani Goo. 2004. 'Database on U.S. Visitors Set for Huge Expansion: Reston Firm's Contract Worth Up to $10 Billion', *Washington Post*, 2 June, E01.

Reich, S. 2006. In Janine R. Wedel and Simon Reich, 'Conspiracies, Clubs, Competitors and Cliques: The Changing Character of American Politics.' unpublished paper.

Robertson, D. 2004. *The Routledge Dictionary of Politics*, 3rd ed. London and New York: Routledge.

Rozen, L. 2008. 'Investigation Update: Three Days in Rome', *Mother Jones*, 20 June.

Rycroft, R. and D.E. Kash. 1999. *The Complexity Challenge: Technological Innovation for the 21st Century*. London and New York: Pinter.

Senate Select Committee on Intelligence. 2004. 'Report on the U.S. Intelligence Community's Prewar Intelligence Assessments on Iraq', 7 July: 457.

———. 2008. 'Report on Intelligence Activities Relating to Iraq Conducted by the Policy Counterterrorism Evaluation Group and the Office of Special Plans Within the Office of the Under Secretary of Defense for Policy', June.

Seymour-Smith, C. 1986. *Dictionary of Anthropology*. Boston: G.K. Hall & Co.

Shafer, J. 2003. 'Richard Perle Libel Watch. Week 4: He's Just Too Busy Resigning to Sue this Week!' *Slate*, 2 April. Retrieved 2 November 2010 from http://slate.msn.com/id/2081053.

Shore, C. and S. Nugent (eds). 2002. *Elite Cultures: Anthropological Perspectives*. New York: Routledge.

Silverstein, K. and C. Neubauer. 2003. 'Consulting and Policy Overlap', *Los Angeles Times*, 7 May.

Strobel, W.P. 2004. 'Alleged Pentagon Leaks May Be Connected to Battle Over Iran Policy', *Knight Ridder Newspapers*, 3 September.

Varese, F. 2003. 'Mafia', in Iain McLean and Alistair McMillan (eds), *The Concise Oxford Dictionary of Politics*. Oxford: Oxford University Press.

Verkuil, P.R. 2007. *Outsourcing Sovereignty*. New York: Cambridge University Press.

Wald, A.M. 1987. *The New York Intellectuals: The Rise and Decline of the Anti-Stalinist Left From the 1930s to the 1980s*. Chapel Hill, NC: University of North Carolina Press.

Wedel, J. 2004a. 'Blurring the State-Private Divide: Flex Organisations and the Decline of Accountability', in Max Spoor (ed.), *Globalisation, Poverty and Conflict: A Critical 'Development' Reader*. Dordrecht: Kluwer Academic Publishers, pp. 217–35.

———. 2004b. 'Flex Power: A Capital Way to Gain Clout, Inside and Out', *Washington Post*, 12 December, B04.

———. 2009. *Shadow Elite: How the World's New Power Brokers Undermine Democracy, Government, and the Free Market*. New York: Basic Books.

Wilkerson, L.B. 2005. 'The Whitehouse Cabal', *Los Angeles Times*, 25 October, B11.

Chapter 9

Espionage, Policy and the Art of Government: The British Secret Services and the War on Iraq

Cris Shore

Introduction: Anthropology, Policy and Ethnography of the State

The conceptual theme I explore in this chapter is the idea of policy as a legal-rational tool of governance that simultaneously provides an instrument for the operation of state power and a lens for analysing the operation of state power and what is sometimes called the 'art of government'. My concern is with how policy makers and politicians use policy to construct the public sphere, classify populations and define problems so that particular solutions appear natural and unavoidable, i.e., how policies are discursively managed in an attempt to control public debate and forge specific outcomes.

The case study I use to exemplify these points is the scandal that erupted in February 2004 following disclosures that British security services were spying on the United Nations (UN) before a crucial vote on war in Iraq. Although this episode was eclipsed by more high-profile events (including allegations that a dossier used by the Blair government to justify invading Iraq had been 'sexed up', and the subsequent suicide of the Ministry of Defence senior biological weapons adviser Dr David Kelly), the story has particular significance for the anthropological study of policy. The public debate these revelations provoked offers critical insight into the more 'occult' practices of government, or how states operate 'backstage', and the tactics politicians and governments use to manage knowledge. In documenting this episode, I hope to contribute to the broader goal of this book: namely, to develop the theoretical and methodological contours of an anthropology of policy as a distinctive disciplinary subfield. I also want to explore how a policy focus can contribute to anthropological analyses of the state. The modern state may be invisible as an empirical entity (Abrams 1988), but it can nevertheless be tracked and studied through its 'effects' and through the mundane encounters and conflicts that are brought into being by its presence (Trouillot 2001; Krohn-Hansen and Nustad 2005).

The scope and content of the anthropology of policy is still largely unchartered terrain (Shore and Wright 1997; Wedel et al. 2005). Its primary subject matter lies in the interface between anthropology and politics, but includes input from several cognate disciplines, including linguistics, science and technology studies, sociology and interpretive policy studies (Yanow 2000; Yanow and Schwartz-Shea 2006). However, gaining entry to study the worlds of policy elites is often fraught with difficulty. Typically, access is granted by people with careers at stake and who dislike being made objects of academic research (Shore 2002). As Gusterson (1997: 115) observes, 'participant observation is a research technique that does not travel well up the social structure'.

My analysis is understandably not based on conventional fieldwork (i.e., long-term immersion among a community of actors). Studying the state and systems of governance calls for a more 'nonlocal ethnography' approach (see Feldman, Chapter 2, this volume). I therefore make no claims for any privileged 'insider' perspective that speaks to (or for) the 'native point of view'. What I offer instead is an anthropological analysis of the multiple voices and intersecting stories that became entangled in this tale of espionage and diplomacy. My aim is to construct an ethnographic reading of the narratives and texts involved, and the way in which different actors, institutions and discourses were brought into alignment as the events leading up to the Iraq war unfolded. Wherever possible, I have substantiated my arguments with references to verifiable public documents and I have 'triangulated' these against other sources and informant narratives. With these caveats in mind, I have structured my chapter as follows.

First, I outline some key methodological issues for an anthropology of policy and suggest how we might develop a more critical understanding of policy processes. Secondly, I explore one particularly salient story that exemplifies these themes: the scandal that emerged in the U.K. following revelations that the Blair government had bugged the office of Kofi Annan, then head of the UN, prior to a crucial UN vote over war in Iraq. In tracking this story, I also reflect on the historical and legal aspects of this covert government policy and the narratives used to legitimise it. Finally, I conclude by examining the broader conceptual themes that this study reveals about power, diplomacy and governmentality, and the way policy processes relate to, or are indicative of, deeper changes in the British system of governance.

Looking at Policy from an Anthropological Perspective

Three general points can be made about policy as an object of anthropological study, which provide the theoretical context for my case study.

(1) Policy as 'Political Technology'

First, policies are inherently political phenomena, yet it is a characteristic of many policies that their political nature is disguised by the neutral, legal-rational idioms in which they are portrayed. Policies are presented as objective instruments – simple tools for promoting efficiency or for achieving the rational objectives of an organisation or government. This veiling of the political under the cloak of legal-rational neutrality is a characteristic feature of modern power. As both Foucault (1997: 15) and Bourdieu (1977) have observed, power disguises the mechanisms of its own operation. The most effective way to disguise power is by making a particular discourse appear so 'natural' that its ideological content comes to be regarded as common sense and therefore beyond question (what Bourdieu termed 'doxa'). In this sense, policies function as 'political technologies' – i.e., they 'advance by taking what is essentially a political problem, removing it from the realm of political discourse, and recasting it in the neutral language of science' (Dreyfus and Rabinow 1982: 196)

(2) Policy as Statecraft: Sovereignty, Legitimacy and the 'Policy Effect'

Secondly, a characteristic of policy is the way it is often used to disguise authorship and self-interest. Like bureaucracy, policy often functions to cloak subjective, ideological and highly 'irrational' goals in the guise of rational, collective and universalised objectives. A key function of policy is legitimation: not only does it outline a particular course of action, it also fixes that course within a framework of universal and sacrosanct principles (such as 'natural justice', the 'rule of law', 'individual freedom', 'constitutional rights', etc.). As anthropologists who study elites have often observed (Bloch 1975; Cohen 1981; Paine 1981), this universalising of the particular functions to rule out disagreement, since any challenge to the policy can be construed by those in positions of authority as a challenge to the principles upon which their policy is founded. An illustration of this emerged in the final presidential debate between President George Bush and Senator John Kerry in 2004. When asked 'what part does faith play in your policy decisions?', President Bush's seemingly naïve reply effectively portrayed God as a cosponsor of his policies:

> [W]hen I make a decision, I stand on principle ... I believe God wants everybody to be free. That's what I believe. And that's been part of my foreign policy. In Afghanistan, I believe that the freedom there is a gift from the Almighty. (Bush 2004)

In analytical terms, we might call this an example of the 'policy effect'. By this I refer to a process similar to what art historian Svetna Alpers (1991) called the 'museum effect', i.e., once an object (or a goal or 'target') is elevated to the status of 'official policy', it is given institutional legitimation and becomes an apparatus of power endowed with an aura of institutional authority. Alpers's theory explains how objects can be transformed into works of 'art' through the structure of presentation and the context in which they are displayed – i.e., the act of exhibiting transforms objects into 'art'. In a similar vein, declaring a policy to be 'official' endows it with a certain authority, although we might then ask what is the ontological status of a policy – like espionage – that is officially denied? This 'policy effect' also implies a calculated and coherent course of action. Policy not only gives the legal-rational coherence and direction to individual aims, it also endows that course of action with a dignity and morality it might not otherwise possess, in much the same way as nineteenth-century European colonialism cloaked itself under the comforting French notion of Europe's civilising mission or *mission civilisatrice*. As Edward Said notes, Joseph Conrad's novel *Heart of Darkness* provides an ironic yet terrifying enactment of this thesis. As the novel's narrator, Marlow, explains it:

> The conquest of the earth, which mostly means the taking it away from those who have a different complexion or slightly flatter noses than ourselves, is not a pretty thing when you look into it too much. What redeems it is the idea only. An idea at the back of it, not a sentimental pretence but an idea; and an unselfish belief in the idea – something you can set up, and bow down before, and offer a sacrifice to. (Said 2002: 574)

Morally repugnant practices are often justified by rhetorical claims to a higher principle (colonialism's *mission civilisatrice*) or a more urgent policy priority (the nation's defence against terrorism). Whether explicit or covert, directed from on high or agentless, most policies thus express a will to power and offer a programme for acting upon the world.

(3) Policy as Method: Beyond 'Studying Up'

Thirdly, if public policy is an instrument of government, it also an instrument for analysing how government and forms of governance work. This is not so much 'studying up' as teasing out connections and observing how policies bring together individuals, discourses and institutions into new formations, and the new kinds of networks, relations and subjects this process creates. A policy perspective therefore has major implications for anthropological method, offering a useful alternative to Marcus's (1995) much-cited (but less often practised) call for 'multi-sited ethnography'. It does not rule out traditional fieldwork, but it does expose the limits of empiricism or the 'ontological imperative of being there' as the be-all-and-end-all of anthropological knowledge (Gupta 1995: 376). Once we acknowledge that cultures, societies and nations cannot be unproblematically mapped onto different spaces, we need to rethink the relationship between fieldwork and the generation of anthropological data. It forces us to turn to other sources of anthropological knowledge. Government reports, speeches, official documents, minutes of meetings and newspaper articles become far more prominent – both as sources of data and as narratives to be analysed. Like Gupta (1995: 377), I see newspapers as valuable cultural texts that should be accorded far more anthropological importance. I am often struck by the paradox that a ninety-year-old newspaper is treated as a precious (and 'authentic') historical document and archival source, whereas a nine- or ninety-day-old newspaper is typically dismissed as 'journalism' and therefore of little anthropological value. Anthropological analysis needs to rethink the methodological significance of using broadcast media and print journalism, as these are increasingly fundamental aspects of the ethnographic present we seek to interpret. With those considerations in mind, let us now turn to the main case study of this chapter. The story of the British government's covert operations prior to the Iraq war illustrates what can happen when statecraft and policy management are out of alignment.

Case Study: The Bugging of the UN by the British Secret Services

My interest in this incident was sparked during a visit to the U.K. in November 2003. I had been discussing Tony Blair's predicament with a friend and colleague – a political historian and arguably one of Britain's foremost analysts of Whitehall and the U.K. government system. My colleague was angry about the war on Iraq. In his view, the legal case for going to war had been 'stitched up'. A key factor which few newspapers had commented on, he added, was that the Deputy Legal Advisor to the Foreign and Commonwealth Office (FCO), Elisabeth Wilmhurst, had resigned the day that war was declared, saying that she disagreed with the Attorney General's opinion that war against Iraq was legal even without a further explicit Security Council resolution authorising it. The Attorney General, Sir Oliver Goldsmith, had previously shared the Foreign Office view that war with Iraq without a second UN resolution would be illegal, but had changed his mind at the last minute. Only one leading U.K. international jurist, Professor Christopher Greenwood of the London School of Economics, was known to hold the contrary view that existing Security Council resolutions provided legal authority for the use of force against Iraq and it was to him that the Attorney General had turned for advice. But Greenwood was now allegedly having pangs of conscience. 'If he were now to come out saying *"mea culpa"*, Tony Blair could be seriously undermined', I was told (and I sensed that my colleague was rather hoping he would). 'Goldsmith had been told what to write.' What worried my colleague most of all was the increasing politicisation of the Civil Service:

Blair now wants applicants to senior posts to submit 'position statements'. He wants ministers to have more say over appointments. He has tried to set up a rival to the Foreign Office in his own Prime Minister's Office. Never has the FCO been so ineffectual – all the key decisions about Iraq were taken by Number 10.[1]

As for the Foreign Secretary, Jack Straw, he added, 'he will accept anything for the price of staying in office'. Blair had seemingly pushed Britain into an illegal war and was now undermining a cherished principle of British democracy: the political independence of the Civil Service and the judiciary. Three months later, events developed in ways few could have predicted. The sequence of events was captured in the *Economist* (2004) report summarised below:

> Katharine Gun, a 29-year-old mandarin translator, was being prosecuted under Section 1 of the 1989 Official Secrets Act, a draconian piece of legislation most often used to prevent disillusioned spies from spilling the beans after they have left the service. Ms Gun had taken it upon herself, as a matter of conscience, to leak to a national newspaper a secret email from an official working for America's National Security Agency that allegedly revealed plans to bug members of the UN Security Council before a crucial vote on the conflict.

> A pretty open-and-shut case by the look of it, given that Ms Gun did not dispute the facts. However, just before proceedings were about to start, the Crown Prosecution Service announced it had decided to offer no evidence against Ms Gun. As she walked free from the Old Bailey, speculation began about why the government had decided to pull the case. Ms Gun's lawyers helpfully suggested that the attorney-general had acted to prevent scrutiny of his only-partially published advice on the legality of the war – a key element in Ms Gun's defence. Absolutely not, huffed officials: the case had been dropped for legal and technical reasons, not for reasons of political sensitivity.

Ministers insisted the case collapsed because the Crown Prosecution Service had decided that it could not secure a conviction, not because of fears that politically sensitive document relating to the Iraq war would come to light. As Lord Goldsmith told the House of Lords: 'The attorney makes his decisions in the public interest, and not in the interests of the Government.'[2] He also told the Lords that he could not comment on the reasons why counsel had reached its decision 'as the matter concerns issues of intelligence [therefore] it is not appropriate for me to do so, even to this House'.

When the BBC invited ministers to comment on the Gun affair, no government spokesperson was available apart for Clare Short, former Secretary of State for Overseas Development, who had resigned in May 2003 in protest over the government's policy on Iraq. Short was interviewed on the BBC's *Today* programme by the veteran journalist John Humphrys. Since that interview provides the ethnographic data for the analysis that follows, I reproduce it here in full:

Interview with Clare Short (CS) by BBC Journalist John Humphrys (JH): 26 February 2004

JH: What do you make of it all [the dropping of charges against Katherine Gun]?

CS: Well I think it centres on the Attorney General's advice that war was legal and resolution 1441, which was published, as a matter of fact, but was very, very odd. The more I think about it the more fishy I feel it was. It came very, very late, he came to the cabinet the day Robin Cook resigned and sat in Robin's seat; two sides of A4; no discussion permitted. We know already that the Foreign Office legal advisers had disagreed and one of them had said there was no authority for war … So my own suspicion is that the Attorney has stopped the prosecution because part of her [Gun's] defence would be to question the legality and put his advice in the public domain again and there was something fishy about the way in which he said the war was legal.

JH: What this memo showed – the secret memo that Katharine Gun disclosed – was pressure from the United States on other countries to get support for a second UN resolution and spying indeed on those countries. Do you believe that Britain, our government, might have been involved in that with the United States?

CS: Well … they were going to war anyway and they were going to bully and pressurise countries to vote for it. I mean enormous pressure was brought to bear, Valerie Amos, Lady Amos, went round Africa with people from our intelligence services trying to press them. I had to make sure that we didn't promise the misuse of aid in a way that would be illegal.

JH: Did you? Was it being suggested then?

CS: There was worry about her brief and making sure that there was no such suggestion because it would have been a breach of the law. Britain also…

JH: But did someone suggest … that might have been the right strategy?

CS: We were worried that was going to be done and went to some trouble to make sure her briefing made it clear that that could not legally be done. I mean the U.K. in this time was also spying on Kofi Annan's office and getting reports from him about what was going on. The U.S. was pressing Chile and Mexico, enormous pressures were brought to bear – I mean what was remarkable was that these countries didn't break. And if you remember, the other part of the context is we were then all deceived about the French position and told the French had said they would veto any second resolution, which wasn't true, we now know. Chirac had said we veto now because Blix needs his time but if Blix failed then of course we would vote with others to authorise military action.

JH: Pressure is one thing, you expect that I suppose, spinning is another thing – you expect that I suppose, spying, spying in the United Nations is something quite different isn't it?

CS: Well indeed, but these things are done. And in the case of Kofi's office it's been done for some time.

JH: Let me repeat the question then, do you believe Britain has been involved in it?

CS: Well I know, I have seen transcripts of Kofi Annan's conversations. Indeed, I have had conversations with Kofi in the run-up to war thinking 'Oh dear, there will be a transcript of this and people will see what he and I are saying'.

JH: So in other words British spies – let's be very clear about this in case I'm misunderstanding you – British spies have been instructed to carry out operations inside the United Nations on people like Kofi Annan?

CS: Yes, absolutely.

JH: Did you know about this when you were in government?

CS: Absolutely, I read some of the transcripts of the accounts of his conversations.

JH: Is this legal?

CS: I don't know, I presume so. It is odd, but I don't know about the legalities. But the major issue here is the legal authority for war and whether the Attorney General had to be persuaded at the last minute – against the advice of one of the Foreign Office legal advisers, who then resigned – that he could give legal authority for war and whether there had to be an exaggeration of the threat of the use of chemical and biological weapons to persuade him that there was legal authority – that's the big question. (Short 2004b)

John Humphrys (2004) later wrote that he had been taken aback by this 'bombshell'. So too had Tony Blair. Clare Short's revelation wrecked his monthly press conference, which he had hoped to use to showcase his new British initiative in Africa. He called her comments 'deeply irresponsible', but refused to confirm or deny whether her allegations were true. Instead, he told reporters: 'I cannot comment on individual court cases or about intelligence matters', adding: 'I, like previous prime ministers, am not going to talk openly about the work of the security services or their operations. To do so would put at risk the security of this country and I will simply not let that happen.' He said that those who commented on intelligence matters 'attack the work that our security services are doing and undermine the security of this country'.

What we have here is both the Prime Minister and the Attorney General invoking the discourse of 'public interest' and 'security' to legitimate their actions and to bring about closure on the debate. Mr Blair was then repeatedly asked whether Short should be prosecuted or face Labour Party discipline. He said he would 'have to reflect upon' her comments. Short later retaliated, saying that Blair would be lying if he denied her claims:

He can say I'm not telling the truth, in which case he's a liar, or he can say it's all true and that would quite simply be too shocking to cope with. Or he can come after me and that's what he's chosen to do. Me, I have nothing to lose. (Blitz 2004)

Reaction from the UN was phlegmatic. The UN secretariat spokesman, Fred Eckhard, said cautiously that if reports 'that the secretary-general's phone conversations were tapped by British intelligence' were true, 'such activities would undermine the integrity and confidential nature of diplomatic exchanges' and that Mr Annan 'wanted this practice stopped, if indeed it exists' (Turner 2004). That was the official reaction. Unofficially, the allegations apparently provoked private amusement. Within the UN, it is common knowledge that the secretary-general's office is bugged. Indeed, from the very first day it convened, the UN has been a magnet for spies, according to UN diplomats and U.S. intelligence experts. The tapping of phone lines and planting of microphones in U.N. offices is so common that the organisation employs a team of debuggers, headed by a former New York police officer, to routinely sweep offices and respond to requests from nations that suspect their officials are being monitored. In the words of Inocencio F. Arias, Spain's ambassador to the UN:

> In my opinion everybody spies on everybody, and when there's a crisis, big countries spy a lot ... I wouldn't be surprised if this secretary general and other secretary generals have been listened to by a handful of big powers, and not only the ones you are thinking. (Cited in Turner 2004)

An ambassador of a Security Council member nation, speaking on condition of anonymity, said it would almost be an insult to be spared the attention of foreign intelligence agencies. 'It used to be a shame; now it's a matter of status. If your mission is not bugged, then you are really worth nothing' (Priest and Lynch 2004). For historians of the secret services, none of this comes as a surprise. James Bamford's book on the U.S. National Security Agency, *Body of Secrets*, records how President Franklin D. Roosevelt fought hard for the U.S. to host the opening session of the UN in San Francisco in April 1945. While this may have looked to some like a magnanimous gesture, his main reason was better to enable the U.S. to eavesdrop on its guests. Roosevelt gave executive authority for the U.S. Attorney General to approve wiretapping when necessary in 'defence of the nation'. The U.S. then listened in on all the delegations, especially the French, who had a complex six-wheel cipher machine, but one that the U.S. codebreakers were able to read (MacAskill 2004b).

Bugging the UN is an 'open secret' among insiders: as long as no one speaks out in public, those in power are able to draw a veil of silence over the subject. This raises questions about the legality of spying on the UN. Somewhat surprisingly, the interception of communications by listening posts on British soil is legal if the Home Secretary has sanctioned it. However, the Vienna Convention governing the conduct of diplomatic relations explicitly bans spying on foreign embassies. The UN is an anomaly. Alex Standish, editor of *Jane's Intelligence Digest*, notes that the UN headquarters is sovereign immune territory and that installing devices there is a 'grey area' (Turner 2004). Yet, under a secret pact between the U.K., Canada, Australia and the U.S., Washington has responsibility for surveillance and sharing information on targets within the U.S. In the U.S., no wiretapping is allowed without a court order. When eavesdropping involves foreign officials, the Federal Bureau of Investigation or the National Security Agency/Central Security Service (NSA/CSS) must obtain a Foreign Intelligence Surveillance Act order. Besides U.S. law, there are three treaties that affirm the inviolability of UN premises – to which the U.K. and the U.S. are both signatories.[3] Yet most diplomats acknowledge that spying is a fact of life and has been since the Cold War. That acknowledgement, however, does not render eavesdropping any more diplomatically palatable. Nor does the knowledge acquired through spying necessarily allay mistrust or encourage tolerance even when it promotes better understanding. For example, Cantaloube and Vernet (2004) argue that the deterioration of French-U.S. diplomatic relations during the Iraq crisis was partly a result of the personal relationship between President Chirac and President Bush. A U.S. diplomat is reported as telling a French military official that the relationship between the two presidents became irreparable because President Bush knew exactly what Chirac thought of him (BBC 2004). Contrary to what anthropologists often assume, understanding how 'natives think' does not always overcome ethnocentrism or prejudice.

How the Crisis was Contained

Clare Short's revelations provoked an immediate damage-limitation response from the government. Ministers and officials drew a distinction between the bugging accusation itself and the fact that a serving minister had revealed it. Short's disclosure was treated as a far more serious offence than the bugging claim itself. As Tony Blair declared: 'Our intelligence services perform a vital task' and it was 'totally irresponsible … to expose them to this public questioning' (MacAskill 2004a). What began as a scandal over revelations of state-sponsored spying on friends now became a tale of ministerial treachery and betrayal. As one senior official declared, 'there is absolutely no precedent for any minister talking about foreign intelligence operations in this way' (Blitz 2004). Her actions constituted not only a breach of trust between the security services and ministers, but also a breach of the 1989 Official Secrets Act and of her Privy Councillor's Oath of loyalty to the Crown (an archaic pledge requiring that members 'keep secret all matters committed and revealed unto you'). Attention therefore turned to the question of whether Short should be prosecuted or publicly sanctioned. In the end, the government did neither, arguing that it did not want to make her a martyr. However, a few days later, it instructed Sir Andrew Turnbull, the highest ranking civil servant, to issue a 'solicitors letter' reminding Short of her responsibilities under the ministerial code and threatening legal action if she gave further interviews on the subject.

This rare rebuke from a Whitehall mandarin produced a scathing response from Short. She accused Turnball of allowing Britain 'to rush to war with Iraq without proper ministerial oversight and without looking at all the diplomatic or political options, and blamed him for allowing Alastair Campbell, the Prime Minister's press officer, to chair the influential Joint Intelligence Committee; and for having 'allowed our decision-making system to crumble' (Hall 2004: 2). For Short, the real breach of protocol was to put the Prime Minister's chief press spokesman and spin doctor in charge, as she saw it, of this major policy committee.

By April, however, this row had been totally eclipsed by the continuing news of bombings and insurgency in Baghdad and Falluja, the seizure of Western hostages and the rising death toll of U.S. servicemen. The position adopted by both the U.S. and U.K. governments was that the run-up to war was now 'history'. Whatever the rights or wrongs of the decision to overthrow Saddam Hussein, the priority was to deal with the problems facing Iraq now. However, attempts to bring closure to the debate were undermined by Kofi Annan. Having studiously refrained from commenting in public on the politically sensitive issue of the legality of the U.S.-led war on Iraq, Mr Annan, in an apparently unguarded moment during an interview with the BBC World Service in September, admitted that in his view the war was illegal, as the UN Security Council had not sanctioned the invasion, nor were the U.S.-led coalition's actions in accordance with the UN's founding charter (MacAskill and Borger, 2004: 1).

If the 2004 Butler Inquiry highlighted weaknesses in the government's claims about Iraq's supposed weapons of mass destruction (WMDs), the leaking of confidential Cabinet Office papers and minutes of meetings of Tony Blair's inner circle illustrated graphically just how flimsy the government's case was for going to war. A leaked memorandum from the head of British Secret Intelligence, Sir Richard Dearlove, dated 23 July 2002, revealed that a notable shift in attitude had occurred in Washington:

> Military action was now seen as inevitable. Bush wanted to remove Saddam, through military action, justified by the conjunction of terrorism and weapons of mass destruction (WMD). But the intelligence and facts were being fixed around the policy. (Simpson 2005: 50–51)

Dearlove read into the minutes to the Prime Minister that President Bush had already decided to attack Iraq several months before he took the question of Iraq to the UN. The leaked memorandum also showed that Blair had promised Bush Britain's full support. The main problem, as FCO Political Director Peter Ricketts wrote, was 'bringing public opinion to accept the imminence of a threat from Iraq' (Simpson 2005: 37). Yet the day after that meeting – on 24 July – Blair explicitly told the House of Commons that 'we have not yet reached the point of decision ... How to deal with [Iraq's weapons] is an open question' (cited in Coates 2005: 6). Lying to the House of Commons is an offence that has ended many a political career in the U.K., but in Blair's case this charge was not easily verified.

In the U.K., that controversy was continued thanks not only to the publication of two government-sponsored reports by Lord Hutton (2004) and Lord Butler (2004) which dealt, *inter alia*, with issues surrounding Iraq's alleged WMDs, but also with publication in November of Clare Short's book, *An Honourable Deception?* This book rejected Butler's conclusion that the Prime Minister had acted in 'good faith' and alleged instead that Blair had knowingly misled Parliament and the British public over Iraq's WMDs. Had it been proven, the charge would have forced Blair's resignation.

Conclusions: Policy as a Window onto Regimes of Governance

Returning to themes outlined at the beginning, what does this story tell us about the relationship between policy, the modern state, and the art of government in contemporary Britain? Let me conclude with four observations.

(1) Governmentality: Liberal, Neoliberal and Illiberal

At the heart of this curiously British controversy were three tangled policy disputes: one about the remit of the intelligence services and the ethics of spying; the second about ministerial discretion and Privy Council codes of honour; and the third about the legality of the government's case for declaring war on Iraq. Contrary to what one might conclude from reading Foucault (1991), the 'art of government' is not just about the rationality of liberal government; rather, it also entails the more traditional tasks of shaping political agendas and controlling the terms of debate. This not only means controlling what is said or goes unsaid, it also requires more subtle, discursive tactics aimed at reinforcing particular norms and behaviours. Alex de Waal (1994: 8) has noted that in any policy area that provokes controversy, there are usually two competing narratives: 'the conflict, and the meta-conflict – the conflict about the nature of conflict itself'. In this case, the metaconflict was the legality of the war against Iraq and the secretive, informal and undemocratic manner in which that decision was made. This was arguably why Clare Short gave her BBC interview – and what provoked her indiscretions about Britain's intelligence services. Until shortly before war, the invasion of Iraq, or 'Operation Iraqi Freedom' as it was code-named, Britain's Chief of Defence Staff and his colleagues were allegedly deeply worried about the uncertainty over the legality of a war lacking new UN authority, and might even have refused to obey ministerial orders to begin hostilities for fear of exposing themselves and their servicemen to the charge of committing war crimes. That would explain the Attorney General's change of position. After 9/11, Tony Blair had stood 'shoulder-to-shoulder' with George W. Bush, pledging Britain's unwavering support for its friend and ally in its 'war on terrorism'. The U.S. had made it clear that it would go to war with or without a second UN resolution. For Blair, pulling out at the eleventh hour would have been politically (and morally) unthinkable. These factors help explain the extraordinary effort he and Jack Straw went to in order to obtain a second UN resolution and why the 'facts' about Iraq's WMDs were being made to fit the policy.

(2) Locating Agency and the Individual in Regimes of Governance

What is significant about this story is that commitments appear to have been made before their legality had been firmly established (Smith 2004). Some pundits believe Tony Blair was convinced that his famous powers of persuasion would swing the wavering states to back a second UN resolution. What we have here is a good example of an arbitrary and subjective decision being cloaked by rational and legal principles of morality and international law. The government was trying to claim that, following the independent advice of its chief law officer, it had simply acted on UN Resolution 1441, despite the fact that the majority of UN and Security Council members held views to the contrary.

This recalls the NATO attack on Kosovo in 1998, which also lacked UN backing and, in terms of international law, was also illegal. Robin Cook, Britain's Foreign Secretary at the time, had also tried to get Security Council approval for military action, much to the anger of the U.S. administration. James Rubin, Madeline Albright's press spokesman at the time, noted a series of strained phone calls between Cook and Albright in which Cook cited problems 'with our lawyers'. Albright's curt answer was 'get new lawyers' (Rubin 2000: 5). The Blair government evidently took that lesson on board when constructing its legal case for the war against Iraq.

Bugging the UN was a side issue. In fact, a closer reading of Katherine Gun's infamous leaked email which sparked this controversy shows that the U.S. did not actually ask Britain to help 'bug' the UN; it merely requested help from British intelligence analysts concerning UN Security Council debates: 'any information that could give US policy makers an edge in obtaining results favourable to US goals or to head off surprises' (Bright et al. 2004). Clare Short's point was simply to illustrate how determined the U.S. and Britain were to secure the consent of the wavering countries (Angola, Cameroon, Chile, Bulgaria, Guinea and Pakistan) whose votes were needed for a second UN resolution. In the event, her breach of ministerial protocol became the lead story, albeit temporarily, rather than Blair's 'agency' in promoting the U.S. agenda and pushing the country into war.

(3) Covert Policy and Cultural Intimacy

Eavesdropping on the UN is evidently a policy sanctioned by the British government and by many other governments. However, whereas most policies derive their institutional legitimacy and authority precisely from their status as 'official policy' (what I called the 'policy effect'), spying belongs to a special category of 'covert policy', i.e., policies that are unethical or illegal, that 'dare not speak their name' or that must be officially deniable. Most diplomats know perfectly well that spying happens and adapt their behaviour accordingly, but protocol requires that they feign surprise or indignation should this ever be made public.

From a theoretical perspective, these behaviours reflect many of the characteristics of what Michael Herzfeld terms 'cultural intimacy': cultural practices that are 'considered a source of external embarrassment but that nevertheless provide insiders with their assurance of common sociality' (Herzfeld 1997: 3). The work of the secret services is widely regarded as part of the 'privacy of nations'. Why, though, should there be a taboo on talking about things that are common knowledge? There are parallels here with the Sicilian Mafia's traditional code of silence, *Omertà*. As Arlacchi (1988: 3) observes, '[t]o keep to the rules of *omertà* was to follow a *double moral system*, with one set of norms applying among the members of a given group, and another, opposing set governing relations with those outsiders'. The code that governs conduct among British diplomats and ministers seems to be 'I'm sorry, but we do not comment on such matters', particularly if they are either *sub judice* or individual cases – which would seem to cover a very large number of circumstances (Paris 2004: 12). This functions to prevent the shattering of delicate but important myths. By refusing to have things said out loud, governments protect themselves from having to confront them, the maxim being 'don't ask, don't tell'.

This case study provides a good illustration of the operation of power through the management of discourse and how certain political tropes (in this case, those of 'national security', 'ministerial responsibility' and 'Privy Council Oaths') are used to control what can be said or what must remain unsaid. As Herzfeld notes (1993: 159), bureaucracy, like policy, provides 'absolution from personal responsibility'.

(4) Rise of the Unelected: The Informal Structures of Government

The fourth point to conclude from this study concerns the 'messiness' of the policy process and the apparent shift in the locus of government decision making. The story of Britain's bugging of the UN not only offers valuable insights into the structure of modern government, it also reveals some of the key major tensions within the British state, particularly between the Prime Minister's Office (which desperately sought to legitimise the war on Iraq) and the Foreign Office, most of whose legal experts could find no plausible legal case. There are parallels here with the Suez Crisis of 1956, when Prime Minister Anthony Eden, together with his French and Israeli counterparts, launched an abortive military invasion of Egypt in order to seize control of the Suez Canal. Like Tony Blair, Eden disregarded the advice of the Foreign Office – including that of his Attorney General, Reginald Manningham-Buller (whose daughter, coincidentally, was head of MI5 during the 2003 Iraq invasion) – and went outside of government to take legal advice from Professor Arthur Goodhart, a lone academic who favoured his Suez policy.

This study also highlights the Hutton Inquiry's (2004) main criticism of the British government: namely, the 'kitchen cabinet' style of government that emerged during the Blair era. This system led to many key national and international policy decisions being made by a small clique of Mr Blair's personal friends and advisers, without the involvement of the Cabinet and without any formal minutes being taken. Clare Short drew particular attention to the implications of this 'informal' system of decision making that runs parallel to the more formal structures of government:

> The question we must all address is whether it is acceptable for the Prime Minister to deceive us in the making of war and the taking and sacrificing of human life because he personally believes it was the right thing to do. Do we want to live under a constitutional system that allows decisions to be made in this highly personalised way? (Short 2004a: 23)

Short's question highlights a significant point about the changing character of governance in contemporary Britain. These changes include the erosion of the Westminster system of government with its tradition of an independent civil service; growing political intervention in the judiciary, which would be unconstitutional and perhaps illegal in many democracies; and a state in which the fundamental decision of whether to take the country to war resides not with its elected representatives in Parliament but with its Prime Minister, invoking the archaic claim to 'Crown prerogative'.

The prosecution of five peace activists from Oxford and Bristol in June 2004 who had attempted to delay U.S. bombers taking off from RAF Fairford in the week before the Iraq war illustrates all of the above. These activists sought a ruling that they were entitled to plead in their defence that they had acted to postpone the start of a war because they believed it to be illegal. A High Court judge had ruled in May 2004 that British foreign policy (including waging war) was an exercise of Crown prerogative that could not be examined in the courts. But although the defendants could not raise the legality of the war itself, they could mount defences of 'necessity', prevention of crime and 'lawful excuse' based on the 'secondary effects of the war'. Just before the trial, however, the Foreign Office asked the appeal court judges to refrain from ruling on the legality of war in Iraq. A witness statement handed in just ten minutes before the hearing began by Sir Michael Jay (Permanent Under-Secretary of State) argued that '[i]t would be prejudicial to the national interest if the courts expressed a view which differed from the government's on the legal justification' (Dyer 2004: 4).

Taking action to defend the 'national interest' is the prerogative of any government, but to prohibit the courts from expressing views on matters of such national importance for fear that these may 'differ' from the government's represents a worrying erosion of the principles of constitutional democracy. Anthropological approaches to policy can offer a valuable diagnostic for understanding how modern states operate in practice, as well as continuities and changes in regimes of governance. They also help to shed light on the complex ways in which individuals, institutions and events interact to give shape to new – as well as perhaps older – ways of governing.

Notes

1. 'Number 10' refers to the Prime Minister's official residence in Downing Street, Whitehall.
2. Lord Goldsmith (House of Lords Debates), *Hansard*, 26 February 2004: www.publications.parliament.uk/cvibin/ukparl.
3. These are the 1946 Convention on the Privileges and Immunities of the United Nations, the 1947 agreement between the United Nations and the U.S. regarding the headquarters of the UN and the 1961 Vienna Convention on Diplomatic Relations.

References

Abrams, P. 1988. 'Notes on the Difficulty of Studying the State (1977)', *Journal of Historical Sociology* 1: 58–89.

Alpers, S. 1991. 'The Museum as a Way of Seeing', in I. Karp and S. Levine (eds), *Exhibiting Cultures*. Washington DC: Smithsonian Institution Press.

Arlacchi, Pino. 1988. *Mafia Business. The Mafia Ethic and the Spirit of Capitalism.* Oxford: Oxford University Press.

Bamford, James. 1982. *The Puzzle Palace: A Report on America's Most Secret Agency.* Boston: Houghton Mifflin.

———. 2001. *Body of Secrets: Anatomy of the Ultra-Secret National Security Agency.* New York: Anchor Books/Doubleday.

BBC. 2004. 'US "Bugged" France's Chirac Calls', 5 October. Retrieved 2 November 2010 from http://news.bbc.co.uk/go/pr/fr/-/1/world/europe/3715980.stm.

Blitz, J. 2004. 'Ex-minister Says UK Bugged Annan's Office', *Financial Times*, 27 February, p. 1.

Bloch, M. (ed.). 1975. *Political Language and Oratory in Traditional Society*. London: Academic Press.

Bourdieu, P. 1977. *Outline of a Theory of Practice*. Cambridge: Cambridge University Press.

Bright, Martin, Gaby Hinsliff, Antony Barnett, Paul Harris, Jo Tuckman and Ed Vulliamy. 2004. 'Whistleblower', *The Observer*, 29 February, pp. 9–10.

Bush, George 2004. Transcript of the third presidential debate between between President Bush and Senator John F. Kerry. *The Washington Post.* 13 October. Retrieved 7th December 2010 from http://www.washingtonpost.com/wp-srv/politics/debatereferee/debate_1013.html.

Butler (Lord Lord Butler of Brockwell). 2004. 'Review of Intelligence on Weapons of Mass Destruction', London: HMSO. Retrieved 2 November 2010 from http://www.butlerreview.org.uk/report/index.asp.

Cantaloube, T. and H. Vernet. 2004. *Chirac contre Bush, L'autre guerre.* Paris: Lattes (Jean-Claude).

Coates, Ken. 2005. 'Foreword', in T. Simpson (ed.), *DowningStreetGate: The Dodgiest Dossier.* London: Spokesman.

Cohen, Abner. 1981. *The Politics of Elite Culture: Explorations in the Dramaturgy of Power in a Modern African Society.* Berkeley: University of California Press.

De Waal, Alex. 1994. 'Meta-conflict and the Policy of Mass Murder', *Anthropology in Action* 1(3): 8–11.

Dreyfus, Hubert and Paul Rabinow. 1982. *Michel Foucault: Beyond Structuralism and Hermeneutics*, Brighton: Harvester Press.

Dyer, Clare. 2004. 'Foreign Office Asks Judges Not to Rule on Iraq War Legality', *The Guardian*, 1 July, p. 4.

Economist. 2004. 'Bugging the UN – Security Services Bugging Activities', *Economist*, 28 February. Retrieved from http://www.highbeam.com/doc/1G1-113730906.html

Foucault, Michel. 1977. *Discipline and Punish: the Birth of the Prison*. Harmondsworth: Penguin.

——. 1980. *Power/Knowledge: Selected Interviews and Other Writings 1972–1977* (edited by Colin Gordon). New York: Pantheon Books.

——. 1991. 'Governmentality', in Graham Burchell, Colin Gordon and Peter Miller (eds), *The Foucault Effect: Studies in Governmentality*. London: Harvester Wheatsheaf, pp. 87–104.

Gupta, Akhil. 1995. 'Blurred Boundaries: The Discourse of Corruption, the Culture of Politics, and the Imagined State', *American Ethnologist* 22(2): 375–402.

Gusterson, H. 1997. 'Studying Up Revisited', *PoLAR: Political & Legal Anthropology Review* 1: 114–19.

Hall, Ben. 2004. 'Short Trades Charges with Top Mandarin Spying Allegations', *Financial Times*, 1 March, p. 2.

Herzfeld, Michael. 1992. *The Social Production of Indifference: Exploring the Symbolic Roots of Western Bureaucracy*. Oxford: Berg.

Herzfeld, Michael. 1997. *Cultural Intimacy. Social Poetics in the Nation-State*. London and New York: Routledge.

Humphrys, John 2004. 'Yes, Big Brother Should be Watching Us – Sometimes', *Sunday Times,* 29 February, p. 21.

Hutton, Lord. 2004. 'Inquiry into the Circumstances Surrounding the Death of Dr David Kelly C.M.G.', London: HMSO. Retrieved 2 November 2010 from http://www.the-hutton-inquiry.org.uk/content/rulings.htm.

Krohn-Hansen, Christian and Knut Nustad. 2005. *State Formation: Anthropological Perspectives*. London: Pluto Press.

MacAskill, Ewen. 2004a. 'Did We Bug Kofi Annan?', *The Guardian*, 27 February, p. 1.

——. 2004b. 'How Britain and the US Listen to the Rest of the World', *The Guardian*, 27 March, p. 3.

MacAskill, Ewen and Julian Borger. 2004. 'Iraq War was Illegal and Breached UN Charter, Says Annan', *The Guardian*, 16 September, p. 1.

Marcus, George. 1995. 'Ethnography In/Of the World System: The Emergence of Multi-Sited Ethnography', *Annual Review of Anthropology* 24: 95–117.

Martin, Emily. 1997. 'Managing Americans: Policy and Changes in the Meanings of Work and the Self', in C. Shore and S. Wright (eds), *Anthropology of Policy*. London and New York: Routledge, pp. 239–57.

Paine, R. (ed.). 1981. *Politically Speaking: Cross-Cultural Studies of Rhetoric*. Philadelphia: Institute for the Study of Human Issues.

Paris, Matthew. 2004. 'I Won't Tell if You Don't', *The Times*, 28 February, p. 12.

Priest, Dana and Colum Lynch. 2004. 'Spying Much Denied but Done a Lot at U.N., Experts Say', *Washington Post*, 27 February, p. 14.

Rubin, James. 2000. 'A Very Personal War – Countdown to a Very Personal War', *Financial Times*, 30 September.

Said, E.W. 2002. *Reflections on Exile and Other Essays*. Cambridge, MA: Harvard University Press.

Shore, C. 2002. 'Introduction. Towards an Anthropology of Elites', in C. Shore and S. Nugent (eds), *Elite Cultures*. London: Routledge.

Shore, Cris and Susan Wright (eds). 1997. *Anthropology of Policy*. London and New York: Routledge.

Short, Clare. 2004a 'How Tony Blair Misled Britain', *The Independent*, 23 October, p. 23.

———. 2004b. 'Transcript: Full Text of John Humphrys' Interview with Clare Short on BBC Radio 4's *Today* Programme', 26 February. Retrieved 2 November 2010 from http://www.guardian.co.uk/politics/2004/feb/26/iraq.iraq1.

Simpson, Tony (ed.). 2005. *DowningStreetGate: The Dodgiest Dossier*. London: Spokesman.

Smith, Michael. 2004. '"Failure is not an Option, but it Doesn't Mean They Will Avoid it". THE memo from Tony Blair's Foreign Policy Adviser', *Daily Telegraph*, 18 September, p. 4.

Trouillot, M.R. 2001. 'The Anthropology of the State in the Age of Globalization 1', *Current Anthropology* 42(1): 125–38.

Turner, Mark. 2004. 'Diplomats Take UN Bugging Allegations in Stride', *Financial Times*, 27 February, p. 3.

Turner, Victor. 1967. *The Forest of Symbols: Studies in Ndembu Ritual*. Ithaca: Columbia University Press.

Wedel, J., C. Shore, G. Feldman and S. Lathrop. 2005. 'Towards an Anthropology of Public Policy', *Annals of the Academy of American Political Sciences* 600: 30–51.

Yanow, D. 2000. *Conducting Interpretive Policy Analysis*. London: Sage.

Yanow, D. and P. Schwartz-Shea (eds). 2006. *Interpretation and Method: Empirical Research Methods and the Interpretive*. Turn: M.E. Sharpe.

Chapter 10

The (Un)Making of Policy in the Shadow of the World Bank: Infrastructure Development, Urban Resettlement and the Cunning State in India

Shalini Randeria and Ciara Grunder

The government agreed to the World Bank policy, it was worked out together. Why does the government not keep to the policy? We don't want much; we simply want our problems solved according to World Bank policy. We are prepared to resettle but following World Bank policy ... We are fighting because our project is a World Bank project.

> (Interview with a displaced resident of Gazi Nagar (Mumbai) who filed a complaint before the Inspection Panel of the World Bank in 2004)[1]

The World Bank should make reasonable demands. The government of Maharashtra was forced to accept the policy. But it was not possible for us to implement it. Conditions should be set which can also be met. The World Bank should also respect property rights. Those affected by the project have no licences (for business) and no legal titles (to land).

> (Interview with the Secretary Special Projects, Government of Maharashtra)

The juridification of ever more domains of our lives today increasingly blurs the distinction between law in the strict sense of the term (i.e., rules enacted by a body with legitimate authority) and policy. Juridification denotes the creation and interpretation of rules, regulations and new soft law instruments by a range of actors – public and private, national and international. Policies and procedures of international financial institutions, development agencies and humanitarian organisations belong to an ill-defined domain at the intersection of international private law, public international law, technical norms and soft law. These policies lack legislative basis but nonetheless acquire law-like qualities and produce effects similar to the workings of law in the everyday life of individuals and communities in the global South. This new architecture of governance has important implications for sovereignty and citizenship rights. Its study calls for a closer dialogue between fields that have hitherto developed relatively independently of one another: the anthropology of law, of development and of policy.

The proliferation of juridification is also accompanied by the institutionalisation of new quasi-judicial arenas of mediation, arbitration and inspection at various scales. One consequence of this development is an increasing judicialisation of politics, or 'lawfare' to use Jean and John Comaroff's term (2006). We argue that the expansion of legal forums and their increased use by citizens to influence policy outcomes neither necessarily strengthens the rights of citizens nor furthers the accountability of public institutions. Paradoxically, the spread of quasi-judicial bodies can create greater legal uncertainty for citizens, who are forced to navigate a maze of unfamiliar institutions with unclear, overlapping jurisdiction. States and international institutions are often able to render themselves unanswerable by passing the responsibility for policy design and execution to one another or to non-state actors involved in the process of its implementation. Ethnographic inquiry can fruitfully examine the effects and experiences of juridification, its ambiguities and limits, from the vantage point of actors in locations constituted as 'local'. Moreover, it can trace how the relationships between the national and international, internal and external or public and private are reconfigured through the transnationalisation of soft law and public policy. Analyses of the making and unravelling of policy call for sensitivity to its diachronic dimension too, for only a study of the worlds of policy over time can map 'deformations of the planned and the formation of the unintended', as Sally Falk Moore (2005: 3) has pointed out.

Our ethnography explores some paradoxical outcomes of current processes of juridification that seek to regulate forced displacement in a World Bank-funded infrastructure development project in Mumbai (formerly Bombay). It delineates the dynamics of the direct involvement of the international financial institution in the formulation of resettlement policy within the ongoing Mumbai Urban Transport Project (MUTP). The making and unmaking of this policy highlights the interplay between four actors (the World Bank, the MUTP project authority/the Maharashtra government, nongovernmental organisations [NGOs] and private firms of real estate developers). Yet neither the joint formulation of policy by the World Bank and the regional government nor its execution by NGOs and the private sector contribute to 'good governance'. On the contrary, a proliferation of policy actors leads to a dispersal of power and dilution of accountability. Those adversely affected by the project seek in vain to hold the state and the World Bank accountable for problems of resettlement.

The chapter analyses the strategies of the World Bank and the state government as they act against one another or in tandem to disavow responsibility for the policy jointly negotiated between them. The World Bank takes credit for an innovative policy design but disclaims responsibility for its implementation. Government officials in turn claim an inability to put into practice an untenable policy, which there was no choice but to accept. Our case study aims to capture the politics of mutual complicity between, on the one hand, the World Bank and the borrower and, on the other hand, the politics of sovereignty used by the cunning state to render itself unaccountable to citizens and to international institutions alike. We use the notion of the cunning state (Randeria 2003, 2007a) to focus on the strategies of the state rather than its presumed (in)capacities. We argue against the view of subordinate states in the international system as being merely weak either in terms of their capacity to govern populations or territory or in terms of their capacity to negotiate with powerful international financial institutions. Instead, we seek to capture the constrained agency of states in the South in order to understand how it is used to legitimate certain policy options and outcomes. The idea of a cunning state is thus a useful way to delineate a range of tactics deployed at sites of negotiation where the state appears only to disappear, and where it constructs and dismantles itself in ways that renders it unanswerable.

Despite sustained demands from social movements and NGOs over the past three decades, the Indian state has yet to formulate a national resettlement policy. It has a dismal record of the expropriation of the poor, having displaced some 500,000 people every year throughout the country since independence. Most of the over thirty million people forcibly evicted have neither received compensation nor been adequately resettled. The courts have been less than sympathetic to their grievances. The involvement of the World Bank in the MUTP introduces fairer standards of resettlement by way of credit conditionality into the national arena. However, citizens are unable to influence through elected representatives the course and content of policy negotiations between the World Bank and the administration. Disaffected citizens therefore try to secure their rights to information, consultation, participation, resettlement and compensation using legal remedies within a labyrinth of administrative, judicial and new quasi-judicial institutions at various scales. We map this shift in the exercise of citizenship rights (i.e., from political participation to inspection and surveillance), which accompanies the transnationalisation of policy formulation.

This chapter analyses the ambiguities of these processes as experienced by two sets of actors in highly asymmetrical positions: officials of the regional government responsible for the implementation of the MUTP and a group of persons displaced by the project. On the one hand, we discuss the complex process of negotiation of the resettlement policy between the World Bank and bureaucrats of the Maharashtra government and, on the other hand, trace the tenacious use of the Bombay High Court and the inspection mechanism at the World Bank by citizens protesting against violations of the policy. Policy outcomes, we argue, thus vary with the local constellation of actors, who implement and contest it on the ground. The involvement of the World Bank alters the dynamics of such conflicts, for it introduces a powerful actor with norms and institutional mechanisms, which can be used by activists in their attempt to set aside national laws and policies (Randeria 2003, 2007b).

The Mumbai Urban Transport Project

With a population of some eighteen million people, Mumbai, the capital of the province of Maharashtra and the commercial and finance metropole of India, is one of the largest cities in the world. The MUTP aims to improve the inadequate transport infrastructure in this megacity in order to further the mobility of people and goods. The World Bank views inadequate transport as a bottleneck for the economic development of the city and especially as a constraint for the poor, who require much longer travelling time to work (World Bank 2002: 6). The project consists of three components: the extension of the suburban railway network, the expansion of highways within the city, and a programme of resettlement and rehabilitation for those displaced as a result. Of the project's estimated total cost of $945 million, the World Bank has lent more than half ($542 million). The rest comes from Indian Railways, the federal and the regional governments (World Bank 2004a, 2004b).

The project loan includes a big budget for the resettlement and rehabilitation of some 120,000 people, whose homes, shops, businesses and small industrial establishments are situated on land needed for the enlargement of the city's transport infrastructure (World Bank 2002, 2004a and 2004b).[2] The massive scale of urban resettlement is unprecedented for a World Bank-funded project anywhere in the world except China. The inclusion of a resettlement policy into the project design and a large loan for this purpose are also exceptional. In fact, the MUTP is unique in being the first infrastructure project financed by the World Bank that includes a budget for resettlement. However, issues of resettlement and rehabilitation have turned out to be the Achilles' heel of the project. No other project funded by the World Bank has led to so many complaints about trenchant violations of the institution's own safeguard policies being filed before its Inspection Panel, a quasi-judicial body. The report of the latter led the World Bank management in 2006, for the very first time, to temporarily suspend credit for a project in India. The reaction of the project authorities was as revealing as the subsequent actions of the lending institution. The former publicly welcomed the withdrawal of the imperious institution, which had infringed on national sovereignty and imposed impracticable conditions. The latter soon resumed the credit despite the absence of significant improvement in the conditions of the displaced families. It is this dance of donors with dependent states, to use Sally Falk Moore's evocative expression (2002), and its consequences for affected citizens that our ethnography details.

Planning for the gigantic project of improving the suburban railway infrastructure began in 1995. The project was represented as pivotal to economic growth, the improvement of the quality of life and the reduction of poverty in the city. But a second component, namely the extension of the highways, was added to the original plan shortly before the loan document was finalised in 2002. By then, the resettlement policy for the project had already been drafted with a view to the needs of those families, whose homes along the railway tracks were to be demolished. The belated inclusion of the extension of the highways along the Santa Cruz-Chembur Link Road and the Jogeshwari-Vikroli Link Road into the MUTP created several problems. The costs for the resettlement of those displaced by the road expansion had not been adequately budgeted for in the loan agreement. Moreover, those displaced due to the new highways included owners of shops, businesses and small industrial units, whose rehabilitation needs were different. It is this group that has been at the forefront of legal action against violations of the MUTP resettlement policy. The Regional Safeguards Advisor of the World Bank felt that the inability to design differential compensation packages for various groups of displaced persons was an important factor in precipitating the conflict around resettlement.

However, officials of the government of Maharashtra took a different view. They pointed out that it was not the application of the policy to an additional set of persons that was problematic, but that the basic premises of the resettlement policy itself were flawed. In their view, the government was being forced to violate its own laws on land acquisition and its policy on slum rehabilitation in order to comply with the World Bank's unreasonable demands on the question of resettlement. During the policy negotiations, officials were opposed to the acceptance of resettlement norms at variance with the country's laws and policies, which provided no compensation for those without legal titles to land acquired by the state for a public purpose. Partial and selective implementation of the policy was therefore justified by bureaucrats with reference to its utter unsuitability for the local context and its disregard for national policy, as the quotation from an interview with a senior bureaucrat at the beginning of the chapter illustrates.

Negotiations on Resettlement Policy

The World Bank, wary of repeating its earlier mistake in seriously underestimating the nature, extent, cost and massive problems of displacement caused by the dams on the Narmada river that it had financed in part, insisted on incorporating a resettlement policy within the MUTP from the start. In the late 1980s and early 1990s, a transnational advocacy network had mobilised public opinion worldwide against the Sardar Sarovar Dam that caused the forcible displacement of nearly 200,000 people without adequate compensation measures (Randeria 2003). The successful campaign led the government of India to forego the remaining credit for the Narmada project. This terminated the involvement of the World Bank in probably the most controversial infrastructure project in its entire history. The campaign also brought about significant policy changes at the World Bank, including the formulation of its current policy on involuntary displacement (Fox and Brown 1998).

The World Bank's Operational Policy (OP)/Bank Procedure (BP) 4.12 (Policy on Involuntary Resettlement) is binding on all borrowers for projects involving displacement (World Bank n.d.).[3] The safeguard policy enjoins prior consultation with those to be displaced in order to ensure their participation in the planning and implementation of resettlement programmes. These programmes are to be executed with a view to sustainable development that enables those affected by a project to share in its benefits. The policy also aims to assist those to be displaced 'to improve their livelihoods and standards of living or at least to restore them, in real terms, to pre-displacement levels or to levels prevailing prior to the beginning of project implementation, whichever is higher'. Many of these norms, which were incorporated into the MUTP resettlement policy, originally stem from demands advocated by environmental NGOs in the North and social movements in the South in the course of the campaign against the Narmada Dam. Understanding paths and patterns of diffusion and domestication of policy in various locations thus calls for a study of connections across sites and scales as well as over time. What appeared to Maharashtra government officials to be unfeasible policies imposed by the World Bank top down turn out on closer examination to incorporate norms originating from civil society actors, including some from India. These norms are subsequently diffused to borrowers in the South through their incorporation into the operational policies of the World Bank. Such circuitous policy making increasingly blurs the boundaries between actors within and beyond the nation-state.

A close reading of the documents on the MUTP project, supplemented by interviews with some of the Indian bureaucrats involved in the negotiations, reveals the process by which policy prescriptions of the World Bank were turned into policies of the government of Maharashtra. As the World Bank, for example, notes in its Project Appraisal Document:

> GoM [Government of Maharashtra] had issued a Government Resolution [GR] adopting the policy in March, 1997 which was later amended in line with the Bank's OD [Operational Directive] 4.30 on involuntary resettlement. The modified version was reviewed and endorsed by the World Bank in February, 2000. Subsequently, the GoM has brought out a Government Resolution [Prakalpa 1700/CR 31/Slum 2, dated December 12, 2000] signifying the adoption of the revised policy for the project. (World Bank 2002: 98)

Interventions in the formulation of policy by donors are thus represented and justified as the consent of the recipient state (Anders 2008). Or, as Sally Falk Moore (2002) has put it, the command of aid conditionalities is couched in the language of contract. Such a 'construct of presumed consent' (Mattei 2003: 385) inverts accountability by shifting responsibility for the implementation of the World Bank's operational policies (OP) and directives (OD) onto an often unwilling borrower who has no choice but to accept the terms of a loan agreement. But the cunning state can use its latitude in the interpretation and execution of policy to undermine the agreed-upon policy. It is able to get away with even gross infringements of policy with impunity by raising the sensitive issue of violation of national sovereignty by the World Bank.

The incorporation of the World Bank's operational policy norms into the resettlement policy of the MUTP resulted in protracted negotiations with the government of Maharashtra. The latter instituted a working group on resettlement policy comprising of senior government officials and the private sector to iron out differences behind closed doors. The adviser to the Society for the Promotion of Area Resource Centres (SPARC), an NGO entrusted with implementing MUTP resettlement programmes, notes that: 'The World Bank required that there be civil society representation on the Task Force to formulate R&R (resettlement and rehabilitation) policy' (Burra 2001: 5). The task force, which included representatives of NGOs, recommended that each family to be evicted be given 225 sq. ft. of accommodation free of cost. Government officials gave in to the World Bank's demands to provide alternative housing to those evicted, but insisted on limiting its size. However, they refused to acquiesce to the World Bank directive to provide compensation for loss of income or restoration of the existing standard of living. Moreover, officials warned against setting a precedent within the MUTP which they would be hard put to replicate elsewhere. As a senior bureaucrat in charge of infrastructure projects put it: 'We (the government of Maharashtra) have nine such projects, the World Bank only one. It is impossible to implement the other projects according to the same resettlement standards as the World Bank one. The state simply does not have the funds for this.' However, affirmations of state incapacity by government officials must be seen as strategic. Bureaucrats reacted in press interviews to the temporary suspension of the World Bank credit due to gross violations of the resettlement policy by stressing the ability of the state to implement the project without the pressure of World Bank aid with strings. They faulted the rigorous MUTP resettlement policy for having slowed down progress on the project, led to an increase in expenditure , and thus ultimately held the Bank policy to be responsible for the inability of the project authorities to meet the demands of the World Bank for speedy implementation and a positive cost-benefit ratio.

The MUTP resettlement policy grants far more rights to persons forcibly displaced by the project than any other policy for expropriation of land for public purpose or slum demolition followed in India so far.[4] Small wonder then that those adversely affected by the project are adamant that the World Bank policy (and not national law) applies to them, as the displaced resident insists in the interview from which we quote at the beginning of the chapter. Policies tied to development projects, however, raise vexed issues of legal pluralism and the fragmentation of citizenship rights. World Bank structural adjustment policies, for example, affect all citizens even if their impact is far from uniform within the borrowing country. Yet policies framed within a particular development intervention carve up state territory into project areas and populations to whom norms negotiated with a particular international organisation apply. These norms may differ with the donor in question and may also be at variance with national laws and policies. Only those who have been displaced by a World Bank funded infrastructure project such as the MUTP are eligible to stake claims for compensation according to World Bank lending norms as incorporated into project policy. Those displaced by other infrastructure development projects in Mumbai can only claim compensation according to national laws and polices.

The existence of dual standards caused dissatisfaction among those displaced due to different infrastructure development projects in the city. The plurality of resettlement norms was also partly responsible for considerable confusion in identifying beneficiaries as claimants swelled the ranks of those eligible for compensation under the MUTP. Government officials sought to reclassify the homes and shops of many of these protestors as falling under the plans for eviction as part of the Mithi river project, a project without World Bank involvement. The policy framed within the MUTP was limited to the duration of the project. Yet the World Bank entertained the vain hope that it would form the prototype of future regional and national policy. Officials of the Maharashtra government, however, stated in no uncertain terms that it would not be extended beyond the ambit of the MUTP.

The World Bank Policy on Involuntary Resettlement, which enjoins compensation regardless of the duration of residence prior to eviction or possession of legal titles to property, also contravenes earlier policies of the government of Maharashtra. Although the Maharashtra government was averse to keeping its own policy temporarily in abeyance for households dislocated due to the MUTP, it was forced to accede to the demands of the World Bank management. Almost all those displaced by the MUTP belong to the official category of 'slum-dwellers' without legal title to their homes or business properties (World Bank 2004a: 5). This is not surprising, as more than half of the population of Mumbai inhabits so-called 'slums' (MTSU 2006) built on either private or public land. Government officials objected strongly to the demand of the World Bank for the rehabilitation of those who in the eyes of the law are 'illegal encroachers'. Officials went so far as to append a note of dissent to the MUTP policy, stating that the World Bank's insistence on compensating illegal 'slum-dwellers' set a dangerous precedent that would encourage lawlessness and reward the illegal occupation of land. The fact that MUTP policy was at odds with the international financial institution's insistence on respect for property rights did not escape notice either, as exemplified by the quotation from an interview with a senior bureaucrat at the beginning of the chapter.

Policy Implementation by Non-State Actors: Real Estate Developers and NGOs

During the protracted negotiations on the project, Maharashtra government officials had strongly opposed the World Bank's initial suggestion that the responsibility for the resettlement programme be fully given over to a private corporation. They had advocated instead the choice of the Mumbai Metropolitan Regional Development Authority (MMRDA). Yet neither the MMRDA nor even the World Bank for that matter had any experience of urban resettlement on such a large scale, as the former Chief of Resettlement and Rehabilitation at the MUTP conceded. The World Bank solved this problem by redefining it as one of the weaknesses of urban governance institutions in India, which suffered from a fragmentation of functions and responsibilities as well as from a lack of overall coordination. The Project Appraisal Document for the MUTP therefore proposed reforming the MMRDA into an efficient and transparent organisation according to the 'good governance' criteria of the international financial organisation (World Bank 2002: 37).

Interestingly, there was no disagreement between the World Bank and the Maharashtra government about the involvement of private real estate developers, a component of the MUTP resettlement policy that was imported from the slum rehabilitation scheme in the city. Private firms were selected to build the new apartment blocks for resettlement. In exchange for the construction of these buildings, they were given permission to develop property in prime areas of Mumbai. World Bank documents were full of praise for this 'innovative' market-oriented approach using so-called Transferable Development Rights (TDRs) (World Bank 2004b: 7–8 and 2006: 44), which enabled the state to acquire additional private land for the purposes of infrastructure development (World Bank 2002: 99). TDRs give the developer the right to build at another location or to sell to a third party the right to build, 2.5 times the floor space index (FSI) generated for resettlement. In return for providing 1,000 sq. m. of built space to house those affected by the MUTP, for example, a firm of developers would acquire the right to construct commercial or residential space of 2,500 sq. m. elsewhere in the city. Noting the extremely poor quality of the new buildings for displaced families, an activist of the Bombay Environmental Action Group remarked: 'Instead of the earlier horizontal slums now vertical ones have been built and that too on a much smaller area of land than earlier. Those who have profited are the builders thanks to the TDR.' The choice of new locations for resettlement on the outskirts of the city reflected the interests of powerful firms of developers and not the preferences of the displaced for accommodation close to their original homes and business premises. The latter had not been consulted prior to relocation, in violation of the World Bank's policy, as the Inspection Panel found upon its investigations into complaints.

The involvement of non-state actors to implement resettlement policy reflects the World Bank's neoliberal prescriptions for development. But it may also be seen as a reaction to the Indian state's recalcitrant attitude towards questions of forced displacement in the past. Having learnt its lesson from the controversial Narmada Dam project, the World Bank insisted on entrusting responsibility for MUTP resettlement programmes to NGOs with high local legitimacy. The NGOs contracted for the purpose were the SPARC, the Slum Rehabilitation Society (SRS) and the National Slum-Dwellers Federation (NSDF), which includes the Railway Slum Dwellers Federation that represents the interests of families living along the railway tracks in Mumbai. All three organisations have a long record of active involvement in furthering the right to housing for the urban poor. They have furthered dialogue between the slum-dwellers and the state to solve problems arising from a lack of civic amenities, evictions and relocation. The NGOs see themselves as facilitators who enable local communities to organise themselves through participatory processes (SPARC/NSDF n.d.; SRS n.d.). Whereas the SPARC represents itself as 'one David against three Goliaths' (the World Bank, Indian Railways and the government of Maharashtra) (Patel and Sharma 1998), for those protesting against inadequate resettlement, the battle-lines were drawn differently.

The NGOs were contracted to carry out baseline socioeconomic surveys of the households to be dislocated, to draw up resettlement plans and to implement them. The MUTP project authorities had to be pressurised by the World Bank into giving up responsibility for the implementation of these parts of the project. Thus, the NGOs took over the burden of determining eligibility for compensation and issuing identity documents in the absence of any existing system of identity cards or registration of residence by the state. Among the contentious issues which were left to the NGOs to resolve were: what constituted a family, which kin and affinal relatives could be counted as belonging to a household, whether they had to be resident in the structure to be demolished at the time of relocation, whether those currently absent from Mumbai in the village could be counted as family members, and who should bear the cost of their travel to the city to be photographed for purposes of identification and compensation. Moreover, the SPARC and the NSDF were also given a contract to construct the 2,500 flats necessary to temporarily house those who had to be urgently relocated before the flats at the resettlement site had been built. The NGOs offered to construct these 'transit tenements at about 75% of the estimated cost, making the offer attractive both to the (World) Bank and the MMRDA (Mumbai Metropolitan regional Development Authority in charge of project implementation)' (Burra 2001: 6). The responsibility for the identification and resettlement of nearly 120,000 persons thus rested with the NGOs, who also bore the brunt of the criticism that was deflected away from the World Bank and the state government or the MMRDA, the nodal agency that coordinates the project. Disaffected citizens in the MUTP case simultaneously filed a petition before the Bombay High Court and asked the Inspection Panel of the World Bank to inquire into a breach of resettlement policy.

The Futile Search for Quasijudicial Remedies: Inspection Mechanisms at Various Scales

Established in 1993, the Inspection Panel is by no means a fully-fledged body for adjudication, but provides a forum for a complaint by any party adversely affected by a World Bank-funded project. The independent body represents an innovation in international law, whereby individual citizens are for the first time formally allowed access to an international financial organisation. Its establishment responds to a long-standing demand by civil society actors, which was also voiced forcefully by the transnational coalition against the Narmada Dam. They demanded the accountability of the World Bank not only to its member states but equally to citizens in debtor countries, who, though affected by its lending policies, had no voice in its functioning. Although the (in)action of borrower governments is beyond the purview of the Inspection Panel, it has been used not only to ensure compliance with World Bank safeguards policies but primarily to pressurise one's own government to adhere to World Bank's norms or standards (Clarke et al. 2003; Randeria 2003, 2007). The primary purpose of the Inspection Panel, a three-member body with investigatory and advisory powers, is to examine the compliance by World Bank staff with the safeguard policies and procedures laid down by the institution that are also binding on the borrower. Its establishment does not render the World Bank legally liable, nor does it provide compensation, even to those whose complaints are found to be justified. In using it as a forum to seek remedy, citizens and civil society organisations also challenge the nation-state's exclusive claim to speak for its citizens and represent their interests at the international level.

In 2004 and 2005, four requests for investigation into infringements of the MUTP resettlement policy were made to the Inspection Panel. Complaints concerned the lack of consultation with the community, the choice of inappropriate relocation sites and inadequate restoration of incomes and living standards due to the unavailability of access to essential services such as schools, medical services, water and waste removal facilities. It was contended that relocation in far-away areas inaccessible by public transport had led to severe problems of mobility, an increase in travel expenses and commuting time to work, and a loss of daily wages for poor households, who could least afford such costs. Petitioners claimed that adequate rehabilitation according to World Bank policies must therefore compensate for the disruption to livelihoods and a decline in standards of living.

However, as the conflict between the MMRDA, the project implementing authority, and those who filed a request for inspection made clear, the cunning state had little intention of abiding by the policy negotiated with the World Bank. The petitioners drew attention to the callousness and the high-handedness of MMRDA officials, who had consistently failed to address their concerns. In a letter to the Inspection Panel, the representatives of the families to be displaced from Gazi Nagar recorded their altercation with the then head of the project implementation authority as follows: 'The head of MMRDA proudly replied [*sic*] us that this is India and not America. One cannot hold us that much accountable and responsible as Americans are! When we told him that it means you people are not as accountable and responsible as expected by the World Bank, he replied in yes [*sic*] and further stated that the people of Gazi Nagar should not expect any such accountabilities and transparencies from him nor from the government [*sic*] ... Now we the poor residents of Gazi Nagar are unable to understand where to go for justice in such circumstances' (World Bank Inspection 2004b: 47 Annex 6).

Residents of Gazi Nagar recalled that members of the Inspection Panel had explained to them during the site visit to Mumbai that it could merely document violations of policy but had no powers to take decisions to improve implementation. In its view, the power to improve the situation of the displaced lay with the World Bank management. Once management responds to the report of the Inspection Panel by putting before the Executive Directors of the World Bank an 'action plan' for improvement in the implementation of the project, which it devises together with the borrower, neither the complainants nor the Inspection Panel have the right to comment on the plans further (Clarke et al. 2003: 267). Besides formulating such a plan jointly with the MMRDA, the World Bank management also reacted to the numerous complaints to the Inspection Panel by prevailing on the project authorities to activate the grievance redress mechanisms established within the MUTP.

A case before the Bombay High Court and the complaint to the Inspection Panel compelled the MMRDA to take steps towards the formalisation of the functioning of these grievance instances. But even in 2006, no regular hearings took place and complaints to the Field Level and Senior Level Grievance Redress Committees responsible for assessing the eligibility for compensation were summarily dismissed. Indignant at being forced to institute complaints mechanisms within the MUTP at the behest of the World Bank, and distrustful of the urban poor, bureaucrats saw to it that the new instances remained totally ineffective. Following criticism by the Inspection Panel, the Independent Monitoring Panel (IMP) within the MUTP, a third body instituted under pressure from the World Bank, was broadened to include independent members from outside the state bureaucracy. But in the absence of any competence to take binding decisions, the IMP too remained ineffective. Nevertheless, the chief of resettlement and rehabilitation at the MUTP and the director of the MUTP were impatient with all the discussions within the IMP. The latter felt that: 'In projects one must bridge the gap between two aims: follow procedures and realise project aims. If one always only focuses on procedures, then no progress is possible.'

Not surprisingly, these dysfunctional quasi-judicial instances brought no relief to those who had lost their homes and businesses, but their existence on paper relieved the World Bank of its responsibility to address problems of implementation. It also deflected demands for accountability addressed to the World Bank management onto the project authorities, who in turn pointed to the existence of the three-tier grievance redress mechanism within the MUTP in order to demonstrate compliance with credit conditionality in the area of 'good governance'. Citizens remain sceptical of these internal mechanisms. As a member of the United Shop Owners Association that filed a request to the Inspection Panel remarked; 'What kind of a bureaucracy is this, which is defendant, judge and lawyer in one? How can one expect justice here?' Moreover, these various MUTP bodies do not seem to have any legal status or established procedures. Their main function seems to be to prevent complaints to, and further investigations by, the Inspection Panel of the World Bank, an aim that both borrower and lender wished to achieve.

Matters came to a head, however, as the MMRDA, the project-implementing authority, seemed to be unable or unwilling to resolve the serious problems of resettlement. Following a spate of complaints, the Inspection Panel went ahead with a limited field investigation into allegations of policy violations. Its highly critical report detailed infringements of the policy on environmental assessment, on project supervision and on involuntary displacement. It was critical of the choice of resettlement sites, the overestimation by the World Bank management of the capacities of the NGOs and the project authority to carry out resettlement programmes on such a large scale, the ineffectiveness of the grievance redress mechanisms within the MUTP, and the deterioration in living standards after relocation (World Bank Inspection Panel 2005 and 2006). The report forced the World Bank to temporarily suspend the disbursement of the remaining twenty per cent of the IDA credit and the $150 million loan for the controversial road and resettlement components of the project in March 2006. The cunning state, however, welcomed the suspension as a blessing in disguise, as it provided an opportunity to sidestep the stringent standards of the World Bank. The then head of the MMRDA stated in an interview to the press that it would be cheaper, quicker and less cumbersome to implement the project without World Bank policies and standards, which push up the costs of resettlement and rehabilitation to a level that was not feasible for the project authority to meet. According to him, 'The World Bank has a lot of harsh impractical conditions. They want us to use global laws for local conditions' (Deshmukh and Mehta 2006). He announced that the MMRDA would consider turning to Japanese banks to complete the project, which lent funds at lower rates without social and environmental conditions attached to them. This turned out to be an empty threat. The federal government prevailed on the project authority and the Maharashtra government not to exacerbate the conflict so as not to jeopardise relations with the World Bank.

The Exercise of Citizenship Rights through Legal Action

Defining democracy as the 'politics of the governed' (2004: 4), Partha Chatterjee points to the emergence of a new distinction between citizens and populations in contemporary regimes of power, following Foucault's idea of the 'governmentalisation of the state'. He argues that these regimes do not secure legitimacy through the political participation of citizens. Instead, their legitimacy rests on claims to provide for the well-being of statistically defined populations as the objects of social and economic policies. Policy thus comes to replace politics, just as the rule of experts replaces political representation. Whereas the right to vote in a representative democracy still remains tied to a world of territorial nation-states, the right to inspect and to judge, the right to evaluate or denounce have not merely gained significance but are also being exercised both within and beyond state boundaries, as our case study shows. Although those at the margins of the nation-state may have recourse to new transnational arenas like the Inspection Panel of the World Bank, this does not mean that they live in a world of 'postnational' or 'pluri-national' citizenship, which is a privilege reserved for another class of citizens. Pierre Rosanvallon (2006) has identified the tendency towards increasing surveillance and control as a central aspect of what he calls 'counter-democracy' at the national level. But even at the transnational scale, it is easier for citizens to inspect or name and shame governments than it is to improve access to, and gain representation in, international institutions.

One aspect of this shift is the increasing use of courts at all levels by citizens rather than participation in elections to render governments accountable. Political mobilisation, parliamentary debates and street demonstrations are conspicuous by their absence in the Mumbai case. These have been increasingly displaced by litigation in the High Court and the international arena. The MUTP case is remarkable for the tenacity with which those seeking adequate rehabilitation have focused almost exclusively on the search for legal remedies. However, claims in the judicial or quasi-judicial arena also require extensive prior mobilisation on the ground. Their outcome in these arenas may also depend to a considerable extent on the success of marshalling resources, capturing media attention and sustaining political pressure. The media (especially the English-language press in Mumbai) has been rather hostile to the rights of slum and pavement-dwellers in the city. The middle classes consider them to be lawbreakers who illegally occupy valuable public or private land and create a public nuisance. There has been a sustained campaign to 'beautify Bombay' by summarily evicting those who disfigure the city by using public space for sleeping, cooking and defecating. The urban poor are represented as 'free riders', who use amenities that middle-class taxpayers sustain.

Interestingly, in the early stages of the MUTP, a public interest litigation petition was filed by an NGO asking for the demolition of all slums along the railway tracks without compensation (Burra 2001). The High Court in all likelihood would have conceded the demand had it not been for the assurance of the government of Maharashtra that it would urgently implement a resettlement programme for the affected families. It is unlikely that the government would have taken this view if it had not known itself to be under scrutiny from the World Bank in this regard. However, the petition by those seeking to avert eviction due to the extension of highways under the MUTP was turned down by the Bombay High Court.[5] They were asked to present their problems to the internal grievance redress mechanism within the MUTP as requested by the defendants, the project authorities. But the court also ruled that no evictions were to be undertaken until rehabilitation according to the norms of the MUTP resettlement policy was provided. The court thus held World Bank policy rather than national law to be applicable in this case. Disregarding the court judgment and its own policy, the project authorities went ahead with evictions and demolitions while complaints by residents were pending before a grievance committee. By filing a compliant to the Inspection Panel of the World Bank, the petitioners could circumvent the administrative and judicial machinery of the state temporarily, but they remained dependent on it in the long run. Disappointed by the lack of improvement in resettlement programmes despite the Inspection Panel having recorded serious violations of policy, citizens turned once again to the Bombay High Court to complain against corruption and mismanagement in the MUTP. This case is still pending.

Efforts by citizens to organise and press claims in legal fora at the national or transnational level are concerned with issues of inspection and judgment rather than with the core classical concerns of citizenship around questions of legitimacy, participation and representation. A broader grammar of governance has thus emerged, one that has extended the vocabulary of citizenship both within the nation-state and outside of it. One of the dilemmas faced by citizens in the new architecture of non-accountability is to identify the addressee of the protest. Activists differ in their assessment of the efficacy of using local, national or transnational arenas exclusively, consecutively or simultaneously. The strategic choices they make also vary depending on the issue in question, as well as their location and ideology. Moreover, the resources available to local actors vary and also determine the levels of support they can marshal at different scales, the networks they are able to tap into or the coalitions they can build and sustain. As the Mumbai case demonstrates, the addressee of the protest, the scale at which it is voiced and the strategy used to further claims can also shift in the course of a struggle.

Conclusion

An anthropology of policy provides a useful vantage point to map processes of the restructuring of the state and its relationship with international financial institutions and citizens. It is well suited to capture shifts in rhetoric and practices of sovereignty as well as the exercise of citizenship rights. Our ethnography of the (un)making of resettlement policy within the MUTP has explored how soft law attains efficacy in everyday life in a particular place. An understanding of processes of juridification in a developmental state, aptly termed 'a state of endemic expropriation' by Jean and John Comaroff (2006: 15), requires the study of dynamic and conflict-laden fields. The boundaries of these fields are not given in advance but are empirically determined in relation to our objects of enquiry. Processes of policy making cannot be understood without reference to the workings of larger forces, which are global in reach but local in their manifestations.

We have shown that the same World Bank policy can produce very different outcomes in different contexts, depending on the bargaining strength of the borrowing state and the extent to which it is able to circumvent policies negotiated under conditions of unequal power. Yet the state is neither a passive recipient of external policy prescriptions, nor without the means to affect their realisation in a local context. While it is an object of neoliberal restructuring, the state actively shapes these policy outcomes too. We use the idea of the cunning state to counter discourses of state weakness that proliferate in academic and policy circles. The cunning state can successfully render itself unaccountable by legitimising its lack of political will to implement a policy in terms of its inability to do so. Partial compliance and foot-dragging can be interpreted in turn by the World Bank as the need to improve state capacities and governance. The dispersal of power in transnationalised worlds of policy leads to a loss of transparency in decision-making as well as to a dilution and divestment of responsibility. The proliferation of a plurality of norms and of new quasi-judicial arenas are experienced by various actors as both empowering and disempowering. Our ethnography has explored the equivocal nature of some of these developments that hold out a promise they have yet to fulfil.

Notes

1. Direct quotations and paraphrases of views expressed by actors derive from interviews carried out by Ciara Grunder during her fieldwork on the MUTP project in Mumbai from September 2006 to March 2007 (Grunder 2008).
2. This final figure has had to be continually revised upwards over the years pushing up project costs and complicating the implementation of the plans for rehabilitation. See the Resettlement and Rehabilitation Policy for MUTP, March 1997 (amended 2000) for the broad definition of 'Project Affected Persons' adopted at the behest of the World Bank.
3. OP/BP 4.12 together have replaced the earlier Operational Directive (OD) 4.30 on Involuntary Displacement.
4. Activists of the National Working Group on Displacement have advocated norms for fair resettlement and rehabilitation that go far beyond those adopted by the World Bank (Randeria 2003, 2007a).
5. Bombay High Court, Writ Petition No. 1161 of 2004, *USOA (United Shop Owner's Association) v. MMDRA*.

References

Anders, G. 2008. 'The Normativity of Numbers: World Bank and IMF Conditionality', *PoLAR: Political and Legal Anthropology Review* 31(2): 187–202.

Burra, S. 2001. 'Resettlement and Rehabilitation of the Urban Poor: The Mumbai Urban Transport Project'. Retrieved 2 November 2010 from www.sparcindia.org.

Chatterjee, P. 2004. *The Politics of the Governed: Reflections on Popular Politics in Most of the World*. New York: Columbia University Press.

Clarke, D., J. Fox and K. Treakle. 2003. *Demanding Accountability: Civil Society Claims and the World Bank Inspection Panel*. India: Rainbow Publishers Ltd.

Comaroff, J. and J.L. Comaroff. 2006. *Law and Disorder in the Postcolony*. Chicago: University of Chicago Press.

Deshmukh, S. and R. Mehta. 2006. 'World Bank Stops Aid, State Not Perturbed', *DNA: Daily News & Analysis*, 3 March. Retrieved 2 November 2010 from http://www.dnaindia.com/mumbai/report_world-bank-stops-aid-state-not-perturbed_1015967.

Fox, J. and D.L. Brown. 1998. *The Struggle for Accountability: The World Bank, NGOs, and Grassroots Movements*. Cambridge, MA: MIT Press.

Grunder, C. 2008. *Wer macht sich hier breit? Transformation in eine 'Weltklasse-Stadt': Das Mumbai Urban Transport Project und die Umsiedlung von SlumbewohnerInnen*, masters thesis, Institute of Social Anthropology, University of Zurich.

Mattei, U. 2003. 'A Theory of Imperial Law: A Study on U.S. hegemony and the Latin Resistance', *Indiana Journal of Global Legal Studies* 10(1): 383–449.

Moore, S.F. 2002. 'An International Regime and the Context of Conditionality', in M. Likosky (ed.), *Transnational Legal Processes: Globalisation and Power Disparities*. London and Edinburgh: Butterworths and LexisNexis, pp. 333–52.

———. 2005. 'Comparisons: Possible and Impossible', *Annual Review of Anthropology* 34: 1–11.

MTSU (Mumbai Transformation Support Unit). 2006. *Strategy for Land and Housing Development*. Mumbai: All India Institute of Local Self-Government.

Patel, S. and K. Sharma. 1998. 'One David and Three Goliaths: Mumbai Transport Case Study', Mumbai: Society for Promotion of Area Resource Centres (SPARC). Retrieved 2 November 2010 from www.sparcindia.org.

Randeria, S. 2003. 'Cunning States and Unaccountable International Institutions: Legal Plurality, Social Movements and Rights of Local Communities to Common Property Resources', *European Journal of Sociology* 44(1): 27–60.

———. 2007a. 'The State of Globalization: Legal Plurality, Overlapping Sovereignties and Ambiguous Alliances between Civil Society and the Cunning State in India', *Theory, Culture and Society* 24(1): 1–33.

———. 2007b. 'Global Designs and Local Lifeworlds: Colonial Legacies of Conservation, Disenfranchisement and Environmental Governance in Postcolonial India', *Interventions: International Journal of Postcolonial Studies*, 9(1): 12–30.

Rosanvallon, P. 2006. *Democracy Past and Future*. New York: Columbia University Press.

Slum Rehabilitation Society, (SRS) NGO. n.d. 'About us'. Retrieved 2 November 2010 from http://www.srsindia.org/default.asp?linkid=5&filename=aboutus.

SPARC/NSDF, NGO. n.d. 'About Us'. Retrieved 2 November 2010 from www.sparcindia.org.

World Bank. 2002. 'Project Appraisal Document. Mumbai Urban Transport Project'. Retrieved 2 November 2010 from http://www-wds.worldbank.org/external/default/WDSContentServer/WDSP/IB/2005/07/19/000112742_20050719101432/Rendered/PDF/240040IB0multi0page.pdf.

———. 2004a. 'Bank Management Response to Request for Inspection Panel Review of the India – Mumbai Urban Transport Project'. Retrieved 2 November 2010 from http://siteresources.worldbank.org/EXTINSPECTIONPANEL/Resources/MumbaiManagementResponse.pdf.

———. 2004b. 'Bank Management Response to Request for Inspection Panel Review of the India – Mumbai Urban Transport Project'. Retrieved 2 November 2010 from http://siteresources.worldbank.org/EXTINSPECTIONPANEL/Resources/ManagementResponseGazi.pdf.

———. 2006. 'Management Report and Recommendation in Response to the Inspection Panel Investigation Report: India Mumbai Urban Transport Project'. Retrieved 2 November 2010 from http://siteresources.worldbank.org/EXTINSPECTIONPANEL/Resources/INDIAManagementResponse.pdf.

———. n.d. 'Policies and Procedures'. Retrieved 2 November 2010 from http://web.worldbank.org/WBSITE/EXTERNAL/PROJECTS/0,,contentMDK:20120722~hlPK:581478~menuPK:41392~pagePK:41367~piPK:51533~theSitePK:40941,00.html.

World Bank Inspection Panel. 2005. 'The Inspection Panel Investigation Report'. Retrieved 2 November 2010 from http://siteresources.worldbank.org/EXTINSPECTIONPANEL/Resources/IPNMUTPFINAL.pdf.

Chapter 11

Sweden's National Pension System as a Political Technology

Anette Nyqvist

This chapter examines Sweden's national pension system, focusing on how the design of the new pension scheme functioned as a political technology to simultaneously depoliticise and 'responsibilise' the subjects of the reform. My analysis sheds light on how tools of new governance may be embedded in the construction of a public policy. The design of Sweden's new pension system recasts what was previously a political issue into a neutral, purely technical one to be dealt with by experts, not by elected politicians. I also explore how the construction of the policy effectively relocated responsibility for future pension levels from the state to the individual citizen.

The Scale and Scope of Pensions

A national pension system covers enormously large issues, both in terms of scale and scope. It stretches from the individual, through the national level and further out to global levels. A pension system is simultaneously of public and private concern. It deals with the past, present and, not least, the unknown future. It is about welfare, security, risk and responsibility. With such a wide social and temporal reach in society, a national pension system connects the state with its citizens in a most general fashion, defining and shaping the relationship between state and citizen in myriad ways. What is interesting here, from an anthropology of policy perspective, is the way that reform of the welfare system changes the relationship between citizens and the state. The design of Sweden's new national pension system relocated the responsibility for, and agency to affect, future pensions to mathematical formulas and to each individual taxpayer.

The reform and design of national pension systems have become important political and economic issues in many countries over the past few decades and a major focus of media attention. For demographic and economic reasons, many national pension schemes were considered too generous and 'the problem of an ageing population' and 'the pension bomb' quickly became issues of both political and public debate. It was after the Second World War that the welfare state shifted gear and expanded rapidly in Europe. In the post-War period, most Western capitalist nation-states sustained high economic growth that allowed them to develop generous social policies, including national pension systems. Social policy designs that assumed sustained high national growth were called into question by the general economic stagnation in the 1970s. In many countries, policy makers and politicians began to consider alternative pension scheme solutions. The 'twin pressures of economic and demographic change' (Bonoli 2000: 1) were the motives most commonly referred to as governments throughout the industrialised world set about reducing their generous post-War national pension systems (Pierson 1996; Lundberg 2005). By the 1990s, most Western European nations began restructuring their national pension systems. In fact, nearly all of the Organisation for Economic Cooperation and Development (OECD) countries have reformed their national pension systems since 1990. Germany introduced a reformed system in 2001, France in 2003, and Italy and the U.K. did so in 2004 (OECD 2007; IMF 2005). These reforms, which generally entailed reducing pension benefits and/or higher retirement ages, have often met with public outcry and extensive media coverage. Large demonstrations and even strikes against proposed changes in national pension systems occurred, for instance, in France and Italy in 2003.[1] This was, however, not the case in Sweden, where a new and fundamentally different national pension system was constructed relatively swiftly and quietly.

'Studying Through' Sweden's Pension Policy

My approach was inspired by the notion of 'studying through' a policy (Reinhold, in Shore and Wright 1997: 14) and the idea of attempting to grasp 'the interactions (and disjunctions) between different sites or levels in the policy processes' (Shore and Wright 1997: 14). Following Hannerz (2001), I defined three 'fields within the field' that represent the production, distribution and receiving levels of the current national pension system in Sweden. In the subfield of the production of policy, my interest focused on the origins of the particular design of our new pension system. My aim was to examine the construction of the pension scheme, why it was designed the way it was, and how the policy process began. Legislation on the current national pension system follows the fundamental reform suggestions published in a 1994 parliamentary committee report (SOU 1994: 20).[2] The parliamentary committee consisted of ten elected politicians (representatives from all seven parties represented in parliament at the time), six 'experts' and six individuals who worked as committee secretaries, all of whom I contacted and interviewed about the making of the pension system.

In order to study the distribution of the policy, I obtained access to the two government bureaucracies in charge of administering the pension system. While observing the work of a group of bureaucrats charged with developing the new communication policy and plan for the national pension system, I became a familiar face in the corridors of the two pension bureaucracies. After a while, I found myself being able to participate in other groups and meetings at different levels within the hierarchy of the bureaucracies, all the way up to the top level among director generals, heads of departments and cabinet ministers.

The third subfield of this attempt to 'study through' Sweden's national pension system placed me at the receiving end of the policy. During the summer of 2005, I hit the road with my car and camping-trailer to 'collect voices' about the pension system from Swedish citizens all over the country.[3] I stopped to interview people in city squares, parks and markets; at cafes and stores; at festivals, beaches and in their gardens. This ad hoc approach resulted in a collection of eighty-three different voices from 'ordinary Swedes' expressing emotions and attitudes as well as accounts of practices concerning the national pension system. The collections of voices are part of my attempt to study all the way through Sweden's national pension system and as a way to 'engage ethnographically with emerging resonances of society' (Holmes 2006: 6).

The Politics of Pension Systems

Pensions became a highly politicised subject in Sweden during the 1950s. After heated political debates, a public referendum (in 1957) and a close-call round of votes in parliament (in 1958), the ATP system (whose full name is *Allmän tilläggspension,* or National Supplementary Pensions Scheme) came into effect in 1963. The reform came to be seen as the one great and symbolic success, 'the crown jewel', of Swedish Social Democratic welfare policy (Lundberg 2003; 2005; Åmark 2005; Elmér 1960). But the ATP reform came to be used, through a defining political struggle, by both the Social Democratic Party and the parties on the right wing as a political tool. To the conservative opponents of the reform, it came to symbolise 'everything that was wrong with the Swedish Social Democratic welfare state model' (Kangas, Lundberg and Ploug 2006: 14). The ATP system, arguably one of the most generous pension schemes in the world, was an earnings-related benefit in which the pension level was calculated on the basis of the fifteen best annual incomes out of thirty in total. The retirement age was set at sixty-five and pensioners were expected to receive the equivalent to around sixty per cent of their previous salary in pension benefits. It was a typical post-Second World War pension scheme built on the assumption that Sweden's national growth of around four per cent would continue indefinitely.

Sweden's new national pension system – designed, legislated upon and launched between 1991 and 1999 – is both the result of political consensus and of political negotiation. Fundamental political differences were bridged by a common aim to construct a new national pension system, while the unusual construction of combining redistribution and funding into one national pension system was the result of political negotiation within the parliamentary committee (Palme 2001; Lundberg 2003). The new system is a universal, defined-contribution and earnings-related pension system. 'Universal' here simply means that the national pension system is designed to include all citizens. 'Defined contribution' means that the payments into the system are fixed – in this particular case at 18.5 per cent of each citizen's taxable monthly income – throughout a person's working life: 16 per cent of this goes to the redistributory part called the income pension and 2.5 per cent to the funded part of the system, the premium pension.

This pension scheme consists of three different parts: the income pension, the premium pension and the guaranteed pension. The income and premium pensions are earnings-related, that is, the size of pension benefits in these parts is adjustable in relation to the demographic and economic conditions that determine the financial development of the entire pension system. The third part, the guaranteed pension, designed to provide basic security for those with little or no income, is financed directly by the tax revenue of the central government budget. Income pensions and guaranteed pensions are administered by the Social Insurance Agency and the premium pension by the Premium Pension Authority (PPM).

To sum up, the main differences between Sweden's previous and current national pension systems are that in the former, pensions were fixed and payments to it were adjustable, while in the latter, payments to it are fixed and pensions are adjustable. A novelty with the current pension system design is that each individual's pension benefits are based upon the sum of an entire life of employment and that each person makes an individual choice regarding what age he or she wants (or is able) to retire from the age of sixty-one with no upper limit. Another important novelty is the funded premium reserve part of the pension system involving an annual, mandatory and individual placement in up to five funds as part of one's future pension. There are approximately 800 different funds, consisting of shares and/or interest-bearing securities, both domestic and international, registered with the PPM. If no choice is made, the person's contribution is, by default, pooled to one particular global share-fund. Yet another novelty introduced in the new national pension system was the government's decision to annually send out individual pension information to each Swedish citizen.

Sweden's national pension system is now constructed so that it is a closed financial and self-regulating system where nothing more than what is paid into it is paid out. The system is revised every year and if the intricate equation does not add up, the entire pension system is 'automatically balanced' and pensions are lowered so that the incomes and expenditures of the pension system do add up. Each individual's lifetime income and years of employment regulates that person's level of pension in the future, as does the nation's 'economic growth', demographic statistics and each citizen's ability to place part of his or her future pension on a global stock market. The technicalities of the pension scheme mean that responsibility for the difficult political decision of adjusting pension levels with the design of the current system is divided and relocated to both an individual level (where it is up to each citizen to secure his or her future pension) and to the distant national and global economic level of demography, growth rates and market mechanisms.

The Depoliticisation of Pensions

Before illustrating how some of the technicalities of the new system work to relocate responsibility and agency, let us take a closer look at how Sweden's national pension system was moved from the political sphere, where it had previously been located. The producers of the pension system were pleased with their product. The interviews with the members of the parliamentary Pension Committee system were filled with exclamations describing it aesthetically as: 'fantastic', 'genial', 'graceful' and 'awesome'. In the words of Anna Hedborg, one of two Social Democratic representatives in the pension committee: 'What seduced me, as an economist, investigator and social constructor was the beauty of the way that the system would buffer its own reserves in a perfectly obvious way.' Highlighting their political differences, Social Democrat Hedborg is sometimes called 'red Anna', while the committee's conservative party representative, Margit Gennser, is referred to as 'blue Margit' by other committee members.

But a comment by 'red Anna' illustrated how such political differences were set aside. Reflecting on her supposedly 'blue' opponent Gennser, she remarked: 'She gets totally seduced by a logical enough line of reasoning. And so do I. So we found each other, often enough, while putting together the logic. We could, from our different viewpoints, ascertain what the logic in the system demanded.' Other members of the pension committee bore witness to the fact that the political opponents came to mutual understandings on the fundamentals of the pension system by setting aside party politics to agree on technical solutions from an economic perspective. The 'red' and 'blue' politicians were talked about in admiring terms by their committee colleagues as being 'extremely intelligent individuals who saw the craft of engineering within the pension system', and further: 'there were analyses and conclusions drawn seemingly not at all directed by party political interests. Instead there were intellectual logic and analyses and an interest in finding the best solutions'.

The view of the national pension system's constructors had seemingly narrowed their concerns to the well-being of the system itself. They agreed that a self-regulating, automatic and autonomous financial system would be the best solution for Sweden. Being 'stable' and 'robust' were the unanimously agreed criteria that defined the political success of the system. Conservative politician Gennser offered her explanation of the term 'robust': 'It simply means that the system is symmetric, and that it is a closed system. It is genial!' One of the Left Party's representatives, Per Lennart Börjesson, explained that: 'What creates the stability, from the state's perspective, is that there is a connection between assets and liabilities. The real and most important change is that we created a system where the payments out of it are decided by how much goes into it.'

What these accounts from the architects of the new pension system highlighted is how the once highly politicised and contested issue of national pensions seems to have been shifted to a seemingly apolitical sphere where political opponents agree that what is important is the architecture of the system itself rather than its overall implications and consequences for those on the receiving end. The way in which the pension system was removed from the political sphere is perhaps best illustrated through a closer look at the world of pension system technocrats. During my fieldwork, I 'shadowed' (Czarniawska 2007) one of the inventors of several of the technical solutions within the current pension system design. This part of my fieldwork took me to sites within the executive levels of the pension system bureaucracy as well as the corridors and closed seminar-rooms at the Ministry of Health and Social Services, as well as a couple of after-hours bar sessions, where more informal discussions of pension system designs took place among a small elite group of pension system technocrats.

What is explained here, from the technocratic point of view, is that decisions made by elected politicians are not stable and reliable, but instead undermine and destroy the work of the economists and technocrats. As one pension technocrat remarked at a hearing at the Ministry of Health and Social Services: 'This pension reform means that we now have a financially stabile system. And I think that is good, because the political decisions about pensions have not represented any stability at all.' The previously political decisions on pension levels are now to be 'formalised', as one of the economists in the pension committee opined, in order to avoid 'ad hoc decision making in Parliament'. After an intense afternoon involving considerable disagreement over the benefits of the technicality, a handful of senior officials and technocrats decided to 'cool off' by having a few beers at a nearby pub. A discussion of decision making in the sphere of pensions soon took off around the small table in a corner of the pub:

> 'With this system the politicians have at least admitted that they are not good at making economic decisions.'
> 'Right, with this we have tied them to the mast.'
> 'Yes, let's see if it works.'
> 'Yeah, because regulations are, in fact, now being made in the parliament in an unpleasant way.'
> 'And that is why having as much automation as possible is good, because otherwise they will want to get their fingers into this.'

By making the national pension system an automatic and self-regulating financial system based on defined contribution, the architects of the system – politicians, experts and technocrats – constructed it to appear as somehow beyond the sphere of politics. The political representatives seemed pleased to be relieved of the burden of uncomfortable decision making concerning future pension levels, while pension system technocrats seemed equally pleased to have removed the politicians from this previously political sphere altogether.

Causing Anxiety and Distrust

However, people at the receiving end of the policy were not quite so happy. Many of those that I talked to expressed a significant lack of trust and confidence towards both the politicians responsible for changing the pension system and towards the design of the pension system itself. Some of the individuals I met and talked to explicitly expressed their lack of trust in the politicians after the introduction of the new national pension system. They reasoned that the politicians in charge merely look after themselves: 'I have absolutely no faith in this. They changed it so that it was good for the state, for the government, but not for us' says one notably upset woman in her forties who I interviewed in central Gothenburg. The owner of a restaurant in a small town in Västergötland took a break to talk to me about the pension system. Towards the end of the interview, he got upset and slammed the palm of his hand on the top of the table: 'I don't trust this pension system at all! I have realised that my pension is not secured at all. I think the politicians have gotten away very easy here ... They give absolutely no guarantees at all now.'

My old car broke down several times during the interview journey. Once it refused to leave central Örebro and, while waiting for the delivery of a necessary spare part, I took the opportunity to interview a man who had stopped to help me. At one point he threw up his arms in the air, exclaiming: 'OK. So the politicians are not capable of dealing with the economy ... They don't understand those things. So how the hell are the rest of us going to understand it all?' Up in north Sweden, in Jämtland, I spent an evening talking to a young couple who had decided to try a different pace and lifestyle, leaving their city life to run a small inn in what seemed like the middle of nowhere. The woman, who was in her early thirties, said: 'I have many years left to retirement, and things will change several times before then. I feel as if the politicians admitted to not being able to handle this with the pensions, and now they tell us to sort this out for ourselves.' The young man expressed his distrust in political decision making: 'I cursed the government when this was introduced. I thought they had lost grip on things totally. They had no control over our future pension money, so they handed over the entire responsibility for that to us. And we only had ourselves to blame if we couldn't take care of it. That's when I decided to get a private savings account. The pension system constantly reminds me about the fact that the state has lost its grip of things. I certainly don't think I will get by on anything coming from the state in the future.'

The design of Sweden's national pension system effectively divided and relocated the responsibility of future pension benefits to a technological sphere of self-regulating automation within the system while simultaneously handing over the responsibility and agency to each individual citizen. While both policy makers seem satisfied with their construction, it appears that citizens regard this as a political 'cop out' that feeds a sense of distrust and hostility towards politicians and the government in general.

Opening Up the 'Black Box' of Pensions

A closer analysis of the technicalities that work to relocate the responsibility within Sweden's current national pension system reveal that a dual shift has occurred, taking agency away from the political sphere to a sphere of both automatised mathematical calculations that I call 'out there' or 'elsewhere' and to a sphere of individual life choices and personal capabilities that I call 'in here'. The particular design of the technical solutions and the decision-making process that precede the solutions is erased and neutralised once the technicalities are in place. From a Foucauldian perspective, the technicalities of the national pension system can be viewed as 'political technologies' that disguise a political problem in a seemingly neutral language of science and technique (Foucault 1991: 99; Dreyfus and Rabinow 1982: 196). As we shall see, statistics also play an important role here, especially in the technicalities that work to relocate agency elsewhere – as Foucault (1991: 99) has observed in other contexts. Numbers, as Theodore Porter argues (1995: 8), often work to disguise the political and the ideological under the cloak of neutrality and scientific objectivity.

The technicalities within the national pension system can also be seen in terms of the 'black boxes' metaphor that Latour uses to describe those scientifically created artifacts – such as a law or a technology – that no one is able to take apart or look into (Latour 1987). Three such 'black boxes' of Sweden's national pension system are the adjustable indexation, the automatic balancing and the annuity divisor. Two of the technicalities – the adjustable indexation and the automatic balancing – regulate the pension system in terms of assets and liabilities. That is, they insure that 'nothing more than what is paid into it is paid out', as the government's information leaflets explain, by connecting it to 'growth' and 'how well Sweden does'. A third technique, the annuity divisor, links the pension system to statistical calculations of the population and prognoses of average life expectancy.

The numerical construction called the 'adjustable indexation' connects the calculations of pension levels to an index based on the development of average income levels in Sweden. In other words, when the entire income pension system is revised at the end of each year, the recalculation of the pension levels is based on statistics of the average income growth in Sweden, but is adjusted using the growth norm so as to smoothen out the edges of the changes. So, in effect, the pension levels are linked to both calculations of changes in income levels and of price levels in society.

Per, one of the inventors of the adjustable indexation, described how the group of technocrats came up with the idea of linking the pension system to both an income-index and a price-index. In an interview, he recalled how the group of technocrats wanted to use an average income index in their preliminary calculations on how the new pension system would work, but that the politicians 'did not dare' to legislate on using an income index, since it 'created unpleasant waves in the system'. Per then 'came to the realisation that we could take the bottom-line of every individual's contributions and entitlements ... It was then entirely possible to calculate the pension debt without looking ahead at all'. And, concludes Per: 'This led to the system being accountable and without forward projection. It totally disregards everything surrounding it.'

The technicality officially called the automatic balancing is popularly dubbed 'the Brake'. This equation annually balances the input to the pension system with the output, thus effectively relocating the responsibility for adjusting pension levels to a seemingly neutral and apolitical equation while simultaneously shifting the financial risk from the pension system to the individual citizen. One of the 'experts' on the Pension Committee explained it as 'a method to quickly and smoothly get the system to follow the national economy. This means that the risk for the insured is altered. It means stability in the system'.

At a strategy meeting, pension bureaucrats discussed what would happen when 'the Brake' hits and reduces pension levels:

'Journalists can sense when something is going on and it will be an opportunity for them to put pressure on the politicians. They will want to see if someone begins to shiver.'

'In Sweden we are not used to things happening without the politicians making the decisions. Well, they did make a decision a long time ago ... but not now. It is going to be interesting to see how they react.'

'I have told the politicians to do the footwork now. They have to talk with their party members.'

'Yes, the Founding Fathers have to get back on track now. They have to be there when the wind begins to blow too. They have to stand up and say: "This is how we planned it. What happens now is nothing strange".'

'The Problem' of Longevity

My third example of a technology that masks a political relocation of responsibility (and risk) for pension benefits and recasts it in the shape of a seemingly neutral and statistical 'black box' is the 'annuity divisor'. The annuity divisor divides the pension fund, adjusted and balanced through the previous techniques, by the amount of individuals who are to share it. To get around the problem that officials cannot know how many years each individual pensioner will live – and therefore how many years the fund must last – statistics are used to determine the average life expectancy, which is then divided by the pension funds accordingly. Put simply, when more people live longer, each one get a smaller share of the pension pot. With the help of the annuity divisor, regulating the pension levels to the demography is no longer a political decision but the result of a calculation.

The situation often called 'the problem of an ageing population' has been the subject of much debate among politicians in most European countries during the past decade (see, e.g., Pierson 1996; Bonoli 2000). It refers to the fact that people live longer and if they do not also work longer, the pension systems created fifty years ago will crumble under the pressure of an increasing amount of years of pension payments. The problem of longevity in Sweden is, with an intricate formula, made quite literally into a problem of the ageing population, since it is the pensioners themselves who solve the situation by receiving a reduced pension, which is now divided into increasingly smaller shares.

Börjesson, the Left Party's first representative in the pension committee, explained the technique in a straightforward manner: 'We live too long, so there is less per year. That is what creates the stability in the system. It is contradictory to the principle [of the previous pension system] of counting on a certain pension in relation to one's salary.'

One pension system technocrat explained the effects on future pension levels as people are expected to live longer: 'Those born in 1990 will live forty-one months longer than those born in 1940. That is, if the prognoses from the Swedish National Central Statistical Bureau come true. Based on this, the scenario is that pensions will be lowered from sixty-five per cent of average income to fifty-five per cent. Just on the effects of the increased average life expectancy. But that can be done away with if people work longer.'

These two accounts reveal how the economic responsibility and demographic risk of lower pensions, thanks to the annuity divisor, has shifted away from the arena of political decision making to the individual citizen. The comments on how people can compensate for lower pension levels by working longer highlights how the uncomfortable political decision of raising the retirement age is built into the very construction of Sweden's current pension system and is hidden within an intricate equation. This also shows how the responsibility for securing one's level of future pension benefits has also shifted to the individual citizen.

Creating Responsible Individuals

The design of the system makes each citizen's life choices important for the outcome of his or her future pension. Each seemingly private consideration of whether one should get married, have a second child, get another degree or file for divorce now matter, since the level of each individual's future income pension is based on the sum of a life's taxable income. Correspondingly, within the funded part of the national pension system, the individualisation of decision making and responsibility is particularly explicit. The official government information published by the PPM is personal and direct, communicating and promoting individual agency and personal responsibility when choosing the right fund in which to place part of one's future pension capital. The official website of the government authority in charge of the funded part of the pension system underlines the theme of individual responsibility. The headline and three bullet points read:

> The size of your premium pension is determined by three factors:
> The amount of money paid into your premium pension account.
> Value fluctuations and withdrawal fees for the funds that you choose to invest your premium pension money in.
> At what age you decide to draw your pension.

The individual pension information, which is sent out annually, illustrates this new emphasis on personal choice and responsibility. This process, by which state agencies seek to make the individual citizen aware of his or her personal responsibility in what was formerly the concern of the government, exemplifies what sociologist Nikolas Rose has termed 'responsibilisation' (Rose 1999: 139ff) and is typical of the new norms of conduct that are associated with neoliberal forms of governance.

As the new pension system was created, politicians agreed on the importance of sending out annual written information on the pension legislation to each citizen. The political representatives and the experts of the Pension Committee describe, in various ways and using different terms, how an idea of 'a general public education' was embedded within the construction of the new national pension system. Every spring, more than six million Swedes receive a bright orange envelope from the government. The colourful envelope contains various prognoses, in exact figures, about each citizen's expected future pension. The variations of the prognoses show different levels of expected GNP growth depending on the age that one chooses to retire. The envelope also contains a page that shows the accumulated value of both the recipient's income pension and his or her premium pension, as well as a printed statement of the funds in which he or she has chosen to place part of his or her future pension, and of the value they held on the last day of the past year. Also included in the orange envelope is the government decision stating how much pension credits he or she is to be granted for his or her last taxable annual income. There is also an informational text explaining how the national pension system works and what factors influence the level of each citizen's future pension. Stated here are the three factors of 'your income', 'the economic growth' and 'when you retire'.

The orange envelope soon became a symbol and a successful trademark of Sweden's national pension system, and it works as an instrument of governance aimed at teaching the Swedish citizens to take individual responsibility for their own future pension. The orange envelope works as a messenger, carrying disciplining messages from state to citizen. Based on the texts and figures in the orange envelope, it might be concluded that the messages are: 'Work more. Earn more. Save money. Learn how to invest in funds.' The producers of the national pension system talk about the importance of teaching people to handle the novelties of the system and raising the level of public knowledge about the pension system and about the idea of the pension system. For the example, the Conservative Party representative Margit Gennser brought up issues of 'learning processes' and what the politicians of the Pension Committee hoped that the pension system would teach the citizens:

> One of the reasons Sweden did so well in the industrialisation was that we, thanks to the primary education code of the mid nineteenth century, got a literate population. And now we have a pension system leading the way. We now learn how to see certain economic contexts. And we learn that others cannot create welfare for us, but that we actually need to participate in that too. And we learn to see how much we ourselves must save for the future. But I believe it is a learning process and what may seem very difficult now will not become standard until, perhaps, in ten or fifteen years.

Another veteran member of the Pension Committee, a nonpolitical representative, reasoned around the same lines:

> There seemed to be, from the conservatives and the center party, a certain interest in of educating the people with the premium reserve part of the pension system. They wanted to create an interest in that sort of capital accumulation. I'd say they wanted to make the Swedish people into little capitalists and shareholders in general.

During an interview with one of the old-timers within the pension bureaucracy of the Social Security Agency, a bureaucrat who had worked with the pension system and its information since the very beginning revealingly talked about the governing function of the national pension system. Illustrating how the very construction of the national pension system in general, and in particular the government information concerning it, work as instruments of governance in a process of responsibilisation, he talked about how the aim of the state authority should be to get people to think about their individual responsibility for future pensions:

> The responsibility must be made clear. It is their own responsibility. No one should be able to come and complain about their low pension if they have been bumming around the world for several years instead of working. So, it is about informing people what they themselves can do to affect the size of their pension. People should, in an intuitive way, understand in order to comply. People will not want to lower their standard of living when retiring, so I think they will choose to work longer.

Politicians, bureaucrats and technocrats alike seem to be more or less clear about how the design of Sweden's national pension system works to relocate the responsibility and agency of future pensions away from the political decision making to both seemingly apolitical numerical constructions and to the individual citizen, and further how the financial risk that a national pension system entails rests with the individual as opposed to the state.

The Meaning of 'Ought to'

At the receiving end of the national pension system, ordinary Swedes talked candidly about the new responsibility the Swedish state has loaded them with, symbolised in the bright orange envelopes that arrive each spring. Most people I met and interviewed during that cross-country journey said that their reaction on receiving the orange envelope was to open it, briefly scan its content and then save it in one way or another. One woman in her forties that I met in a small town in southern Sweden said what many others phrased in similar ways: 'When that orange envelope arrives I open it and look inside. I don't exactly throw myself at it though. And I still don't know how much I will receive the day I retire.' A young man I stopped to talk to on a parking lot outside a huge shopping centre in Halland shook his head when I asked him what he did with his orange envelopes: 'I just get depressed when that notice arrives. And there's not much one can do about it. I just bury it in a pile of papers somewhere.' At a camping ground by a lake in Västmanland, I sat down to talk to a couple in their fifties. They were having coffee in the shade outside their camper and took turns as they got involved in talking about the pension system in general. When I asked them what they usually did with their orange envelopes, the woman quickly and quite animatedly responded, speaking for both of them: 'The orange envelopes? Well, we open them and we look inside and then we say: "Oh, my God! How are we to survive on this?!" And then we throw them away and deny we ever saw them.'

While conducting the interview-study among ordinary Swedes, one particular expression kept coming up spontaneously and with surprising frequency in the interviews – the words 'ought to'. People kept telling me things like: 'I ought to know more', 'I ought to do more', 'I ought to be more active' and 'I ought to save more'. Here is what a young man, a university student still only in his twenties, told me as I began asking him about his thoughts on the pension system. Carefully choosing his words, he said slowly: 'It all seems so far away, but I feel I ought to get more informed about this. It's all in the back of my head somewhere, and I do know where I put those papers. So, I know where the papers are and I know I ought to get involved, but no one I know talks about these things and I don't think anyone does anything either, and the information is too difficult anyway.'

A woman in her mid thirties who I sat down to talk to at a lakeside child-friendly beach illustrated well the recurring use of the phrase 'ought to'. We were both monitoring our children who were playing in the shallow water and she punctuated her thoughts on the national pension system with heavy sighs: 'I don't know where to begin. It's as if those who know of stocks and such have an advantage. Oh, it's embarrassing to be so ignorant about all this. When I've been into the bank I actually feel like getting involved in it. I know I ought to and they make it seem so easy, but I still don't do anything.'

What the frequent and varied use of 'ought to' might indicate is that the Swedes have understood that the responsibility for their own pension has been handed to them through the design of the current national pension system. An additional meaning of 'ought to' might be that the process of responsibilisation has not been completed, since the individual citizen still struggles with what to actually do with this novel responsibility handed to them. A man that I met in a harbour town in the most southern part of the country seemed to express something along those lines. I caught him and his friend at their lunch break, and his remarks were stressed by the eager nods that his friend kept doing across the table at the outdoor restaurant where I found them: 'I'm afraid I don't know that much about the pension system. I ought to though. But I don't know anything about the pension system or how it works. But I'm self-employed so I really ought to know more. But I've really tried to get involved in all this. I've tried to get my act together and do something about it; I've talked to people at the bank and at the insurance company about this, but they are sellers and not advisors.'

I suggest that one interpretation of the frequent reoccurrence of the expression 'ought to' among Swedish citizens who talk about the national pension system is that people are aware of the demands and expectations that are being placed upon them from the state, but they generally do not – at least not yet – act upon them. This gap between knowing and doing is highlighted by the particular expression 'ought to'. An additional aspect of the phrase 'ought to' might be that it is an expression of bad conscience, that is the person knows of his or her new responsibility but has not yet acted upon it and feels a little bad for not having done so.

Conclusion: Insecure Outcomes of New Forms of Governance

'Ought to' seems to imply that a responsibilisation process among Swedish citizens is, in fact, underway. However, the outcomes of such a process are still unclear. The questions of what happens at the receiving end of responsibilisation still remain to be answered. What happens if individuals understand but do not accept that they have been handed a responsibility that was previously held by the state? Embedded in the policy design are expectations that the individual citizen will choose, for instance, to work more, earn more, save more, retire later and learn how to invest in funds in order to secure his or her future pension. What happens if citizens do not act as they are supposed to? While some of the effects of a national pension system, such as the received level of pension benefits, are hidden in the distant future, others might already be detected. Increased public distrust in political decision makers, a devaluation of the collective as each citizen must now look out for himself or herself, a greater level of anxiety and a sense of insecurity in relation to the national security system – these might be some of the 'unexpected' effects of the depoliticisation and responsibilisation inscribed in Sweden's new national pension system.

Sweden's national pension system is seen as a political technology that recast formerly political issues as apolitical and technical concerns, and simultaneously made each individual citizen personally responsible for something that the state had previously handled. Such forms of governance may, as we have seen, come in the shape of intricate equations as well as orange-coloured envelopes. They are masked as neutral mathematical constructions and are presented as objective government information to the public. In either instance, these political technologies of Sweden's national pension system are, as Dreyfus and Rabinow suggest, 'taking what is essentially a political problem, removing it from the realm of political discourse, and recasting it in the neutral language of science' (1982: 196).

The change in governance that the political technologies help to advance is one that shifts responsibility from the political arena to a sphere of abstract automation on the one hand and to the individual citizen on the other. In doing so, the relations between actors involved in this policy process are altered. We have seen how elected politicians are pleased to be relieved of the burden of making difficult decisions concerning pension levels. In addition, we have heard how technocrats of the pension system seem equally relieved and pleased with the fact that formerly political decisions about the national pension system now have been relocated to technicalities designed by them within the system.

The forms of governance that relocate agency away from the political sphere are significantly less communicated than the forms of governance that work to relocate responsibility for future pensions to the individual level. The technologies that are designed to promote the processes of individualisation and responsibilisation carry disciplinary messages from the state about the desired conduct of the citizens. However, whether a process of public education is underway is not certain. What my interviews with Swedish citizens hint at is that many seem to have understood that there is a new element of individual responsibility embedded in the construction of the pension system; exactly what this means and what they can, should and are able to do to secure their financial situation in a distant future is, however, not as clear. And even if people understand what they should and can do in order to secure their future pension, they also understand that there are a number of other factors over whch they have absolutely no control that significantly affect each citizen's level of pension.

It might be said that one of the effects of the major restructuring of an important social security policy in a nation famed for its welfare system is, quite paradoxically, a dispersion of a sense of insecurity.

Notes

1. See, e.g., 'Workers March Through Paris to protest Pension Reform', *New York Times*, 26 May 2003; 'Italians Protest Pension Reform', *Deutche Welle*, 12 June 2003; 'Italians Protest at Pension Reforms', *BBC News*, 24 October 2003.
2. SOU is short for *Statens offentliga utredningar* – the Swedish Government Official Reports.
3. I owe the conceptualisation of this interview study as 'a collection of voices' rather than research interviews to Daniel Rothenberg and his monograph *With These Hands* (1998).

References

Åmark, Klas. 2005. *Hundra år av välfärdspolitik: Välfärdens framväxt i Sverige och Norge*. Umeå: Boréa förlag.

Bonoli, Giuliano. 2000. *The Politics of Pension Reform: Institutions and Policy Change in Western Europe*. Cambridge: Cambridge University Press.

Czarniawska, Barbara. 2007. *Shadowing and Other Techniques for Doing Fieldwork in Modern Societies*. Malmö: Liber.

Dreyfus, Hubert L. and Paul Rabinow. 1982. *Michel Foucault Beyond Structuralism and Hermeneutics*. Chicago: University of Chicago Press.

Elmér, Åke. 1960. *Folkpensioneringen i Sverige med särskild hänsyn till ålderspensioneringen*. Lund: Gleerups förlag.

Foucault, Michel. 1991. 'Governmentality', in Gordon Burchell, Colin Gordon and Peter Miller (eds), *The Foucault Effect. Studies in Governmentality*. Chicago: University of Chicago Press.

Hannerz, Ulf. 2001. *Flera fält I ett. Socialantropologer om translokala fältstudier*. Stockholm: Carlssons förlag.

Holmes, Douglas R. 2000. Integral Europe: Fast-Capitalism, Multiculturalism, Neofascism. Princeton, N.J.: Princeton University Press.

IMF. 2005. *Ageing and Pension System Reform: Implications for Financial Markets and Economic Policies*. IMF Report Series, September.

Kangas, Olli, Urban Lundberg and Niels Ploug. 2006. *Three Routes to a Pension Reform. Politics and Institutions in Reforming Pensions in Denmark, Finland and Sweden*. Report 2006: 10. Stockholm: Institute for Future Studies.

Latour, Bruno. 1987. *Science in Action*. Cambridge, MA: Harvard University Press.

Lundberg, Urban. 2003. *Juvelen i kronan. Socialdemokraterna och den allmänna pensionen*. Stockholm: Hjalmarson & Högberg Bokförlag.

———. 2005. 'Social Democracy Lost: The Social Democratic Party in Sweden and the Politics of Pension Reform, 1978–1998', in E. Carroll and L. Eriksson (eds), *Welfare Politics Cross-Examined: Eclecticist Analytical Perspectives on Sweden and the Developed World, from the 1880s to the 2000s*. Amsterdam: Aksant Academic Publishers, pp.117–45.

OECD. 2007. *Pensions at a Glance. Public Policies Across OECD Countries*. Paris: OECD Publishing.

Palme, Joakim (ed.). 2001. *Hur blev den stora kompromissen möjlig? Politiken bakom den svenska pensionsreformen*. Stockholm: Pensions Forum.

Pierson, Paul. 1996. 'The New Politics of the Welfare State', *World Politics* 48(2): 143–79.

Porter, Theodore. 1995. *Trust in Numbers: The Pursuit of Objectivity in Science and Public Life*. Princeton, NJ: Princeton University Press.

Rose, Nikolas. 1999. *Powers of Freedom. Reframing Political Thought*. Cambridge: Cambridge University Press.

Rothenberg, Daniel. 1998. *With These Hands. The Hidden World of Migrant Farmworkers Today*. Berkeley: University of California Press.

Shore, Cris and Susan Wright (eds). 1997. *Anthropology of Policy. Critical Perspectives on Governance and Power*. New York: Routledge.

SOU. 1994. *Reformerat Pensionssystem*. Stockholm: Socialdepartementet.

SECTION III

SUBJECTS OF POLICY: CONSTRUCTION AND CONTESTATION

Introduction

Davide Però

This volume has so far addressed two key aspects of the anthropology of policy: first, the ways in which policy processes connect different sites and scales (local, national, supranational) in order to reveal the way power operates and the broader political systems in which polices are embedded; and, secondly, the ways in which the study of local manifestations of policy can serve as a vantage point for examining deeper historical changes in the structures of governance that shape people's lives. This part of the book addresses a third set of questions, namely those concerning the role played by the governed in the everyday shaping of policies devised by powerful institutions to organise individuals, their behaviour and their social relations. Whereas much of the international relations and political science literature tends to assume that subjects are passively constructed by the policies that act upon them, here we examine how policy recipients actively negotiate and contest the policies of the powerful. As John Clarke pointed out, sometimes people are 'recalcitrant' to governmental efforts to construct them in particular ways. They 'refuse to "know their place"' (2005: 460) and they contest and redefine the terms of the policy that acts upon them. Given their traditional interest in people's lived experiences, anthropologists are well positioned to examine how policy recipients – including subaltern or dissenting groups – engage with and impact on the life of a policy.

At a time when neoliberal regimes have deepened social divisions within and between borders, it is especially important to include the policy engagements of the governed when we study policies directed at disadvantaged groups or geographical regions. Attention to how subaltern groups engage with policy can help shed light on the nature and the working of such neoliberal policy processes and regimes, and on how they can be influenced, resisted or challenged most effectively.

In the following chapters, the policy engagement of subaltern and dissenting groups is addressed through case studies which differ in focus and scale. In terms of focus, the chapters range from protests against nuclear waste dumping in Italy (Zinn) to strategic participation in supranational policy making concerning genetically modified crops (Müller), and from ethnic minority associations' negotiating regulations that limit their activities (Kugelberg) to migrant workers' collective action in the fields of housing, immigration and employment policy across Europe (Però). In terms of scale, the chapters range from the 'local' small town level (Kugelberg) to the 'global'/supranational level (Müller) via the combined analysis of large cities (Però) and regional areas (Zinn).

These chapters are connected by two main interrelated themes that I call the dynamics of 'bridling' and 'unbridling'. The first refers to the neoliberal state's efforts to bring under control or neutralise civic organisations and individuals, especially when these challenge its policies. The second refers to the efforts of these organisations and individuals to 'break free' and articulate alternative visions and policy agendas. A central question in the debate over bridling addressed in the following chapters is: how does the neoliberal state seek to involve civil society organisations in the making and implementation of policy in ways that simultaneously extract legitimisation from them while producing their political quiescence?

The problematic involvement of civil society in policy-making mechanisms is well illustrated by Clarissa Kugelberg, who discusses bridling dynamics by exploring the domesticating and exploitative character of the integration policy for ethnic minorities of the Swedish state. Ethnic minority associations, as a condition of receiving government funds, have to: (i) comply with regulations restricting the range of their initiatives; (ii) demonstrate that they are actively contributing to the state's national and local integration policies; and (iii) subject themselves to its bureaucratic scrutiny. This policy significantly affects the activity and the ambitions of the women's association that Kugelberg studies. These women inhabit a transnational space but the nationalist character of the policy prevents them from operating in such a space. They have to abandon their goal of engaging in international cooperation and fulfilling their responsibilities to help women in Africa. Kugelberg illustrates how the self-governing (or self-censoring) of such ethnic minority organisations is reinforced by the state's audit procedures. In a context of public spending cuts, market-based solutions are introduced in order to manage the relationship between government and civil society.

Birgit Müller examines a well disguised effort to co-opt civil society organisations into the United Nations' Food and Agricultural Organisation (FAO) and its policy-formulation activity on biotechnologies to enhance legitimisation and deflate dissent. Through a discussion of policies which the FAO typically presents as rational, scientific and representative of the interests of all the parties concerned, Müller shows how these policies in reality tend to favour the interests of the most powerful. Drawing on Foucault, she critiques the professed political neutrality of the FAO and its claims to have created a mechanism that reconciles the competing interests of such diverse interlocutors as farmers, multinational corporations and environmentalist nongovernmental organisations (NGOs).

Bridling dynamics are also examined by Davide Però, who discusses the use of policy as a mechanism for co-opting and controlling interest groups and minorities. His first case study concerns the supposedly progressive, multicultural and democratic immigration policy of the City Council of Bologna. Their management of a residential centre, far from empowering migrant workers as claimed, was driven by cost-saving and managerial priorities. His second case study concerns the socialist municipality of Barcelona and the limited and conditional support that 'pro-migrant' NGOs offered migrants who protested against a new restrictive immigration law introduced by the right-wing Spanish government.

Dorothy Zinn's chapter differs from the others as it does not discuss a policy developed with the intention of bridling civil society through co-optation but through an authoritarian use of state powers. Through her study of the right-wing Italian government's attempt to establish a nuclear waste storage facility in the southern Italian region of Basilicata, Zinn reminds us how neoliberal policy implementation not only entails 'soft' strategies to involve civil society organisations (often in co-optative ways) but also authoritarian and top-down use of the coercive apparatuses of the state.

Taken together, these chapters illustrate how the new governmental relationship between the neoliberal state and civil society, despite its participatory and empowering rhetoric of governance, often works to disempower, co-opt, neutralise or marginalise the disadvantaged sectors of the population in practice. In particular, they reveal how policy – which is presented as good, democratic, authoritative, rational and techno-scientific – is a profoundly political technology which serves the interests of powerful groups and is often detrimental to subaltern groups, who may have no other option but to resist it.

The second and perhaps most important theme addressed in these chapters concerns 'unbridling', i.e. the strategies and practices that subaltern and dissenting groups adopt in the attempt to engage effectively with oppressive policy and avoid the co-optative and neutralising attempts of the state. The minority women's association studied by Kugelberg seems to accept the bridling policy restrictions that prevent it from operating transnationally. The association did not attempt to challenge or subvert the terms of the policy, although they did engage in an active process of negotiation. The association reluctantly gave in to the policy prescription in order to retain the possibility of participating in and influencing the local (Swedish) political process, and to access resources.

By contrast, the subaltern and dissenting groups described by Zinn succeeded in their unbridling efforts to disrupt the Italian government's plan to set up a nuclear waste storage facility in Scanzano. Their policy impact was achieved by simultaneously contesting the national government's plan at the institutional level (with active opposition from regional, provincial and local governments, as well as public petitions and appeals) and through mass mobilisation (by physically – but peacefully – blocking the policy implementation with marches and road and rail blocks). In contrast to the Swedish women's association, the Scanzano protest was characterised by the unbridling articulation of alternative discourses that challenged those of the national government on both techno-scientific grounds and on grounds of the local population's right to self-determination. Interestingly, the protest managed to involve sectors of the state itself (the regional and local authorities) in the articulation of its unbridling efforts.

The issue of people's policy engagement and its impact is also addressed by Però. Each of his cases in Bologna, Barcelona and London highlights the importance of migrants finding appropriate 'allies' and developing unbridling strategies that enable them to turn small-scale undeclared resistance into large-scale public opposition if they want to influence policy. Such alliances are especially effective in enabling migrants to transcend the dominant logic of liberal multiculturalism based on narrow conceptions of ethnicity, and to link their cause to wider and more universal struggles for social and economic rights. Però argues that in order to recognise the migrants' agency and its unbridling significance, it is important to broaden the idea of policy change from below so as to include not just formal policy change – which is often hard for powerless groups like migrants to achieve – but also more modest transformations such as policy neutralisation.

Dynamics of unbridling and their 'policy impact' are further explored by Müller, who shows how civil society organisations involved in seemingly neutral and inclusionary bodies such as the FAO need careful strategising if they are to influence policy and avoid being co-opted or used to legitimise policies they do not agree with. This strategising, as Müller explains, involves actively refusing to play a merely 'technical' role in favour of a 'political' one when participating in decision-making mechanisms such as those of the FAO that she examines.

The overall point that these chapters make is that a comprehensive anthropological study of policy requires the analysis of bridling–unbridling dynamics and, in particular, of the engagements of the governed and their impact on the actual life of policy. At times, the policy impact of these engagements can be negligible or modest, while at others, it can be very substantial. In all cases, the examination of the policy engagements of the governed facilitates a more thorough and nuanced understanding of how policy works and impacts on target populations, as well as how it can be transformed, sometimes radically, by the policy subjects themselves.

References

Clarke, John. 2005. 'New Labour's Citizens: Activated, Empowered, Responsibilized, Abandoned?', *Critical Social Policy* 25(4): 447–63.

Chapter 12

The Case of Scanzano: *Raison d'État* and the Reasons for a Rebellion

Dorothy Louise Zinn

For two weeks in November 2003, a massive protest of unprecedented proportions shook the Basilicata region (Lucania) in southern Italy. The action took place as a response to Legislative Decree 314, which paved the way for a nuclear waste storage facility in the coastal town of Scanzano Jonico. The Lucanians' practices of resistance operated through the institutional actions of local politicians and non-governmental bodies, as well as through a vast mobilisation on a popular level. During the protest, which garnered widespread solidarity and participation from the inhabitants of neighbouring regions, thousands and thousands of people participated in roadblocks, demonstrations and rallies; protesters occupied the designated site for the facility and a railway station. All of this action, which culminated in the historic 'March of 100,000' of 23 November, took place in a region best known in the social sciences as the place where Edward Banfield (1958) developed his influential concept of 'amoral familism' – that the inhabitants of this land were incapable of collective action beyond the nuclear family.

The protest was widely recognised for its great composure and civicness, even by those who supported the government's position.[1] Some observers have gone so far as to speak of a 'Scanzano model' of resistance (*Carta* 2004); this is perhaps excessive, but in fact several subsequent protests have explicitly referred to Scanzano. The motivations triggering the Scanzano revolt would seem rather obvious, and in fact some government officials admitted afterwards that they had expected some reaction, but nothing like the extent of what actually occurred. Environmentalist protest and opposition are no novelty in Basilicata; with Scanzano, however, a rupture with the government took place that coagulated a spontaneous, shared and determined reaction unlike anything seen in the past. This was no longer a matter of protest by the radical Left or a handful of environmentalists, carried out largely by activists from outside the area. Instead, a vast movement was formed that cut across all lines of difference: gender, generation, politics, class and locality. Together with all of the local institutions, the people managed to organise, act and make their influence felt.

I focus here on the point of rupture between the narratives that informed and expressed the government's action on the one hand, and the discourses and practices of resistance on the part of the Lucanian population on the other hand.[2] The resistance fought the government's project not only in its technical-scientific terms but also by presenting an alternative 'moral economy' (Scott 1985; Vike 1997), effectively reconfiguring the concept of a 'common good'. The revolt of Scanzano began as an action to defend the territory, but it turned out to be strongly marked by a claim to direct participation in decision-making processes. The analysis is based on the examination of government documents and acts, journalistic accounts and my own participation (more than participant observation) in the events, as well as conversations with people actively engaged in the protest.[3]

Birth of a Decree: The Background in Earlier Policies

In order to understand the Scanzano revolt, it is necessary to trace the essential lines of the policies that led to the government's decision. What follows is a summary of the terms that shaped the nuclear waste debate, simultaneously shedding light on the state's modes of governmentality. One must bear in mind not only a context of moving towards neoliberal policies, but also a post-9/11 climate that transformed the question from one of environmental safety to one of national security.

Italy actively pursued nuclear power as an energy source in the 1960s and 1970s, but following the Chernobyl incident, a popular referendum in 1987 halted the production of nuclear energy: the four functioning reactors stopped working and the construction of two more were blocked. Even so, Italy has continued to purchase nuclear energy from France, with the agreement that it must accept a proportion of the waste; moreover, the medical, scientific and military sectors have constantly generated radioactive waste. Presently, there are some 80,000 cubic metres of nuclear waste in Italy, stored in twenty sites in various regions, eight of which are particularly significant.

In 1999, the Centre-Left government made the first moves towards liberalising energy in Italy. One of the provisions (D.L. 79, 16 March 1999, Article 13, comma 2e) sanctioned the creation of a separate company to manage the dismantling of the old nuclear reactors and the disposal of the waste. The Sogin company was formed that year, which was part public property and a member of the Enel group (Enel itself no longer held a public energy monopoly). Sogin's mission was to 'be responsible for the efficiency of the program, valorise company resources and reduce the costs of decommissioning [the reactors]'.

The problem of radioactive waste disposal began to crop up with some insistence from 1996 onwards.[4] A document dated 29 April 1999, approved by the Scalia Parliamentary Commission, referred to a national site or sites for storing nuclear waste and considered the hypotheses of surface or geological sites, arguing that the latter required further study. In a 1999 document, the Ministry of Industry spoke of a strategy for nuclear waste disposal in terms of national energy policy and environmental safety. This document underlined the need for transparency in the process in order to reach a definitive solution, whose premise was the development of a consolidated storage site, as suggested in reports from ANPA (the Environmental Protection Agency) conferences in 1995 and 1997. Solutions were to be developed in close collaboration with local authorities, trade unions, environmentalist groups and public opinion, and a variety of alternatives were on the table.[5]

In 2001, Silvio Berlusconi returned to the office of Prime Minister for his second administration. His project of 'Great Works' (promised during his campaign in a 'Contract with the Italians') was the centrepiece of his first 100 days in office. The so-called 'Objective Law' (L. 443) passed on 21 December of that year had the aim of accelerating projects considered to be 'strategic and of preeminent national interest' for the modernisation and development of the country (Article 1, comma 1). Besides streamlining procedures, especially with regard to inspection and environmental impact evaluation, the Objective Law modified decision-making processes, delegating a substantial part to the executive branch. Except for consultations with regional governments, decision making no longer involved the lower levels of the government. Additionally, for 2002 and 2003, the government had the mandate to emanate 'one or more legislative decrees bearing definitive approval ... of specific projects for strategic infrastructures' (Article 4).

The situation of nuclear waste in particular was addressed by a Cabinet President Ordinance (no. 3267) of 7 March 2003. The document referred to a 'declaration of a state of emergency in regard to the activity of disposing radioactive waste' located in various regions[6] and considered 'the inevitable need to take extraordinary and urgent measures for securing radioactive waste, with the aim of protecting essential interests of State security'. Based on the premise that 'the value of public interests involved makes it indispensable to provide for a concentration of powers aiming to fulfil the objective in a single decision-making body', Article 1 nominated the President of Sogin 'Authorised Commissioner for securing nuclear materials'. In Article 4, the Commissioner was given vast powers 'with the goal of guaranteeing the unitary character, rapidity and economic efficiency of the operations' and 'having heard the Regions directly involved, will take every necessary initiative for managing this activity'. The Ordinance also instituted a Commission 'with the task of evaluation and great vigilance for the technical-scientific aspects inherent in the objectives'. The Ordinance's text did not outline any plan of action for securing the waste, but simply spoke of 'any necessary initiative'.

About two months later, word circulated publicly that Sardinia was to be selected to host the national storage facility. Many Sardinians began to protest, forcing Commissioner (cum Sogin President) General Carlo Jean to announce that the question required another year of study and that the citizens would be involved in the choice of the site (*Manifesto*, 22 June 2003). The storm died down only after Berlusconi himself promised that 'touristic Sardinia would never undergo an outrage of the sort' (Soave 2004: 30). In the meantime, in that summer's torrid heat, a series of blackouts took place. The most serious one occurred in September, and subsequently various ministers and politicians pointed to these blackouts in suggesting the need to return to the domestic production of nuclear power.

Legislative Decree 314 was passed in a Cabinet meeting during the night of 12 November. Apparently, its conception was supposed to be immaculate, given that there was no trace of it on the agenda. Its official paternity was supposed to be attributed to the President of the Republic, Ciampi, but since he was abroad, Senate President Marcello Pera underwrote the document. While the Cabinet worked on the Decree, Italians were mourning the nineteen Carabinieri who died in a suicide attack in Nassiriya, Iraq.

Legislative Decree 314: Explicit and Implicit Discourses

When it formulated Decree 314, the Cabinet apparently operated through association, starting with Nassiriya and finishing with abstract Islamic terrorism, because it reiterated the concerns for security already present in the 7 March Ordinance: 'the extraordinary necessity and urgency to take initiatives'; 'the wide-ranging international crisis, which requires the urgent creation of initiatives of an extraordinary nature with the aim of protecting the national security interest of the State'. Article 1 provided for the 'safe stowage' of the radioactive waste in a national storage facility, 'a work of military defence and property of the state' whose site would be Scanzano Jonico. The facility was further defined as a 'work of public utility, declared unpostponable and urgent', which could employ the Objective Law's streamlined procedures (Article 1, comma 3). Additionally, the Decree foresaw 'other structures aimed at high-technology services and promoting the territory's development'. The concept that collateral 'development' might be favoured by the dump echoed a document of the Minister of Industry of 14 December 1999, which suggested that sites for nuclear waste treatment and storage could become poles for development, because these activities would be compatible with other technological and scientific activities.

To carry out the initiative, the Cabinet nominated the Sogin President, General Carlo Jean, to the post of Special Commissioner; Jean was already designated authorised commissioner for nuclear security in the March Ordinance. Article 4 stated that 'at the Special Commissioner's proposal, having consulted the Regions involved, measures for territorial intervention are established, of an economic nature as well, for compensating the obligations imposed on the territory by the creation of the National Storage Facility'. Finally, the same article states that 'Sogin will promote ... a national information campaign regarding the safe management of radioactive waste'.

The militarisation of the project was an element of continuity between the 7 March Ordinance and the 14 November Decree: by making reference to the post-9/11 climate, the government argued that the current multiple storage sites were unsafe and were possible targets for terrorist attacks. From the Ordinance onwards, the waste problem was no longer predominately defined as an environmental question but as a national security issue. The 7 March Ordinance cited general measures for securing the waste, but nowhere did it specify that the single national facility must be the sole or mandatory solution. Although it did not specify whether it must be a 'geological' site or an 'engineered' one, this point was given in Decree 314.

The two documents had differing views on lower-level government participation: the Ordinance cited the involvement of the regional governments, while the Decree wholly lacked any mention of local or regional participation, except for 'hearing' the Region in order to determine its compensation. This compensation was foreseen for 'obligations' (*vincoli*), but not for risks: the legislation did not consider the risks of transporting nuclear waste across the country to the dump or the risks inherent in the creation and maintenance of the facility. Instead, the law underlined the terrorist risks implicit in the present situation. I will return below to the concept of compensation.

As those anthropologists analysing the state have noted, one of the clear modes of governing through policy is the creation of certain forms of subjectivity (Shore and Wright 1997). Explicitly and implicitly, Decree 314 created or indexed forms of subjectivity which, on the one hand, were thought to be acquiescent and, on the other, lacked prospects for an alternative subjectivity and provoked resistance. In press comments, some members of the government applauded the Decree, defining it a 'courageous' move, a break with the 'typically Italian' *modus operandi* of putting off difficult choices; they further argued that the facility was urgently needed to meet European requirements. The nuclear waste dump, then, like the other 'Great Works', was to be a step forward on the road to progress and Europeanness.[7] The government's role in the tutorship of the population found a counterpart in the description of the people as needing 'defence' and 'information': since there was a 'wide-ranging international crisis', the national population was at risk of terrorism and thus a military defence was justified; the population also needed to be 'informed' about nuclear safety. In effect, the citizenry became constructed here in terms of 'feminine' passivity, the object to be transformed and protected under the state's aegis, with all of its masculine military power. We might consider the policy of creating a nuclear waste dump to be part of a wider neoliberal project, along the lines of what Sharma (2006: 69) describes: 'The massive, corrupt, slow, ignorant and weakened state that neoliberalism seeks to transform and cut to size is an "emasculated" state.

What neoliberalism seeks to conjure instead is a strong "hypermasculine" state that is lean, mean, and devoid of excesses.'

By combining a military approach with neoliberal streamlining, local participation and the local citizenry were cut out of the picture; the government took for granted that, as a 'rational and free subject', the local population would accept compensation for hosting the dump. It was further assumed that this population shared the government's particular vision of 'development'. The government's perspective was also informed by the relatively low population density of the region, seemingly comparable to the desert areas of the two U.S. sites – Yucca Mountain and WIPP – constantly cited in its technical-scientific studies. The government calculated that of the 'few' people to be impacted, only the usual protesters would complain, but everything would finally pass through just fine.

After the Decree was issued, the regional government of Basilicata and the Conference of Regional Presidents observed that, on the basis of the 7 March Ordinance, the decision of the location of the site should have been made with their participation. The government's piqued response in turn was that the Regions themselves were responsible for delaying matters, justifying its own decisive action. Thus, the only subjects authorised to speak – the Regions – were blamed for the government's heavy-handedness.[8] According to the latter, the Lucanians were afflicted with the 'NIMBY' syndrome and were irrational and particularists of the sort who 'say no to everything' and are 'against progress'. But, as we shall see, the sense that the government had of the subjects it governed is one thing, while the sense of self of the subjects governed is another.

The Lines of Resistance

The resistance moved on two parallel and complementary levels – the institutional and the popular – and there was a continuous interchange of discourses between them. The people generally moved independently, but they looked to their institutions for active support and for a dignified representation in the national arena. Intervention by local representatives of the Catholic Church also figured prominently, under the energetic guidance of Scanzano's parish priest, and other institutions participated in the protest: the governments of neighbouring regions, the Conference of Regional Presidents, and various trade unions and associations.

The city, provincial and regional administrations of Basilicata opposed Decree 314 by carrying out a series of counter-moves: the regional government's Internet site gave real-time news of all developments, gathered signatures for an electronic petition, opened a forum space on the topic and invited the citizenry to send postcards of protest to Prime Minister Berlusconi. Scanzano became the symbolic capital of the region, hosting various provincial and regional council meetings. The regional administration and several city councils passed ad hoc ordinances, declaring their respective territories 'denuclearised' and forbidding the transport of nuclear materials. The regional government also contested the Decree legally, questioning its constitutionality and at the same time officially raising the seismic risk rating of Scanzano to levels indicated in more recent geological surveys.

Within Scanzano itself, the leadership of Mayor Mario Altieri created a much more delicate question: rumours circulated that the Mayor had met with General Jean and had consented to the project; the national news weekly *Panorama* even stated that in a telephone exchange, Altieri had personally reassured Berlusconi: 'Don't worry, President, we'll make a top-notch dump' (Oldani 2003). Despite denials on all sides, it is at least conceivable that Altieri – a member of a party in the governing coalition – might have been 'fraternising with the enemy'; the Mayor's personal safety was jeopardised, but in the end the local population decided to momentarily suspend judgment on him in order to remain united. In the meantime, Altieri sought to position himself unequivocally against the dump, ordering the confiscation of the rock-salt mines that were to receive the radioactive waste.

The Lucanian politicians belonging to the government coalition were in a particularly complex position. All of them insisted on their ties to Basilicata and their opposition to the Decree's contents; those who were not parliamentarians tended to disassociate themselves from the government and several suspended themselves from their political parties, while the parliamentarians instead positioned themselves as strategic and necessary intermediaries to reach Berlusconi and gain his good offices. The local Centre-Left parliamentarians contested the Decree in the Chamber of Deputies, in Environment Commission hearings and in the Chamber itself.

At the beginning of the tumult, the government's deployment of technical-scientific 'facts' seemed unimpeachable: both the Lucanian politicians and the masses were unprepared, and throughout the events of those two weeks, the legitimacy of technical-scientific discourse as a mode of argumentation was never questioned. Quickly, however, the protest showed that it was capable of mustering its own 'facts'. As a result, what was cast in doubt was not scientific discourse *tout court*, but rather the hypothesis that Scanzano was the best choice for pursuing the announced aims of efficiency and security. Thus, far from arguing a perfect case, the government seemed to present shoddy and superficial science. If the government thought the people needed to be 'informed', the latter responded by holding counter-information lessons with local schoolteachers and university professors at the occupied site and the roadblocks.

Reversing the Moral Frame

Alongside but paramount to the institutional level of resistance was the reaction of the local population and its many sympathisers, who together conducted a strenuous opposition to the Decree with a mobilisation whose breadth surprised everyone. I return here to a question posed at the beginning of this analysis: why was there a reaction of such proportions? Surely the symbolic charge of the nuclear aspect provoked fear in the populace, and yet Basilicata had been storing nuclear materials since 1968, when the Itrec-Trisaia facility in Rotondella was opened, only a few miles from Scanzano. 'La Trisaia', as it is commonly called, was to have handled the reprocessing of nuclear fuel. Since the collapse of the Italian nuclear energy programme, the facility has continued to store, among other things, sixty-four bars of uranium from the U.S.'s Elk River reactor. In the 1970s, only a few environmentalists protested against the nuclear presence in Trisaia, and despite the fact that through the years there had been many rumours of accidents, up until the events of Scanzano, no one said much.

In my view, it would be rather reductive to attribute the Scanzano revolt exclusively to the spectre of the radioactive waste, though this aspect might appear predominant. It is instead useful to consider Halvard Vike's suggestion (1997), inspired by the work of James C. Scott (1985), regarding the 'moral economy' of resistance. In this sense, the revolt of Scanzano acted by reversing the moral frame of the question and redefining the concept of 'common good'. An examination of this moral economy illuminates the meaning of the collective subject as embedded in history and society, a subjectivity here denied by the government's policies.

As the analysis of the relevant legislation has shown, the government attempted to frame its position on Scanzano as an action conducted in the general interest and in contrast to the emotional and particularistic reaction of the local population. This *raison d'état* is, in part, an effect of what Ferguson and Gupta (2002: 982) have called 'vertical encompassment', in which the Western conception associates the state with a 'higher' position over the territory, 'possessing such "higher" functions as reason, control and regulation', while the lower levels are associated with 'irrationality, passion and uncontrollable appetites'. The resistance put forth in Scanzano, however, turned out to be capable of reversing this frame by demonstrating that the government was by no means so 'universal' and demonstrative of 'dispassionate reason'; on the contrary, it bore its own particularism, if not – still worse – a resurgence of an archaic patrimonialism, despite its neoliberal rhetoric.

As Nikolas Rose (1996) has observed, the 'destatalisation' of governmental practices constitutes one of the techniques through which an 'advanced liberal' regime operates, thereby creating its own inevitability by presenting a presumed neutrality of the agents of its policies. The creation of the separate public company Sogin offers an example of these 'measures whose emphasis upon the apparent objectivity and neutrality of numbers underpins a claim that they now operate according to an apolitical agenda' (Rose 1996: 56). The status of Sogin is by no means unambiguous: it is a company whose stock is held by the government and which is part of the partially privatised Enel group. During the events of Scanzano, Sogin President General Carlo Jean catalysed a great deal of negative attention among the local populace. Jean was a retired general and military strategist who had a past history with the military secret services; to the Lucanians, he appeared to be a Dr Strangelove-type figure. In the regional government's Internet forum on the Decree, many postings discussed whether or not he belonged to the P2 Masonic Lodge, the latter being the *Ursprung* of Italian conspiracy theories. As we will see below, Jean's Piedmontese origins provoked a vehement personal reaction against this 'general with a foreign surname', the 'Piedmontese invader'. According to the protesters, Jean was anything but a neutral and authoritative actor to whom radioactive waste security should be entrusted. While it is true, as Burchell (1991: 144) notes, that a citizenry turns to its government for security issues, in the case of Scanzano, the people felt the need to be defended from the government itself, not from hypothetical terrorists.

The idea that the government's interest was 'universal' was cast into doubt by the revelation of a substantial conflict of interest. Many noted that Paolo Togni, Chief of Staff in the Environment Ministry, was also the Vice-President of Sogin. In other words, a key figure in the watchdog agency was simultaneously a key figure in the agency being supervised. Moreover, before his role at the Ministry, Togni held the office of President of the Italian affiliate of Waste Management, a large corporation in the field of energy production and waste disposal. The hurry and urgency so strongly emphasised by the government, according to the Lucanians, were dictated not so much by public security concerns – the waste had been in the same condition for years and no European country had yet taken definitive measures – as by the hundreds of millions of Euros estimated to surround the project. Local hearsay claimed that the dump was an excuse to hand out generous contracts and probably generated 'business' for disposing waste from other countries.

Finally, Berlusconi himself was a target of protest discourse: his figure had personalised and polarised politics during his entire term, and the question of Scanzano was no exception. The local protesters wrote to him directly and mocked him in banners and posters; one of the most popular slogans suggested sending the waste 'to Arcore', Berlusconi's private residence. Yet another slogan wryly suggested that the people of the Ionian coast give Berlusconi a vacation home there, since his well-known luxury villa in Sardinia was evidently the reason why that region was not chosen to host the facility. During the two weeks of the crisis, Berlusconi remained entirely behind the scenes, never making any public statement on the matter; his ministers implied that he was reconsidering the question, while the Lucanian politicians of his coalition sought to demonstrate their positive influence in reaching the chief, in the classic style of a patrimonial regime.

By identifying the actors within the government and in personalising their role, the Lucanians confuted the government's projected image of objective neutrality and thereby depicted the government's interests as themselves particularistic, reversing the accusations that sought to discredit the protest. Moreover, the rebels interpreted the conditions in which the Decree was prepared – off the agenda, at the time of the Nassiriya tragedy and with the President of the Republic abroad – as proof that the government, far from making a bold and decisive move to draw Italy closer to Europe, was instead pulling a shifty and underhanded move more in line with the usual, deplorable Italian craftiness (cf. Zinn 2001). As I discuss below, beyond these single actors involved, the entire governing coalition seemed caught up in its own particularism in favour of northern Italy.

Redefining the Common Good

From the government's perspective, a rational calculation of the common good considered the entire national population to be pre-eminent to the relatively few people populating the presumably desert-like land of the waste dump site. In the Lucanians' view, however, their region was selected because it was small, politically insignificant and decisively left-wing. In this context, the people were infuriated to see themselves wholly ignored in the decision-making process and treated as if they were nonexistent.

Although the government insisted that the consolidated site was necessary for the country's security and progress, the discourses arising from the local protest reformulated the notion of 'common good' in terms of substantial, not formal, rationality: that is, a rationality oriented towards outcomes and values like solidarity (Weber 1961; Brubaker 1984). The South, it was argued, was already penalised vis-à-vis the North, and the waste dump would have unjustly exacerbated the divide. The parameters of substantial rationality were put forth in contrast to the government's hegemonic framework of 'federalism' and its perceived 'anti-southern' bent. In effect, among the population in revolt, but also among sympathisers in neighbouring regions, there was a widespread perception that the policies of the Berlusconi government seconded the positions of the Northern League (cf. Loiero 2003); Decree 314 was roundly interpreted as an anti-southern move.[9]

The basis of this redefinition of the common good comes from the historical experience of the people of Scanzano and the surrounding area. As Vike concludes in a case of resistance to local policies in Norway, 'history is invested with a moral force of its own. The power of this moral force is drawn from the way members construct a link of identity between the heroes of the past and the here-and-now' (Vike 1997: 205). Decree 314 discursively reduced the local populace to being a 'people without history'. In order to reconfigure the moral economy of the common good, the revolt reappropriated two critical moments in Lucanian history: Italian unification and the post-Second World War peasant struggles for land. With reference to unification, the historical figure of the brigand became widely adopted as a powerful symbol for the Scanzano protest. Here, as Ana Alonso (1992) says, a 'dominant history of origins' was contested: the brigand no longer represented southern criminality or beastliness, as in old Italian unity narratives, but was rather the defender against the 'Piedmontese invader'. In this revisionist history, the North's sack of the South began with unity and continued today with Scanzano.

We can further see a substantive definition of the common good in the local interpretation of 'development'; here, too, history cannot be ignored in people's subjectivity. The Lucanians were very mindful of the history of the Metapontine area and its particular path to development in the second half of the twentieth century. Many elderly people recalled the 'struggles for land', when the peasants' centuries-long ambition clashed with the small but powerful landowning elite. At the end of the 1940s, this area was a theatre to many conflicts, which were often violent, and peasant occupations of the estates finally led to a land reform which expropriated some of the larger properties, subdividing them into plots. This land reform created a patchwork of small farms that formed the backbone of today's Metapontine economy. The historical memory of this is still quite important, even for those lacking a direct tie to the land; it became common heritage for the different socioeconomic classes active in the protest (cf. Zinn 2007).

From the end of the 1950s until the early 1980s, here (and elsewhere in the South) the central government launched an unsuccessful project of creating industrial complexes aimed at stimulating endogenous development. In contrast to this picture, agriculture and tourism in the region have enjoyed a relatively florid growth: in the last two decades, seaside tourism has thrived along the Ionian coast; at the same time, farmers have focused on advanced forms of agriculture, quality and organic produce. During what has become known as 'the Days of Scanzano', the Lucanians represented these forms of development as 'slow' and 'green' alternatives to the grey and industrial North, and held them to be incompatible with nuclear waste. In point of fact, local environmentalists had previously protested against excessive construction along the coast and the presence of radioactive waste at Trisaia. The defenders of Scanzano roundly ignored this reality in their struggle against Decree 314, insisting that the consolidated waste facility would represent a contradiction that would void the millions of Euros spent in investments in tourism and agriculture. In short, in the protesters' view, the dump would constitute an injustice for the inhabitants of this 'green' region, which – after a long period of 'modernisation without development' – was finally getting ahead on its own two feet. For them, any suggestion of 'compensation' was unthinkable and provoked indignation (cf. Della Corte 2004: 37).

From the Lucanians' perspective, then, the 'common good' could not be defined without taking into account their historical specificity, one which directly referred to the historical and social position of their collective subjectivity. The populace considered the nuclear waste dump to be an impending hazard that could very well lead to physical annihilation; on a discursive level, too, the government's actions amounted to an annihilation of subjectivity precisely by ignoring this specificity. As Burchell writes, '[People] are most profoundly affected when the way they are governed requires them to alter how they see themselves as governed subjects ... It is then ... that individuals may be led to resist or even revolt' (Burchell 1993: 119).

Participation: The Importance of Being There

In affirming subjectivity, the protest also asserted the moral value of its participation in decision-making processes, in contrast to the 'efficiency' of centralised approaches. I would like to suggest that, above and beyond being a rigorously defensive action, the spontaneous and massive uprising of Scanzano sought to propose itself as a claim or even a surrogate of true participation in decision making. In this sense, I examine here the practices of popular resistance in the Scanzano revolt. If, as many stated, Decree 314 was completely unexpected and seemed an all-out military blitz, the popular mobilisation remained determined but pacific. Numerous measures were taken: as soon as news of the Decree spread, the citizenry of Scanzano occupied the Town Hall, which remained open in a permanent assembly throughout the entire crisis. A short time afterwards, the first roadblocks were formed along State Road 106, which passes through Scanzano. A group of protesters headed towards the designated site for the dump, and they created a stronghold that was soon called 'Base Camp', presided over by citizens and whole families. Numerous tents and a field kitchen were set up there, together with a camper for logistics and communications. The Scanzanesi, joined by citizens of other towns along the coast and the interior, organised four committees for coordinating action. When the government's position began to harden in the first days, roadblocks multiplied throughout the region, sealing off Basilicata from the rest of the country.

Since the Decree was to take effect immediately, there were fears among the populace that the nuclear waste would arrive by train; for this reason, people occupied the Metaponto railway station. In the meantime, numerous other demonstrations took place throughout the region, signatures were gathered on petitions, and even the electronic community was mobilised, including Lucanian associations abroad. Graffiti appeared everywhere against the nuclear waste and against the government, on road signs and on banners. Daily life in the coastal towns came to a halt, businesses and schools closed, and there was a general siege atmosphere. In the provincial capital, Matera, a demonstration or a rally took place in the main square nearly every day. The protest began to involve the dams supplying water to Apulia, the oil wells in Val d'Agri and the Fiat plant in Melfi. The culminating moment was the 'March of 100,000' of 23 November, stretching from State Road 106 to Scanzano's centre. Four days later, the government announced that the name of Scanzano would be struck from the Decree.

This very brief description of the popular measures of resistance in the case of Scanzano cannot adequately render the widespread feeling and action of *communitas* (in Turner's [1969] sense) during those days. Emotions of being under siege alternated with carnivalesque states that implied the suspension of order and hierarchy, but also the presence of the collective subject. The roadblocks and Base Camp created domestic spaces at the heart of the public sphere, spaces of social reproduction where people slept, shared meals and local dishes, where people had fun and learned. Agricultural products were displayed as if at a town fair. Slogans and proclamations not aimed at criticising the government expressed a strong sense of caring for the future generations and the celebration of the bond between land and life. Orange and olive trees were planted on the uncultivated site of Base Camp. One of the most intense images of the protest was that of the women nursing their infants while seated on the train tracks of Metaponto. Expressive forms belonging to local traditions were used, making reference to the community's cultural intimacy (Herzfeld 1997): the use of dialect in the banners and signs, ritual lament in a mock funeral for the land, and folk Catholicism. Cold nights spent at the roadblocks and Base Camp featured storytelling, as the older generations told youths of their struggles for the land. People spontaneously organised roadblocks, and the supplies for the people on the frontline arrived in a solidarity chain from throughout the region. The 'March of 100,000' was marked by a fully carnivalesque atmosphere, with people in costumes, grotesque bodies of 'nuclear monsters' that marched between the town delegations and ordinary people, banners and slogans in dialect, at times quite vulgar with reference to the government, traditional music with cowbells and bagpipes (*zampogne*).

However, within this picture of unity among the Lucanians, there were two faultlines which were potentially capable of creating irreparable divisions: one between the extreme Right and the radical Left, and one between the people and the political class. In the former, there was a continuous tension generated by the simultaneous presence at the roadblocks and protests of members of Forza Nuova – an extreme Right movement with strong roots in the Metapontine region – with others associated with the radical Left. The populace constantly feared that some hothead might create a provocation that would be utilised to justify police intervention; even so, the two politically opposed sides maintained a tacit truce. The other division, which was more muted and ambivalent, was between the political class and civil society. I have already mentioned the controversy surrounding Mayor Altieri; if his case was an extreme example of this rupture, the people still harboured a lingering doubt about what other local politicians might have known about the dump. During the crisis, the entire Lucanian political class attempted to prove its 'street credentials' and was appreciated for concrete actions, but the populace and nongovernmental bodies did not stand idly by while awaiting the politicians. In this discussion, I can only hint at what was certainly a complex dynamic, one which merits greater attention than can be given here.

Despite the militaristic stance of the Decree and rumours that the army was arriving to force the roadblocks open, the people of the Scanzano revolt kept true to their pacific rebellion, despite the at times militaristic language of the protest and the references to brigands. The Days of Scanzano challenged, if symbolically, what feminist scholar Wendy Brown has called the masculine 'prerogative dimension' of the state: 'The prerogative dimension of the state pertains to that which marks the state as a state: legitimate arbitrary power in policy making and legitimate monopolies of internal and external violence in the police and military. As the overt power-political dimension of the state, prerogative includes expressions of national purpose and national security as well as the whole range of legitimate arbitrary state action' (1995: 192). With Decree 314, the government thought that it had made a decisive move. Its militaristic approach demonstrated the crudest face of masculinist domination; in order to discredit the local community, the government silenced it, feminising it, and then accused it of (feminine) particularism.

The state's vertical encompassment acted to suffocate the voice of revolt and, in effect, not all of the Lucanians were completely convinced that the protest would work: some were resigned to a fait accompli. Vertical encompassment also has a gendered dimension, as Sharma notes: 'Verticality symbolically encodes social conventions of masculinity that represent men as dominant and authoritative. Encompassment expresses the ability to define and control particular discursive and sociopolitical terrains. It arguably connotes both masculinist power and the hegemonic image of the state as a sovereign entity with the legitimate power to define, manage and protect (often through violent means) territories and populations and regulate proper subjectivity' (2006: 68).

And yet the protest was gradually able to subvert the effect of vertical encompassment. The local population turned to 'Europe' (the EU) to find alternative solutions that would negate the inevitability of the choice. Looking at EU legislation (and, internationally, the Rio Declaration of 1992), the protesters reaffirmed the principles of local participation in decision making. In the attempt to make their voices heard, the rebels formed horizontal ties with a panoply of other movements – the Zapatistas of Chiapas, but also various antiglobalisation and antinuclear organisations – and drew on ties with Lucanian emigrant communities from around the globe.

The Scanzano revolt offered a point-by-point refutation of the government's arguments, defeating instrumental rationalism on its own terms, but it did not respond to the government with 'an ethic of activism that confronts domination with the smashing and terror so characteristic of masculinist revolutionary action' (Diamond and Quinby 1988: xvi). Instead, it demonstrated a powerful affective and experiential dimension: the protest articulated a sense of connection and embeddedness in the social fabric that can be easily overlooked in what Kathleen Jones calls dominant masculine forms of authority: 'The rational modes of speech taken to be constitutive of authority exclude certain human dimensions, voices, and "interests" from the public realm' (1988: 130).

In this sense, the affinities between Scanzano and antiglobalisation movements can be seen as an expression of the two tendencies indicated by Paolo Ceri (2000) in his analysis of the Seattle protests. Ceri notes that in these new protests we see a collective current that 'bears with it ... a group of moral claims that confer strength and legitimacy to *demands for equity,* though no longer for equality as happened in the past' (Ceri 2000: 21). But there are also impulses toward social integration: here, we find both elements of cooperation and protection described by Ceri, but especially the 'recomposure of the existential and systemic division between economy and culture, between the claims of instrumental rationality and those of belonging and sentiment' (2000: 21).

Conclusion

In commenting on the Habermasian ideal of 'discursive democracy', Simone Chambers writes the following:

> In a world where negotiation, instrumental trade-offs, and strategic bargaining are the most common routes to reaching collective 'agreement' and resolving disputes, it is plausible that the most serious barrier to discourse can be found in the conversational habitus that citizens have become used to ... Implementing practical discourse ... involves fostering a political culture in which citizens actively participate in public debate and consciously adopt the discursive attitudes of responsibility, self-discipline, respect, cooperation, and productive struggle necessary to produce consensual agreements. (1995: 176–77)

The Scanzano revolt was capable of galvanising the majority of the population into the type of active participation described by Chambers. It was transformative of the sense of collective subjectivity as an object of governmental policies and, on the basis of this subjectivity, the people mobilised in an exemplary fashion. Those who crafted the government's policy were blinded by assumptions regarding the governed subject and, on this basis, they were convinced that they could simply erase any voice of dissent. The discourses and practices of the protest successfully reversed the moral battleground, revealing an ontologically plural state and the patrimonial and particularistic features hiding behind its universalistic and rational facade. Along with its own technical-scientific discourse, the protest managed to affirm that the 'common good' is not to be considered a given together with *raison d'état.*

Notes

1. Even a newspaper such as *Il Giornale*, closely linked to the Berlusconi government, described the 'March of 100,000' as 'proof of great civility that honors all Lucanians' (24 November 2003, p. 17).
2. Living in Basilicata, I was a participant in the events of November 2003. I therefore situate myself as an activist, yet I hope to avoid an excessively romanticised view of the struggle. I aim here to make a scientific reflection on Scanzano, which to date has received only journalistic treatments or marginal consideration in scientific debates.

3. A previous version of this chapter was published in *Quaderni di Sociologia* (2007, LI(44): 151–74), whose editors kindly granted permission for an English adaptation. I would like to express my gratitude to all those who contributed to this work. My first attempt at thinking of Scanzano in these terms was a presentation at the EASA Conference in Bristol (18–21 September 2006) in the 'Policy Worlds' Workshop; I thank Susan Wright, Davide Però, Cris Shore and the Workshop participants for their comments. I must also acknowledge Paolo Ceri, who expressed great interest in my analysis of Scanzano and whose questions provoked further reflection. Finally, I thank Gianni Palumbo and Nuccia Nicoletti for their generous comments. All translations from Italian are my own.

4. In 1996, the Civil Protection Agency formed a Nuclear Section, and the ENEA research agency was given the responsibility of constituting a task force to study the question.

5. For middle- and long-life waste, the document (p. 15) supported a deep geological site, but at the same time it left alternatives open in terms of international collaboration, the study of innovative solutions and the possibility of creating multinational storage facilities.

6. This declaration was made a few weeks prior to the Ordinance (Cabinet President Decree, 14 February 2003).

7. See Zinn (2001) for a discussion of Italian identity vis-à-vis Europe.

8. The regions' response claimed that the delay on their part was due to the fact that Sogin's technical-scientific report was too vague and did not meet the Ordinance's criteria. Moreover, Sogin's report was presented even before the members of the scientific commission were nominated (Soave 2004).

9. On the importance of southern identity in the Scanzano revolt, see Zinn (2007).

References

Alonso, A.M. 1992. 'Gender, Power and Historical Memory: Discourses of *Serrano* Resistance', in J. Butler and J.W. Scott (eds), *Feminists Theorize the Political.* New York: Routledge, pp. 404–25.

Banfield, E. 1958. *The Moral Basis of a Backward Society.* Glencoe: The Free Press.

Brown, W. 1995. *States of Injury: Power and Freedom in Late Modernity*, Princeton: Princeton University Press.

Brubaker, R. 1984. *The Limits of Rationality: An Essay on the Social and Moral Thought of Max Weber.* London: George Allen & Unwin.

Burchell, G. 1991. 'Peculiar Interests: Civil Society and Governing "The System of Natural Liberty"', in G. Burchell, C. Gordon and P. Miller (eds), *The Foucault Effect: Studies in Governmentality*, Chicago: University of Chicago Press, pp. 119–50.

Carta. 2004. 'Modello Scanzano. Un anno fa è nato il nuovo Sud', *Carta Quaderni 3*, supplement to Carta, VI, 42, 18 November.

Ceri, P. 2000. 'A Seattle è nato un movimento globale', *il Mulino*, XLIX(387): 15–24.

Chambers, S. 1995. 'Feminist Discourse/Practical Discourse', in J. Meehan (ed.), *Feminists Read Habermas: Gendering the Subject of Discourse.* New York: Routledge, pp. 163–79.

Della Corte, E. 2004. 'Fiat-Sata: exit e voice sul prato verde di Melfi. Condizioni di lavoro, lotte e desideri', in V. Della Sala, F. Caruso, I. Di Sabato and G. Pittà. (eds),

Globalizzazione e Mezzogiorno. Percorsi di Democrazia Partecipativa. Ferrazzano: Ondeserene, pp. 37–57.

Diamond I. and L. Quinby 1988. 'Introduction', in I. Diamond and L. Quinby, eds. *Feminism & Foucault: Reflections on Resistance*. Boston: Northeastern University Press, pp. ix–xx.

Ferguson, J. and A. Gupta 2002. 'Spatializing States: Toward an Ethnography of Neoliberal Governmentality', *American Ethnologist* 29(4): 981–1002.

Herzfeld, M. 1997. *Cultural Intimacy: Social Poetics in the Nation-State*. New York: Routledge.

Jones, K.B. 1988. 'On Authority: Or, Why Women are Not Entitled to Speak', in I. Diamond and L. Quinby (eds), *Feminism and Foucault: Reflections on Resistance*. Boston: Northeastern University Press, pp. 119–33.

Loiero, A. 2003. *Il patto di ferro. Berlusconi, Bossi e la devolution contro il Sud con i voti del Sud*. Rome: Donzelli Editore.

Manifesto, 22 June 2003.

Ministero dell'Industria, del Commercio e dell'Artigianato (14 December 1999). 'Indirizzi strategici per la gestione degli esisti del nucleare'. Document transmitted to Parliament on 21 December 1999.

Montemurro, R. 2004. *I giorni di Scanzano. Cronaca di un accidente nucleare*. Rome: Ediesse.

Oldani, T. 2003. 'Il generale in un labirinto chiamato Scanzano', *Panorama*, 48: 86–88.

Rose, N. 1996. 'Governing "Advanced" Liberal Democracies', in A. Barry, T. Osborne and N. Rose (eds), *Foucault and Political Reason*. London: UCL Press, pp. 37–64.

Scott, J.C. 1985. *Weapons of the Weak. Everyday Forms of Peasant Resistance*. New Haven: Yale University Press.

Sharma, A. 2006. 'Crossbreeding Institutions, Breeding Struggle: Women's Empowerment, Neoliberal Governmentality, and State (Re)Formation in India', *Cultural Anthropology*, XXI(1): 60–95.

Shore, C. and S. Wright 1997. 'Policy: A New Field of Anthropology', in C. Shore and S. Wright (eds), *Anthropology of Policy: Critical Perspectives on Governance and Power*. New York: Routledge, pp. 3–39.

Soave, E. 2004. *Dopo Scanzano. Storia di scorie*. Venosa: Osanna Edizioni.

Turner, V. 1969. *The Ritual Process: Structure and Anti-structure*. Chicago: Aldine.

Vike, H. 1997. 'Reform and Resistance: A Norwegian Illustration', in C. Shore and S. Wright (eds), *Anthropology of Policy: Critical Perspectives on Governance and Power*. New York: Routledge, pp. 195–216.

Weber, M. 1961. *Economia e società*, vols. 1–2, P. Rossi (ed.). Milan: Edizioni di Comunità.

Zinn, D.L. 2001. *La Raccomandazione. Clientelismo vecchio e nuovo*. Rome: Donzelli Editore.

Zinn, D.L. 2007. 'I Quindici Giorni di Scanzano: Identity and Social Protest in the New South', *Journal of Modern Italian Studies* 12(2): 189–206.

Chapter 13

Migrants' Practices of Citizenship and Policy Change

Davide Però

In the seminal introduction to their book Anthropology of Policy (1997), Cris Shore and Sue Wright argued for the inclusion of policy in the domain of anthropological inquiry. Since then, the anthropology of policy, with its approach to policy as 'practice of power' (Levison and Sutton 2001), has been growing steadily in terms of contributions and gained progressive recognition. However, this growth has taken place more in terms of studying the powerful actors at the top of the policy chain and less in terms of the powerless, especially with regard to the policy change they produce.

But what is policy and how do we define policy change? As Shore and Wright (this volume's Introduction) have pointed out, policies are contested practices that both reflect and create the social and cultural world in which they are embedded. They are the key tools through which governments and other power bodies organise the spaces and the people they seek to govern. However, as this chapter will show, policies are not merely the performative acts of powerful collective actors but are also the result of the creative practices of a number of other actors – including the governed themselves – who engage with them voluntarily or because they are forced to. Building on this definition of policy, we could – very schematically – distinguish between two ideal typical forms of policy change. The first refers to the top-down transformations produced by powerful governmental actors. The second refers to the bottom-up activities of the governed.[1] In this chapter, I focus on the policy responses of the governed and I contend that – alongside studying how policy operates as an instrument of governance – it is important to examine how policy comes to be transformed, challenged, resisted, neutralised or improved from below, through the creative engagements of disadvantaged recipients and other actors (e.g., trade unions, nongovernmental organisations [NGOs], social movements and other civil society organisations) who work with these disadvantaged groups to protect their interests. This focus on the agency of the governed is relevant not only to complement the anthropological studies of policy makers but also to rebalance the prevailing attitude in mainstream policy studies which typically treats people as 'objects', 'targets' or passive 'recipients' of policy (see, for example, the influential article by Schneider and Ingram [1993]). Such prevailing policy studies shed little light on the experience or agency of the governed. For instance, they do not ask what disadvantaged and marginalised groups do to ameliorate their conditions, or how they respond to unfavourable policies and with what implications.

The critical issues to consider in this context concern the way those who are targeted by particular policies and their advocates engage with and respond to such policies. In particular, this chapter highlights the importance of considering how and when targeted groups 'scale up' their policy responses, taking them to a higher level where, for example, additional actors and advocates become involved in their support. It is also important to pay attention to how and when the governed abandon undeclared practices of resistance to 'come out' into the open to challenge policy overtly. Moreover, these policy responses and engagements should also be looked at in terms of their 'impact', i.e., in terms of how they affect policy. Appreciating the bottom-up initiatives of the governed, I would argue, requires a more comprehensive idea of policy change from below than that of formal policy transformations currently in use. For example, in an article by Meyer highlighting the importance of studying the effects of social movements (2003), policy impact, while recognised as crucial, is narrowly conceived as being limited to formal policy change. Accordingly, the more comprehensive idea of policy change being suggested in this chapter includes not only bottom-up induced formal transformations to policy produced by explicit and larger scale collective mobilisations, but also the 'smaller' policy changes produced by the everyday practices that people deploy to cope with, neutralise or resist policy. James Scott's work on resistance and 'weapons of the weak' is particularly helpful in identifying a wide range of resistance practices (Scott 1985, 1990).[2] Moreover, this idea of policy change from below should include the demands that the governed articulate (through mobilisations, campaigning, etc.) to apply existing 'favourable' policies and legislation when these are not implemented.[3]

Although I argue for a comprehensive idea of policy change from below, I also stress that this idea should be critically and carefully applied. In particular, efforts to appreciate the policy responses of the governed, expressed in the form of undeclared and unorganised resistance, should be made neither at the expense of addressing larger scale, more overt and organised practices nor at the expense of examining how these practices come about, scale up or become overt challenges. This critical application seems necessary to avoid some of the pitfalls that have affected resistance studies lately. As Fletcher (2001) reminded us, so-called 'resistance studies' emerged in an attempt to explain how those who see their lives as oppressed rise up in defiance of the causes of such oppression. However, this original project got lost along the way, stretching the concept of resistance into a catch-all category to cover virtually any practice deemed oppositional. In other words, resistance studies have moved away from a concern with explaining forms of opposition to descriptions of copying strategies and symbolic expressions of undeclared dissent, leading some authors to call for the end of resistance studies altogether. This chapter builds on Fletcher's critique by exploring examples of how subaltern groups 'scale up' their dissent and openly challenge the hegemonic policy terms set by powerful institutions, and by looking at the policy impact of such subaltern practices.[4]

In addressing the agency of the governed, this chapter is situated in the long-standing critical anthropological tradition of looking at how oppressed groups seek to alter the terms of their oppression. This theme has been particularly addressed in the anthropological literature on development and social movements. Critical anthropologists have looked at a broad range of ways in which people across the world engage to change (or preserve) power relations. While some have examined everyday instances of infrapolitical resistance that are kept undeclared and disguised to avoid a backlash and sanctions (Scott 1985, 1990), others have focused on contestation in rituals which were previously conceptualised as moments of power assertion sustaining the social order (Comaroff 1985; Dirks 1994; Kertzer 1980). Another area of such critical research is the study of large-scale social movements that emerge at moments of socioeconomic crises to openly challenge powerful institutions and elites (Fox and Starn 1997; Gough 2002; Hale 1997; Nash 1992; Pratt 2003; Smith 1999; Starn 1999; Wolf 2002).[5] While many of these works contain relevant policy contextualisation, their theorisation of engagement is seldom made in terms of 'policy change from below' or as part of a wider anthropological effort to understand the policy field.

In focusing on policy change from below as an integral component of the wider anthropological study of policy, this chapter develops a sort of 'meso-level' approach to political engagements, one that is situated somewhere between the study of copying strategies and undeclared resistance and larger scale organised mobilisations. This meso-level approach is characterised by a focus on the dynamics of smaller scale collective engagements such as the transition from individual to collective action or undeclared to declared resistance, and the impact this has on policy.

Migrants constitute an important context in which to apply the approach to policy change outlined above, because of their typically marginal and disadvantaged position within the policy process from which they start mobilising for policy change. For example, migrants are normally deprived of the ultimate political right – the right to vote – and often even of the right of being in the 'host' society by a gamut of exclusionary and exploitative policy measures.

The treatment of migrants as objects rather than subjects of politics has not only characterised the approach of policy-makers but also of many scholars, particularly those who have uncritically embraced the perspective of the nation-state and the legitimisation of the 'national order of things' (Malkki 1995). This approach is what Wimmer and Glick Schiller (2003) call 'methodological nationalism'. Scholars addressing issues of migrants and politics tend to do so at the macro-level, often in the abstract and in isolation from the lived experiences and practices of citizenship of the migrants themselves. For example, they do so by: abstractedly counterposing integration models (e.g., assimilationism versus multiculturalism); focusing on the effects of migration on the politics and policies of the receiving state and on the electoral patterns of the 'host' population; addressing the politics and policies of 'homeland' governments and diplomacies toward their expatriates; and considering migrants in connection to the rise of the extreme Right, or in terms of security threats and manoeuvrable electoral blocs (for an overview of the existing work on the subject, see Castles and Miller 2009).

Migrants have 'existed' as political actors only when they have been entitled to vote or when they have put themselves forward as political candidates. Of course, this narrow understanding of political engagement cannot account for the political practices of migrants, especially in the countries in which they do not enjoy formal political entitlements (Però and Solomos 2010).

Moreover, for the most part, the limited literature on migrants' mobilisation has been concerned with explaining the emergence of migrants' political behaviour in terms of 'political opportunity structure' (POS) (Però 2008a). This largely abstract theoretical concern with the 'origin' of migrant collective action (mono-causally attributed to POS) shifts attention from the objects of migrants' contention (e.g., mobilisations for regularisation of status, less exploitative working conditions and recognition as ethnic groups) and promotes a more 'detached' and apolitical rather than 'engaged' approach to research on the topic.[6]

By focusing on migrants' policy engagements, this chapter will simultaneously address issues of multiculturalism and injustice in contemporary neoliberal democracies, and will illustrate the creative role that subaltern groups can play in affecting policy in practice. In particular, it will address the question of policy change from below by ethnographically and comparatively considering three different instances of migrants' engagement with policy. The first instance is from Bologna and examines how a seemingly progressive package of housing policies for migrants was in fact experienced as oppressive and was resisted by migrants through participation in the local polity and an unusual alliance with the Right. The second is from Barcelona and explores the protest of a group of undocumented migrants and advocacy organisations who successfully challenged a new immigration law that worsened their already vulnerable conditions. The third instance is from London and considers migrants and advocacy groups' policy engagements demanding the application of existing policies protecting workers' rights so as to combat their exploitation more effectively. All three cases explore the questions of finding appropriate 'allies', strategies and niches in the receiving society to enhance their policy impact.

Case 1: Migrants' Protest in Municipal Housing in Bologna

Context

Towards the end of the 1980s, after being a country of emigration for many decades, Italy turned into a country of immigration (King et al. 1997). At the beginning of the 1990s, housing constituted the most urgent and eye-catching problem affecting migrants in Italy, including in Bologna where I conducted fieldwork. Many migrants had to sleep in fields, cars, abandoned houses, old caravans or rental accommodation that was often illegal, unhealthy and unsafe. To address this problem, the municipal administration of Bologna,[7] instead of favouring migrants' residential distribution across the city, set up ad hoc residential structures – called 'centres of first shelter' or CPAs (*Centri di Prima Accoglienza*) – to house migrants according to ethnocultural criteria (i.e., Moroccans were housed with Moroccans, Pakistanis with Pakistanis and so forth). The municipality initially subjected them to a management policy called 'strong management' which involved the firm running and control of the centre through the twenty-four-hour presence of social workers and armed guards. In a top-down and authoritarian manner, the municipality subsequently decided to turn such structures into 'self-managed community centres' in which residents would appoint their own ethnic community leader to act as interlocutor with the City Council. In particular, the community leader would have been responsible for running the centre and for managing the municipal resources, as both the social workers and the armed guards were being removed. The nomination of a 'community leader' in the self-managed centre was made into a prerequisite for receiving resources, services and assistance from the municipality, when previously these had been 'automatically' provided (alongside social workers and security guards).

When I started my fieldwork in one such centre (for Moroccans)[8] in early 1995, it soon became clear to me that in the year since the introduction of this self-management policy, the control of the centre had increasingly been taken over – through the use of intimidation and violence – by a group of North African 'squatters' who, together with some gypsies, had turned the residential complex into a centre for selling stolen goods and drugs as well as for the consumption of the latter. This situation strongly affected the legitimate residents' security (who were being harassed and physically assaulted) as well as their ability to sleep and work effectively.

The legitimate residents attributed the cause of their insecurity and degraded environment to the policy of *autogestione* imposed by the municipal administration, which they rejected and interpreted as 'abandonment', as well as a lack of care and respect. Not surprisingly, the relationships between the legitimate CPA residents and the council administration had not only deteriorated, but the migrants were also less inclined than ever to adopt the *autogestione* policy. In fact, they had decided to resist such a policy.

Strategy

We can distinguish three stages in the migrants' strategies of resistance. The first was to deal directly with the top of the political hierarchy (namely the municipal councillor for immigration) and to bypass the intermediate administrative levels (i.e., of the municipal officials) held responsible for the implementation of the policies. Although the migrants had a clear idea of where things were going wrong in the municipal apparatus, this strategy was not very effective. Its ineffectiveness was due not only to the migrants' powerlessness but also to the fact that the city councillors and top politicians (besides having authored the policies) could not do without – but instead had to rely on – their own administrative apparatus of policy implementation. Nevertheless, the migrants' refusal to deal with the intermediate levels of the administration (the communication between migrants and the administration had broken down) seemed to work at least as a strategy of basic resistance. This resistance significantly disrupted the municipality's policy plans and implementation, and, increasingly, was also becoming a source of potential embarrassment for a municipality which prided itself on its reputation for progressive social policies in favour of the disadvantaged sectors of the population.

The second strategy developed as a result of the activity connected to a subsequent participatory action research (PAR) project that connected the CPA residents to the local political society of their district but with which the migrants had hitherto had no connection. This PAR project was carried out by an NGO that the municipality had hired not to empower the migrants (as would have been typical of this radical methodology) but as a twisted attempt to induce the migrants to accept and implement the management policy of *autogestione*. The PAR project was eventually brought back, at least to some extent, to an actual participatory process which was directed at building bridges to connect the isolated residents of the CPA to the local polity of the District.

Interestingly, after realising that, while sympathetic to their disadvantaged conditions, the local progressive society was not going to stand on their side against the City administration and therefore their problematic situation was unlikely to change, the migrants developed a third and unexpected strategy. Taking advantage of the new contacts established in the local polity (e.g., through participating in the District Commissions which are consultative bodies made up of residents and District politicians), the migrants developed a collaboration with the local political Right of the post-fascist Alleanza Nazionale and Berlusconi's Forza Italia. The Right had not reacted to the 'arrival' of the migrants on the local political scene by ignoring or antagonising them, as was its custom, but by adopting a politically shrewd, instrumental and opportunistic strategy of support to the migrants in an attempt to create difficulties for the 'progressive' city administration. This collaboration soon made the migrants feel 'stronger' and able to challenge the municipality openly. One of the most visible manifestations of this new political course were the two eye-catching *striscioni* (banners) hung on the fences surrounding the CPA which read: 'Many billions spent! Horrific health and hygienic conditions. Houses denied. Council absent' and 'Enough with concentration camps!' At this point, the CPA residents had broken with the undeclared practices of resistance (or infrapolitics – see Scott 1990) in favour of an explicitly contentious stand.

Achievements and Assessment

The achievements of the alliance with the Right included the following. First, their complaints (about security and hygienic conditions for instance) had increased their effectiveness, weight and resonance. This was achieved through the involvement of a lawyer (allegedly of right-wing affiliation) which was apparently paid for by the money saved from the migrants' ongoing rent strike. Partly as a result of this strategy, some urgent and long overdue repairs were at last carried out, and the public phone was finally reinstalled in the Centre. The second achievement was the acquisition of the necessary self-confidence to challenge the Council openly and publicly. Thirdly, largely as a result of their new strategic alliance, the migrants obtained greater consideration and respect from the administration, and above all improved efficiency in the provision of services, including the return – albeit for fewer hours than in the past – of the social workers in the CPA, and a systematic control and removal of unauthorised residents. However small, for the migrants, these achievements constituted a significant moral as well as material success against a powerful institution – the municipality – whose policies they had regarded as oppressive for several years.

The reading that the left-wing administration officials and activists of the Party of the Democratic Left (PDS) gave to the forging of this unusual collaboration between the CPA migrants and the Right was that the migrants had been duped and manipulated. The Right was notoriously anti-immigration and nationalist, and often portrayed migrants (in Bologna as elsewhere) as 'criminals', 'threats', 'rapists', etc. The Left saw the migrants as politically naïve and inexperienced, passive, short -sighted, unwise, Rightists and opportunists who did not understand the local political system. They even called them ungrateful and disrespectful to those (of the left-wing administration) who had made cheap accommodation available to them for many years. The Left's negative interpretation denied the legitimacy of the migrants' politics and also denied them recognition as political subjects with their own specific disadvantaged conditions and contentious claims. There seemed to be no space to discuss how the Left had set up a system which – despite being perhaps originally intended to support the migrants – had ended up malfunctioning. Rather than interpreting the migrants as being duped, it is preferable to view them in terms of Scott's notion of resistance. In fact, the migrants' acts were intended to mitigate and/or deny claims made about them by the left-wing administration. One obvious instance of that was the migrants' rejection of the policy requiring them to self-organise and act as an ethnic community.[9] The encounter with the Right offered them the possibility of significantly increasing the pressure on the municipality to improve their residential conditions, as well as of gaining greater recognition. The migrants, whose situation had deteriorated to such an extent that they reckoned they had little to lose, were very quick to recognise the political weight that a collaboration with the Right would add to their cause, and decided to go for it.

Here are some examples of conversations I had with the CPA leadership on their alliance with the Right, which provides a sense of how the migrants were not as politically naïve as the Left portrayed them:

> It is obvious that those of the District [the Right] are making an instrumental use of us but there wasn't any other choice if we wanted to wake up the others [the Left] ... for example also the *Resto del Carlino* [the local conservative newspaper] is using me, but the left-wing press never showed up when we called them ... I have kept the postal receipts! ... my task is that of raising the issue, of pointing out the problem ... like when you go to the doctor and you tell him 'I have a pain here' ... immigrants are waking up and want to enter into the system!

The following statement gives a sense of the level of frustration and discontent felt by the CPA residents: 'Everybody gets a share of the pie [the funds allocated to immigrant policies] except us, we remain here with the cockroaches. Enough!'

The epilogue to this story is that the CPA continued its difficult existence for a few more years until it was demolished to make way for a new road that apparently had been planned over a decade earlier – that is, before the creation of the CPA and the subsequent decision to turn it into a self-managed Moroccan 'community centre'. While I was conducting fieldwork, the migrants knew nothing about such a plan, and the municipal immigration officials themselves, if they were at all aware of it, did not speak about it beyond a very restricted circle.

Conclusions

The case study presented in this section illustrates how a seemingly progressive municipal residential policy requiring migrants' self-management was contested and neutralised by its powerless recipients. The impact of the recipients on the policy became stronger after they developed an alliance with the local political Right, which enabled them to publicly challenge the left-wing administration (coming out) and bring the policy negotiations to a 'higher' level involving new influential players (scaling up).

This case illustrates how policies are not only the result of the top-down initiatives of powerful actors but also of the bottom-up practices of the powerless. Indeed, it shows that policies are complex processes of negotiation involving numerous actors, both powerful and powerless. The case study also shows how contemporary Italian policies toward multiculturalism – which claim to recognise and empower migrants – were, in practice, detrimental to migrants' interests. It was only when these migrants allied across ethnic lines and against the multicultural logic that had grouped them together as ethnics (and expected them to act as a community in a context of marginality) that they were better able to represent their interests.

Case 2: Immigration Law and the Sin Papeles Protest in Barcelona

Context

At the beginning of the 1990s, Spain – like Italy – had begun to change from a country of emigration into one of immigration (Mendoza 2003) characterised by increasingly restrictive policies measures. This section discusses one such policy and the responses it generated. On Tuesday 23 January 2001, the new Spanish *Ley d'Estranjeria* (immigration law) designed and approved by Prime Minister José Maria Aznar's Partido Popular became effective. The new law reclassified as 'clandestines' over 100,000 migrants who had failed to 'regularise' their position, subjecting them to deportation (within a week) and preventing them from working legally, demonstrating, forming associations or affiliating to trade unions. This law was so draconian in denying migrants their rights that many of them felt they had little to lose from confronting the Spanish government head-on.

Strategy

Three days before the law came into force, approximately 360 'irregular' migrants locked themselves into the central Church of Santa Maria del Pi in Barcelona with the permission of the parish priest, Josep Vidal. They protested against the new law and sought to obtain a permit to stay and work. Some 328 of these *sin papeles* (undocumented migrants), who were mostly from the Indian sub-continent, north and sub-Saharan Africa, started a hunger strike. As one of them put it, 'we are against a law that discriminates against us, that separates us from the rest of the citizenry, making us inferior'. The protest was soon to extend to other churches in Barcelona and other Spanish cities, and became one of the most significant and successful migrant protests taking place in Southern Europe to date.

The *sin papeles*' struggle was critically supported by Barcelona's well-developed progressive civil society. By and large, this support ranged from the strong collaboration offered by 'radical' left-wing and Christian organisations and individuals to the moderate support declared by the socialist municipality of Barcelona and by well-established and institutionalised Christian and lay charities and NGOs. To the first group belonged significant sectors of the

Catholic Church, which crucially hosted the protest in some of its churches. 'Radical' groups but also many 'independent' volunteers provided most of the daily, face-to-face and physical support to the *sin papeles* both in the churches (providing for the migrants' basic needs) and outside (helping them to negotiate with the national government and so forth). These groups included the movement *Papeles para Tod@s* (Papers for All), the CGT union, the Neighbours Association, *Servicio Civil Internacional*, the Greens, *Izquierda Unida*, the Republican Left, etc.

To the second group belonged the 'progressive' institutions such as the municipality of Barcelona, the Socialist Party and the organisations, charities and NGOs working for or with them in the process of governance (e.g., as subcontractors for public service-delivery). This included the mainstream unions of CCOO and UGT, SOS Racisme, Caritas, IBN Batuta, etc. This second group supported the protest mostly 'in words' by stating their sympathy for the protesters' vulnerability and by criticising the new law.[10]

The protest also enjoyed large and sympathetic coverage by many well-known journalists and editorialists in the national and local media, who contributed considerably to making the Catalan and Spanish public opinion broadly sympathetic and supportive of the *sin papeles'* cause (e.g., by pointing out how inhumane and unjust the new law was). By and large, the migrants' protest was represented as a legitimate initiative of a group of powerless people against a new draconian policy. Renowned artists also publicly endorsed the protest in the media as well as at public events.

In addition to the occupation of a number of churches (*encierros*), the protest also involved several demonstrations and marches with thousands of people, including a memorable one featuring some 40,000 participants (an extraordinary figure for pro-migrant issues) as well as a petition signed by 60,000. Clearly, crucial to the success of the protest was the remarkable determination of the migrant protesters themselves, who kept struggling against a myriad of linguistic, cultural, organisational, financial and logistical obstacles.

Achievements and Assessments

As anticipated, the migrants' mobilisation was successful and within forty-eight days, they had managed to obtain the much-desired permit to stay and work in Spain for 'extraordinary reasons' such as 'humanitarian reasons' or 'settlement in the receiving society' (*arraygo*). The mobilisation was also successful because it triggered protests from progressive elements in Spanish and Catalan civil society, media and public opinion against the new policy, providing a concrete focus (the first victims of the new draconian law) around which to coalesce. While failing to formally change the law, this civic and media response discouraged the national government from fully enforcing its new policy. They did not go into the churches and deport the occupants or carry out stop-and-search practices. Most likely, this 'soft' implementation was to avoid escalating the protests and undermining the government's popularity among Spanish citizens. As a result, the new policy was de facto neutralised in several of its harshest aspects.

One aspect of the protest worth reflecting upon in our analysis of policy change from below is the split that took place in the 'pro-migrant' front described above, when the migrants occupying the churches decided to undertake the hunger strike. This split largely reflected pre-existing and latent divisions and alliances, and featured on one side those institutions and organisations belonging to the local 'governance' bloc. This side asked the migrants to cease the hunger strike, as this form of protest allegedly did not constitute an appropriate form of protest in Europe. It was regarded as too extreme for local customs and too dangerous for the health of the protesters themselves – as if the protesters did not know. Instead, they wanted the migrants to delegate to them the representation of their interests vis-à-vis the government. This side of the 'pro-migrant' front saw the other side as 'idealist', 'utopian', 'unreasonable', 'unrealistic', 'irresponsible', 'unreliable', 'ultra-lefty', 'disorganised' and 'unprofessional'. For instance, in an interview with a spokesperson of the well-established SOS Racisme, the organisations and collectives external to governance were regarded and dismissed as 'manipulating' migrants.

On the other side of the 'pro-migrant' movement clustered the 'alternative' leftist and Christian groups (ranging from monks to members of the *okupas* libertarian movement) as well as many individuals who, unlike the governmental Left, respected and supported the format of protest chosen by the migrants, including the hunger strike, without necessarily agreeing with it. As one of the Spanish activists who supported the protest put it, 'we were more inclined to conduct a softer type of struggle but the majority of the migrants decided for the hunger strike, especially the Hindus and the Pakistanis'.

This 'alternative' sector of the 'pro-migrant' front tended to view the other with suspicion and described them as 'collaborationists', 'after power and careers', 'quiescent', 'charitable', 'patronising' and 'paternalist'. The 'mainstream' Left was also referred to as *la bella izquierda* (the good-looking Left) to signal its concern with appearance, form, institutions and procedures, and which was viewed as no longer being bothered about the disenfranchised sectors of the population and or wishing to get its hands dirty over them.

Some of these critical views of the mainstream Left were also present among the migrant protesters, as the following quote from one of my informants illustrates:

Since the PP [Partido Popular] came to power, none of the main trade unions, none of the main organised groups had confronted it [on immigration policy], it was us the *sin papeles* – those without rights to organise and demonstrate – who are challenging the new immigration law … We are seen [by the moderate pro-migrant side] as incapable of self-organising, of taking decisions, and worse of negotiating. This protest has shown that undocumented migrants can negotiate with the government, can negotiate with the institutions.

Migrant protesters had, on the contrary, a very appreciative view of the Church and of ordinary people:

> Without the Church [which hosted the protest in a number of its churches] we from the streets would have not been able to do anything because the police would have quickly dislodged us.[11] … The support of the city population and of the neighbours has to be pointed out. Without them as well we wouldn't have had blankets, mattresses, food, water and so forth because the [local] institutions did not provide them.

While both sides, the moderates and the alternatives, contributed to the success of the mobilisation, it was the latter group that crucially sustained the migrants in their struggle for regularisation, especially during the hardest and most delicate moments of the protest.

Conclusion

This case study of a mobilisation against a new immigration law enacted by migrants and involving advocacy groups and the media shows how 'policy targets' and dissenting citizens can have a significant effect on how a policy is implemented and works in practice.

Unlike the Bologna case, the migrants in Barcelona enjoyed the support of local political and civic organisations as well as the media from the outset. This support enabled them to start straight away with an open and large-scale challenge to the policy, which eventually led to the neutralisation of the policy for all those involved in the protest, who obtained permits to stay on in Spain.

As in Bologna, in Barcelona, the migrants' mobilisation was about rights and material (rather than cultural) aspects of recognition (as defined by Yar 2001; see also Però 2005). This mobilisation sought to secure the right to stay on to live and work in Spain, i.e., the possibility of legitimately supporting themselves and their families there, and of not wasting the resources they had invested in the migration journey. Issues of ethnocultural recognition typical of a (neoliberal) multicultural agenda – such as being recognised as distinct communities or being entitled to specific cultural rights – were clearly peripheral to the need to be recognised as human beings, citizens or legitimate residents.

Case 3: Latin American Workers' Mobilisations in London

Context

In the early 1990s, the U.K. – like Italy and Spain – experienced a large wave of immigration. However, unlike Italy and Spain – which were receiving international migrants in high numbers for the first time – for the U.K., this population inflow represented a second wave, the first one being that of the 'colonial workers' of the post-War years (Castles and Miller 2009) who turned into long-standing ethnic minorities. However, it was only in the mid-2000s that the U.K. came to recognise that it is no longer a post-migration country (Martiniello 2005) but rather one of new immigrations as well, and was indeed a country of 'superdiversity' (Vertovec 2006), one where new migrants (this time from countries without colonial links to the U.K.) were arriving into an already multi-ethnic society. Latin Americans are perhaps one of the most typical groups of this second migration wave.

The Latin American Workers Association (LAWA)[12] was set up in the second half of 2004 by three Colombian and one Chilean trade unionists as part of the British Transport and General Workers Union (hereafter T&G-Unite). Forming LAWA was seen as a necessary step to protect and support more effectively the large number of Latin American workers experiencing super-exploitation and abuses of various types in the workplace. Until the creation of LAWA, employment had been a crucial aspect of life which was left 'uncovered' by existing Latino organisations. In the words of one of its founders:

> LAWA is the product of a necessity, which has emerged progressively after that many Latinos had solved their immigration, housing and benefits problems ... Besides addressing some of the exploitative aspects experienced by Latinos workers in Britain, LAWA struggles for helping the Latinos workers coming out of the invisibility with dignity not by 'asking' [*pedir*] but by 'demanding' [*exigir*]. Together with other workers organisations – the Portuguese, the Turkish, the African – we share the same class need [*necesidad de clase*].[13]

The kind of problems that Latin Americans experience and the nature of LAWA's activities are illustrated by Ines:

> Sexual harassment, psychological maltreatment ... abuses concerning working time, verbal abuses and discrimination of all sorts. Essentially all that happens because one doesn't know the [British] laws ... and people [employers and managers] take advantage of that and abuse the power they've got ... I myself had a case and after solving that, I stayed on working with them [LAWA] as a volunteer. I was abused verbally and psychologically by my managers ... It happened in a clothes shop for which I worked.

Although support in the field of employment was, in principle, available to Latino workers through the existing British trade unions, such support was not, in practice, accessible to them, for reasons of communication/language, trust, lack of relationships or links between T&G-Unite and the Latin collective, and a lack of adequate efforts on the part of the union to reach out for migrant workers.

An important concern in setting up LAWA was the preservation of its autonomy. LAWA founders had always been determined to form a political rather than a civic or community 'charitable' organisation. They wanted to avoid relying on public funding – as these organisations often do – because this would entail economic dependence on the state (an institution that they did not see as promoting the interests of working people and in particular of migrant workers) and political restrictions (for receiving public funding and a 'charitable' status). In the end, the four founders' assumption about the need for LAWA proved correct and the organisation 'boomed' straight away (and with it Latino affiliations to T&G-Unite) to the extent that after a few months of activity, LAWA was already struggling to keep up with the demand for assistance.

Strategy

The field of political initiative in which LAWA operates can be described as 'socio-political'. LAWA is neither interested in party politics nor in lobbying national and local politicians and officials (as other Latin American organisations such as the Latin Front do; see Però 2008a). They privilege political initiative in the socioeconomic sphere, focusing on issues of workers rights and, more generally, material justice issues. In addition to the protection of Latin-American workers in the U.K., they are connected to the initiatives of social forums and of the global justice movement. For example, in 2004, they participated in the European Social Forum in London. They have also been developing international/transnational links with trade unions in Latin America.

In terms of 'identity politics', LAWA articulates a particular blend of class and ethnicity. It aims to promote greater ethnocultural recognition of Latin Americans within the marked class framework of the trade union movement. Overall, LAWA considers it important to be fully part of a large and organised British trade union, but its leaders feel there are ethnocultural specificities which require a 'customised' treatment, hence their organisation as Latinos within T&G-Unite. However, as Fernando said, 'the objective and the essence of the struggle, as well as what unites us with other immigrant groups, is a question of class'. The attitudes that LAWA members have towards unauthorised migrant workers further help us to understand LAWA's political vision. As Irene put it: 'Work is a right that all human beings have. Whether they are illegal or not makes no difference to us ... and this is why we also fight for illegal immigrants.'

Since 2004, Latin Americans have also become increasingly active through the 'mainstream' T&G-Unite (rather than through LAWA). For many of them, this 'direct' involvement with T&G-Unite developed largely as a result of the recent large-scale efforts – like the 'Justice for Cleaners' campaign – to organise migrant workers in the cleaning sector. In terms of politics, this second and 'direct' engagement of Latin-American migrants with T&G-Unite represents a rather 'classic' form of class politics, i.e., one in which the focus on the 'socioeconomic' dimension of the migrants' needs at the workplace is central and the 'ethnocultural' dimension – while present (e.g., in the resorting to migrant organisers in order to carry out the campaign) – is complementary. This politics is also one that targets all workers independently of their ethnocultural background, who in the cleaning sector happen to be essentially migrant (with a significant quota of Latin Americans). Recently, T&G-Unite has also strengthened its pro-migrant stand by starting to campaign for a regularisation of unauthorised immigrants, as it recognises that their 'irregular' immigrant status makes them vulnerable to super-exploitation and abuses, and condemns them to a position of permanent exclusion, marginality, vulnerability and fear. As for LAWA, the prevailing attitude within T&G-Unite towards unauthorised migrants is inclusionary – they are seen as workers regardless of the legal status attached to them by the state. T&G-Unite has recently subscribed to a major campaign for the regularisation of unauthorised migrant workers in the U.K., in which it features as one of the key players, together with the Catholic Church and others.

Achievements and Assessment

In terms of achievements, LAWA and T&G-Unite have unionised a remarkable number of Latin-American workers (apparently in 2006, these numbered about 1,000). This process has taken place in a relatively short period of time and by overcoming a number of fears and prejudices, including the fear of deportation (a recurrent fear among unauthorised migrants) and the view (recurrent among Colombians) that trade unions are guerrilla supporters. The second achievement is the operationalisation of the protection of Latino workers which both LAWA and T&G-Unite have performed. Thirdly, they have also gained a greater visibility and popularity in the eyes of the Latin-American collective and among employers, who are becoming aware that there is an increasing chance of facing the trade unions if they abuse migrant workers.

Finally, all this activity has strengthened the overall integration of Latin-American migrants into British society, particularly in the socio-political sphere.

Conclusions

More generally, the case study of the Latino migrants in London has revealed that the trade union is a growing form of Latino engagement which is not only important in itself but is also one which is crucial to recognise if we want to avoid the 'ethnicist' (Brah 1996) or 'culturalist' (Vertovec 1996) reductionism typical of much of the literature on migrants and minorities, which tends to conceive and represent them only as ethnocultural subjects while overlooking their other political identities, relationships and engagements.

The case of London confirms the point made earlier in the chapter that the form that policy assumes in practice is the result of the activity not only of 'powerful' institutional actors but also of 'powerless' ones who – by organising within a trade union, as in this case – were better able to demand the application of the existing legislation that protects workers from employers' abuse. It also reveals how the policy engagement of subaltern actors is not restricted to resistance or opposition to oppressive policies, but can also be found in efforts to have existing (but unapplied) equitable policies applied in practice.

The possibility for migrants to influence policy in this case was enhanced greatly when they scaled up their policy engagement and found allies and advocates among the native citizenry. Once again, the case of the Latinos shows that migrants' needs are not just ethnocultural, as the prevailing ideas of multiculturalism seem to maintain, but material too. It also shows that the best way to achieve working rights is not by following the prevailing multicultural organising model encouraged by the receiving society and forming ethnic community organisations with apolitical/charitable status, but by organising into more politicised and 'confrontational' ways around material issues and through class organisations.

Conclusions

Following an approach that appreciates not only how people see policies but also how they concretely act to transform them, this chapter has discussed policies concerning migrant workers in Europe. Most of the migrants I have described in this chapter lack voting rights, have limited social or political capital and are positioned within a system that seeks to exploit them as much as possible. Under these circumstances, the room for migrants to induce formal policy changes appears on the whole modest. However, this chapter has shown that it is still possible for migrants to influence policy, for example, when they mobilise to mitigate exclusionary policies (as in the case of the *sin-papeles* in Barcelona or in that of the migrants of a residential centre in Bologna) or to request the application of already existing inclusionary policies (as in the case of LAWA and T&G-Unite in London).

The ethnographic material presented suggests that to increase their chances of influencing policy, it is particularly important for migrants to make allies beyond their ethnic circles and to forge links with 'mainstream' collective actors (like unions, parties and churches), as well as to garner more sympathetic coverage in the media. Political isolation contributes to the vulnerability and marginalisation of migrants.[14] Migrants' 'best allies' in their struggles to improve their conditions in the receiving context seem to be committed autonomous civil society organisations, i.e., those organisations that are not hired by governmental bodies to deliver policies and that are 'free' to be openly 'political' (e.g., when they do not have to observe – like T&G-Unite in the U.K. – the restrictions inherent in 'charity' status). Less effective and more risky strategies seem to be those collaborations with organisations that have instrumental or exploitative attitudes (like that of the CPA migrants with the Right in the Bologna case) or with organisations that are subordinated to governmental bodies (such as the NGOs subcontracted by the municipality of Barcelona).

In the U.K. case study, as in Italy and Spain, breaking out of the migrant-ethnic group circuit to collaborate with 'non-migrant' organisations entails going against the norms of civic engagement that are typically encouraged by neoliberal multiculturalism. For those migrants concerned with overcoming policy denials, exploitation, lack of rights and marginalisation, 'ethnicist' attitudes that reduce the migration-integration problematic to a merely 'cultural issue' are misleading and unproductive. It is perhaps with some of the organisations that articulate interests of class (like T&G-Unite in London) – which neoliberalism and 'Third Way' politics represent as obsolete – that migrants appear better off collaborating in an attempt to produce tangible policy change.

In other words, the three case studies suggest that to be successful at influencing the policies affecting their lives, migrants have to transcend the dominant multicultural paradigm that persistently constructs them in terms of ethnocultural otherness and expects them to organise primarily as ethnic subjects. This construction is one of the key characteristics of the politics of multiculturalism in the current age. Multiculturalism is supposed to be about recognising difference and empowering migrants and minorities, but its effects, as seen in this chapter, appear more aligned to those of neoliberal governamentality than its advocates care to admit (see Mulhern 2001).

Finally, this chapter has highlighted one of the possible directions for future anthropological studies of policy, namely the examination of policy changes produced through the bottom-up initiatives of the governed. In order to recognise the agency of the governed, we need to adopt a broader and more comprehensive definition of policy change, one that conceives of change as not just the result of top-down initiatives of powerful institutions but also of the bottom-up engagements of subaltern individuals. Analytically, this attention to the engagement of subaltern individuals should include not only large-scale successful initiatives that lead to formal changes in law and policy but also a much wider spectrum of initiatives entailing: (a) in the case of oppressive policies, their full or partial neutralisation (as in the Bologna case) or their more 'relaxed' enforcement (as in the Barcelona case); and (b) in the case of already existing 'positive' policies, their fuller application (as in the London case). A focus on the bottom-up collective and infrapolitical actions through which the governed seek to transform policy constitutes an important way for the anthropology of policy to enhance our understanding of the complex and unequal policy worlds that people inhabit while staying committed to the cause of deprived social groups. Strategic foci for future critical and transformative research on resistance and policy change are those of 'scaling up' and 'coming out', whereby individualised and informal resistance is transformed into more collective and organised resistance. Focusing on how and under what circumstances policy resistance comes to be 'declared' and articulated on a larger scale, and with what impacts, seems to constitute a productive avenue for moving resistance studies out of the impasse produced by the proliferation of merely descriptive accounts of copying strategies and symbolic dissent.

Acknowledgements

I am very grateful to Cris Shore, Sue Wright, Dvora Yanow and Elisabetta Zontini as well as the anonymous readers for the precious comments and suggestions they provided on earlier drafts of this chapter.

Notes

1. Clearly, this is a simplification as there are social actors and organisations acting on policy that find themselves somewhere inbetween the makers and the recipients.
2. Scott defines 'resistance' as: 'any act(s) by member(s) of a subordinate class that is or are intended either to mitigate or deny claims (for example, rents, taxes, prestige) made on that class by superordinate classes (for example, landlords, large farmers, the state) or to advance its own claims (for example, work, land, charity, respect) vis-à-vis those superordinate classes' (1985: 290). Scott also highlights the importance of focusing on intentions rather than consequences in trying to understand resistance, since many acts of resistance may not succeed in achieving the intended results (1985: 290).
3. This idea of policy change from below represents an even broader concept than Levison and Sutton's appropriation (2001: 3), as it also encompasses those policy engagements of marginalised actors that 'simply' resist policy without necessarily laying claims to create policy or to become formally involved the process of governance.
4. Fletcher (2001) notes the importance of focusing on how subalterns come to articulate practices of resistance, particularly through alternative counter-hegemonic elaborations (see also Però 2008a).
5. For a review of the anthropological work on social movements, see Burdick 1995; Edelman 2001; Escobar 1992; Gibb 2001; and Nash 2005.
6. Not all scholars fall into these categories. Some, especially those from the anthropology and feminism fields, have recently developed approaches that seek to reconcile the microlevels and the macrolevels, the experiential and the abstract, and to be more 'people-centred' and cognisant of migrants' agency and subjectivity (for an overview, see Però 2008b).
7. In accordance with Law 39/90, which devolved to local authorities the responsibility for many immigration issues.
8. For a 'thicker' ethnographic account, see Però 2005 and 2007a.
9. Others involved delays in the payment of rent, an undeclared rent strike and several forms of transgression of the regulations of the Centre.
10 For an ethnography of the governance of migrants in Barcelona, see Però 2007b.
11 Here the term 'Church' does not refer to the Catholic Church in its entirety, but only to specific sectors and individuals particularly committed to the cause of the marginalised, like Josep Vidal – the priest of Santa Maria del Pi who in line with its personal trajectory (he had actively opposed Franco's regime) hosted the *sin papeles'* protest in his church after they had been rejected by the Cathedral of Barcelona.
12 The initial acronym of LAWA was later changed to LAWAS
13. For a more detailed account of LAWA, see Però 2008b.

14. All numerically small groups arguably need to forge allegiances with stronger organisations and movements in order to have greater policy impact. For migrants – who lack voting rights, sociopolitical capital and often even the right to be in the country of immigration – this allying out of the (ethnic) group seems particularly compelling.

References

Brah, A. 1996. *Cartographies of Diasporas. Contesting Identities.* London: Routledge.

Burdick, J. 1995. 'Uniting Theory and Practice in the Ethnography of Social Movements', *Dialectical Anthropology* 20: 361–85.

Castles S. and Miller M. 2009. *The Age of Migration*, 4th ed. Basingstoke: Palgrave Macmillan.

Comaroff, J. 1985. *Body of Power, Spirit of Resistance.* Chicago: University of Chicago Press.

Dirks, N. 1994. 'Ritual and Resistance: Subversion as a Social Fact', in N. Dirks, G. Eley and S. Ortner (eds), *Culture/Power/History.* Princeton: Princeton University Press, pp. 483–503.

Edelman, M. 2001. Social Movements. Changing Paradigms and Forms of Politics', *Annual Review of Anthropology*, 30: 285–317.

Escobar, A. 1992. 'Culture, Practice and Politics: Anthropology and the Study of Social Movements', *Critique of Anthropology* 12(4): 395–432.

Fletcher, R. 2001. 'What Are We Fighting For? Rethinking Resistance in a Pewenche Community in Chile', *Journal of Peasant Studies* 28(3): 37–66.

Fox, R. and Starn, O. 1997 'Introduction', in R. Fox and O. Starn (eds), *Between Resistance and Revolution: Cultural Politics and Social Protest.* New Brunswick, NJ: Rutgers University Press, pp. 1–16.

Gibb, R. 2001. 'Towards an Anthropology of Social Movements', *Journal des Antropologues* 85–86: 233–53.

Gough, K. 2002 [1968]. 'New Proposals for Anthropologists', in J. Vincent (ed.), *The Anthropology of Politics.* Oxford: Blackwell, pp. 110–19.

Hale, C. 1997. 'Cultural Politics of Identity in Latin America', *Annual Review of Anthropology* 26: 567–90.

Kertzer, D. 1980. *Comrades and Christians.* Cambridge: Cambridge University Press.

King, R., Fielding, A. and Black, R. 1997. 'The International Migration Turnaround in Southern Europe', in R. King and R. Black (eds), *Southern Europe and the New Immigrations.* Brighton: Sussex Academic Press, pp. 1–25.

Levinson, B. and Sutton, M. 2001. 'Introduction: Policy as/in Practice. A Sociocultural Approach to the Study of Educational Policy', in M. Sutton and B. Levinson (eds), *Policy as Practice.* Santa Barbara: Greenwood Press, pp. 1–22.

Malkki, L. 1995. 'Refugees and Exile: From "Refugee Studies" to the National Order of Things', *Annual Review of Anthropology* 24: 495–523.

Martiniello, M. 2005. 'The Political Participation, Mobilization and Representation of Immigrants and their Offspring in Europe', in R. Bauböck (ed.), *Migration and Citizenship: Legal Status, Rights and Political Participation*, Amsterdam: IMISCOE, pp. 52–64.

Mendoza, C. 2003. *Labour Immigration in Southern Europe.* Aldershot: Ashgate.

Meyer, D. 2003. 'How Social Movements Matter', *Contexts* 2(4): 30–35.

Mulhern, F. 2001. *Culture: Metaculture*, London: Routledge.

Nash, J. 1992. 'Interpreting Social Movements: Bolivian Resistance to Economic Conditions Imposed by the International Monetary Fund', *American Ethnologist* 19(2): 275–93.

———. 2005. 'Social Movements and Global Processes', in J. Nash (ed.), *Social Movements: an Anthropological Reader*, Oxford: Blackwell, pp. 1–26.

Però, D. 2005. 'Left-wing Politics, Civil Society and Immigration in Italy. The Case of Bologna', *Ethnic and Racial Studies* 28(5): 832–58.

———. 2007a. *Inclusionary Rhetoric/Exclusionary Practices. Left-wing Politics and Migrants in Italy*. Oxford: Berghahn Books.

———. 2007b. 'Migrants and the Politics of Governance in Barcelona', *Social Anthropology* 15(3): 271–86.

———. 2008a. 'Migrants' Mobilization and Anthropology. Reflections from the Experience of Latin Americans in the United Kingdom', in D. Reed-Danahay and C. Brettell (eds), *Citizenship, Political Engagement, and Belonging. Immigrants in Europe and the United States*. New Brunswick, NJ: Rutgers University Press, pp. 103–23.

———. 2008b. 'Political Engagements of Latin Americans in the UK: Issues, Strategies and the Public Debate', *Focaal* 51: 73–90.

Però, D. and Solomos, J. 2010. 'Migrant Politics and Mobilisation: Exclusion, Engagements, Incorporation', *Ethnic and Racial Studies* 33(1): 1–18.

Pratt, J. 2003, *Class, Nation and Identity. The Anthropology of Political Movements*, London: Pluto Press.

Schneider A. and Ingram, H. 1993. 'Social Construction of Target Populations: Implications for Politics and Policy', *American Political Science Review* 87(2): 334–47.

Scott, J. 1985. *Weapons of the Weak: Everyday Forms of Peasant Resistance*. London: Yale University Press.

———. 1990. *Domination and the Arts of Resistance. Hidden Transcripts*. New Haven and London: Yale University Press.

Shore, C. and Wright, S. 1997. 'Policy a New Field of Anthropology', in C. Shore and S. Wright (eds), *Anthropology of Policy. Critical Perspectives on Governance and Power*. London: Routledge, pp. 3–30.

Smith, G. 1999, *Confronting the Present*. Oxford: Berg.

Starn, O. 1999. *Nightwatch. The Politics of Protest in the Andes*. Durham, NC: Duke University Press.

Vertovec, S. 1996. 'Multiculturalism, Culturalism and Public Incorporation', *Ethnic and Racial Studies* 19: 49–69.

———. 2006. *The Emergence of Super-Diversity in Britain*. COMPAS Working Paper No. 25. Oxford: Centre on Migration Policy and Society.

Wimmer, A. and Glick Schiller, N. 2003. 'Methodological Nationalism, the Social Sciences, and the Study of Migration: An Essay in Historical Epistemology', *International Migration Review* 37(3): 576–610.

Wolf, E. 2002 [1971]. 'National Liberation', in J. Vincent (ed.), *The Anthropology of Politics*. Oxford: Blackwell, pp. 120–26.

Yar, M. 2001. 'Beyond Nancy Fraser "Perspectival Dualism"', *Economy and Society* 30(3): 288–303.

Chapter 14

Integration Policy and Ethnic Minority Associations

Clarissa Kugelberg

Sweden is a country with very many associations and you learn a lot by being active in associations. To participate and be involved in a society, you have to take part in what there is. This is our new country and we have children, so we have to participate. And we think that we need competence and education for this. This is integration, is it not?

This is what a young woman, Frances, told me when I asked her about an ethnic minority association she and some friends had formed. The association brought together women from many African countries.

In Sweden, non-profit associations are indeed considered a significant part of social life and have received financial assistance from the state and local communities for decades. In this chapter, I will illustrate how national policies were converted into principles for allocating financial support to ethnic minority associations and how these principles were turned into decisions through a local interplay between members of ethnic minority associations and local bureaucrats. I will highlight how these procedures influence association activities. The discussion is based on fieldwork in one local community in Sweden. During my fieldwork, a new administrative procedure was developed both to create a more efficient and impartial tool for allocating financial support, and to direct the associations' activities towards those that fulfilled the political goals of the local authority. A new policy for ethnic minority integration stated that financial support should facilitate democracy, gender equity and integration, and these motives were integrated into the new administrative procedures.[1]

This chapter focuses on the encounter between individuals' life worlds[2] and the abstract world of political institutions, with their stereotyping and institutionalised classifications. When exploring how the processes of governing and self-governing are intertwined, it is of crucial importance to investigate the taxonomic activities of local civil servants – the ways in which they classify and make distinctions, exclusions and inclusions (Douglas 1987; Handelman 1990; Herzfeld 1992). But it is equally important to explore how classifications are understood and received by members of ethnic minority associations – how well they correspond with members' experiences and knowledge, social conditions and daily activities, and the consequences that such classifications have on interactional dynamics. Classifications entail power and are a means of control and management, but institutions' activities and decisions need to appear rational and fair if they are to justify their authority and power. There is an intrinsic tension between institutions' classification systems and people's life worlds and expectations. Taking a phenomenological approach to the meaning of association life in Sweden in order to uncover the complexities and divergent perceptions involved, I have followed concrete interactions and listened to participants' accounts of what they actually do and how they experience their work.

The field for my study is a middle-sized Swedish town with around 100,000 inhabitants. Ten per cent of the inhabitants have a foreign background.[3] The town has a diversified economy and is situated in a region that had a high level of unemployment at the time of my research. In 2007, Sweden received 100,000 immigrants (SCB 2008a) and 17.5 per cent of the population had a foreign background (SCB 2008b). The immigration pattern was the same as in the rest of Sweden. During the 1960s and 1970s, most immigrants came from Finland and Yugoslavia as labour immigrants. In the 1970s and 1980s, the majority were refugees from Latin America, followed by refugees from Iran and Kurdistan in the late 1980s, while in the mid 1990s, refugees from Bosnia were in the majority. At the time of my fieldwork, the majority of refugees came from Iraq.

My fieldwork took place between 2005 and 2006. I participated in public meetings as well as in association meetings and activities. I interviewed members of associations, politicians and bureaucrats, and investigated national and local policy documents. I presented myself as a researcher from the university who wanted to learn about the conditions for ethnic minority associations. I was welcome to attend meetings, and association members let me read their documents without restrictions. The bureaucrats and politicians took time for the interviews and they seemed interested in informing me about their new administrative procedure, of which they were apparently very proud. However, when I asked if I could attend an internal meeting for allocating funding, I was not invited. This might have been due to the fact that the administrative procedure was under construction, but I assume that it also showed the politically sensitive character of their work. Migration is a highly debated political issue in Sweden. However, during the 2006 election, it had almost disappeared from the agenda, compared to the election four years earlier, when it was a major campaign topic. Migration has an impact on the whole of Sweden, but its significance varies strongly. In the large cities, ethnic segregation and discrimination has become a great problem and the source of considerable debate, whereas in middle-sized towns, such as the one in which I conducted my fieldwork, the issue appears less often on the political agenda.

In the next section, I outline two policies – one for popular movements in general and the other for ethnic minority integration – which together shape the national discursive frame for the local governing of ethnic minority associations. I point out an inherent tension between the objective to support associations in their own right and the ambition to govern and exploit them. Thereafter, I will present one ethnic minority association and will discuss the impact of the local policy on its formation. In the last section, I describe how the process of funding allocation reflects and is framed by policy structures surrounding ethnic minority associations on a national and a local level. I show how the policy is produced by the civil servants' concrete procedures, together with the associations' efforts to adjust to institutional rules.

Ethnic Minority Associations in the Intersection of Two Policy Domains

In Sweden, a particular domain of policy making has been generated by the existence of popular movements (*folkrörelser*). These movements have had an important role in the development of the welfare state, and selected movements have been integrated into the mainstream corporate political system of Swedish decision making (Micheletti 1994). These popular movements are surrounded by an ideology praising their role as a democratic force in Swedish society. This ideology embraces normative ideals, and associations are seen as schools for democracy (Lindgren 1999; Wijkström, Einarsson and Larsson 2004). They are also believed to give politically under-represented individuals opportunities for political participation.

During the 1990s, a new public management philosophy introduced an instrumental attitude towards associations, which resulted in an increasing proportion of their financial support being targeted at specific objectives in line with political goals (Regeringens proposition 2005/06: 4: 9, Wijkström, Einarsson and Larsson 2004). This development was part of wider political and economic changes not only in Sweden but throughout Europe, characterised by cutbacks in the public sector, new network forms of governance and various collaborations between authorities, civil society and the private sector, and emerging market relations between the state and nonprofit organisations (Rhodes 2000; Però 2005). Increased regulation was justified by the need to control the use of public expenditure so as to guarantee efficiency.

Critics, however, pointed out the risks of threatening the independence of associations. A growing political concern to strengthen associations has emerged during recent years, partly owing to a drop in members (SOU 2000: 1; Svenska Kommunförbundet 2001). The normative ideal of valuing commitment to all kinds of organisations as a bedrock of Swedish democracy has remained.

As a result, there are conflicting attitudes towards associations in general, which also affect ethnic minority associations. There is a strong belief in the benefits of active ethnic minority associations, not least for the Swedish policy on ethnic minority integration. But the policy has changed significantly several times since it was first outlined in the 1970s. In 1974, support was motivated primarily in terms of the associations' importance for identity and social unity within ethnic minorities. Ethnic minority associations were also seen as representing their members and as such were assumed to promote the interests of the ethnic group, thereby making them an important part of democratic processes. In 1984, the significance of associations as representatives for immigrant society was again stressed, but this time only for their role in maintaining and promoting culture and identity (Borevi 2002). In the 1990s, the government's objective to regulate associations also affected ethnic minority associations (Lindgren 1999). By tying part of the state's financial support to prioritised issues and specified projects and activities, associations were to be pushed towards working for the political goals of integration, and their role as culture and identity builders was given less importance.

Today, the support for associations as such is combined with compelling them to act in accordance with the political goals of integration. Can these objectives be combined? Political scientists depict this problem as an inherent dilemma of democracies (Dahl 1982; Borevi 2002). On the one hand, independent associations are seen as fundamental to the reproduction of society by giving citizens opportunities to take part in democratic processes. With increased governing, there is a risk of undermining this force for democratic development by hampering members from creating their own order and, as a consequence, reducing their engagement. On the other hand, the state must exert certain forms of control in the name of national and democratic protection.

Following these lines of argument, we can see that ethnic minority associations fall within two policy domains: the domain of popular movements and the domain of ethnic minority integration. This double inscription has positioned them as special and different from other associations. In the following sections, I will show how this positioning is reproduced at the local level and how the same ambiguous attitudes frame local governing and the allocation of financial support to ethnic minority associations.

Ethnic Minority Associations in Research

Research has shown the multidimensional and changing meanings of ethnic minority associations (Aytar 2009; Rex, Joly and Wipert 1987). This research has revealed a number of common grounds for founding an ethnic minority association. One is the objective to protect and nurture ways of life that deviate from the ways of life in the host society. Seeing to immigrants' needs and wishes in the host country constitutes another ground for forming an organisation, either by providing for these needs themselves or by persuading the government of the host country to do so (Rex, Joly and Wipert 1987; Wingborg 1999). A third ground is for an association to serve as a link between the diaspora and the country of origin. This transnational perspective on ethnic minority associations has deepened our understanding of their meaning for immigrants' identity and life situations, as well as of their significance in the surrounding societies (Faist 2004; Glick Schiller 1992). Such findings have situated ethnic minority associations in a broadened contextual framework and have revealed the important role they play in sustaining the double existential framework of migrants (Rex, Joly and Wipert 1987).

Research indicates that political and institutional opportunity structures have a major impact on the emergence and development of associations (Ireland 1994; Wahlbeck 1999; Knocke and Ng 1999: 111). Others have criticised this perspective, which was developed in policy science for comparative research on social movements, for being too narrow. Besides the political and institutional conditions in the host society, critics argue that members' experiences from their country of origin and their actual experiences in the host country must be included in the analyses if we are to understand the differences between associations (Però 2007; Aytar 2009; Bengtsson and Kugelberg 2009).

In Sweden, we find an idealised view of associations not only in politics but also among many researchers. This view also seems to underlie the perspective of critical researchers, even when their research reveals a lack of democratic values in associations (Lindgren 1999; Micheletti 1994). Political scientist Robert Putman has been particularly influential with regard to this perspective. His argument that a civil society with active associations creates a democratic spirit, cohesive norms and a strong trust in the political system has gained particular attention (1993). Scholars have shown great similarities between Putman's ideas and the Swedish ideology of popular movements (Bengtsson 2004; Borevi 2002).

Some critical perspectives on civil society have given more nuanced pictures of non-profit organisations and have shown how dimensions such as gender, age and ethnicity intersect and reproduce unequal relations (SOU 2004: 59: 202–8; Però 2005). The marginal position of women in ethnic minority associations has been exposed in international research (Knocke and Ng 1999; SOU 2004: 59). Like society as a whole, associations are found to be male-dominated and it is suggested that authorities' administrative procedures and requirements put women at a disadvantage.

The interplay between policies, local political institutions and ethnic minority associations is complex and insufficiently studied. In the following discussion, I address these questions by trying to 'study through' the implementation of these policies on a national and a local level in order to explore how they influence gender relations and the scope for agency of ethnic minority associations (Shore and Wright 1997). I will in particular focus on the interaction between civil servants and members of a women's association.

A Women's Association

When I contacted the Bureau for Immigrant Issues for the first time, the African women's association was described as fulfilling all the criteria for a desirable association. But ten months later, the civil servants said that they were disappointed that the association had not yet accomplished the goals it had set out for itself. When the group of friends started the association, they had several motives. They wanted to assist women who had recently arrived from their countries of origin, to create a circle for their mutual benefit and a place where they could talk about their experiences in Swedish society. As the quotation in the introduction indicates, they saw managing an association as one way of participating in Swedish society. But, in addition – and perhaps most of all – the women wanted to raise money to support other women in their countries of origin. Ann, one of the other founders, said:

> Ann: In all kinds of activities you have a vision that changes as time passes, we wanted to help African women in our home countries, this was our vision - we wanted to do something. And when we think about a woman, she knows which needs she shall fulfil to benefit the whole village. This was our ambition.
> Clarissa: Was this as important as helping women in this town?
> Ann: Of course, this was our main vision, but somehow we got to know that, well, we have to think about the women who are here as well. Because it is the bureaucracy that reigns. You can't get financial support here to help people in another country. The needs also exist here.

Thus they postponed their vision. At first this was because of advice they received from the Swedish Foreign Office, which they had contacted to get information on how to start an aid project for women and children. Foreign Office officials advised them not to reveal this aspect to the local authorities, as public financial backing is supposed to be used for activities in Swedish society. Later they obtained the same information from the Bureau for Immigrant Issues in the local community. They therefore started an organisation in accordance with the local rules, but hoped to realise their vision of providing aid in the future.

Aid objectives of this kind are understood to be outside the realm of publicly funded ethnic minority associations, despite the fact that international solidarity work has been an accepted activity of traditional popular movements. The daily life of women in the countries of origin is part of these African women's transnational life worlds and when they are not allowed to develop such aid objectives, a significant part of their life worlds is excluded. The lives of these women do not stop at the national borders, but cross them. They feel solidarity with several localities, and their family networks are spread across the borders of several nation-states (Faist 2004; Glick Schiller 1992). Thus, their transnational condition conflicts with the notion of the local community as a delimited geographic and political entity.[4] This conflict exists on several dimensions. For the African women discussed here, an important motive for establishing their association was defeated, and this could diminish their enthusiasm for running the association. As mentioned above, officially, one important reason for supporting ethnic minority associations involves helping migrants maintain their multidimensional existential base. This conflict between the transnational and local purposes of associations indicates uncertainty and disagreement as to what a multi-cultural nation state is or should be today. This issue emerged at several meetings I attended and where involvement in aid projects was discussed. Aid to the victims of the Tsunami in 2005 was discussed several times, and this was clearly considered to be something to which we should all contribute. But when a small association was discussed, whose major activities were aid to women and children in the country of origin, some doubt was expressed by a civil servant. These contradictory examples reveal an uncertain perspective on the part of the local authority and politicians in relation to today's growing global and transnational conditions.

When starting the association, the women had been methodical. They told me that they wanted to understand every single detail in order to manage things well. They had appreciated a lecture from a civil servant and were planning to ask him for another, as they were eager to understand more and emphasised that they had not yet acquired all the vital skills. Both Ann and Frances assumed that membership of an association would teach them Swedish democratic principles.

> Ann: Associations adhere to the same democratic principle as the government, … you have to follow certain norms.
> Clarissa: I wonder, could you run the same activities without following these rules?
> Ann: Then you have to figure out how to do it …It would have become private and then it's not an association. If Frances and I were to start something [like that], then it would have been a financial association. Do I answer your question? But we feel that you can't do that in Sweden, you must always look at the rules. Am I doing the right thing now? All the time you have to wait, and be careful even when you are zealous, that's what I have learnt anyway. We have to adapt to something, to what, I don't know.
> Frances: I believe that it is difficult to run an association without these norms; I don't think it would be good. Everyone would present their thoughts about how to organise, what to do, it would become rather chaotic. It's good to know that you have to have a secretary, we have to have a chairman, and we've got to have this and that.

However helpful the rules for establishing associations were for creating order, they still stressed the need to adjust to the Swedish vision of democratic order. As the above quote reveals, the administrative rules had a strong impact on the formation of the association, and I suggest that the women's course of action illustrates how governance works both on and through individuals, as Shore and Wright argue (1997: 6). Public support for popular movements is strongly institutionalised in Sweden, and the women's arguments, when related to their eager ambition to be part of Swedish society, appear as fully rational.

For these African women, it had been out of the question to start a mixed-gender association. They wanted a place for women's talk. 'When in a democratic society', Ann said, 'we believe that the African woman, who has so much to give and whose opinions often are silenced and hampered by dominating men – we thought it was clear that we wanted an African women's organisation.' Their perception is in accordance with the view of feminist researchers, who stress that women's associations are necessary for creating an arena in which women as political subjects can act on women's interests and experiences (Eduards 2002). However, as discussed below, this view conflicts with a dominant political assumption that the main issue is to have an equal number of men and women in organisations and on their boards.

When I met with the African women, there were just over ten active members. Most of them were employed and had young children, and thus they had very little time for the association. The women were also disappointed that it had been so difficult to enrol more members. But now, after investing so much time and effort into the association, they wanted to continue. They still spent a great deal of time building the organisation and recruiting new members. They arranged walks, activities for children, parties and information meetings. They accepted the fact that support for newly arrived women would be a major part of their activities. The association was active together with others in many contexts where ethic integration was discussed, and it was involved in public events in the town.

Implementing an Integration Policy

We have seen that the women in the African women's association worked hard to adjust to the advice and norms of the authorities. In the introduction, I described the national policies governing financial support to ethnic minority associations and pointed out a growing instrumental attitude. In this section, I will show how these policies affected local governing and framed the daily work of the bureaucrats. One of my informants was the politician who was responsible for support to associations; the others were three civil servants. The bureaucrats had long experience of associations and two of them, Peter and Henrik, had been involved in immigration issues for many years. Henrik had himself founded an ethnic minority association and had been heavily involved in multi-cultural activities in the town.

The political authority in the local community where I conducted my fieldwork reached a unanimous agreement on a policy for ethnic minority integration in 2005. The first sentence in the document states: 'An integrated society is based on democracy and participation, on the fact that all citizens feel responsibility for, affiliation with and are part of the local community.' Integration is defined as a mutual process in which everyone is involved and influenced, ethnic Swedes as well, but it is also stated that individuals and groups shall not have to give up their distinct character. The authorities, the document says, must work towards the political goals for integration sanctioned by the national assembly. The backing of ethnic minority associations is discussed under the section 'Culture and Leisure'. In the introduction it is established that:

1. the financial backing for ethnic minority associations is to be scrutinised and constructed so that activities favourable to integration and gender equality and the needs of newly arrived groups are prioritised;
2. new routines shall be developed to offer financial support to association activities and cultural activities that strive for integration;
3. public culture institutions shall seek cooperation with ethnic minority associations to make use of their commitment and to give them opportunities to participate and gain influence.

The first goal expresses an ambition to push the associations towards facilitating integration. This is in accordance with the national ambition to direct the orientation and activities of associations to help achieve the policy objectives of politicians. The second goal is also in agreement with national policies, by seeking more efficient use of the financial support available to associations. The third goal is closer to the discourse of multiculturalism, as it aims at helping associations to influence institutions. It also connects to the policy of popular movements by emphasising the democratic role of associations. Local government's interest in making use of associations' capacities is in line with the general development towards the increased regulation of associations. The problematic combination of governing associations and protecting their independence was not discussed. The local policy, which constituted the framework of action for the civil servants, consisted of goals that were difficult to combine.

The local administration, responsible for contacts with associations, categorised them in general by the nature of their activities or by their target group. But ethnic minority associations were defined by ascribing members to a common ethnic minority background. The label 'ethnic minority association' separated them from other 'Swedish' associations and classified them as different, no matter how old and established they were, how integrated their members were in Swedish society or what kind of activities they pursued. In fact, many had a number of different activities that could have put them in some of the other categories. All associations had to follow a number of general requirements in order to receive financial backing. First, their work had to be voluntary and valuable to society, and all activities had to be open to the public. They had to be democratic and have a board, with a president, a secretary and auditors, and there had to be democratically established rules. The associations had to acquire an organisation number through the assessment authority before being registered at the local authority. A minimum of ten members was required, and the activities had to take place primarily within the boundaries of the local community.

The special position of ethnic minority associations was underlined with a few extra requirements. They had to be politically and religiously independent. Ethnic minority associations were guaranteed subsidies if they met the authority's requirements, but at the same time, it limited their freedom to apply for subsidies for other reasons.

Until a few years ago, the amount of financial support to ethnic minority associations was simply based on the number of members; now the ambition was to base the assessment on information about the associations' performance and to create a system that would lead to a fair and efficient allocation and would also make associations adhere to the government's goals. The system was developed by two civil servants, who had made a list of ten criteria that would meet the political objectives. That list was then used as a neutral measure for assessing the performance of an association. The size of an association's membership was still important in determining the amount of funding, but with the new measures, an association could get a great deal of money if it adapted its activities to the list of objectives. Ethnic minority associations now received increased funding depending on how well their activities were found to facilitate integration, democracy, gender equity, stopping drug use and assisting the elderly, children and young people. Each criterion could give zero to three points. Newly started associations received an extra point. Financial support was then allocated on the basis of the number of points that each association had received, which meant that if one association received more points, there was less to be distributed to the others. Finally, a contract was to be signed in which association members ensured that they would follow what was stipulated in their annual plan. This procedure can be compared with business procedures in which a contract confirms the financial agreement, thus reflecting the new management philosophy.

The largest amount of money that was distributed to an association was 35,000 SEK and the smallest was 3,000 SEK. Naturally, the significance of the funding varied with the amount – some associations were able to rent a place with the money, while others were able to arrange some regular activities such as renting a sports ground once a week or arranging a public meeting.

The Ambiguous Meanings of Gender Equality

What were the consequences of the system of funding allocation for the African association? Here I will limit my discussion to the way the officers inspected association activities for gender equality. The association was not given even one point for gender equality, and when I asked why, Fredrik, the civil servant responsible for funding allocation, answered that there were only women on their board. By not having an equal number of men and women on their board, this women's association did not meet the official definition of gender equality. If they had had a project for gender equality, they might have been given one point. Could a single-sex association facilitate gender equality? The civil servants had discussed this issue. One could easily say, they told me, that an association exclusively for old men, which they said was the case in some associations, did not facilitate gender equity. But what about an association only for women: did it promote gender equality? Based on the criterion of equal representation, it did not. But was the composition of the board really a sign of gender equality? When the civil servants discussed this issue, two problems were revealed. First, they themselves had observed deficiencies in gender equality in associations with an equal number of men and women on the board. They had attended meetings at which women were silenced or openly criticised men for limiting their influence. The civil servants also noticed that, in practice, equal representation may be nothing more than a ploy for getting funding. Despite this, Fredrik talked about having women on a mixed board as a taken-for-granted sign that resulted in giving an association a point for gender equality. He told me about a multi-ethnic women's association to which they had given two points for gender equality, and I asked him whether it was because this was a women's organisation:

> Fredrik: Well ... we discussed this quite a bit. Can we see it the other way around in this case? If they let men take part would that mean gender equality? We discussed this back and forth, but we also thought that an association that actually is for women, where women decide for themselves, may be good. This is uncommon.

When Fredrik talked about that association, he brought up the notion that a single-sex association may be good, and his argument was similar to that of Ann and Frances. But Fredrik and the politician pointed out to me on several occasions that some men had participated in that association's activities and that they saw this as facilitating gender equality. But they also said that the multiethnic women's association had received funding primarily because it arranged many activities for immigrant women. Having a women's section within an association was another taken-for-granted reason for giving points for gender equality. In the following, Fredrik talked about a large Bosnian association that received one point:

> They have a special women's section and the chair of this section is of course on the board of the association ... but when you look at the annual report, you can see that they not only have football and well typically male activities, but also rather many activities for women.

The Bosnia association's documents described many activities that can be seen as gender-neutral and interesting for women, and as they also had a section for women, they received one point. Their activities were primarily for members, but they also took part in other activities in cooperation with other organisations. I will compare the judgment made about this association with that made about another small association that had received two points. The major objective of the latter association was to inform about the situation for children in their country of origin, but it also arranged public meetings to provide information about violence towards and the oppression of women and children in Sweden. The association did not have many activities for members. Fredrik motivated his judgment by saying that they had an equal number of men and women on the board. The association also received one point for extraordinary activities, namely their meetings about violence and circumcision. He stressed to me that he had noticed on one occasion how democratically the members behaved towards each other and that he had continuous contact with the organisation. It was a small association that did a great deal to facilitate integration, he said. However, he also informed me that it was a problem that their major objectives were in the country of origin, as financial backing was supposed to benefit activities for citizens in the community, and he discussed the problem with the board. But the positive virtues were great.

When these two so very different associations are compared, the difficulties in applying the principles appear. The small association's more outwards-directed actions for the sake of children and women seem to be more in accordance with the opinions of the civil servants than the activities for women run by the large association. With regard to the African women's association, whose whole purpose could be seen as an equality project from a gender perspective, it was clear that the bureaucrats did not recognise these qualities at all (Eduards 2002). In practice, the civil servants' assessments seemed to be based on a number of relatively subjective observations and experiences, and on implicit ideas about the ability of activities to promote gender equality as well as on ideas found in the dominant discourse on gender equality in Swedish politics. Any elaborate discussion of gender equality was absent, and the observation of the civil servants that the presence of women on boards did not always lead to gender equality did not influence the funding allocation.

Conflicting Goals

Let me now return to the civil servants to investigate the interaction between their assessments and the policies on ethnic minority integration at different levels. The assumption that associations had a special responsibility and role in facilitating ethnic minority integration emerged recurrently in the interviews with the bureaucrats and the politician. However, directing other associations to facilitate ethnic minority integration seemed to be out of the question. What assumptions underlie the distinction between ethnic minority associations and other types of associations in this respect? Fredrik answered my question about whether they had any plans to push other associations towards ethnic equality.

> Fredrik: No, from what I know there is no such consideration.
> Clarissa: Why is that?

> Fredrik: Well of course the people who mostly have to be integrated into our society are the ones who were not born here ... I don't exactly know how you reason or if I have blinders on and can't see what you mean, and there are of course young Swedish people today who were born in Sweden, who are not particularly integrated, but we haven't thought about it, not as far as I know.

Here he constructed the meaning of integration more or less as assimilation, a way of thinking that makes ethnic minority associations responsible for the integration of people with foreign backgrounds in the sense of making them adjust to Swedish society. He also stressed that ethnic minority associations have an important objective in informing their minorities about mainstream Swedish society and its basic values. Henrik, working at the immigration bureau, asked rhetorically if it was OK to control associations and answered that when an association turns to the authorities for support, the authorities have a legal reason to exert control. He said:

> If we as authorities are to, what can we say, bless an association ... We must see to it that the basic values are respected in all institutions and associations in our society, this is the frame within which we will inspire [them].

The basic values were exemplified as gender equality and democracy. Through relating these values to the law, he made the control legitimate and natural. The dilemma that arises between governmental control and the autonomy of associations was not mentioned. He and his colleague Peter explicitly stated that they expected their activities to promote integration. However, they admitted that ethnic minority associations had a complex and differential value for their members (which is in line with research findings – Aytar 2009). They described life cycles of these associations from the first stage, when a new association is formed to unite refugees or working immigrants, to a point when the first generation of immigrants continues to uphold traditions and to socialise, but where the younger generation no longer takes part.

Fredrik said that he questioned the method of allocating funds from the moment when he started working with ethnic minority associations. He needed new principles for controlling the use of money and began to collaborate with Henrik, who had long worked on supporting ethnic minority associations. He described the new system and how they applied it:

> We put all associations in an Excel file together with the criteria that we thought ought to be there ... and ended up with the number of points that associations had received together, which we divided into 330,000, this showed how much money one point gave. In this way, the associations themselves decide how much they shall have. It is not I as a civil servant who decides.

The quote shows how Fredrik constructed an image of a neutral system by making the associations responsible for the distribution of funds. One could say that the dilemma between control and autonomy was solved by this creation. This way of thinking is the logic of bureaucracy. But from a critical theoretical perspective, I have shown that it was developed to create a system appropriate for governing the associations. The system created a group of associations that received a great deal of financial backing and a group that received less; some associations were included in the group of valuable associations and some were excluded. The system reflected not only dominant political interests but also personal interests and the assumptions of the civil servants who had created it. Their personal experiences and judgments determined what the consequences would be for the associations (cf. Douglas 1987; Handelman 1990; Herzfeld 1992; Shore and Wright 1997). By making the associations responsible for the outcome of the funding allocation procedures, Fredrik concealed the fact that the definition of the criteria as well as the judgment about each association was based on his and Henrik's perceptions of the local policy together with their personal perspectives.

The contract that accompanied the offer of funding constituted a new way of governing associations and has led to negative feelings among the members of leading associations. Previously free to use the money as they wished and as they saw this as their right, they questioned the bureaucrats' right to direct their priorities and judge their performance. They pointed out that only ethnic minority associations were directed. The bureaucrats claimed that ethnic minority associations were treated discretely in a positive rather than negative sense, as they were the only associations to receive financial support for the organisation as such, besides associations with activities for children, young people and the disabled.

Could the civil servants have acted in another way? As I have shown, their elaborate system and assessments were in line with the goals of the local authority and the national policies. The bureaucrats' ambition to support association activities was subordinated to the explicit demands for handling tax money efficiently and for using associations to achieve political objectives. The civil servants reproduced and consolidated the policies' discursive and institutional structures by inventing a new institutional practice based on payment for performed objectives. By adapting their activities to the rules, the women in the African association can be said to be part of this consolidating process.

Support and Exploitation – an Ambiguous Combination

By scrutinising a local system for distributing financial support to ethnic minority associations, this chapter has revealed an increasingly dominant attitude about regulating and exploiting such associations. This move reflects a general tendency in Swedish society that can be related to overall changes such as cutbacks in the public sector, and more market-like relations between the state and non-profit organisations. Using financial support to exploit associations is part of a general attitude related to the new forms of governance.[5] As seen in this example, the interplay between local civil servants and an ethnic minority association can lead to self-regulation based on the great efforts of members to adapt to the rules and principles of the local administration. In Sweden, the positions of ethnic minority associations vary, as do local policies. In the Stockholm metropolitan area, much more elaborated forms of governance are found that involve politicians, officials, ethnic minority associations and financial support on quite another scale (see Hertting 2009). Further comparative research would deepen our understanding of these policy processes.

This chapter shows an ambiguous political framework for the bureaucrats' endeavours and points out the tensions between, on the one hand, efforts to create fair and suitable guidelines embedded in a multicultural discourse and, on the other hand, objectives to control and make use of ethnic minority associations by compelling them to promote integration and other governmental goals embedded in the new governance perspective. The example of an African women's association suggests the existence of complex negotiations in which governmental goals, the personal experiences of bureaucrats and association members' experiences and visions are in motion and intertwined. Classifications and allocation guidelines were ambiguous and difficult to apply in concrete cases. It is not surprising that a subjectively informed assessment system emerged, as every system of classification is founded on the interests and discourses of dominant actors and is applied subjectively in relation to the interests and perspectives of the individuals involved. But when, as in this case, the system is treated as neutral, it becomes difficult to create an open and democratic discussion about the allocation of financial support. This attitude also clearly conflicts with the view that nonprofit associations are important democratic actors and vital organisations for a dynamic democracy. The visions of the members of the women's association were clearly hampered by the authorities' principles and by the women's significant efforts to adjust to the rules for constructing an association in 'the Swedish way' and for being part of Swedish society.

The present discussion shows how the inspections and classifications carried out by local bureaucrats reduce and simplify the often multifunctional qualities and directions of ethnic minority associations. I have described how the African women's organisation was credited with zero points for gender equality because their efforts were not recognised by the bureaucrats. But I suggest that a more serious aspect was that the women felt that they had to change the objectives of their association. Postponing the solidarity project for African women may create a risk in the form of members' diminished interest in and enthusiasm for the association in the long run.

Notes

1. The official term for Swedish immigration policy today is integration policy and it is presented as conveying an inclusive attitude towards migrants, where equal rights, equal treatment and gender equality are founding principles. It is a highly debated policy, and the concept of integration is disputed. One reason for the new

concept was to disassociate the policy from assimilation in the sense of imposing Swedish culture and identity on immigrants. Integration policy has been widely criticised for creating immigrants as a special category that is different from ethnic Swedish people.

2. I use life world in Merleau-Ponty's sense as the concrete world which we can experience and where we live our every day lives. It is a world of meaning and is related to us as perceiving subjects (Bengtsson 2001: 69).

3. This is a statistical definition meaning that they or both of their parents were born abroad.

4. This attitude is to be related to the notion of the nation-state as a delimited cultural, economic, political and geographical realm. Malkki discusses its taken-for-granted concreteness in ordinary talk, ideological propaganda and research; she points out its impact on anthropological thinking and discusses the correspondence between the concepts of nation and culture (1992). See also Anderson (1991) and Hylland Eriksen (1993).

5. Governance refers to the growing manifestations of collaboration and coordination between the government, nonprofit organisations, institutions, private actors, etc., and is related to the erosion of traditional bases of political power (Pierre 2000). However, the concept also signifies theoretical perspectives. For an elaboration of the meanings of governances, see Rhodes (2000).

References

Anderson, B. 1991. *Imagined Communities. Reflections on the Origins and Spread of Nationalism*. London: Vergo.

Aytar, O. 2009. 'Organisering, diaspora och statslöshet', in B. Bengtsson and C, Kugelberg (eds), *Föreningsliv, delaktighet och lokal politik i det mångkulturella samhället*. Lund: Égalité.

Bengtsson, J. 2001. *Sammanflätningar. Fenomenologi från Husserl till Merleau-Ponty*, 2nd ed. Gothenburg: Daidalos.

Bengtsson, B. 2004. 'Föreningsliv, makt och integration – ett inledande perspektiv', in B. Bengtsson (ed.), *Föreningsliv, makt och integration*. Rapport från Integrationspolitiska maktutredningens forskarprogram, Ds. 2004: 45. Stockholm: Justitiedepartementet.

Bengtsson, B. and C. Kugelberg. 2009. 'Föreningsliv, delaktighet och lokal politik i det mångkulturella samhället – ett inledande perspektiv', in B. Bengtsson and C. Kugelberg (eds), *Föreningsliv, delaktighet och lokal politik i det mångkulturella samhället*. Lund: Égalité.

Borevi, K. 2002. *Välfärdsstaten i det mångkulturella samhället*. Uppsala: Acta Universitatis Upsaliensis.

Dahl, R. 1982. *Dilemmas of Pluralist Democracy: Autonomy vs. Control*. New Haven: Yale University Press.

Douglas, M. 1987. *How Institutions Think*. London: Routledge & Kegan Paul.

Eduards, M. 2002. *Förbjuden handling. Om kvinnors organisering och feministisk teori*. Malmö: Liber.

Faist, T. 2004. *Multiple Citizenship in a Globalising World: The Politics of Dual Citizenship in a Comparative Perspective*. School of Migration and Ethnic Relations, Malmö University. http:hdl.handle.net/2043/685.

Glick Schiller, N. (ed.). 1992. *Towards a Transnational Perspective on Migration: Race, Class, Ethnicity, and Nationalism Reconsidered*. New York: New York Academy of Sciences.

Handelman, D. 1990. *Models and Mirrors: Towards an Anthropology of Public Events*. Cambridge: Cambridge University Press.

Hertting, N. 2009. 'Etnisk organisering i den lokala nätverkspolitiken', in B. Bengtsson and C. Kugelberg (eds), *Föreningsliv, delaktighet och lokal politik i det mångkulturella samhället*. Lund: Égalité.

Herzfeld, M. 1992. *The Social Production of Indifference. Exploring the Symbolic Roots of Western Bureaucracy*. New York: Berg.

Hylland Eriksen, T. 1993. *Etnicitet and nationalism*. Nora: Nya Doxa.

Ireland, P.R. 1994. *The Policy Challenge of Ethnic Diversity. Immigrant Politics in France and Switzerland*. Cambridge, MA: Harvard University Press.

Knocke, W. and R. Ng. 1999. 'Women's Organizing and Immigration: Comparing the Canadian and Swedish Experiences', in L. Brisking and M. Eliasson (eds), *Women's Organizing and Public Policy in Canada and Sweden*. Montreal: McGill-Queen's University Press, pp. 87–116.

Lindgren, L. 1999. 'Det idealiserade föreningslivet', in L. Bennich-Björkman and E. Amnå (eds), *Civilsamhället*. Stockholm: Fakta info direkt, Statens Offentliga Utredningar, no. 1999: 84, pp. 213–46.

Malkki, L. 1992. 'National Geographic: The Rooting of Peoples and the Territorialization of National Identity among Scholars and Refugees', *Current Anthropology* 7(1): 24–44.

Micheletti, M. 1994. *Det civila samhället och staten, Medborgarsammanslutningarnas roll i svensk politik*. Stockholm: Publica.

Però, D. 2005. 'Left-wing Politics, Civil Society and Immigration in Italy: The Case of Bologna', *Ethnic and Racial Studies* 28(5): 832–58.

———. 2007. 'Anthropological Perspectives on Migrants' Political Engagements'. Working Paper no. 50, Centre on Migration, Policy and Society, University of Oxford.

Pierre, J. 2000. 'Introduction: Understanding Governance', in J. Pierre (ed.). *Debating Governance. Authority, Steering, and Democracy*. Oxford: Oxford University Press, pp. 1–10.

Putnam, R.D. 1993. *Making Democracy Work. Civic Traditions in Modern Italy*. Princeton: Princeton University Press.

Regeringens proposition 2005/06: 4. *Statligt stöd för kvinnors organisering*. Stockholm: Regeringen.

Rex, J., P. Joly and C. Wilpert (eds). 1987. *Immigrant Associations in Europe*. Aldershot: Gower.

Rhodes, R.A. 2000. 'Governance and Public Administration', in J. Pierre (ed.), *Debating Governance. Authority, Steering, and Democracy*. Oxford: Oxford University Press, pp. 54–90.

SCB (Statistiska CentralByrån). 2008a. *Pressmedelande Nr 2007:362*. Stockholm; Statiska CentralByrån.

———. 2008b. *Befolkningsstatistik i sammandrag 1960–2007*. Retrieved 18 March 2008 from Statistiska CentralByrån database: www.scb.se.

Shore, C. and S. Wright. 1997. 'Policy. A New Field of Anthropology', in C. Shore and S. Wright (eds), *Anthropology of Policy. Critical Perspectives on Governance and Power.* London: Routledge, pp. 3–39.

SOU (Statens Offentliga Utredningar). 2000 *En uthållig demokrati! Politik för folkstyrelse på 2000-talet*: *Demokratiutredningens betänkande.* Stockholm: Fritzes offentliga publikationer, Statens Offentliga Utredningar, no. 2000: 1.

———. 2004. *Kvinnors organisering. Betänkande av Utredningen statligt stöd för kvinnors organisering.* Stockholm: Fritzes offentliga publikationer, Statens offentliga utredningar, no. 2004: 59, pp. 202–8.

Svenska Kommunförbundet. 2001. *Föreningspolitik och föreningsstöd.* Stockholm: Svenska Kommunförbundet.

Wahlbeck, Ö. 1999. *Kurdish Diasporas. A Comparative Study of Kurdish Refugee Communities.* Basingstoke: Macmillan, in association with Centre for Research in Ethnic Relations, University of Warwick; New York: St Martin's Press.

Wijkström, F. and S. Einarsson. 2006. *Från nationalstat till näringsliv? Det civila samhällets organisationsliv i förändring.* Stockholm: Handelshögskolan, EFI.

Wijkström, F., S. Einarsson and O. Larsson. 2004. *Staten och det civila samhället: idétraditioner och tankemodeller i den statliga bidragsgivningen till ideella organisationer.* Stockholm: Socialstyrelsen.

Wingborg, M. 1999. *Invandrarföreningarna och integrationen. Utvärdering av föreningarnas verksamhet i Stockholm.* Stockholm: Integrationsförvaltningen i Stockholms stad.

Chapter 15

The Elephant in the Room: Multistakeholder Dialogue on Agricultural Biotechnology in the Food and Agriculture Organization[1]

Birgit Müller

The planting and patenting of transgenic plants has sparked unprecedented and multifaceted controversies all over the world. The introduction of genetically modified organisms (GMOs) raises at least three contentious issues. First, proponents of genetic modification see GMOs as a means to reduce chemical use and to overcome environmental constraints on agricultural production. Opponents warn of the unforeseen potential implications that a release of genetically modified plants into the environment would pose, as they could cross-pollinate, contaminate and outcompete indigenous plants. Secondly, it raises issues of health and food safety with proponents advertising the technology as indispensable for fighting hunger and malnutrition, and opponents warning that consuming GMOs could be potentially dangerous as health risks have not been sufficiently researched. Thirdly, it raises issues about the redistribution of profits and the control over agricultural production (Müller, 2006a, 2006b, 2008) as only five agrochemical corporations, Bayer Crop Science, Monsanto, Syngenta, BASF and DuPont, hold most of the patents on GM seeds.

The issues raised by these controversies have fundamentally affected the Food and Agriculture Organization (FAO) of the United Nations (UN), which is the main body in the international system with a mandate to promote action to secure sufficient and adequate nutrition for the world's population. With hunger increasing and food riots in many parts of the world, the normative status of the FAO's scientifically based policy advice to governments has been challenged. The FAO's practices of international governance dilute controversies between administrators, experts, government representatives and civil society activists because they provide a gloss of harmony and consensus, whereas in fact there are a wide variety of viewpoints. Drafts of policy recommendations are tamed until they become acceptable and polite, cleansed of any conflictive elements and rendered 'technical'. The mechanism that makes a technical issue out of a conflict about resources and control obscures differentials in power and economic inequalities. How can people challenge the ways they and the issues that affect them are constructed?

In a practical sense, the public that is governed by the FAO's policies are all food consumers and citizens worldwide. Yet it is the producers of food (peasants, farmers, herders, hunters and gatherers, workers in the agro-industry and agricultural labourers) who are especially concerned by the FAO's policy guidance, as well as the entrepreneurs and shareholders in the agro-food industry, whose profits are affected. In a more restricted sense, the FAO's public is those individuals or groups who interact with the FAO through its membership forums and technical assistance programmes, or through the Internet or letter-writing campaigns. Among these, the 'rural poor' have emerged as a new force and they play a special role for the FAO, considering that the organisation's basic objective is 'to improve the welfare of the rural and urban poor' and to encourage their participation in 'field action and policy dialogue' (FAO 1999: 5). Peasants who were previously reduced to the role of 'victims without a voice' now organise themselves, propose alternatives and make their presence felt in civil society forums parallel to FAO conferences.

This chapter examines how individuals and groups interact with the FAO. To do this, I look at the institution not as a bounded entity but as a *dispositif* [2] (Foucault 1994), which is translated into English as 'assemblage' or 'apparatus'. For Foucault, the general target of a *dispositif* is not socialisation, structural stability, equilibrium or the reduction of complexity, but 'the ordering of human multiplicities' (Foucault 1975: 218). In the case of the FAO, the organisation continually draws in new actors as experts, interlocutors and opinion-givers, engaging them with forms of calculation, technical reasoning, human 'capacity building' and with non-human objects and devices such as GMOs. The FAO's *dispositif* attempts to produce coherent policy narratives, which become integrated or contested and consequently have effects. In Foucault's terms, a *dispositif* liberates while it regulates; in other words, it regulates liberty. The role of a *dispositif* is not to prevent a certain type of behaviour but to organise a space that constrains behaviour according to determinate objectives (Fusulier and Lannoy 1999: 189). Actors are simultaneously instituting and instituted, that is, they participate in the production of norms and rules and are themselves integrated into the system of constraints (Abélès 1986: 73; Boudon and Bourricaud 1986: 327).

Whilst actors are drawn into the space organised by the FAO's *dispositif* which produces de-politicised policy guidance, this chapter explores how they struggle to maintain a counter-conduct (*contre-conduite*: Foucault 2004) that allows for conflict, contention and strategic action. They thus attempt to look at the organisation as a distinct entity from which they have to hold themselves at a critical distance. De Certeau calls 'strategy' the calculation of power relations that becomes possible when subjects with a will of their own act from a vantage point that is their own and that serves as a basis for their relations with a separate and distinct exteriority. In contrast, when a person cannot count on a space of his or her own, or cannot maintain a clear boundary to distinguish himself or herself from the other as a clearly visible totality, then that person can only make 'tactical' calculations (de Certeau 1990: xlvi). Tactics operate in the space of the other in which one insinuates oneself without being able to step out of its logic – as in Foucault's *dispositif*. Then actors must constantly play with events in order to transform them into opportunities for making an impact that may not last.

Discussing GMOs in terms of health and environmental consequences and in terms of how GMOs could improve the living conditions of 'the poor' opens up a technical debate that assumes a common moral basis for all the participants in the debate. Improving the health of the world population, feeding the hungry and reducing environmental destruction are objectives spelled out in the UN's Millennium Development Goals. They are the basis for a global consensus. Only the technical means to achieve these goals are debated. These debates are part of what Marc Abélès (2006) calls the politics of survival. Focusing on the common survival of humankind, this politics blurs political faultlines and abstracts from power and economic differentials. Instead of asking what mechanisms make the poor become and remain poor, or through which practices does one social group impoverish another (Murray Li 2007: 7), the debates focus on how the poor could be empowered to help themselves out of poverty or to protect their own health and environment.

In contrast, debating GMOs in terms of intellectual property rights over agricultural plants poses the issue in political terms, emphasising conflicts between farmers and corporations and between northern holders of patents (US, Canada, China and Europe) and southern providers of germ plasma. For a long time, questions of corporations' appropriation of resources and control over the means of production have been blanched out of the FAO's policy documents on the grounds that they are 'political questions'. These political questions of appropriation and control are 'the elephant in the room' – as the saying goes – the problem that everyone knows exists and that will not go away even if it is not talked about. The process of rendering political questions into technical issues should be seen 'as a continuous project, not a secure accomplishment' (Murray Li 2007: 10).

In the first section of this chapter, I will analyse how the FAO attempted to become a neutral broker in the biotechnology debate by arbitrating on political-economic questions from a neutral technical vantage point. In the second section, I will analyse how the FAO tries to neutralise conflict through consultation. Here I will examine the biotechnology forum that the FAO launched on the Internet in 2000. In the third section, I will examine how political controversy re-emerges in unexpected ways. I will look at the production of, and reactions to, the FAO's first thematic annual report, *The State of Food and Agriculture. Agricultural Biotechnology: Meeting the Needs of the Poor?* For this chapter, I draw on the FAO's documents and website, on fieldwork at the FAO's regional and international conferences in 2003, 2004 and 2006, and on extensive interviews with FAO administrators and with members of the international coordination of civil society organisations (International Planning Committee).

The Broker: Honest, Neutral, Objective

The role that the FAO has attempted to carve out for itself in recent years, and which corresponds to similar tendencies in other UN institutions, is that of a 'broker' between governments, the private sector and civil society organisations. A broker, in its most basic sense, is an intermediary between the buyer and the seller who helps to negotiate an economic transaction to the satisfaction of both parties. The FAO has come closest to this economic broker role when called on to negotiate between donor and receiver countries. As the FAO's funding has been considerably reduced since the beginning of the 1990s, the institution has in many cases been reduced to brokering projects financed by individual donor states with receiver countries. The political equality that all states have in the FAO's assembly becomes questionable when projects are financed through a 'donor-driven approach'. Instead of intervening on issues of world agriculture and nutrition, the FAO assumes the role of a development agency split between those who claim the status of being 'developed' and who are thus outside of its realm of influence, and those who are to be 'developed'. The FAO thus partakes in a 'will to improve' (Murray Li 2007) that it shares with other development agencies. Its claim of expertise in optimising the lives of others is in itself a claim to power (Murray Li 2007: 5) as its experts feel legitimated to act on the conduct of others supposedly in their own interests. The irony of this type of authority is that it makes bureaucracies powerful precisely by cultivating the appearance of being depoliticised, that is, not driven by conflicting interests (Barnett and Finnemore 1999: 708).

This broker role exists in tension with the normative role for which the institution is mandated. The FAO formulated and promoted individual human rights to food (Voluntary Guidelines to Right to Food 2004) and to land (Final Declaration of the ICARRD International Conference on Agrarian Reform and Rural Development 2006), and promoted farmers' rights to use their own seeds (the International Treaty on Plant Genetic Resources for Food and Agriculture 2004). Some administrators have coined the term 'strong broker' or 'objective broker' for the FAO – that is, a broker whose strength is based on 'competence' and 'knowledge'. In short, this role for the FAO depends on its capacity to be an expert who can claim superior normative authority over donor and receiver countries alike. In this formulation, though formally still an international democratic institution with an assembly of member nations where different worldviews and values could be expressed, the FAO becomes de facto an institution governing world affairs by searching for 'truth' based on expert knowledge.

Regarding debates over biotechnology, the FAO claims for itself the role of an 'independent honest broker' of controversial information. The ambiguity of this broker role comes out in the following self-presentation of the FAO's work on biotechnology:

> Whenever the need arises, FAO acts as an 'honest broker' by providing a forum for discussion … FAO is constantly striving to determine the potential benefits and possible risks associated with the application of modern technologies to increase plant and animal productivity and production. However, the responsibility for formulating policies towards these technologies rests with the Member Governments themselves. (Retrieved 2 November 2010 from http://www.fao.org/biotech/stat.asp)

Thus, the FAO provides the analysis, determines risks and benefits and, from its position of superior knowledge, mediates the discussion of others. This does not necessarily mean that any discussion would have an impact on its own analysis. At the same time, the institution rejects any responsibility for the effect that its policy guidelines might have on others. It claims instead that responsibility rests entirely with the governments who endorse the FAO's analysis.

In its comprehensive effort to categorise and measure 'hunger', 'food' and 'agricultural production', the FAO has contributed to a system of governance that relies on 'normalising' the hungry. That is, the hungry person is transformed into a statistical unit and part of the 850 million 'hungry' that need to get fed in order to reach the commitment of the World Food Summit 1996 to halve the number of the 'hungry' by 2015. This style of reasoning has produced particular ways of finding out the 'truth' about peoples, populations, commodities and nutrition. These become new objects of inquiry and eventually the known objects, disrobed of their mystery (Ilcan and Phillips 2003: 450). Hunger, intellectual property, biosafety and even free trade are treated as technical problems for which technical solutions can be found.

The power of the FAO as an international bureaucracy lies precisely in its capacity to make, order and 'know' social worlds through the impressive statistical apparatus it produces. It does this 'by moving persons among social categories or by inventing and applying such categories' (Handelman 1995: 280):

> The power resides in the fact that the institution presents itself as impersonal, technocratic, and neutral – as not exercising power – but instead as serving others; the presentation and acceptance of these claims is critical to their legitimacy and authority. (Barnett and Finnemore 1999: 708)

By promising technical solutions to the sufferings of powerless and oppressed people, FAO policy making expunges reference to the political forces that oppose each other, creating what Ferguson calls 'the anti-politics machine'

(Ferguson 1990: 256). As I will show, consulting with different 'stakeholders' and providing them with a neutral forum for expressing diverse opinions is part of this search for truth and also of this effort at de-politicisation.

Non governmental organisations (NGOs) and civil society organisations (CSOs) have played an increasing role in initiating international regulatory and voluntary frameworks negotiated under the aegis of the FAO. An official FAO strategy paper (1993) stresses the mutual benefits of cooperation with NGOs and CSOs: the latter seek the FAO's help to influence government policies, while the FAO seeks their support to 'enhance the validity of decision-making'. Both affirm that policy making within and by the FAO is tied to the complex relationships that the civil society organisations and the FAO secretariat have with the governments whose policies they want to influence and who ultimately give the mandate and assume the responsibility for the policies that are pursued. However, at the World Food Summits of 1996 and 2002, some NGOs that were not officially accredited to the FAO devised strategies diametrically opposed to those envisaged by the government delegations. Instead of presenting hunger as an ethical problem to which technical solutions could be found, they drew attention to the inequalities in power and access to resources that caused hunger and poverty. Their alternative forum rejected what it called 'the productivist politics of the FAO' and its support for free trade. Instead, they launched the concept of 'food sovereignty' as the 'right of peoples, communities and countries to define their own agricultural labour, fishing, food and land policies which are ecologically, socially, economically and culturally appropriate to their unique circumstances'. Their views received considerable media attention. In 2002, the FAO's Director General invited the International Planning Committee (IPC), which had organised the alternative forum and publicised its criticisms of the FAO, to facilitate new forms of 'dialogue' of NGOs/CSOs and social movements with the FAO.

The IPC reacted cautiously to this offer. It emphasised its autonomy and insisted that it was not seeking official accreditation to the FAO. It would not become a liaison committee or act as an official representative or intermediary of NGOs and social movements with the FAO. Formally, the IPC included all the organisations that participated in planning the alternative forum parallel to the World Food Summit 2002 and while it did not want to exclude others, it also wanted to ensure that participants in this FAO 'dialogue' adhered to the principles laid down in the IPC's platform on food sovereignty formulated in 2002. It also demanded a quota system that would prioritise the representation of 'social movements from developing countries' and sought assurances that governments would not screen out members of CSOs whose attendance the IPC had facilitated.

Nonetheless, the FAO's offer of dialogue was extremely challenging for the IPC. The IPC was walking on a tightrope between formalising its internal relationships and preserving its character of an open forum. Its internal meetings spent considerable time devising systems of representation and accountability. The IPC accepted dialogue with the FAO under the condition that it be based on 'mutual recognition' and respect for their 'own spaces'. To use de Certeau's (1990: XLVI) distinction, the IPC tried to move 'strategically' as opposed to 'tactically'. Its explicit strategic aim was to reinforce the part of the UN that dealt with food issues against the impact of the free trade politics and intellectual property regimes upheld by the World Trade Organization. It wanted the FAO to become an institution 'for the people and not only of governments' (IPC interview, 5 May 2006) and appealed to the FAO's initial mandate to stand above day-to-day politics, power differentials and particular governments' short-term interests. Members of CSOs that were part of the IPC cooperated with those FAO administrators who were responsive to their concerns and open to their suggestions, and who saw it as part of their mission to spread, inculcate and enforce global values and norms, such as the right to food, to land and to seeds. While members of the IPC had easy access to particular sections of the organisation, they had no access at all to other sections that pursued policies and delivered analyses that stood in contrast to their political analysis and visions for the world.

To pursue these norms, the FAO secretariat and the CSOs made influencing governments a key objective of their cooperation. As an NGO representative put it: 'For Diouf [the Director General of the FAO] the NGOs are a sort of lobbying tool. It is not only the general gloss of civil society and of showing: Oh I am so democratic! He also wants NGOs to lobby governments on certain issues' (IPC interview 3 November 2006). Conversely, NGOs expected to increase their negotiating power with governments when they had the support of the FAO. Some organisations openly stated that they wanted the FAO secretariat to put pressure on governments to accept the participation of NGOs more readily. NGOs and the FAO secretariat attempted to achieve a strategic position with respect both to governments and to each other, and to affirm a moral legal authority beyond particularistic governmental interests.

The Biotechnology Forum on the Internet

A fundamental tension between mobilisation and expertise appears when the institution attempts to transform politically engaged and concerned citizens into experts it 'consults' with. The 'expert' has become the favoured interlocutor of public agencies and supranational organisations, drawing his or her legitimacy from a supposedly scientific objectivity. Citizens feel compelled to resort to 'counter-expertise' to make their point and contest 'official expertise', as shown in the organisation of a Forum for Food Sovereignty in 2002. Citizens who participated in planning procedures as a civic and political act wanted their personal experience to be taken as seriously as experts' supposedly objective science. They either claimed that their daily experience had the same status as scientific expertise or they challenged the latter with counter-scientific arguments. Relationships between professionally engaged experts and citizens pursuing a cause on a voluntary basis become complex here, because both are often aware that no scientific truth is devoid of interest and independent of normative frames. As soon as specialised knowledge is used to solve 'problems of regulation that are significant from a political point of view, the normative imprint of this knowledge can be felt and it provokes controversies among the experts themselves that have a polarizing effect' (Habermas 1987: 378). A multiplicity of truths stand side by side (Beck 1986: 277) and the so-called 'sound science' of expert statements enters into direct competition with the global political objectives advanced by CSOs.

In 2000, the FAO launched its Biotechnology Forum, a series of moderated email conferences on biotechnology, in an attempt to let the controversies be played out and become politically neutralised in a space that the FAO controlled and over which it exercised moral and scientific authority. The declared objective was to open 'international discussion from a credible organization that is both independent and authoritative'. I focus here on one of these conferences, 'Participation of Rural People in Decision Making Regarding GMOs', which aimed to provide a neutral platform for 'quality balanced information' on this 'sometimes controversial subject'(FAO 2006: IX). Over five weeks there were 508 subscribers, coming equally from developed and developing countries, of whom seventy submitted at least one message (116 messages in total). Messages came from university academics (thirty-seven per cent), independent consultants (twenty-two per cent), research centres (twenty per cent), NGOs (eleven per cent), farmers' organisations (six per cent), government ministries (three per cent) and the UN (one per cent). The conference addressed 'participation' on two levels. First, it directly involved those academics and experts with knowledge about 'rural people' who knew about the Biotechnology Forum and had internet access. Secondly, these participants discussed an imaginary amorphous mass of 'rural people', whom they described as the 'unheard voices' of people who were 'pushed against the wall unable to participate', 'ignorant', 'easy to persuade', 'echoing pressure groups' and 'suspicious'. Contributors gave different reasons for not wanting to involve 'rural people' directly. Those critical of biotechnology thought it 'hypocritical' and 'useless' to involve people who were 'not listened to' and 'did not own' a process that was characterised by 'huge power asymmetries' and in which 'decisions were taken on the international level'. Those in favour of introducing biotechnology into the agriculture of developing countries thought that the participation of rural people would 'deter progress', 'create chaos' and 'delay sound projects'. Instead, they thought experts should make decisions based on facts and evidence, not on 'majority rule and feelings'. A minority who favoured participatory processes saw these as a way to provide education and 'quality information', 'stop scare mongers', and 'create a culture to make people be in favour'.

The Forum gives people a 'voice' in an unorganised inconsequential fashion, addressing people in rather central positions linked to opinion making, universities and research centres as individuals with personal opinions. Participants are part of a potential pool of 'experts' – intermediaries between 'rural people' and governments, industry and international institutions such as the FAO – all claiming to provide 'credible, true information'. The Forum informs the active and passive participants of a wide range of arguments; actual discussion and debate is the exception. It is thus in a way a concert of individual voices. These opinions are addressed to a virtual international community on the World Wide Web. One of the participants questioned for instance whether 'neutrality' was at all possible in the biotechnology debate:

> FAO forum organizers would like that we exchange on how to involve farmers when a preliminary question remains to be addressed: do we dispose of a basic un-biased and clear information for a neutral and non-oriented involvement of farmers? … People who answer yes have not a neutral position. When they are defending their own job, it is clear that it is difficult for them to be neutral. (Ferry message 67)

Another pointed out that the social dimensions of biotechnology were left out of the considerations: 'I detect some Margaret Thatcherism in the debate we are having, namely … there is no such thing as society!' (Dunn message 96). Forum participants made suppositions, as experts, about an abstraction they called 'the rural people' and focused on the channels through which to reach them with messages about biotechnology. The FAO webmaster's final summary of the Forum drowned out any strong individual arguments with sentences such as: 'there was broad agreement that citizens including rural people should be involved in decision making' (FAO 2006: 139). Contentions were smoothed over and statements by participants questioning the appropriateness of the Biotechnology Forum itself did not appear in the summary. The main purpose of the Forum seemed to be to produce a fiction that the FAO offered and stood for a 'neutral' platform for all these voices, which in turn spoke for an even wider muted audience: 'the rural people'.

Lynne Phillips and Susan Ilcan's analysis of the FAO's biotechnology debate concludes that the FAO wants to construct the individual, the everyday person, as what they call 'a responsible expert' (Phillips and Ilcan 2007: 118). Responsible expertise is an orientation to the world that meshes with and depends upon expert knowledge and moral judgment in everyday decision making (Phillips and Ilcan 2007: 105). Through the global expansion of responsible expertise, populations are supposed to become responsible decision-making entities armed with the appropriate knowledge to deal with the future. Once they get involved in the decision of adopting biotechnology, they become entwined in the management of risk and have only themselves to blame for the consequences of their decisions. As Mary Douglas and Aaron Wildavsky (1982) affirmed, risk points at not only how populations and their environments are classified in different ways, but how these distinctions hold a moral judgment about who is to blame and who is to be rewarded when problems arise. She finds in risk certain structural principles, which provide a guide to how people, events and objects are made accountable within a particular moral framework. Through involving rural people in decision -making on biotechnology, the FAO both mobilises their agency in risk-related projects and, by reframing those projects as participatory, deflects the blame for encouraging the technology away from the international institution and onto those who adopt it.

In its consultations on the Internet, the FAO transformed 'citizens' embedded in complex social and political structures into 'individuals', who were not merely 'free to choose' but were obliged 'to understand and enact their lives in terms of choice' (Rose 1999: 87). The *dispositif* of depoliticisation worked fully in the electronic Biotechnology Forum, where strong opinions and differentiated analysis were neutralised by the mechanisms set up by the FAO. The contributions to the Biotechnology Forum become simply voices in a wilderness where individuals stripped of their context and collective attachments were ultimately disempowered.

Alice in Wonderland and the SOFA Report

In 2004, the FAO added to its annual, mandatory statistical report *The State of Food and Agriculture* (SOFA) an analysis of a theme in agricultural and economic development. It began with the most controversial theme it could have chosen: *Agricultural Biotechnology. Meeting the Needs of the Poor?* As the report of the U.S. Department of Agriculture commented with satisfaction, the SOFA report:

> marks a significant shift in FAO's public posture on biotechnology. The report openly embraces the potential of biotechnology to meet the needs of poor farmers in developing countries. It concludes that biotechnology, while not a panacea, can provide both economic and environmental benefits for developing countries. (Hegwood 2005)

None of the critical arguments voiced in the year-long Biotechnology Forum found their place in the SOFA report. With this report, the FAO ceased to take a 'neutral' approach towards GMOs and it 'came down on the pro-GM side of this global debate' (Paarlberg 2005: 38). How did the FAO report present the wholehearted support of biotechnology as a balanced and scientifically sound analysis of the benefits of biotechnology for the poor?

The Director General of the FAO, by signing the foreword, authenticated the report as an official document. The foreword was probably not written by the Director General himself, but it engages him personally as he appeals to 'the international community' in the first person singular. His foreword distils the content of the report and establishes the typical UN discourse (Rist 2002: 27), which couches its support for the promotion of biotechnology in the rhetoric of neutrality: 'FAO recognizes the need for a balanced and comprehensive approach to biotechnological development taking into account the opportunities and risks.' The Director General gives an assurance that the FAO will 'continue to address all issues of concern to its constituents regarding biotechnology and its effect on human and plant and animal health', and he formally requests trust and support for the policies he pursues in the name of the FAO.

The SOFA report went through three stages of review: first, the subject of the report and its outline were approved by the administrative hierarchy of the FAO; secondly, scientific evidence on biotechnology was collected; and, thirdly, the report was reformulated to fit the policy guidelines the FAO wanted to convey:

> Up to the DG level the focus is primarily on technical issues, accuracy, balance, as you go up the ladder you get more an emphasis on the messages, FAO messages. Is the report framing those messages correctly? (FAO interview 4 May 2006)

Analysing the trajectory of the SOFA report, it becomes clear that the report is not as technical and neutral as it pretends to be, but is clearly a political statement that engages the FAO as an international political institution, transmitting its messages to the member governments. What is also interesting to consider is who was not consulted when the report was produced. Administrators in the institution who did not agree with the message of the report were either not consulted or refused to comment on a report whose overall tendency they thought they could not influence. The publication also ignored the Biotechnology Forum's considerable work of consultation and discussion. The thousands of accumulated pages of diverse opinions and analysis were overwhelming for the small unit responsible for the report, so that it 'did not have the time and resources to go through the material and select a balanced range of inputs' (FAO interview 4 May 2006). The IPC, composed of farmers' organisations, fishing people, environmental groups and indigenous peoples' organisations, to whom the Director General had made a formal pledge that he would enhance their 'participation in the policy research and analysis activities that FAO undertakes', was not consulted at all.

This report combines a language of impartiality and neutrality with a discourse that makes claims to the truth and that asserts its grip on objective realities. Science, or rather an 'international scientific community' whose existence and coherence is assumed, is evoked to give these claims a scientific validity. The existing economic and political structures at the global level are taken to represent an invariable status quo to which all economic and political players have to adapt if they want to succeed in the world of free trade. Corporate interests are presented as the motor for innovation; innovation is positive; intellectual property rights (IPRs) are needed to stimulate innovation; and all countries have to adapt their legislation to these IPR requirements in order to prepare for biotechnology. The 'poor' appear as an entirely abstract category of people who lack resources, power and information, and need to be reassured.

One of the administrators involved in producing the report maintained that:

> To establish truth, we find the best economic and scientific evidence we can. How do we determine 'the best?' 'Best' is based on: has this work been peer reviewed, has it been published in a respectable outlet? Is the person doing the work expressing any obvious bias on the subject? We try to base as best as we can what we say on this best factual evidence. Where there are widely divergent views, we reflect these views. The preponderance of evidence pointing into one direction is this, and we go forward. (FAO interview 4 May 2006)

Scientific truth, as this administrator sees it, is not established on a transcendent principle of objectivity, but on the reputation an author has gained among peers, on the status of the journal publishing the scientific material, on the number of people who hold the same view and on the subjective feeling of the administrator who judges whether the scientist expresses what he thinks could be a bias. This relational view of science, as Latour and Woolgar (1979) have shown, corresponds to the practice of valuing the scientific status of colleagues. In spite of this, the administrator feels that she can establish from the criteria of reputation what is the 'best' evidence and ultimately, by eliminating all the other viewpoints, what is a 'fact'. The report's 'sound science' is thus based on a social process that ultimately establishes a truth that is neither objective nor ahistorical, but that nevertheless has the authority to relegate all other truth-claims to the status of discredited fictions. 'Sound science' is here not just political, but it is playing a very particular sort of power politics; in doing so, it is certainly not disinterested, but is in fact expressing extremely strong and powerful interests.

Integral to this view of sound science is a discourse about scientific 'progress' that stems from the Enlightenment idea that knowledge builds on itself over time and ultimately leads towards improvement. The Assistant Director General of the FAO responsible for initiating the SOFA report used an image from the novel *Alice in Wonderland* to frame her view of scientific progress. She began her speech to the EU Forum on Sustainable Agriculture in 2003 as follows:

> Once upon a time, lost at a crossroads, a little girl meets a cat. The cat told her, 'If you do not know where you want to go, then it does not matter which road you take'... The Cheshire Cat's words have some relevance for our subject today. Like Alice through the looking glass of fast-paced scientific progress, we are catching a glimpse of an exciting world. Like Alice, we are at a crossroads with many paths open in front of us, as new opportunities are created by tremendous technological advances. But we must carefully choose our destination, and the roads we can take to get there.

She concluded by saying: 'As Alice learns in the end, you are sure to get *somewhere*, if only you walk long enough. But let us be aware that time is short' (Fresco 2003).[3] What is notable is that she conceives of progress as a 'progression' that does not necessarily have a destination. The destination can be chosen once the progression has been set in motion. The essential thing is that the movement continues. It becomes thus an end in itself, a motor that sustains the system. This progression is presented as urgent in spite of the fact that the destination and the path to take remain unclear.

For the Assistant Director General, it is the scientists 'who should tell us where to go'. The FAO should support 'science-based' evaluation procedures that objectively determine the benefits and risks of each individual GMO. She assigns a pacifying role to scientific experts as they translate worries into thresholds, that is, figures below which safety could be claimed to be achieved for the time being. Through the process of transforming an open question into a numerically limited one, the whole question is reframed (Pestre 2007: 411). The issue is no longer to contest the necessity for transgenic crops but to define the norms making them 'safe'. The Assistant Director General operates a semantic shift in the FAO's role as a 'broker' by assigning it the 'key role' of an 'objective broker' in the biotechnology controversies. She says: 'it is the duty of FAO to promote a social contract between the North and the South, public and private research and scientists and citizens, based on open dialogue, research and access and benefit sharing to bridge the molecular divide' (Fresco 2003). The need for a social contract acknowledges indirectly that there is a 'molecular divide' between northern economic interests in exploiting patented genetic material and southern interests in preserving control over agricultural production and thus over seeds.

The Assistant Director General suggests that the FAO can set a frame within which biotechnology could be regulated and tamed in the interest of all parties, and made profitable for the corporations in the north and usable for the 'poor' in the south. In this view, the main role of administrative regulation is to find ways to cope with the inevitability of progress and of (economic or political) interests, and to answer the fears and refusals that new systems generate by showing that they are safe – or in this case fair – through the creation of new rules (Pestre, quoting Boudia 2007: 411).

In the SOFA report, the 'poor' appear as a homogeneous category, not as social actors with diverse interests and strategies. Although reference is made almost constantly to the 'problems of the poor', 'seeds for the poor', 'research for the poor' and 'technology for the poor', neither their actual needs nor their capacities and skills are analysed in the report. No mention is made of the complex and resource-efficient farming techniques that many small-scale producers use around the world. What the report describes as the clear advantage of transgenic crops for the 'poor' is that they offer a simple solution for problems of malnutrition[4] and they enhance productivity. As the technology 'is embodied in a seed', the report states that 'it may be easier for small-scale, resource-poor farmers to use than more complicated crop technologies that require other inputs or complex management strategies'.

This view of the 'rural poor' as passive recipients of biotechnology was energetically refuted in a protest letter that 670 CSOs and 801 individuals addressed to the Director General of the FAO on 14 June 2004:[5]

> We, the undersigned organisations, movements and individuals involved in farming and agricultural issues, wish to express our outrage and disagreement with the FAO report ... This report has been used in a politically-motivated public relations exercise to support the biotechnology industry. It promotes the genetic engineering of seeds and the further skewing of research funding towards this technology and away from ecologically sound methods developed by farmers. The way in which the report has been prepared and released to the media, sadly, raises serious questions about the independence and intellectual integrity of an important United Nations agency. The report turns FAO away from food sovereignty and the real needs of the world's farmers, and is a stab in the back to the farmers and the rural poor FAO is meant to support.
>
> We are deeply disappointed that FAO has breached its commitment (and your own personal pledge) to consult and maintain an open dialogue with smallholder farmers' organizations and civil society. By failing to consult such organizations in the preparation of this report FAO has turned its back on those who are most directly affected by the technologies it promotes.

This protest letter raises several issues that bring the elephant in the room into full view: it stresses the political nature of supposedly neutral expert recommendations on agricultural technologies. It underlines the capacity of small farmers to exercise agency and it highlights the controversies over biotechnology as a fight over the control of seeds and over public research money. It underlines that the technological 'fix' proposed through the promotion of transgenic crops strengthens the very structures that enforce hunger by concentrating power and control in the hands of a few agrochemical corporations and by giving farmers 'fewer options to support and further develop their own farming and livelihood systems'. The authors ask whether the FAO, as a UN agency, is fulfilling its constitutional mandate to serve the rural poor or if it has lost its independence to the big economic and political players. They claim that CSOs should occupy the role of a political actor legitimated by the FAO's 'commitment' to consult and communicate with them. They consider it 'a stab in the back of small farmers' that this consultation has not taken place. The authors also stress the internal divisions over agrobiotechnology inside the institution. They declare that the report not only insults those scientists and policy makers within the FAO, but also those FAO member governments that have 'courageously' resisted industrial and political pressures and that put 'the role and rights of farmers first'.

The letter sparked internal criticism in the FAO administration and made the Director General write a letter of justification to his staff, in which he underlined all the other initiatives that the FAO had taken to remedy to the problem of world hunger, distancing himself implicitly from the wholehearted support to biotechnology expressed in the SOFA report. In a meeting with CSOs, he promised to provide them with the opportunity and the financial resources necessary for writing a counter-report. The Assistant Director General responsible for the report resigned in 2006 and her position was taken up by a member of the German Green Party who actively promoted agro-ecology.

What can we make of what seems like a 'strong reaction' to civil society protests against the SOFA report? The impact of the protests against the SOFA report shows the limits of the *dispositif* of depoliticisation. As the NGOs that were part of the IPC had jealously guarded their autonomy and had maintained a strategic position (de Certeau 1990: XLVI) from outside the institution, they were able to communicate with the institution while questioning and cutting across its mechanisms of governance. Their experience seems to confirm Sidney Tarrow's analysis of social movements' relations to institutions: neither full access to the institutions nor its absence produces the greatest degree of influence (Tarrow 1998: 77). Fully integrating into the established mechanisms of consultation would have reduced the impact of their contestation, while no access at all would have made communication impossible. What also enhanced their impact was that the IPC affirmed the collective agency of peasants and of their organisations, in contrast to the FAO's setting out to govern the reified category of the 'rural poor' and to make them individually responsible. From their vantage point, the CSOs were able to bring the elephant in the room into full view, showing that the struggles for control over seeds and over the appropriation of genetic resources were disguised and neutralised in the report under a discourse of scientific objectivity. However, walking the tightrope between integration and maintaining an informal status outside was not always successful, as became apparent in the IPC's inability to seize the opportunity offered by the Director General to write a counter-report.

Conclusion

In this chapter, I showed how 'dialogue' is a mode of governance for the FAO which neutralises political antagonisms and requires careful strategising by civil society interlocutors if they do not want to find themselves legitimising policies they do not agree with and that they are unable to influence. Through the process of rendering issues technical, the FAO is constantly delimiting the possibilities for democratic politics. Democracy, in the Western representative form, comes with ideas of differing interests. Formulating a problem as political means taking into account opposing forces, ideologies and interests that are played out in public. Democratic politics is based on the expression of these antagonisms and the confrontation of different projects for society in the public realm (Mouffe 1994). It is hard to conceive of a democratic project where the neutralisation and displacement of politics are ever-present (Garsten and Jakobsson 2007). I showed in the first part of this chapter that the FAO administration self-eliminates its democratic political role and defends the status quo by playing the role of the objective and neutral broker who obscures conflict rather than making it apparent.

The FAO works constantly at rendering technical political conflicts about access to resources and economic control. It thereby reduces differentials in power, economic inequalities and relationships of exploitation to technical problems. I have demonstrated in the second part of this chapter how the institution renders political controversies ineffective in its consultation mechanisms on the Internet by pulling individuals out of their organisational context and by transforming them into experts. CSOs always have to work on remaining 'political' rather than becoming technical, though they are constantly being pressed to occupy the space of the latter, which reduces their actions to tactics. What is needed is an international institution with adequate funding capable of acknowledging and of publicly exposing that there is in fact an elephant in the room.

Notes

1. 'The elephant in the room' is an English idiom for an obvious truth that is being ignored or goes unaddressed. It is based on the idea that an elephant in a room would be impossible to overlook; thus, people in the room who pretend the elephant is not there might be concerning themselves with relatively small and even irrelevant matters compared to the looming big one.
2. 'Un ensemble résolument hétérogène, comportant des discours, des institutions, des aménagements architecturaux, des décisions réglementaires, des lois, des mesures administratives, des énoncés scientifiques, des propositions philosophiques, morales, philanthropiques, bref : du dit, aussi bien que du non-dit. Le dispositif lui-même, c'est le réseau qu'on peut établir entre ces éléments' (Foucault 1994: 299).
3. The story goes on but this was not in the speech:
   Alice felt that this could not be denied, so she tried another question. 'what sort of people live about here?'
   'In that direction', said the Cat, waving its right paw round, 'lives a Hatter: and in that direction,' waving the other paw, 'lives the March hare. Visit either you like: they're both mad.'
   'But I don't want to go among mad people,' Alice remarked.
   'Oh, you can't help that,' said the Cat: 'we're all mad here. I'm mad. You're mad' (Carroll 1865).
4. Here the slightly betacarotene-enhanced 'Golden Rice' that has never been commercialised is quoted.
5. 'FAO Declares War on Farmers Not On Hunger', retrieved 2 November 2010 from: http://www.grain.org/front_files/fao-open-letter-june-2004-final-en.pdf.

References

Abélès, M. 1986. 'L'anthropologue et le politique', *L'Homme, L'Anthropologie : état des lieux* 26(97–98): 191–212.

——. 2006. *Politique de la survie*, Paris: Flammarion.

Barnett, M.N. and M. Finnemore. 1999. 'The Politics, Power, and Pathologies of International Organizations', *International Organization* 53(4): 699–732.

Beck, U. 1986. *Risikogesellschaft. Auf dem Weg in eine andere Moderne*, Frankfurt: Suhrkamp Verlag.

Boudia, S. 2007. 'Global Regulation: Controlling and Accepting Radioactivity Risks', *History and Technology* 23(4): 389–406.

Boudon, R. and F. Bourricaud. 1986. *Dictionnaire critique de la sociologie*, Paris: Presses Universitaires de France.

Carroll, L. 1865. *Alice's Adventures in Wonderland*. Retrieved 2 November 2010 from http://www.cs.indiana.edu/metastuff/wonder/ch6.html.

De Certeau, M. 1990. *L'invention du quotidien. L'Arts de faire*, Paris: Gallimard.

Diouf, J. 2004. 'Biotechnology: FAO Response to Open Letter from NGOs Director-General Jacques Diouf Outlines His Views on Use of Biotechnology', 16 June 2004, Rome. Retrieved 2 November 2010 from http://www.fao.org/newsroom/en/news/2004/46429/index.html.

Douglas, M. and A. Wildavsky. 1982. *Risk and Culture: An Essay on the Selection of Technical and Environmental Dangers*. Berkeley: University of California Press.

FAO. 1993. *Strategy Paper for Cooperation with NGOs and Civil Society Organizations*. Rome: FAO.

——. 1999. *Poverty Alleviation and Food Security in Asia: Lessons and Challenge.*, Bangkok, FAO Regional Office for Asia and the Pacific. Rome: FAO.

——. 2004. *The State of Food and Agriculture. Agricultural Biotechnology. Meeting the Needs of the Poor?* Rome: FAO.

——. 2006. *Results of the FAO Biotechnology PAIA Stakeholder Survey*. FAO Working Group on Biotechnology, October. Retrieved 2 November 2010 from http://www.fao.org/biotech/docs/surveyfaopaia.pdf.

Ferguson, J. 1990. *The Anti-Politics Machine: Development, Depoliticization, and Bureaucratic Power in Lesotho*. Cambridge: Cambridge University Press.

Foucault, M. 1975. *Surveiller et punir : Naissance de la prison*. Paris: Gallimard.

——. 1994 [1977]. 'Le jeu de Michel Foucault', in *Dits et écrits*, volume II. Paris: Gallimard, pp. 298–329.

——. 2004. *Sécurité, territoire, population: cours au Collège de France, 1977–78*. Paris: Gallimard/Seuil.

Fresco, L.O. 2003. 'Which Road Do We Take? Harnessing Genetic Resources and Making Use of Life Sciences, a New Contract for Sustainable Agriculture', EU Discussion Forum Towards Sustainable Agriculture for Developing Countries: Options from Life Sciences and Biotechnology, Brussels, 30–31 January.

Fusulier, B. and P. Lannoy. 1999. 'Comment aménager par le management', *Hermès* 25: 181–98.

Garsten, C. and K. Jakobsson. 2007. 'Corporate Globalisation, Civil Society and Post-political Regulation: Whither Democracy?', *Development Dialogue* 49: 143–58.

Habermas, J. 1987. *Droit et démocratie. Entre faits et norms*. Paris: Gallimard.

Handelman, D. 1995 'Cultural Taxonomy and Bureaucracy in Ancient China: The Book of Lord Shang', *International Journal of Politics, Culture and Society* 9(2): 263–93.

Hegwood, D. 2005. *FAO and Biotechnology. GAIN Report.* Number: US5001. Rome: USUN.

Ilcan, S. and L. Phillips. 2003. 'Making Food Count: The Global Governance of Food and Expert Knowledge', *Canadian Review of Sociology and Anthropology* 40(4): 441–61.

Latour, B. and S. Woolgar. 1979. *Laboratory Life: The Social Construction of Scientific Facts.* Los Angeles: Sage.

Mouffe, C. 1994. *The Return of the Political.* London: Verso.

Müller, B. 2006a. 'Infringing and Trespassing Plants. Control over and Responsibility for Patented Seeds at Dispute in Canada's Courts', *Focaal. European Journal of Anthropology* 48: 83–98.

———. 2006b. 'On the Ownership of Nature', in G. Laxer and D. Soron (eds), *Not for Sale: De-commodifying Public Life.* Calgary: Broadview Press.

———. 2008. *La bataille des OGM. Combat d'avenir ou d'arrière-garde?* Paris: Editions ellipses.

Murray Li, T. 2007. *The Will to Improve. Governmentality, Development and the Practice of Politics.* Durham, NC: Duke University Press.

Paarlberg, R. 2005. 'From the Green Revolution to the Gene Revolution', *Environment: Science and Policy for Sustainable Development* 47(1): 38–40.

Pestre, D. 2007. 'The Historical Heritage of the 19th and 20th Centuries: Techno-science, Markets and Regulations in a Long-term Perspective', *History and Technology* 23(4): 407–20.

Phillips, L. and S. Ilcan. 2004. 'Capacity-Building: The Neoliberal Governance of Development', *Canadian Journal of Development Studies* XXV(3): 393–409

———. 2007. 'Responsible Expertise: Governing the Uncertain Subjects of Biotechnology', *Critique of Anthropology* 27(1): 103–26.

Rist, G. 2002a. 'Le prix des mots', in G. Rist (ed.), *Les mots du pouvoir: Sens et non-sens de la rhétorique internationale).* Nouveaux Cahiers de l'IUED, vol. 13. Paris: PUF, pp. 9–23.

———. 2002b. 'Le texte pris aux mots', in G. Rist (ed.), *Les mots du pouvoir: Sens et non-sens de la rhétorique internationale.* Nouveaux Cahiers de l'IUED, vol. 13. Paris: PUF, pp. 25–41.

Rosavallon, P. 2006. *La contre-démocratie. Essai sur la société de la defiance.* Paris: Éditions du Seuil.

Rose, N. 1999. *Powers of Freedom: Reframing Political Thought.* Cambridge: Cambridge University Press.

Tarrow, S. 1998. *Power in Movement,* 2nd ed. Cambridge: Cambridge University Press.

AFTERWORD
Chapter 16

A Policy Ethnographer's Reading of Policy Anthropology

Dvora Yanow

Much as anthropologists talk about coming to understand their own cultures better for having lived in other countries, sometimes travelling to a foreign discipline helps see one's own more clearly. Reading in cognate fields can generate oblique visions that enable eureka moments for present-day thinkers, much as displacing bathtub water did for ancient Greeks. So it might be for those reading this book from the tub of political science, policy studies, public administration/organisational studies and international relations – the 'we' of this chapter. For I come to these chapters as someone with a primary disciplinary home in 'politics' and subfield specialisations in public policy and organisational studies, but also as a long-time reader of anthropological literature, especially concerning ceremonies and rituals, myths, language (including metaphors and categories) and other aspects of the symbolic, the social and the cultural. As a methodologist, one of the central questions I brought to this book was: what, if anything, distinguishes policy anthropology from policy ethnography? By the latter I mean studies of public policies and policy processes from a political science background (including public policy, public administration, comparative government and international relations), without formal training in anthropology but informed by ethnographic methods and interpretive methodologies. I use these two terms throughout this chapter in drawing that distinction.

Taken as a whole, these chapters have the potential to enable 'us' political/policy ethnographers to see what has been directly under our noses for some time, but which has been obscured by recent political science's insistence, hegemonically, on turning human action – words, deeds, settings and interactions mediated by physical artefacts – into numbers. Yet, just as that discipline –

from the perspective of understanding human action on and in its own terms – is blinkered by its theoretical heritage, so too can anthropology be hampered – from the perspective of theorising public policies – by its methodological heritage. Strictures and boundaries developed within or imposed by epistemic communities and disciplinary devices can forestall successful communication, learning and even collaboration between the two groups.

These chapters show a way out, for both. They provide a necessary corrective for both fields: an anthropology that increasingly looks to root its studies in domestic governmental, organisational and other urban and trans-local settings, in strong contrast to its traditional 'foreign', bounded, village settings; and a public policy studies, perhaps even a political science, that is increasingly seeking to overcome a behaviouralist hegemony of the last thirty-five years that holds up quantitative methods as the scientific yardstick and expects qualitative methods to aspire to that 'standard' (Brady and Collier 2004).

For anthropological readers who may be unfamiliar with events and trends in political and policy sciences, let me note that the discipline is only now taking its own 'interpretive turn' (e.g., Klotz and Lynch 2007; Yanow and Schwartz-Shea 2006). *Policy Worlds* comes at a time of ferment when ethnography is becoming a serious contender, once again, for attention in North American political science; witness the recent publication of Schatz's *Political Ethnography* (2009) by a major press, the American Political Science Association's (APSA) Qualitative Methods Section's award of its 2007 Best Paper prize to Pachirat's (2009) ethnography, and Routledge's taking over of the rechristened *Critical Policy Studies* journal associated with the Europe-based Interpretive Policy Analysis conference. Yet these efforts still struggle against a strongly entrenched realist-objectivist hegemony, especially within the APSA, the Association for Public Policy and Management (APPAM) and North American public policy and political science curricula and journals.

For those of us in policy and political studies who have been contending with that hegemonic impulse, *Policy Worlds* is a welcome contribution. It should promote dialogue between anthropologists and interpretive policy analysis and political science scholars. To the extent that 'policy anthropology' is marginalised within its disciplinary home as 'applied anthropology' and 'policy/political ethnography' is marginalised within its base for not doing survey or 'mixed methods' (qualitative plus quantitative) research, the two groups might not only find common intellectual ground but also assist each other in their respective science wars. Several themes in the book's chapters, shared by both disciplinary communities, might facilitate that potential conversation.

Shared Meanings

First among these is a shared focus on meaning and its production and contestation. Policy anthropologists and political/policy ethnographers are equally as likely to look for meaning-making not only in the acts and interpretations of decision makers, policy experts and other elites, but also among those on the 'receiving end' of governmental activities with local knowledge of their neighbourhood or agency. Both kinds of researchers ask how governments' ideas about and expectations of individuals and collective entities (neighbourhoods and communities, schools and hospitals, corporations and factories) – whose bodies, identities and behaviours they seek to shape, change and control – are embedded in and expressed through public policies (see, for example, Nyqvist, Chapter 11, this volume). Research conducted by both seeks to elucidate the processes through which this occurs.

In their introduction, as do the chapter authors elsewhere in the book, Cris Shore and Susan Wright bring into the policy arena theoretical developments taking place outside of traditional policy studies (especially its U.S.A. versions). These include the contributions of the French *Sciences Po* school and other post-behaviourist, post-structuralist theories, such as Latour's actor-network theory, Foucault's knowledge/power interrelationships and Bourdieu's habitus. Such theorising has the potential to catapult policy scholarship far beyond its current boundaries, as I note below with respect to the definition of 'policy' itself. This is where these chapters make a major contribution for those coming from the relatively atheoretical background of traditional policy studies. At the same time, some of the analyses presented here would have benefited from a greater awareness of the work done in that discipline. For example, that policies have unintended consequences 'that go beyond the original intentions' (Shore and Wright, Introduction, this volume) was learned by policy studies researchers in the early 1970s, becoming the starting point for many policy implementation analyses. A bit of disciplinary history helps clarify how this came about.

The instrumental-rational model of the policy process (a set of stages that strongly echoes the steps of the 'scientific method'), which Shore and Wright call 'authoritative instrumentalism' (Introduction, this volume), is a received wisdom that is still the starting point of many textbooks today. To the extent that this is a 'practitioner perspective', as they claim, that status derives from the way in which policy analysis developed into a field of professional practice. 'Policy studies' developed in the U.S.A. in the 1960s and 1970s, when the Kennedy and Johnson administrations, supported by primarily federal legislatures and courts, used policies actively as social change instruments (consider, for example, civil rights policies attacking entrenched housing, educational and employment practices). The model, and the conceptualisations associated with it, were exported to the world of practice in a newly created professional degree, the Master of Public Policy (MPP), established at a number of U.S. universities. Chief among these was Harvard's Kennedy School of Government, an analysis-oriented heir of the university's more theoretical Graduate School of Public Administration. Through its training for mid-career policy makers, public administrators and other decision makers, many of whom held positions in Washington, the model was exported to the world of practice, as well as to practice-focused conferences and journals – although many practitioners themselves admitted that their worlds did not operate in such rational-instrumental ways.

It was the practice-informed critique of that model (Pressman and Wildavsky 1984; Lipsky 1978, 1980), including its separation of 'political' policy making from 'apolitical' administration, that launched the field of policy implementation studies, out of which interpretive policy analysis grew (Fischer 2003; Fischer and Forester 1993; Hajer and Wagenaar 2003; Yanow 1993, 1995). These scholars (including critical theorists and political discourse analysts) have common cause with policy anthropologists in showing, as noted in the Introduction to this volume, how policy analysis is in fact 'not a quasi-scientific activity'.

But I am not convinced that it is their anthropological background per se that gives policy anthropologists an edge over policy ethnographers and other interpretive policy analysts in focusing on policy meanings and the (inter)subjective meaning-making of policy-relevant actors, so as to 'challenge received wisdom and think outside of the conventional policy box' (from the Introduction). That is precisely what interpretive policy analysts began doing in the 1970s and 1980s (and what Edelman did even earlier; see, e.g., Ascher 1987; Brunner 1982; DeHaven-Smith 1988; Dryzek 1982; Edelman 1964, 1977; Fay 1975; Goodsell 1988; Hawkesworth 1988; Healy 1986; Jennings 1983, 1987; Rein and Schön 1977; Torgerson 1986; Yanow 1987). Moreover, influenced by Habermasian and other theorising, much interpretive policy analysis took a discursive conceptual turn in the 1990s. In a methodological departure from behaviouralist political science, this led them to go and talk to people – the so-called 'targets' of public policies (Schneider and Ingram 1993). That unfortunate term suggests that the only persons with agency in a policy situation are 'policy actors' – legislators, their staff, lobbyists, implementers and the like. In contrast, those on the receiving end of decisions are sitting ducks just waiting for policy solutions to hit them, like the missiles of Robert McNamara's U.S. Department of Defense (DoD), where so much technical policy analysis (e.g., cost-benefit analysis) was initially developed. Brought by him from the Ford Foundation, from DoD it entered the Kennedy School and other academic curricula.

Administrations of the 1960s and 1970s inherited, and maintained, a highly paternalistic period of governmental policy making (the Ford Foundation's Grey Areas Programs, forerunners of the Great Society programmes, including the Peace Corps and its domestic counterpart, VISTA), which intended to do good, as defined by elites, but which denied recipients' expertise in their own local knowledge and their own agency (a pattern continued by some of the more recent social constructionist treatments of policy analysis). Even the 'participatory planning' movement of this era was critiqued for its cosmetic aspects (e.g., Arnstein 1969). The more recent discursive, dialogical turn counters this denial of agency to those on the 'receiving ends' of policies. It has sparked several authors (Dryzek 1990; Schneider and Ingram 1997) to argue that interpretive policy analysis is much more democratic than the traditional, top-down policy analysis that has become standard in academic curricula for training professionals.

Perhaps, then, *pace* the Introduction to this volume, it is not 'anthropology's more open and democratic approach' *per se* that leads to emphasising situated meaning, policy process' messiness and the complexities, ambiguities and contestations of policy meanings – in short, to the problematising of policy itself. Policy anthropology is not alone in doing this. Rather, it is the ontological and epistemological underpinnings shared by policy anthropologists, policy ethnographers and other interpretive policy analysts, rooted in a phenomenological hermeneutics and manifested in ethnographic sensibilities and/or practices adopted and cultivated by both disciplines, that carry within them the impetus to such analytic starting points.

Policy scholars are, however, still often restricted by the theoretical heritage of their disciplinary base. Here is where the chapters of this book can be enlightening, beginning with the very definition of what 'policy' means.

Defining 'Policy'

Although those coming from political and policy studies backgrounds tend to take for granted much that is highlighted in these chapters, it is very useful to have one's 'common sense' spelt out explicitly and held up as an object of reflection. For example:

> If part of the 'work of policy' is to classify and organise people and ideas in new ways, then it becomes easy to understand why policies can be such powerful vehicles for social change. (Shore and Wright, Introduction, this volume)

That policies are social change mechanisms is, I think, a baseline assumption among policy analysts – that is part of the air we breathe. To have it held up for investigation, however, is a useful reminder that things might be otherwise – and a challenge to return to our assumptions and interrogate them.

Policy and political scientists' present-day conceptualisations of policy processes are constrained or framed by the intellectual history that has shaped that understanding. The institutional approach with which North American studies of governmental action began conceptualises three branches of government, each balancing the others, with the legislative branch passing laws/making policies. Such a formulation restricted policy 'making' to legislative actions and the decision-making acts of legislators; even their staff were an analytic non-entity until the appearance of Redman's participant-observer case study (1973). Even when 'policy making' was expanded on the front end to include 'agenda-setting' and on the back end to cover 'implementation', it was still framed as a linear, assembly-line process. This linear model vests politics and power exclusively in the hands of decision-making elites, reflecting the conceptualisation of authority embedded in Weberian bureaucracy theory (which also undergirds the politics-administration dichotomy). Breaking out of the straitjacket of that disciplinary history to imagine policy in a new way has not been easy.

Anthropologists suffer no such history. Their conceptualisation of policy could catapult us out of our received framing: policy is 'a continuous process of contestation across a political space' (Wright and Reinhold, Chapter 5, this volume). No linearity here! The same sense of multiplicities of actors and settings, of locales of power and influence, of cyclicality of policy proposal and revision as described in the public policy literature comes into focus in this discussion. Moreover, in drawing on other theoretical sources, new potentialities emerge: 'Hegemony and contestation are central to this idea of policy: political conflicts to defend or unsettle established discourses and advance particular ways of conceptualising the role of the individual, social institutions and even of government itself' (Wright and Reinhold, Chapter 5, this volume). Such formulations, looking not to the regularity and control of manufacturing but more to power and conflict, potentially reframe the ways in which we think about 'policy'. So, whereas the critique of a linear, top-down model of the policy process has already been articulated in the policy studies literature, these chapters offer new ways of conceiving of policy itself.

But even more is required. This treatment still encounters the definitional problems found in the policy studies literature. Is 'policy' the formal document that is the outcome of a legislative act? Is it a set of inclinations, as in 'The British Government's policy is ...'? Is it a specific programme? Implicit in some chapters is a sense that the key question is not what is a policy, or even what's happening here, but instead, what work is a policy doing? That kind of question, the sort of focus found in science studies, shifts analytic attention to the meanings of concepts – such as 'policy', in a broader, 'governance' discourse – or of specific terms in particular policy issues – such as 'gay' (Wright and Reinhold, Chapter 5, this volume) or 'housing decay' (Schön 1979).

Other conceptual arenas in which this book's ideas interact generatively with those in (interpretive) policy analysis include the research setting; the up/down direction of study; power and agency; and public perceptions of the power of 'science'. I will take these up in order.

Multi-sited Research, in Space and Time

Anthropologists are also constrained by disciplinary history, although theirs seems more methodological than theoretical. Their battle is against the traditional model of a 'single site', a geographically bounded setting, with its inhabitants, language, tools and practices. Following the policy – the legislative document, for example, or the legislator – moves traditional anthropology to a necessarily 'multi-sited' study, the marked term suggesting the challenge. For policy ethnography, this is a nonissue: we look for the sites of decision-making power and of silent and/or silenced voices without pressure to constrain our study to the borders of a specific physical setting. The policy itself is the site, not some geographically bounded entity.

A policy issue's borders are more diffuse than those of a village or city: no civil administrator or planner has drawn a red line around it on a map. We exchange the boundedness of place (and of time) for the relatively more open domain of a policy issue and the processes through which it comes onto the public agenda (or does not), is legislated (or not), implemented successfully (or not) and resurfaces later (potentially) reframed in a different guise. This typically involves a wide range of policy-relevant actors – those whose behaviour is to be changed, activists both pro and con, gatekeepers, stakeholders, legislators and their staffs, lobbyists, agency directors and their staffs, street-level bureaucrats, other implementers and evaluators. Greg Feldman's 'nonlocal ethnography' (Chapter 2, this volume), then, may be nonlocal in the traditional anthropological sense of setting, but it is very local – very situated – with respect to specific policies and their entailments and policy-relevant documents and actors. It might be considered local with respect to settings as well, but in a rather different sense; consider housing policy, for instance, which is situated not with respect to one specific house, but rather to a category of housing type, and is no less spatial for that.

Space is not only geographic; in policy spheres, it also refers to levels of analysis. 'Public policy studies' in U.S. academia has long meant domestic legislative processes and policies only – welfare, housing, transportation, environment, etc.; foreign policy has more commonly been left to international relations (IR). The creation of the European Union (EU) has made the limitations of this boundary making abundantly clear: environmental problems, after all, cross state lines, and policies must do likewise. Both policy and IR scholars stand to benefit from policy anthropologists' inclination not to recognise boundaries between domestic and 'supranational entities', as Janine Wedel (Chapter 8, this volume) puts it. Cris Shore's exploration (Chapter 9, this volume) of the build-up to the war in Iraq is a wonderful example of analysis that crosses such 'spatial' boundaries.

In shifting to a focus on discourses, which are 'present in multiple locations but are not of any particular location', Feldman (Chapter 2, this volume) gets at precisely this point, to which Shore (Chapter 9, this volume) also turns. To the extent that much interpretive policy analysis engages in discourse analysis of some sort, the two epistemic communities are on the same page. What the privileging of language at the hands of discourse analysis threatens to lose, however, is the ways in which acts and physical artefacts are also significant in policy meanings. This is manifest in methods of policy discourse analysis, which tend to rest on documents and/or interviews, often presenting the latter – wrongly, in my view – as ethnographic research. A policy anthropology that encompasses 'discursive spaces' without abandoning participant-observer ethnography can help interpretive policy analysis gain methodological clarity.

And time? Interpretive policy analysts seem much more cognisant than their traditional policy/political science counterparts of historical antecedents to contemporary policies and the contingencies of present social and political realities. This is the sort of 'writing the history of the present' that Wright and Reinhold (Chapter 5, this volume) discuss. Their 'studying through', following an actor or how a policy issue might be framed at one moment and reframed at another, can apply not only to physical un-boundedness but to time un-boundedness as well (Rein and Schön 1977; Schön and Rein 1994).

Top Down/Bottom Up Meets Studying Down/Studying Up

Traditional policy analysis, as with nearly all political science, engages its subject matter at the top. That is where power, the *leitmotif* of the discipline's work, presumably resides. Anthropologists, by contrast, have traditionally studied down. I cannot, for instance, imagine an anthropologist producing a work that instructs students in 'elite interviewing' alone, although that is a central focus in recent U.S. political science (Leech 2002; contrast Bogner, Littig and Menz 2009). When seeking to overcome disciplinary strictures, the two disciplines use similar language, but look in opposite directions: policy and political scientists study 'bottom-up' processes, such as implementation; anthropologists 'study up'. But that invocation notwithstanding, anthropologists, claim Wright and Reinhold (Chapter 5, this volume), tend to focus on the dominated even when they are interested in domination. If the same holds true for policy/political studies scholars – that we attend to those in power even when thinking to study workers, community residents, etc. – this might explain part of the current scepticism regarding ethnographic work!

What a marvellous opportunity for the two groups to join intellectual forces, drawing on their respective topographical orientations and the strengths of their methods. In fact, interpretive policy analysts and others have studied those in lower positions of bureaucratic hierarchies, including street-level bureaucrats (Lipsky 1980; Prottas 1979; Weatherley 1979) and agency clients' meaning-making of policy implementation (Stein 1984; Yanow 1996), using ethnographically informed research methods. Much methodological potential resides in this possible collaboration.

But we might also take a cue from Shore's (Chapter 9, this volume) idea that policies require not so much studying up – in fact, policy implementation scholars might argue that it requires studying down – as studying across and every which way (perhaps Wright and Reinhold's 'studying through') in a network sort of fashion, something that Wedel also points to. This is what following a policy and policy-relevant actors, objects, acts and language achieves 'teasing out connections and observing how policies bring together individuals, discourses and institutions ... and the new kinds of networks, relations and subjects this process creates' (Shore, Chapter 9, this volume). 'Up' and 'down' are intertwined, conceptually, with methodological issues of place and single-sitedness; dating from anthropology's academic origins, they are, ultimately, increasingly outdated formulations. The study of policy might indeed provide a pathway towards methodological reframing for the discipline as a whole.

Power and Agency: Researchers, Policy-Relevant Actors and Knowledge Claims

Clearly, we need to uproot the language of policy 'targets', as well as the thinking that underlies it. But is there a structural dimension to our conceptualisation of research relationships and the generation of knowledge that promotes such thinking? 'Up' and 'down', both stances reflect the researcher's (felt) cognitive and power position relative to situational members. Does this facilitate a view of some as targets lacking in agency – the idea, as Davide Però puts it (introduction to Section III), that policy's 'subjects are passively constructed by the policies that act upon them'? Gritt Nielsen's discussion (Chapter 4, this volume) of Danish educational policy and Chinese students suggests another direction, her incorporation of a multi-perspectival analysis embodying the networked 'through-ness' noted above. Unhampered by a political scientist's disciplinary restrictions, she draws on actor network/science studies theories of Callon, Latour, Law and others to advance a reconceptualisation of the policy process in terms of students' subjectivities, emerging assemblages and translations. It would be interesting to see this approach brought into dialogue with the classic multi-perspectival works of Graham Allison (1971), offering three interpretations of U.S. decision making in the 'Cuban missile crisis', or Lipsky (1980), looking at street-level bureaucrats' 'policy making' activities as distinct from formal legislative processes. According legitimacy to multiple perspectives – and not just those of policy makers or researchers – is one way of moving beyond 'targets', a perceived lack of knowledge and a lack of agency. Can it also open the door to reconsiderations of the knowledge/power link?

David Mosse uses his experiences with former colleagues and funders who sought to scuttle his book publication to raise a number of related issues with which other literatures also engage and that could make for interesting cross-fertilisation. Organisational studies, for example, addresses the matter of employee loyalty and reactions when that loyalty is breached, a situation not uncommon in the experience of community organisers working for (quasi) governmental agencies. Such discussions recall Hirschman's (1970) classic discussion of exit or voice as strategies when loyalty to the organisation has been betrayed. Argyris and Schön's (1974) analysis shows managers dealing with cognitive dissonance by enacting defences, with disastrous results for their effectiveness. Consultants' experiences of making clients' tacit knowledge explicit (Schein 1992) – when the latter thought it well hidden – parallel what Mosse presents. It is not so much a problem of tension between ethnographers and experts that is at play as it is the complex relationships between knowledge and power, whoever their bearers are.

Anthropologists have long been in the lead in engaging their positionality explicitly in producing knowledge and the need for researcher reflexivity in considering personal as well as physical situatedness in the generation of 'truth claims'. Although *de rigueur* in anthropology, these are still very much contested methodological spaces in policy/political studies. There, researchers are much more likely to consider the 'positionalities', without using that term, of those researched than to explicitly engage their own, something that Tara Schwegler (Chapter 7, this volume) touches upon. Policy anthropologists can be an example to policy ethnographers, linking reflexivity more directly to issues of power – the bread and butter of political scientific inquiry – and not 'just' to the subjectivities of knowledge generation. In so doing, they might enable us to overcome political science's resistance to such considerations. The related methodological issues are well worth elaborating. What are the power/knowledge issues in the common advice that researchers use 'member checking' in qualitative research (Erlandson et al. 1993)? And what characterises research relationships that might provoke a 'native' to exclaim to an ethnographer: 'But I thought we were friends?' (Beech et al. 2009)?

Science and 'the State'

Another dimension of power in the policy process is the societal standing accorded to conceptualisations of science, in particular in policy usages of scientific-sounding terms, which garner them a certain legitimacy. Several chapters touch directly on the relationship between perceptions of science and the state. Drawing on the widespread understanding of science as objective and value-neutral, they succeed, as Shore puts it (Chapter 9, this volume), in making policy discourses 'appear so "natural" that [the policy's] ideological content comes to be regarded as common sense and therefore beyond question'. In one example, Dorothy Louise Zinn (Chapter 12, this volume) remarks on the ways in which in Lucania, Italy, government officials' use of 'technical-scientific "facts"' positioned these beyond political debate. Birgit Müller (Chapter 15, this volume) continues this theme, noting how the United Nations' Food and Agriculture Organization, in rendering policy issues technical, moved them outside the realm of democratic politics. In this process, perceptions of science join with the ideas of technical-rational policy processes, including their instrumentally rational bureaucracies, in promoting values that set them apart from power and politics. Rendering the political technical has profound implications for democratic political ideals. This is something that policy scientists, other than those working within science and technology studies or perhaps environmental policy studies, have rarely engaged. It is a topic that I would hope to see developed in further work in both disciplines.

Prognosis

Stepping outside one's disciplinary training and reframing the way one asks questions or defines concepts is not easy. That is why looking obliquely, through another discipline's eyes and framing devices, can be useful. What public policy scholars stand to gain by looking through the lenses of these chapters is new insights into ways to conceptualise and theorise 'policy'. For political scientists who often conflate ethnographic research with interviewing (by which they typically mean the single, 'one-off' interview rather than the 'intensive interviewing' Wright refers to in the Introduction to Section I of this volume), this book will be a useful antidote. It demonstrates what an 'ethnographic sensibility' and that ineffable quality of 'being there' bring to a research project that interviewing alone does not and cannot. What anthropologists would gain from conversation with their interpretive policy analysis counterparts is greater insight into the methodological implications of studying things that are not bounded by traditional ethnographic space and time. Several chapters note the necessity, in studying public policy making, of drawing on more kinds of data than would be included in a traditional anthropological ethnography. Among them are Wedel, who observes that the 'complexity of governing also calls for the employment of multiple methods', by which she apparently means various sorts of documentary evidence along with interview and ethnographic material, and Shore, who includes 'informant narratives' and official texts, and the triangulation of the latter against the former. Examples of such studies abound within policy studies, especially pre-implementation analyses of public bureaucracies (Blau 1963; Crozier 1964; Kaufman 1960; Selznick 1949). To this list of methods innovations we should add Weldes' (2006) 'low data', such as Shore's nine- or ninety-day-old newspaper, the kinds of sources often dismissed in political science as popular culture or in anthropology, according to Shore, as 'journalism'.

Pace Shore (Chapter 9, this volume), far from posing a challenge to claiming an insider's perspective or 'native's point of view' on the issue, ethnographies of policies, which are perforce non-local in a traditional anthropological sense, are very much 'policy-local' in the ways illustrated in these chapters and thereby potentially provide that insider's point of view. The question has to be who is 'the native' in policy studies – and which 'natives' are we studying? What ethnography can and must do, whether practised by anthropologists or by policy/political studies scholars, is to identify those multiple policy-relevant communities of meaning that are 'native' to the issue under study and seek insiders' understandings of these multiple points of view. For it is in these multiplicities of interpretations and clashes of meaning-making that the complexities of policy making and implementation develop and reside; and it is the explication of these conflicting understandings that both policy anthropologists and policy ethnographers should be after.

There is something distinctive about 'ethnographying' public policies, and joining forces – or at least reading across the boundaries thrown up by our respective epistemic communities – promises to help all of us articulate what that is, something that will at least help us be better teachers of newer generations of scholars.

References

Allison, Graham T. 1971. *Essence of Decision*. Boston: Little, Brown.
Argyris, Chris and Donald A. Schön. 1974. *Theory in Practice*. San Francisco: Jossey-Bass.
Arnstein, Sherry R. 1969. 'A Ladder of Citizen Participation', *Journal of the American Institute of Planners* 35(4): 216–24.
Ascher, William. 1987. 'Editorial', *Policy Sciences* 20: 3–9.
Beech, Nic, Paul Hibbert, Robert MacIntosh and Peter McInnes. 2009. '"But I Thought We Were Friends?" Life Cycles and Research Relationships', in Sierk Ybema, Dvora Yanow, Harry Wels and Frans Kamsteeg (eds), *Organizational Ethnography: Studying the Complexities of Everyday Organizational Life*. London: Sage, pp. 196–214.
Blau, Peter. 1963 [1953]. *The Dynamics of Bureaucracy*. Chicago: University of Chicago Press.
Bogner, Alexander, Beate Littig and Wolfgang Menz. 2009. *Interviewing Experts: Methodology and Practice*. Basingstoke: Palgrave Macmillan.
Brady, Henry E. and David Collier (eds). 2004. *Rethinking Social Inquiry: Diverse Tools, Shared Standards*. Lanham, MD: Rowman & Littlefield.
Brunner, Ronald D. 1982. 'The Policy Sciences as Science', *Policy Sciences* 15(2): 115–35.
Crozier, Michel. 1964. *The Bureaucratic Phenomenon*. Chicago: University of Chicago Press.
DeHaven-Smith, Lance. 1988. *Philosophical Critiques of Policy Analysis*. Gainesville: University of Florida Press.
Dryzek, John S. 1982. 'Policy Analysis as a Hermeneutic Activity', *Policy Sciences* 14(4): 309–29.
———. 1990. *Discursive Democracy*. Cambridge: Cambridge University Press.
Edelman, Murray. 1964. *The Symbolic Uses of Politics*. Urbana: University of Illinois.
———. 1977. *Political Language*. New York: Academic Press.
Erlandson, David A., Edward L. Harris, Barbara L. Skipper and Steve D. Allen. 1993. *Doing Naturalistic Inquiry*. Newbury Park, CA: Sage.
Fay, Brian. 1975. *Social Theory and Political Practice*. Boston: George Allen & Unwin.
Fischer, Frank. 2003. *Reframing Public Policy: Discursive Politics and Deliberative Practices*. New York: Oxford University Press.
Fischer, Frank and John Forester (eds). 1993. *The Argumentative Turn in Policy Analysis and Planning*. Durham, NC: Duke University Press.
Goodsell, Charles T. 1988. *The Social Meaning of Civic Space*. Lawrence: University Press of Kansas.
Hajer, Maarten A. and Hendrik Wagenaar (eds). 2003. *Deliberative Policy Analysis*. New York: Cambridge University Press.

Hawkesworth, M.E. 1988. *Theoretical Issues in Policy Analysis*. Albany, NY: SUNY Press.

Healy, Paul. 1986. 'Interpretive Policy Inquiry. A Response to the Limitations of the Received View', *Policy Sciences* 19(4): 381–96.

Hirschman, Albert O. 1970. *Exit, Voice, and Loyalty: Responses to Decline in Firms, Organizations and States*. Cambridge, MA: Harvard University Press.

Jennings, Bruce. 1983. 'Interpretive Social Science and Policy Analysis', in Daniel Callahan and Bruce Jennings (eds), *Ethics, the Social Sciences, and Policy Analysis*. New York: Plenum, pp. 3–35.

———. 1987. 'Interpretation and the Practice of Policy Analysis', in Frank Fischer and John Forester (eds), *Confronting Values in Policy Analysis*. Newbury Park, CA: Sage, pp. 128–52.

Kaufman, Herbert. 1960. *The Forest Ranger*. Baltimore, MD: Published for Resources for the Future by Johns Hopkins University Press.

Klotz, Audie and Cecelia Lynch. 2007. *Strategies for Research in Constructivist International Relations*. Armonk, NY: M.E. Sharpe.

Leech, Beth L. (ed.). 2002. 'Interview Methods in Political Science', *PS: Political Science & Politics* 35(4): 663–88.

Lipsky, Michael. 1978. 'Standing the Study of Public Policy Implementation on its Head', in Walter Dean Burnham and Martha Weinberg (eds), *American Politics and Public Policy*. Cambridge, MA: MIT Press, pp. 391–402.

———. 1980. *Street-level Bureaucracy*. New York: Russell Sage Foundation.

Pachirat, Timothy. 2009. 'The Political in Political Ethnography: Dispatches from the Kill Floor', in Edward Schatz (ed.), *Political Ethnography: What Immersion Contributes to the Study of Power*. Chicago: University of Chicago Press, pp. 143–61.

Pressman, Jeffrey L. and Aaron Wildavsky. 1984 [1973]. *Implementation: How Great Expectations in Washington are Dashed in Oakland; Or, Why it's Amazing that Federal Programs Work at All...*, 3rd ed., expanded. Berkeley: University of California Press.

Prottas, Jeffrey M. 1979. *People-processing*. Lexington, MA: D.C. Heath.

Redman, Eric. 1973. *The Dance of Legislation*. New York: Simon & Schuster.

Rein, Martin and Donald A. Schön. 1977. 'Problem Setting in Policy Research', in Carol Weiss (ed.), *Using Social Research in Policy Making*. Lexington, MA: Lexington Books, pp. 235–51.

Schatz, Edward. (ed.). 2009. *Political Ethnography: What Immersion Contributes to the Study of Power*. Chicago: University of Chicago Press.

Schein, Edgar H. 1992. *Organizational Culture and Leadership*. San Francisco: Jossey-Bass.

Schneider, Anne and Helen Ingram. 1993. 'Social Construction of Target Populations. Implications for Politics and Policy', *American Political Science Review* 87(2): 334–47.

———. 1997. *Policy Design for Democracy*. Lawrence: University Press of Kansas.

Schön, Donald A. 1979. 'Generative Metaphor', in Andrew Ortony (ed.), *Metaphor and Thought*. Cambridge: Cambridge University Press, pp. 137–63.

Schön, Donald A. and Martin Rein. 1994. *Frame Reflection: Toward the Resolution of Intractable Policy Controversies*. New York: Basic Books.

Selznick, Philip. 1949. *TVA and the Grass Roots*. Berkeley: University of California Press.

Soss, Joe B. 2002. *Unwanted Claims: The Politics of Participation in the U.S. Welfare System*. Ann Arbor: University of Michigan Press.

Stein, Sandra J. 1984. *The Culture of Education Policy*. New York: Teachers College Press.

Torgerson, Douglas. 1986. 'Interpretive Policy Inquiry. A Response to its Limitations', *Policy Sciences* 19(4): 397–405.

Weatherley, Richard. 1979. *Reforming Special Education*. Cambridge, MA: MIT Press.

Weldes, Jutta. 2006. 'High Politics and Low Data: Globalization Discourses and Popular Culture', in Dvora Yanow and Peregrine Schwartz-Shea (eds), *Interpretation and Method: Empirical Research Methods and the Interpretive Turn*. Armonk, NY: M.E. Sharpe, pp. 176–86.

Yanow, Dvora. 1987. 'Toward a Policy Culture Approach to Implementation', *Policy Studies Review* 7(1): 103–15.

——. 1993. 'The Communication of Policy Meanings: Implementation as Interpretation and Text, *Policy Sciences* 26(1): 41–61.

——. 1995. 'Editorial. Practices of Policy Interpretation', *Policy Sciences* 28(2): 111–26.

——. 1996. *How Does a Policy Mean? Interpreting Policy and Organizational Actions*. Washington DC: Georgetown University Press.

Yanow, Dvora and Peregrine Schwartz-Shea (eds). 2006. *Interpretation and Method: Empirical Research Methods and the Interpretive Turn*. Armonk, NY: M.E. Sharpe.

Notes on Contributors

Gregory Feldman teaches anthropology and geography at the University of British Columbia. His research addresses globalisation, the state, migration, population regulation, subjectivity, and methodological questions about transnational ethnography. His book, entitled *The Migration Apparatus: Security, Labor, and Policymaking in the European Union*, is forthcoming from Stanford University Press (2011). He has published numerous articles on the European politics behind Estonia's policy to integrate Soviet-era Russian-speaking immigrants. He cofounded both the Interest Group for the Anthropology of Public Policy and the Network of Concerned Anthropologists and has consulted for the United Nations Development Programme.

Ciara Grunder is a graduate student, who is currently teaching at the Institute of Social Anthropology at the University of Zurich. Her thesis addresses problems of forced displacement and resettlement caused by the largest World Bank-financed infrastructure project in Mumbai. Her research interests focus on legal pluralism, policy negotiations between international organisations and the state, and the transformation of state power and practices in the era of globalisation.

Susan Brin Hyatt is Associate Professor of Anthropology at Indiana University-Purdue University Indianapolis. She earned her Ph.D. in Anthropology at the University of Massachusetts in Amherst. Her primary research focus is on the politics of social policy on poverty and welfare in both the U.S. and the U.K. She is currently working on a book on grassroots activism among women living on peripheral council estates in Bradford, West Yorkshire during the Thatcher and Major eras.

Clarissa Kugelberg is Associate Professor at the Department of Cultural Anthropology and Senior Lecturer at the Institute for Housing and Urban Research at the University of Uppsala. Her research interests are in gender, families with young children, the interface between the labour market and family life, and migration, political participation and governance.

David Mosse is Professor of Social Anthropology at the School of Oriental and African Studies (SOAS), University of London. He is the author of *The Rule of Water: Statecraft, Ecology and Collective Action in South India* (2003) and *Cultivating Development: An Ethnography of Aid Policy and Practice* (2005). Recently he edited *The Aid Effect: Giving and Governing in International Development* (with D. Lewis, 2005), *Development Brokers and Translators: The Ethnography of Aid and Agencies* (with D. Lewis, 2006) and *Adventures in Aidland: The Anthropology of Expert Knowledge and Professionals in International Development* 2011.

Birgit Müller is Senior Researcher at the LAIOS-EHESS in Paris. She has researched in postsocialist factories and on social and environmental movements in Europe and Latin America. She is currently undertaking a multi-sited research project, *Food, Property and Power: Agricultural Technologies as Global Policies and Local Practices*, with fieldwork in the Food and Agriculture Organization and among agricultural producers in Saskatchewan (Canada) and Carazo (Nicaragua). She is the author of, among other titles, *Disenchantment with Market Economics. East Germans and Western Capitalism* (Berghahn Books, 2007).

Gritt B. Nielsen is Assistant Professor in Educational Anthropology at the Danish School of Education, Aarhus University. Her research interests are in internationalisation and marketisation of higher education, human capital, and new forms of student participation. Her Ph.D. focused on recent reforms of Danish universities and the changing notions of students. This built on previous research into academics' perceptions of university reform and their ideas of academic freedom.

Anette Nyqvist received her Ph.D. in Social Anthropology from Stockholm University in 2008 for research into Sweden's reformed national pension system. The title of the published thesis is 'Opening the Orange Envelope. Reform and Responsibility in the Remaking of the Swedish National Pension System' (Stockholm University, 2008). Her research interests are focused on issues of policy and new forms of governance in the nexus of statecraft and market making. She is currently employed as a researcher at Score (Stockholm Center for Organizational Research) engaged in 'the Organising Markets' research programme.

Davide Però is Lecturer in Sociology at the University of Nottingham, where he convenes the Identity, Citizenship and Migration Centre. Previously, he was Researcher at the Centre on Migration, Policy and Society (Institute of Social and Cultural Anthropology, University of Oxford). He has conducted ethnographic research on politics and migrants in the U.K., Italy and Spain, and is now particularly interested in migrants' practices of citizenship and policy change. He wrote *Inclusionary Rhetoric/Exclusionary Practices. Left-wing Politics and Migrants in Italy* (Berghahn Books, 2007).

Shalini Randeria is Professor of Social and Cultural Anthropology at the University of Zurich. She is currently a member of the Senate of the German Research Foundation (DFG) and was President of the European Association of Social Anthropologists (EASA) from 2007 to 2009. Her research interests include the anthropology of law, state and governance, the anthropology of globalisation and modernity, and postcolonial theory. Her most recent publications are the coedited volume *Vom Imperialismus zum Empire? Postkoloniale Perspektiven auf Globalisierung* (2009) and the edited volume *Grenzverschiebungen und Grenzüberschreitungen in einer globalisierten Welt* (2011).

Sue Reinhold owns an investment advisory firm in Berkeley, California, with about $200 million under management. Her methodological approach of 'studying up' has been applied during her work career as a stock analyst, portfolio manager, Fortune 200 company corporate strategy lead, investment advisor and business owner. She has two children, lives in Berkeley, California, and teaches Torah in her free time.

Tara Schwegler is a Lead User Experience Designer at a Fortune 200 financial services company and a former Collegiate Assistant Professor at the University of Chicago. She holds a Ph.D. in Anthropology from the University of Chicago. Her research focuses on the intersection of state power and forms of economic knowledge in the policy-making process, and she is interested in the methodological challenges of conducting ethnographic research in dynamic contexts. Her recent publications include 'Take It From the Top (Down)? Rethinking Neoliberal Economic Expertise and Political Hierarchy in Mexico' (*American Ethnologist*) and 'Trading Up: Reflections on Power, Collaboration, and Ethnography in the Anthropology of Policy' (*Anthropology in Action*).

Cris Shore is Professor of Social Anthropology at the University of Auckland, New Zealand. He has conducted extensive ethnographic research on Italian politics, EU civil servants and university reform in the U.K. and New Zealand. He is the author of nine books, including *Corruption: Anthropological Perspectives* (with D. Haller, 2005). His research interests include the anthropology of politics, governance and the state, and the study of Europe and the EU.

Janine R. Wedel is a professor in the School of Public Policy at George Mason University and a senior research fellow at the New America Foundation. She writes about the privatisation of public and foreign policy, corruption and the state, and development and foreign aid through the lens of a social anthropologist. She is the author of numerous articles and books, including *Collision and Collusion: The Strange Case of Western Aid to Eastern Europe* (2001), which won the Grawemeyer Award for Ideas Improving World Order, and *Shadow Elite: How the World's New Power Brokers Undermine Democracy, Government, and the Free Market*, (Basic Books, 2009). She is cofounder of the Interest Group for the Anthropology of Public Policy (IGAPP).

Susan Wright is Professor of Educational Anthropology at the Danish School of Education, Aarhus University. She has studied how people engage with large-scale processes of political transformation during university reforms in Denmark and the U.K. and through the transformation of governance in 1980/1990s Britain. Informing all her work are insights gained from studies in Iran before and after the Islamic Revolution. She co edited *Anthropology of Policy* with Cris Shore (1997) and is co-editor of the Journal *LATISS (Learning and Teaching: International Journal of Higher Education in the Social Sciences).*

Dvora Yanow is Visiting Professor, Department of Political Science, at the University of Amsterdam. She is the author of *How Does a Policy Mean? Interpreting Policy and Organizational Actions; Conducting Interpretive Policy Analysis* and *Constructing American "Race" and "Ethnicity": Category-Making in Public Policy and Administration,* and co-editor of *Knowing in Organizations: A Practice-based Approach, Interpretation and Method: Empirical Research Methods and the Interpretive Turn* and *Organizational Ethnography: Studying the Complexities of Everyday Life.* Her current research engages state race-ethnic category making in the Netherlands, policy frames/framing, reflective practice, science museums as organisational spaces, and U.S. Institutional Review Board policies and practices.

Dorothy Louise Zinn is an adjunct instructor at the Università della Basilicata (Italy). She received her Ph.D. in social-cultural anthropology from the University of Texas at Austin. Her research interests have focused on various aspects of southern Italian culture and society, including youth unemployment, patronage-clientelism, immigration and multiculturalism. She also has extensive experience as a translator of anthropological works and has published an annotated English edition of *The Land of Remorse,* a classic ethnography by renowned anthropologist Ernesto de Martino.

Index

Index of Names

Aarslund, L. and Svanholm, G. 70
Abel-Smith, B. 2, 20
Abélès, M. 283
Abrams, E. 158
Abrams, P. 170
Abu-Lughod, L. 86
Adler, E. and Haas, P.M. 135
Agamben, G. 47
Albright, M. 181
Allahyari, R. 57
Allison, G. T. 308
Alonso, A.M. 236
Alpers, S. 172
Altieri, M. 233, 239
Amann, R. 21
Amark, K. 207
Amos, V. 175
Anderson, B. 279n4
Anderson, E. 113
Annan, K. 43, 128, 170, 175, 176, 179
Appadurai, A. 3
Argyris, C. and Schön, D.A. 308
Arias, I.F. 177
Arlacchi, P. 182
Arnstein, S.R. 303
Arvidson, M. 57
Asad, T. 87, 96, 97
Ascher, W. 303
Aytar, O. 267, 268, 276
Aznar, J.M. 252

Ball, S. 69, 72, 73, 77
Banfield, E. 227
Barnett, M.N. and Finnemore, M. 135, 285, 286
Barrientos, A. 148n1
Beck, U. 289
Beech, N. et al. 309
Bengtsson, B. and Kugelberg, C. 268

Bengtsson, J. 268, 279n2
Berger, M.T. and Beeson, M. 134, 136
Berger, P. and Luckman, T. 2
Berlusconi, S. 229, 230, 232, 233, 235, 236, 242n1, 249
Berry, F.S. and Berry, W.D. 6
Bertranou, J.F. 138, 139
Beveridge, W. 1
Beveridge Report (1942) 1–2
Blair, T. 16, 17, 128, 169, 173, 176, 178, 179, 180, 181, 182, 183
Blau, P. 310
Blitz, J. 176, 178
Bloch, M. 171
Bloch, M. and Perry, J. 80
Blok, A. 156
Blumenthal, S. 158, 160
Bogdanor, V. 155
Bogner, A. et al. 307
Boissevain, J. 156
Bonoli, G. 206, 214
Borevi, K. 267, 268
Börjesson, P.L. 210, 214
Boudia, S. 294
Boudon, R. and Bourricaud, F. 283
Bourdieu, P. 11, 114, 171, 302
Boyson, R. 103n5
Brady, H.E. and Collier, D. 301
Brah, A. 258
Bratton, W.J. et al. 109
Bright, M. et al. 181
Brooks, S.M. 135, 141
Brown, W. 240
Brubaker, R. 236
Brunner, R.D. 303
Burch, P.H. 156
Burchell, G. 16, 18, 235, 237, 238
Burdick, J. 261n5
Burgess, G. and McLean, D. 98

Burra, S. 193, 196, 200
Bush, G.W. 6, !58, 127, 157, 159, 171, 178, 179, 180
Butler of Brockwell 179

Callon, M. 73, 308
Campbell, A. 178
Cantaloube, T. and Vernet, H. 178
Caplan, J. 100
Carroll, L. 297
Castles, S. and Miller, M. 247, 256
Cattalino, J.R. 107, 114
Ceri, P. 240, 241, 242n3
Cernea, M. 62
Chalabi, A. 158
Chambers, S. 241
Chatterjee, P. 199
Cheney, D. 127, 154, 157, 162, 163
Chesluk, B. 107, 114
Chirac, J. 175, 178, 184
Clarke, D. et al. 197, 198
Clarke, J. 106, 226
Clarke, J. et al. 17, 18, 69
Clausen, A.W. 134
Clay, E. and Schaffer, B. 4, 5
Clifford, J. 46
Clinton, H. 154
Clinton, W.J. 109, 112, 158
Coates, K. 179
Cohen, A. 171
Colebatch, H.K. 4, 12
Comaroff, J. 246
Comaroff, J. and J. 33, 47, 188, 201
Conrad, J. 172
Cook, R. 175, 181
Cooper, R. 80
Craig, D. and Porter, D. 56, 58, 59, 60
Crozier, M. 310
Cruikshank, B. 3, 9, 10, 20, 110, 111, 112
Cruz-Saco, M.A. and Mesa-Lago, C. 135
Czarniawska, B. 210

Dahl, R. 267
Dale, R. 126
Davies, A.E. 12
Davis, D.-A. 108, 110, 113, 121
de Certeau, M. 19, 288, 296
    perspective on strategy 284
de Vries, B.A. 134

De Waal, A. 180
Dean, M. 69, 126, 127
Dearlove, R. 179
DeGenova, N. 45
DeHaven-Smith, L. 303
Deleon, P. and Martell, C. 6
Deleuze, G. 80
Deleuze, G. and Guattari, F. 83n5
Della Corte, E. 237
DePalma, A. 132
Deshmukh, S. and Mehta, R. 199
Diamond, I. and Quinby, L. 240
Dion, M. 130, 135
Diouf, J. 288
Dirks, N. 246
Dogan, M. 156
Dolowitz, D. and Marsh, D. 6
Donnelly, T. and Perle, R. 159
Dorrien, G. 158
Douglas, M. 107, 265, 277
Douglas, M. and Wildavsky, A. 290
Dreyfus, H.L. and Rabinow, P. 11, 44, 46, 171, 212, 219
Drezner, D. 130
Dryzek, J.S. 303
Dyer, C. 183

Eckhard, F. 176
Edelman, M. 303
Eden, A. 182
Eduards, M. 271, 275
Elmér, A. 207
Elmore, R.F. 10
Erlandson, D.A. et al. 309
Escobar, A. 261n5
Evens, T.M.S. and Handelman, D. 27
Eyben, R. 56, 61

Fairclough, N. 14
Faist, T. 268, 269
Faithfull of Wolvercote 103n10
Fay, B. 303
Feith, D. 151, 157, 160, 161, 162, 163
Feldman, G. 14, 15, 16, 27, 28, 29, 30, 33, 170, 306
Feldman, G. and Müller, B. 11
Ferguson, J. 44, 142, 287
Ferguson, J. and Gupta, A. 234
Finlayson, A. 91
Fischer, F. 5, 7, 303
Fischer, F. and Forester, J. 303

Fletcher, R. 245, 261n4
Foucault, M. 11, 17, 28, 32, 69, 77, 80, 108, 126, 171, 180, 212, 224, 283, 284, 297n2, 302
Fox, J. and Brown, D.L. 192
Fox, R. 92, 102
Fox, R. and Starn, O. 246
Franklin, L. A. 163
Fresco, L.O. 293, 294
Friedman, J. 56
Frum, D. and Perle, R. 106
Fusulier, B. and Lannoy, P. 283

Garsten, C. and Jakobsson, K. 296
Gavin, M. and Rodrik, D. 133
Geertz, C. 8, 102
    'doing history backwards' 92
Gennser, M. 209, 210, 216
George, S. and Sabelli, F. 135
Geva-May, I. 7
Ghorbanifar, M. 163, 164
Gibb, R. 261n5
Giddens, A. 17
Giroux, H.A. 106, 119
Giuliani, R. 107
Glick Schiller, N. 268, 269
Gluckman, M. 27
Goldman, M. 60, 135
Goldsmith, O. 173, 174, 184n2
Goode, J. 110
Goodhart, A. 182
Goodsell, C.T. 303
Gottweis, H 7
Gough, K. 87, 246
Grant, W. 155
Green, S. 160, 161
Greenaway, H. 103n9
Greenhalgh, S. 13, 17, 33, 48
Greenwood, C. 173
Griffiths, P. 57, 61
Gun, K. 174, 175, 181
Gupta, A. 172, 173
Gupta, A. and Ferguson, J. 33, 45
Gusterson, H. 12, 45, 170
Guttman, D. 154
Guttman, D. and Willner, B. 155

Habermas, J. 241, 289
Hadley, S. 164
Hajer, M.A. and Wagenaar, H. 303
Hale, C. 246

Hall, B. 178
Hall, S. 94, 97
Halsbury, Earl of 103n11
Handelman, D. 265, 277, 286
Hannerz, U. 56, 206
Haraway, D. 45
Harper, I. 56
Hartung, W.D. 159
Harvey, D. 106
Hastrup, K. 64, 92
Hawkesworth, M.E. 303
Healy, P. 303
Hedborg, A. 209
Hegwood, D. 291
Hersh, S. 159, 160
Hertting, N. 278
Herzfeld, M. 182, 239, 265. 277
Hilzenrath, D. 159
Hirschman, A.O. 308
Hitler, A. 95
Holmes, D.R. 207
Holmes, D.R. and Marcus, G.E. 52, 53
Holzmann, R. 132
Howell, W.G. 155
Humphrys, J. 174, 175, 176
Hussein, S. 158, 159, 161, 162, 179
Hutton, J.P. 154
Hutton of Furness 179
Hyatt, S. 9, 18, 28, 29, 30, 91, 110, 119, 127
Hylland Eriksen, T. 279n4

Ilcan, S. and Phillips, L. 286
Ireland, P.R. 268

Jackson, H.,'Scoop' 160
James, O. and Lodge, M. 7
Jay, M. 183
Jean, C. (Sogin President) 230, 234–5
Jennings, B. 303
Jessop, B. 126
Johnson, L.B. 148n3, 302
Jones, B. et al. 21n2
Jones, K.B. 240

Kaminski, A. 154
Kangas, O. et al. 207
Kapferer, B. 93
Kaufman, H. 310
Kay, S. 130, 135
Kelling, G.L. and Wilson, J.Q. 107

Kelly, D. 169
Kennedy, J.F. 148n3, 155, 302
Keough, L. 121
Kerry, J. 171
Kertzer, D. 246
King, R. et al. 248
Kingfisher, C. 110
Kingfisher, C. and Maskovsky, J. 119
Kirsch, S. 2
Klotz, A. and Lynch, C. 301
Knocke, W. and Ng, R. 268
Kretzmann, J.P. and McKnight, J. 115, 116
Krohn-Hansen, C. and Nustad, K. 170
Kugelberg, C. 18, 224

Labaton, S. 159
Laitinen, I. 41
Larner, W. and Le Heron, R. 3
Latour, B. 3, 14, 30, 51, 55, 73, 80, 212, 308
    perspective on transformation 30
Latour, B. and Woolgar, S. 293
Law, J. 73, 308
Ledeen, M. 163
Leech, B.L. 307
Levison, B. and Sutton, M. 244, 261n3
Li, T.M. 59, 60, 284, 285
Libby, I.L. 157, 163
Light, P.C. 154
Lindgren, L. 266, 267, 268
Lipsky, M. 8, 303, 307, 308
Lobe, J. 162
Loiero, A. 236
Lugo, A. 47
Lundberg, U. 206, 207, 208

MacAskill, E. 177, 178
MacAskill, E. and Borger, J. 179
McGuire, C. 47
McIntyre, M.E. 164
McNamara, Robert 134, 148n3, 303
Madrid, R.L. 130, 134, 135, 138, 139, 145
Makinson, L. 154
Malinowski, B. 64
Malkki, L. 247, 279n4
Mann, J. 158
Manningham-Buller, R. 182
Marchesi, M. 121
Marcus, G. 12, 93, 172

Markon, J. 163
Marshall, J.M. et al. 163
Martin, E. 3
Martiniello, M. 256
Mason of Barnsley 103n13
Mattei, U. 192
Mauer, M. 114
Maxfield, S. 134
Mendez, P. and Wright, S. 47
Mendoza, C. 252
Merleau-Ponty, M. 279n2
Metcalfe, A.W. 88
Meyer, D. 245
Micheletti, M. 266, 268
Mills, C.W. 156
Mitchell, T. 59, 62, 86
Miyazaki, H. and Riles, A. 52, 64
Modell, S. 73, 80
Moe, R.C. and Kosar, K.R. 154
Monson of Burton 103n13
Moore, S.F. 81, 92, 101, 188, 190
Moran, M. et al. 6
Morgen, S. and Maskovsky, J. 110
Morgen, S. et al. 112
Mosse, D. 8, 27, 28, 308
Mouffe, C. 296
Mulhern, D. 260
Müller, B. 7, 16, 17, 224, 226, 309
Müller, B. and Schwegler, T. 7
Müller, K. 148n2

Nader, L. 45, 86, 87, 101
Nader, N. 52
Nash, J. 246, 261n5
Newby, H. and Bell, C. 27
Nicoletti, N. 242n3
Nielsen, G. 27, 30, 308
Nonini, D. 121
Nustad, K. 170
Nyquist, A. 126, 302
Nyquist, A. and Schwegler, T. 20

Oldani, T. 233
O'Leary, T. 109
O'Malley, P. et al. 69
Orenstein, M.A. 130, 134, 135
Osborne, D. and Gaebler, T. 16

Paarlberg, R. 291
Page, E. 11
Paine, R. 171

Palme, J. 208
Palumbo, G. 242n3
Paris, M. 182
Patel, S. and Sharma, K. 196
Pera, M. 230
Perkins, J. 57
Perle, R. 151, 157, 158, 159, 160, 161, 163
Però, D. 16, 18, 242n3, 266, 268, 308
Però, D. and Solomos, J. 247
Pestre, D. 294
Peters, B.G. and Pierre, J. 5
Pfiffner, J.P. 155
Phillips, D.L. 163
Phillips, L. and Ilcan, S. 290
Pierre, J. 279n5
Pierson, P. 206, 214
Pinochet, A. 148n1
Piven, F.F. and Cloward, R. 109
Podgorecki, A. 153
Pollitt, C. et al. 15
Porter, T. 212
Powell, C. 162, 163
Power, M. 3, 21
Prados, J. 163
Pratt, J. 246
Pressman, J.L. and Wildavsky, A. 303
Priest, D. and Lynch, C. 177
Pritchett, L. and Woodcock, M. 60
Prottas, J.M. 307
Putman, R.D. 268

Quiesser, M. 130, 132

Rabinow, P. 32, 74
Randeria, S. 135
Randeria, S. and Grunder, C. 7, 17, 127
Rans, S.A. 116, 118
Reagan, R. 154, 158, 161
Reddy, A. and Goo, S.K. 154
Redman, E. 304
Reich, S. 152
Rein, M. and Schön, D.A. 303, 307
Reinhold, S. 86, 88, 92, 93, 94, 95, 96, 97, 99, 100, 101, 102, 206
Reinhold, S. and Wright, S. 12
Rex, J. et al. 267, 268
Rhodes, R.A. 266, 279n5
Rhodes, R.A.W. and Marsh, D. 11
Ricketts, P. 179
Riles, A. 52, 55, 57, 64

Rist, G. 291
Rizvi, F. 7
Roberts, A. 103n12
Robertson, D. 155
Roosevelt, F.D. 177
Rosanvallon, P. 200
Rose, N. 3, 16, 18, 69, 113, 115, 119, 120, 215, 234, 290
Rose, N. and Miller, P. 15, 69
Rothenberg, D. 220n3
Rozen, L. 164
Rubin, J. 181
Rumsey, A. and Weiner, J.F. 2
Rumsfeld, D. 127, 158, 162
Rycroft, R. and Kash, D.E. 153

Said, E.W. 172
Sales-Sarrapy, C. 138
Salinas de Gortari, C. 145
Sánchez, M. 35
Sanford, J. 134
Sassen, S. 29, 106, 108, 112, 120
Schein, E.H. 308
Schiller, W. and G. 247
Schmidt, J. 60
Schmögnerova, B. 42
Schneider, A. 73
Schneider, A. and Ingram, H. 245, 303
Schneider, B.R. 130
Schön, D.A. 305
Schön, D.A. and Rein, M. 307
Schwegler, T. 14, 17, 62, 126, 309
Schwegler, T. and Nyquist, A. 16
Scott, J. 245, 246, 250, 261n2
Scott, J.C. 13, 17, 228, 234
Selznick, P. 310
Seymour-Smith, C. 156
Shafer, J. 161
Sharma, A. 231, 240
Shore, C. 14, 15, 17, 45, 121, 128, 165n1, 170, 242n3, 261, 306, 307, 309, 310
Shore, C. and Nugent, S. 156
Shore, C. and Wedel, W. 16
Shore, C. and Wright, S. 3, 9, 11, 13, 15, 17, 52, 72, 86, 170, 206, 231, 244, 268, 270, 277, 302, 304
Short, C. 174, 175, 176, 178, 179, 180, 181, 183
Silver, L. 117
Silverstein, K. and Heubauer, C. 159
Simpson, T. 179

Smith, G. 246
Smith, M. 181
Smith, N. 107
Smouts, M.-C. 127
Soave, E. 242n8
Souter, B. 90
Spoelstra, S. 80
Sridhar, D. 51
St Clair, A.L. 60, 61
Standish, A. 177
Stanley, F. 121
Stein, S.J. 307
Steinmetz, G. 126
Stiglitz, J. 60
Stokes, S.C. 130
Strathern, M. 3, 12
Straw, J. 174, 180
Strobel, W.P. 163
Sutton, M. and Levinson, B. 72
Svanholm, G. 70, 71, 77

Tarrow, S. 296
Teichman, J. 130, 134, 135, 150
Thatcher, M. 12, 86, 90, 91, 94, 95, 96,
    97, 100, 103n6, 154, 290, n15
Thompson, J. 94
Tlili, A. and Wright, S. 74
Togni, P. 235
Torgerson, D. 303
Trouillot, M.R. 16, 33, 47, 170
Turnbull, A. 178
Turner, M. 176, 177
Turner, S. 160
Turner, V. 238

Varese, F. 156
Verdery, K. 105
Verkuil, P.R. 154
Vertovec, S. 256, 258
Vidal, J. 252, 261n11
Vike, H. 13, 228, 234, 236
Vives, L. 47

Wacquant, L. 108, 113, 114, 119
Wahlbeck, Ö. 268
Wald, A.M. 158
Watson, G. 34, 35
Weatherley, R. 307
Weber, M. 236
Wedel, J. 7, 15, 16, 17, 60, 101, 128,
    165n1, 306, 307, 310

Wedel, J. et al. 52
Weintraub, S. 148n4
Weldes, J. 310
Wendel, J. and Shore, C. 127
Weston, K. 100
White, H.D. 133
Wijkström, F. et al. 266
Wilkerson, L.B. 162, 163
Wilson, W.J. 113
Wingborg, M. 268
Wolf, E. 246
Wolfowitz, P. 127, 151, 157, 158, 160,
    161, 162, 163, 164
Woods, N. 59, 61, 62, 134
Woods, N. and Martinez-Diaz, L. 147
Woolcock, M. 59
Woolfson, C. 13
Wright, S. 65n1, 87, 94, 121, 165n1,
    242n3, 261, 310
Wright, S. and Reinhold, S. 15, 27, 28,
    29, 305, 307

Yanow, D. 5, 12, 20, 170, 261, 303
Yanow, D. and Schwartz-Shea, P. 5, 7,
    170, 301

Zedillo, E. 144, 145, 146
Zhang, S. 47
Zinn, D.L. 13, 15, 18, 19, 224, 225, 236,
    237, 242n7, 309, n9
Zontini, E. 261

Index of Subjects

accountability 16, 20, 59, 61, 62, 110–11, 152, 159–60
  avoidance of 127–8, 159–60, 188, 192–3
  International Planning Committee (IPC), systems of 287–8
  non-accountability, architecture of 201
  of World Bank, demand for 197, 198–9
acquis communautaire 13
actants 3
  with agency 20
activism (and activists) 9, 51, 92, 97, 195, 227–8, 250, 254, 306
  citizenship, activism and transformation of 108, 112, 114, 121
  ethic of activism 240
  history of participation in activism 116
  peace activists 183
  strategic choices of 201
actor-network-theory (ANT) 61, 302, 308
actors 1–2
  authoritative actors 63, 278
  civil society actors 192
  economic actors 6
  institutional actors 11–12
  key actors 62
  in locations, vantage point of 188
  policy actors 10, 45, 188, 303, 307–8
  social actors 64, 261n1, 294
African women's association 269–71, 278
agency 3, 7, 54, 57, 80, 189, 205–6, 303
  actants with 20
  assignment of creativity and 72
  collective agency 296
  engagement with policy 17–19
  of ethnic minority associations, scope for 268

expert ideas as means of 61
of governed peoples 244–5, 246, 260
incentivisation of 59
individual and, location in regimes of governance 181, 215, 217, 219
of migrants, significance of 226, 261n6
ownership and origin, questions of 73
policy appropriation and 30
of policy ideas 55
power and 77, 305, 308–9
rationality-technology-subjectivity triad, location in 73–4
responsibility and, relocation of 209, 212
of rural people 291, 295, 296
shared meanings and 301–2
subjectivity and 80–81
aging workforce in EU 36
agricultural biotechnology 283, 285, 287, 288, 295–6
aid 50, 53–5, 56–7, 58–9, 60, 61, 62–3, 101, 269–70
Aid to Families with Dependent Children (AFDC) 110
  conditionalities of 192–3
  mutual aid 161
Alliance of Liberal Democrats in Europe (ALDE) 34
ambiguous spaces of governance 16–17
antagonism 296
anthropological fields 72, 261n6, 301
anthropological knowledge 53, 63, 172–3
anthropology of policy 169–70
anti-terrorism 16, 172
  absorption capability 45
  the apparatus 11, 28, 29–30, 283
  challenge to ethnography 33, 45
  control, anonymity of 39–44
  formation and organisation of, crisis and 35, 42, 43–4

non-local ethnography and
illumination of 46–7
policy domains, connections
between 34–5
security as organising metaphor
35–9
studies of 32–4
appropriation 30, 72–3, 74, 80, 81–2
Argentina 137, 143, 148n1
Arms Control and Disarmament
Agency (ACDA) 160
assemblages 11, 13, 20, 30, 77, 80–81,
82, 83n5, 106, 120, 283, 308
assessment 135, 144, 201
achievements of migrants,
assessments of 250–51, 253–5, 258
environmental assessment 199
legal assessment 74, 81–2
systems of 45–6, 272, 273, 275, 277,
278
associations 18, 87, 162, 224, 232, 238,
252
African women's association 269–71,
278
ethnic minority associations,
integration policies and 264–79
exploitation of ethnic minority
associations 267–8
funding allocations and ethnic
minority associations 276–7
Latin American Workers Association
(LAWA) 256–7, 257–8, 259,
261n12
non-profit associations 264
audit
audited subjects 20–21
culture 3, 110–11, 164
practices 164
procedures 224
regimes 20
society 21
systems 111
technologies 3, 111
authoritarianism 8, 106, 109, 114, 118,
127, 153, 225, 248
neoliberalism (and neoliberals) and
118–19, 120, 157–8, 161–2
authoritative instrumentalism 4, 10,
21, 302

banking systems 139
Barcelona 18–19, 225, 226, 247, 259,
260
Sin Papeles protest in 252–5
Basilicata *see* Lucania
Belgium 48n1
benchmarking 3
Beveridge Report (1942) 1–2, 16, 20
integration of strategy 20
bipolar authority 152
Bologna 18, 225, 226, 247, 248–52, 255,
259, 260
boundaries of fields 201–2
bridling (and unbridling) 224–6
broadcast and print media, use of 173
brokers (and brokerage) 53, 59, 157–8,
284, 285–8, 294, 296–7
see also stockbrokers
bureaucracy (and bureaucrats)
absolution from personal
responsibility 182
ambiguity in political framework,
difficulties for 277–8
bureaucratic alliances 136, 142–4
bureaucratic rationality 60, 309
bureaucratic reporting 21
bureaucratic scrutiny 224
bypassing of 157–8
conflicting goals, problem of 275–7
decision-making 4–5
deindustrialisation, effects on 113
flex-nets and processes of 156–7
instrumental rationality 309
integration policy, implementation of
271–3
legitimation 171–2
lethargic processes 53
local bureaucracies 119, 264, 265
Maharashtra government 189–90,
191, 192, 193–4, 198, 199
monitoring of daily lives 108
national bureaucracies 56–7
organising logic 29–30
pension bureaucracies in Sweden
207, 210, 213, 216–17
policy domains, weaving together of
34–5
power of 285
preferment 140
public bureaucracies 310
regularisation 42

reigning bureaucracy 269
ruling relations and bureaucratic
    documents 13–14
'street level bureaucrats' 8, 306, 307,
    308
technologies and processes of 152–3
Weberian bureaucracy theory 204–5
see also Food and Agriculture
    Organization (UN, FAO)

Canary Islands, Operation Hera in 41
capitalism 105, 112
'fast capitalism' 127
Catalunya 253
    see also Barcelona
Centre-Left 228, 233
China 13, 41, 68, 78, 190, 284
citizens 7, 9, 17–18, 87, 230, 238, 241,
    283, 288–9, 290, 291, 294
    Mexican citizens 146, 147
    responsibilisation of 126–7
    Spanish citizens 254, 255
    Swedish citizens 205, 207, 208, 212,
        216, 218, 219, 267, 271–2, 275
    transformation in law-and-order
        state 107–8, 110, 111, 114, 115
    urban resettlement in India 188–90,
        193–4, 196, 197, 198–9, 200, 201
citizenship 2, 9, 40
    activism and transformation of 108,
        112, 114, 121
    core concerns of 201
    migrants' practices of, policy change
        and 244–60
    neo-liberalism and 112–14
    practices of migrants, policy change
        and 244–5, 249, 252–3, 259
    transformation in law-and-order
        state 105–21
citizenship rights 127, 188, 189
    exercise through legal action of
        199–201
    issues in India of 193–4
civil service 173–4, 183
civil society 192, 193, 197, 224–5, 226,
    239, 266, 268
    agricultural biotechnology and 283,
        285, 287, 288, 295–6
    migrants' practices of citizenship,
        policy change and 244–5, 252–3,
        259

class 2, 88, 110, 113, 117, 200, 228, 260,
    261n2
    ethnicity and 257
    political class 239
classification systems 265, 278
cliques 128, 152, 155, 156, 162, 183
cognate fields 170, 300
Cold War (and aftermath) 98, 148n3,
    152–3, 155, 178
collaboration 28, 115, 229, 242n5, 266,
    279n5
    between anthropology and
        ethnology, potential in 307
    migrants' practices of citizenship,
        policy change and 249–50, 251,
        252–3, 254, 259
collective action 18, 227, 246–7
    by migrant workers in EU 224
collective agency 296
collective subject in history 234
Colombia (and Colombians) 148n1,
    256, 258
colonialism 36, 87, 172, 256
    postcolonial perspectives 27, 86
coming out 251, 256, 260
common good 19, 228, 234, 241
    redefinition of 236–8
common sense 4, 15, 97, 108, 171, 304,
    309
communism 148n3, 154, 157
communities
    disciplinary mechanisms and
        300–301, 304
    expert communities, dealing with
        ethical issues and 52–3
Community Development Project
    (CDP, UK) 111–12
complaint systems 76
concepts
    fields 27–8, 45, 101
    governance 127
    transformation 105–9
constitutional systems 183
consumers 17–18, 115, 119, 283
contestations 131, 147–8, 246, 296,
    301–2, 304
contested spaces in methodology 309
    and engagement with policy 17–19
    expressions of 106
    fields of, histories of the present and
        91–4

multiplicities of competing claims,
dealing with 92–3
processes of 11–12, 13–14, 86–8,
94–7, 305
control
anonymity of 39–44
disciplinary mechanisms 106–7
unauthorised residents, control and
removal of 250
cooperation 1, 36–7, 224, 241, 272, 274,
287, 288
on border controls 41
civic cooperation 115
collaboration and, importance of 115
international, on travel
documentation 43
judicial cooperation 40
technical cooperation 53–4
coping strategies 134, 245, 294
corporations 87, 107, 116, 136–7, 152,
195, 225, 235, 282, 284, 294–5, 302
counter-conduit 283–4
courts of law 87, 90, 96, 176, 177–8,
196, 302
Bombay High Court 189–90, 198,
200–201, 202n5
British High Court 183
creativity 21
assignment of creativity and agency
72
criminal justice systems 120
crisis
Cuban missile crisis 308
formation and organisation of the
apparatus, crisis and 35, 42, 43–4
peso crisis (1994) in Mexico 144–6
cultural intimacy 181–2, 239
culture
audit 3, 110–11, 164
cultural transformation 101
customers 17–18, 27–8, 69, 75–6, 78, 82
customer behaviour 77
passive customers 80–81
rights of 74–5, 77
student-customer subjectivity 80, 81
customisation 257

data from fields 29, 30
decision-making systems 178–9, 266
defence 13, 44, 159, 172, 177, 180, 183
military defence 230–31

systems 41
deindustrialisation 112–13
democracy 10, 105, 151, 152, 157, 162,
164–5, 273, 276
constitutional democracy 183
'counter-democracy' 200
discursive democracy 241
dynamic democracy 278
Global Democracy Strategy 158
independence of civic service and
judiciary and 174
liberal democracy 127
parliamentary democracy 16
'politics of the governed' as 199–200
representative democracy 200
schools for, associations as 266
social democracy 126
society based on 271–2
systems of 17
Demographic Trends, Migration and
Integrating Persons Belonging
to National Minorities (OSCE
Conference, 2005) 42
denial of history 60
Denmark 2–3, 27, 30, 68, 70, 73, 75
depoliticization 205, 285, 291, 296
of pension provision 209–11, 219
development 15, 34, 35, 41, 59, 76,
152–3, 230–31, 232, 237, 246, 285
assets-based development 30, 110,
114–19
biotechnological development 291–2
career development 161
community development 18, 27–8,
110, 112, 114–19
culture of 64–5
economic development 36–7, 190,
291
expertise in 51, 52–5
financial development 208
infrastructure development 134,
187–202
international development 18, 27–8,
51, 52, 56–7, 58, 62, 63, 65n1
Millennium Development Goals
(UN) 284
participation in 61
professionalism in 57–8, 59–60, 63
rural development 50, 109, 285–6
social development 60, 61–2
sustainable development 192

development projects 7, 127
diplomacy 170, 176, 177, 178
disciplinary mechanisms
  communities, homes, bases 300–301,
    304
  control 106–7
  devices 301
  ethical guidelines 51
  framework 164
  histories 302, 305
  messages 219
  power 17
  research 61
  restrictions 308
  space 11
  strictures 307
  'techniques of self' 3
  training 308
disciplinary obscurity 33
discourse 46, 90, 95–6, 98–9, 171, 182,
    241, 293
  customer discourse 75
  dependency discourse 110
  discourse analysis 102, 306, 307
  dominant discourse 18, 19, 93, 97, 275
  emergence of 29–30
  empowerment discourse 119
  of governance 86, 88, 101, 305
  ideology or 94
  institutional discourse 64
  migration policy discourse 39
  of multiculturalism 272, 278
  policy convergence discourse 136,
    147, 148
  political discourse 219, 303
  poverty discourse 113
  protest discourse 235
  public discourse 106, 132, 141, 176
  security discourse 35–6
  technical-scientific discourse 233,
    241, 293, 296
  UN discourse 281–2
discursive tactics 180, 189
dispersed sites 45, 87–8, 93, 102
displacement 33, 34, 46–7, 114, 188,
    191–2, 195–6, 199, 296–7
dispositif, concept of 11, 14, 19, 28, 29,
    32, 283–4, 291, 296, 297n2

Eastern Europe 148n2, 152, 153, 154,
    157

accession to EU of countries from 13
ecological systems 59
Economic and Monetary Union (EMU)
    13
economists 57, 60–61, 141, 210
ecosystem transformation 152–5
elites 6, 16, 126, 152, 155–6, 170–71,
    246, 301–2, 303
empiricism 33, 45, 47, 172
employment fields 256
energy production fields 235
Environmental Protection Agency
    (ANPA) 229, 235
espionage 160
  policy and the art of government
    169–84
ethics
  of business 127
  ethic of activism 240
  ethical guidelines 51
  politics and 50–65
  of spying 180
ethnic minorities
  agency of ethnic minority
    associations, scope for 268
  associations of, exploitation of 267–8
  associations of, funding allocations
    and 276–7
  associations of, integration and
    275–6
  class and ethnicity 257
ethnographic description 20, 51–2, 54,
    55, 63
ethnographic locations 86
EURODAC (European Dactyloscopy)
    43
European Commission (EC) 34, 42
  Freedom, Justice, and Security, Area
    of 40
European Migration Policy
  Organization (EMPO) 35–6, 37, 38,
    39, 47
European Parliament 33, 34, 35, 43
European Union (EU) 34, 240, 306
  accession of Eastern European
    countries 13
  acquis communautaire 13
  aging workforce 36
  collective action by migrant workers
    in 224
  Economic and Monetary Union 13

EURODAC 43
Europol (criminal law enforcement
  agency) 35
Forum on Sustainable Agriculture
  293
Frontex (border control agency) 35
hunger strikes, inappropriateness in
  254
illegal migration from Africa and
  Middle East to 38
migrant protests in south of 252
migration flows from Africa to 38
migration management policy (the
  apparatus) 14–15, 28, 33, 39–44
new public management philosophy
  in Sweden and 266
Schengen Agreement 39–40, 48n1
Schengen Information System 43
security, urgency post 11 September
  on 40
Visa Information System 43
welfare state, expansion in 206
Europol (criminal law enforcement
  agency) 35, 37, 38
eventalisation 77, 80, 82
events 54–5, 88, 89, 93, 101
expert knowledge, professions
  identity and 51, 56–7, 58
expertise 50, 55, 57–8, 59, 61–3,
  65n1, 136, 285, 290, 303–4
  counter-expertise 288–9
  development expertise 51, 60
  expert ideas as means of agency 61
  expert knowledge, professions
    identity and 51, 56–7, 58
  responsible expertise 290
exploitation 44, 247, 258, 260, 277–8,
  297

'fast capitalism' 127
feminism 261n6
fields
  anthropological 72, 261n6, 301
  boundaries of 201–2
  cognate 300
  collective action in multiple fields
    224
  concept of 27–8, 45, 101
  of contestation 91–4
  data from 29, 30
  dialogue between 188

employment 256
energy production 235
feminism 261n6
fields within 206–7
location within 14–15, 29
micro-political 61
policy field 1, 87–8, 169–70, 246, 301
policy implementation studies 303
political field 136, 142–4, 147, 257
professional practice 302
of research 11–12, 29, 44, 55, 93–4,
  125, 265
sites and 28
fieldwork 12, 28, 29, 36, 51–2, 63–4,
  131, 170, 202n1, 210, 248, 251, 264
  location-specific 33, 264–6, 271–2
  traditional, limitations of 172–3
filtering systems 43
financial systems 137, 139
flex nets (covert cabals)
  neocon flex-nets 158, 161–2
  and processes of bureaucracy 156–7
  in United States 127, 128, 154, 155–
  7, 160–61, 161–2, 164
Folketinget 70
Food and Agriculture Organization
  (UN, FAO)
  biotechnology on Internet and
    288–91
  civilsociety reaction against SOFA
    295–6
  FAO Strategy Paper (1993) 287
  genetically modified organisms
    (GMOs) 282, 283, 284, 289, 292
    and
  honest broker, role as 285–8
  international governance and 282–3,
    286, 296–7
  non-governmental organisations
    (NGOs) and 287–8, 289, 296
  objective realities 292–3
  protest letter to Director General
    295–6
  scientific truth, progress and 293–4
  The State of Food and Agriculture
    (SOFA Report, 2004) 291–6
Forum on Sustainable Agriculture (EU)
  293
fragmented systems 155
France 41, 48n1, 206, 228
freedom 20, 91, 100–101, 106

individual freedom 10, 171
Freedom, Justice, and Security, Area
    of 40
Frontex (border control agency) 35,
    37, 41, 44
funds, allocation of 276–7

gender equality 273–5, 276
genetically modified organisms
    (GMOs) 282, 283, 284, 289, 292
Germany 2, 41, 48n1, 137, 206
global (or international) systems 58,
    189, 282–3
governance
    agency and the individual in regimes
        of 181
    agency of governed peoples 244–5,
        246, 260
    ambiguous spaces of 16–17
    bad governance, results of 58
    concept of 127
    discourse of 86
    'good governance' criteria 188, 195,
        198–9
    ideology of 91–2
    and individuals, working both on
        and through 270–71
    insecure outcomes of new forms of
        218–20
    institutions of 58
    international, FAO and 282–3, 286,
        296–7
    juridification, sovereignty,
        citizenship rights and new
        architectures of 187–8
    liberal frameworks of 59
    liberal governance, instruments of 9
    modes of 9, 115, 296
    multi-level 10, 126–7
    neoliberal forms of 17, 215, 218–20
    network forms of 266
    NPM as technique of 16
    pension system in Sweden as
        instrument of 215–16, 217–18
    policies as instruments of 15–17, 20,
        169, 172–3, 244–5, 305
    policies as reflections on regimes of
        180–83
    policing as primary mechanism of
        106, 108
    post-welfare-state in US 9
    power and 4, 17
    processes of 1
    'progressive' institutions and process
        of 253–4, 279n5
    public policy and tools of 205
    rationalities of 2
    regimes of 125, 180–83
    rhetoric of 225
    security and 120
    structures of 127, 223
    subjects of 17
    systems of 11, 20–21, 27, 78, 92,
        94–5, 128, 164, 170, 173, 182–3,
        277–8, 279n5, 286, 296
    territorial governance 59
    in UK, changing character of 183
    university system of 78
    urban institutions of, weakness of
        195
    vocabulary and grammar of 201
    World Bank and 144, 147–8, 202
governmentality 9, 15, 16–17, 20, 30,
    69, 77, 81, 120, 125–6, 127, 128,
    170, 180, 228
    tactics of governments 169–70

habitus 11, 15, 54, 241, 302
hegemony
    of behaviourism 301
    of 'common knowledge' 46–7
    contestation and 86–7, 305
    of practitioner perspective 10
    realist-objectivist, entrenched 301
history 46, 54, 106
    as 'analytic of change' 120
    collective subject in 234
    denial of 60
    disciplinary 302, 305
    Geertz and 'doing history
        backwards' 92
    historical contingency 46
    historical transformation 92
    intellectual 304
    local 147, 236–7
    Lucanian 236–7
    of Mexico 145
    moral force of 236
    'of the present' 88, 101–2, 307
    of participation in activism 116
    revolution and 1
    of state transformation 29–30

of United States 154, 156, 163
war in Iraq, run-up categorised as
179
of welfare restructuring in US 110
of World Bank 133–4, 191–2
housing policy 306
human service systems 115
human subject in transformation 80–81
Hungary 137
hunger strikes, inappropriateness in
EU 254
hypermasculinity 232

identity 56, 63, 76–7, 92, 95, 111, 196,
236, 267–8
class identity 88
expert knowledge, professional
identity and 51, 56–7, 58
identity card systems 196
identity politics 257
professional identity 52, 54
sexual identity 89–90
ideology
of governance 91–2
ideological transformation 29, 91,
94, 102
locations and 201
implementation 30, 54, 72–3, 74, 76, 77,
80, 81–2, 86–7, 101, 117
integration policy, implementation of
271–3
policy implementation studies 303
sites of 72
'soft' implementation of immigration
law in Spain 253–4
see also policy implementation
incentivisation of agency 59
India 7, 17, 27, 28, 41, 50, 127, 135,
187–202, 252
Bombay High Court 189–90, 198,
200–201, 202n5
citizenship rights, exercise through
legal action 199–201
citizenship rights, issues of 193–4
expropriation of poor, dismal record
on 189
Indian Railways 190, 196
inspection mechanisms 197–9
legal pruralism, issues of 193–4
Mumbai Metropolitan Regional

Development Authority
(MMRDA) 195, 196, 197,
198, 199
Mumbai Urban Transport Project
188–9, 190–91, 192–3, 195, 196,
197, 198, 199, 200–201
Narmada Dam project 191, 192,
193–4, 197
resettlement policy, interventions by
donors in formulation of 192–3
resettlement policy, World Bank and
negotions on 190, 191–4
urban governance institutions,
weakness of 195
individuals
agency and, location in regimes of
governance 181, 215, 217, 219
working both on and through
governance 270–71
information systems 28, 43–4
infrastructure development
urban resettlement in India, NGOs
and 188, 189, 192–3, 194, 196,
199, 200
infrastructure development and urban
resettlement in India 188, 189,
192–3, 194, 196, 199, 200
insecurity 3, 161, 248
of outcomes of new forms of
governance 218–20
inspection, mechanisms of 189–90,
197–9
institutions of governance 58
insurance systems 130
integration policy, implementation of
271–3
intellectual history 304
intelligence experts (and service) 157–8,
159, 162–3, 175, 176, 177, 178, 179,
180, 181
Interdisciplinary Studies Graduate
Program (UBC) 48
International Bank for Reconstruction
and Development (IBRD) 133
international development 18, 27–8, 50,
51–2, 53, 56–8, 63, 65n1, 133
international law 181, 187–8, 197
International Planning Committee
(IPC) 287–8
internationalisation strategy 70

interpretive approach 51–2, 170, 300, 301, 303–4, 305, 306–7, 310
anthropology and 3–8, 12, 14, 15, 20
Italy 3, 41, 42, 137, 206, 224, 227–42
blackouts in 230
Cabinet President Ordinance (No. 3267, 2003) 229, 230, 231, 232
endogenous development aims in south 237
Environmental Protection Agency (ANPA) 229, 235
hypermasculinity 232
immigration, country of 248, 252, 255–6
labour migration quotas, structure of 42–3
Legislative Decree 314, explicit and implicit discourses 230–32
liberalisation of energy in 228
modus operandi of governance in 231
Nassiriya in Iraq, deaths of Carabinieri at 230, 236
nuclear power as energy source, pursuit of 228
nuclear waste storage 228
Objective Law (L. 443, 2001) 229
particularism in favour of north 236
patronage systems in 156
south of 19, 227–42
see also Bologna; Lucania

juridification 127, 201
sovereignty, citizenship rights and new architectures of governance 187–8

keywords 30, 77–8, 80–81, 82, 88, 91, 94, 101, 102
historical trajectories and 97–100
knowledge
anthropological knowledge 53, 63, 172–3
'common knowledge,' hegemony of 46–7
ethnographic knowledge 45, 64
expert knowledge 50, 52, 55, 57, 59, 60, 62, 286, 290
'situated knowledges,' construction of 45
strategy for 11

systems of 62
knowledge processes 58, 60–63
knowledge production 37, 45–6, 46–7, 55, 56–7, 58–9, 64, 293, 309
institutional processes of 60–63

labour migration quotas, structure of 42–3
Latin America 17, 130, 132–3, 134, 135, 138, 255–60, 265
mobilisations of Latin American workers in London 255–60
see also Mexico
Latin American Workers Association (LAWA) 256–7, 257–8, 259, 261n12
law 8, 10, 13–14, 58, 72, 75, 78, 160, 194, 201, 212, 231, 260, 276
criminal law 35–6
defamation law 51
education (postgraduate) in 38
EU law 43–4
homosexuality, law on 'promotion' of (Section 28) 89–90, 92, 96, 97–8, 100
immigration law 225, 247, 252–5
international law 181, 187–8, 197
juridification and 187–8
law-and-order state 105–21
maritime law 34
New Law of Social Security (Mexico) 131, 132–3, 139, 141, 142, 143–4, 145–7
Objective Law (Law 443, Italy) 229
'One-Child Law' in China 13
rule of law 171
systems of 72, 120
The Left 210, 214, 227–8, 239, 250–51, 254, 263
left-wing politics 75–6, 88–9, 92, 250–51, 252–3
liberal frameworks of governance 59
liberal governance, instruments of 9
liberalism 35, 127–8
lived experiences 223, 247
livelihood systems 295
lobbyists 155–6, 164, 303, 306
local
contribution to large-scale transformations 87
history 147, 236–7

sites and processes of transformation
    87–8
location-specificity
    in fieldwork 33, 264–6, 271–2
    of practices 33
locations 136–7, 192, 232
    actors in, vantage point of 188
    ethnographic 86
    within fields 14–15, 29
    finding suitable 15, 27–8
    ideology and 201
    location-specific practices 33
    materials emanating from
        multiplicity of 29
    multiple locations 28, 306
    policy domains and 33
    for resettlement 195, 196–7, 198, 199
    rotation of 37–8
Lucania
    antiglobalisation movements,
        Scanzano protest and 240–41
    common good, redefinition of 236–8
    communitas under siege, feelings of
        238–9
    destatalisation of governemtal
        practices 234–5
    discursive democracy in 241
    history of 236–7
    Legislative Decree 314, explicit and
        implicit discourses 230–32, 238,
        239–40
    militarisation of nuclear waste
        disposal project 231, 239–40
    moral frame, reversal of 233–6
    NIMBY syndrome 232
    participation, importance of 238–41
    radioactive waste disposal, problem
        of 229, 230, 234
    resistance, lines of 232–3
    roles of government actors,
        personalisation of 235–6
    Scalia Parliamentary Commission
        229
    Scanzano revolt in 225–6, 227–8,
        230–31, 232–3, 233, 234–5, 236–7,
        238–9, 240–41
    Sogin company in 228, 229–30, 231,
        234–5, 242n8
    subjectivity, affirmation of 238
    technical-scientific facts, government
        deployment of 233

unity (and faultlines) among
    Lacunians 238–9
vertical encompassment by state in
    240
Luxembourg 48n1

Maharashtra government in India 189–
    90, 191, 192, 193–4, 198, 199
Managed Mediterranean Project (3MP)
    35–6, 37, 38, 39, 44, 47
Manifesto 230
marketisation 73, 76–7, 78, 82
methodological nationalism 247
methodology 51, 125, 169–70, 300–301,
    303
    broadcast and print media, use of 173
    collaboration between anthropology
        and ethnology, potential in 307
    contestations, dealing with
        multiplicities of competing claims
        and 92–3
    contested spaces 309
    expert communities, dealing with
        ethical issues and 52–3
    'methodological nationalism' 247
    multi-sited research, in space and
        time 305–7, 310
    'nonlocal ethnography' as 33–4,
        45–7
    participatory action research (PAR)
        249
    policing policies, tracking
        transformations in 108
    policy perspective and 27–8, 30–31
    policy regimes, strategy for study of
        32–3
    power networks, dealing with
        disguised operations and 87–8
    reflections on 11–15
    'situated knowledges,' construction
        of 45
    'studying through' strategy 12, 27,
        29, 86, 87–8, 101, 102, 206, 307–8
Mexico 126, 130–48
    Administradoras de Fondos de
        Retiro (AFORES) 132
    Autonomous Technological Institute
        of (ITAM) 137
    Averting the Old Age Crisis (World
        Bank, 1994) 141, 144
    bureaucratic alliances 142–4

deniability 140–42
deregulation and privatisation in 126
Finance Ministry 138, 139, 142–3, 144
history of 145
Institute Mexicano de Seguridad
Social (IMSS) 132, 133, 138–9,
140, 141–2, 143
International Bank for
Reconstrucrtion and Development
(IBRD) 133
International Development
Association (IDA) 133
national savings rate 145, 146
pay-as-you-go (PAYG) 132, 138,
141, 145
pension reform 7, 14, 16, 136–40,
141–2
peso crisis (1994) 144–6
policy convergence, politics of
130–31, 134, 135, 136, 146–8
political and economic circumstances
131, 136, 138, 139–40, 144
privatisation (and reprivatisation)
132, 139, 140, 145
Retirement Savings System (SAR)
139
Social Security, New Law of (1995)
131, 132–3, 139, 141, 146–7
Social Union of Mexican
Businessmen (USEM) 139
'space for manoeuvre,' discovery of
135
Stabilisation of Pensions, meeting of
Project on (1991) 137–8
World Bank, influence in 130–31,
132–3, 133–6, 140–42, 142–4
micro-political fields 61
micro-processes of transformation 30,
121
Middle East 38, 41, 157, 158, 161, 162
migrant workers 56, 224–5, 256–7, 258,
259
migrants 16, 18–19, 28, 34, 35, 40–44,
47
agency of, significance of 226, 261n6
practices of citizenship, policy
change and 244–5, 252–3, 259
resistance, strategy for 249–50,
252–3, 257–8
significance of agency for 226, 261n6
unauthorised residents, control and
removal of 250

undocumented 118, 247, 252, 254–5
migration
illegal migration from Africa and
Middle East to EU 38
labour migration quotas, structure of
42–3
management policy (the apparatus)
of EU 14–15, 28, 33–4, 39–44
minimum-state, policy of 127
minorities
African women's association 269–71,
278
Demographic Trends, Migration
and Integrating Persons Belonging
to National Minorities (OSCE
Conference, 2005) 42
disadvantaged 99
ethnic 18, 224, 256, 264–79
homosexuals 95
interest groups and 225
migrants and 258, 260
policy domains, ethnic minority
associations and intersection of
266–9
racial 95
research, ethnic minority
associations in 267–8
see also ethnic minorities
mobilisation 30, 200, 226, 227, 234,
238, 247, 253, 255
expertise and, tension between
288–9
money exchange systems 80
moral economy 13, 228, 234, 236
multi-level governance 10, 126–7
multi-sited ethnography 47, 101, 172–3
multi-sited research, in space and time
305–7, 310
multiculturalism 18, 226, 247, 252, 259,
260, 272
Mumbai
Metropolitan Regional Development
Authority (MMRDA) 195, 196,
197, 198, 199
Urban Transport Project 188–9,
190–91, 192–3, 195, 196, 197, 198,
199, 200–201
mutual aid 161

Narmada Dam project 191, 192, 193–4,
197

Nassiriya in Iraq, deaths of Carabinieri
    at 230, 236
nation-state 34, 126, 128, 192, 197, 200,
    201, 247, 269, 279n4
national order of things 247
national pensions system in Sweden
    126, 205–20
    parts of 208
    scale and scope of 205–6
    self-regulatory nature of 208–9
National Supplementary Pensions
    Scheme (Sweden, 1963) 207
neo-liberalism 106, 109, 111, 112–14,
    118–19, 120
    authoritarianism and 118–19, 120,
        157–8, 161–2
    citizenship and 112–14
    neoliberal forms of governance 17,
        215, 218–20
    neoliberal institutionalism 58–60
neocons 16, 127, 151–65
    collective power of 160–61
    flex-net of 158, 161–2
    organisations associated with 162–3
Netherlands 21n1, 41, 48n1
networks 2, 153–4, 155, 307–8
    advocacy network 191–2
    network analysis 164
    network forms of governance 266
    networked ecosystem 151–2
    power networks 87–8
    railway network 190
neutrality 171, 212, 225, 234, 235, 290,
    291–2
new forms of governance 9, 16, 59, 87,
    218–20, 277–8
new institutionalism 7, 58
New Labour 17
new public management (NPM) 3
    philosophy in Sweden of 266
    as technique of governance 16
newspapers 15, 75, 141, 173
9/11 (and post-attack environment)
    15–16, 106–7, 128, 158, 161–2, 180,
    228, 231
non-governmental organisations
    (NGOs) 2, 7, 19, 29, 152, 154, 156,
    225
    citizenship practices of migrants,
        policy change and 244–5, 249,
        252–3, 259

expert knowledge, professional
    identity and 51, 56–7, 58
Food and Agriculture Organozation
    (UN, FAO) and 287–8, 289, 296
infrastructure development and
    urban resettlement in India 188,
    189, 192–3, 194, 196, 199, 200
non-local ethnography
    illumination of the apparatus 46–7
    as methodology 33–4, 45–7
non-state actors 188, 195–6
nuclear energy 228
nuclear waste
    disposal strategy 229
    sites 229–30, 231–2, 233, 236, 238–9,
        242n5
    storage in Italy 228

Oath of Loyalty 178
Official Secrets Act (UK, 1989) 174,
    178
omertà 182
oppression 99, 117, 245–6, 275
Organisation for Security and
    Cooperation in Europe (OSCE) 34,
    42–3
Organization for International
    Cooperation and Development
    (OECD) 70, 206

participation 9, 15, 61, 147, 224, 247
    agricultural biotechnology, dialogue
        on 283, 288, 289, 292
    citizenship, transformation in law-
        and-order state 111–12, 114,
        116–17
    fee-paying students, conflicting
        subjectivities of 74, 76, 78–9
    infrastructure development and
        urban resettlement in India 189,
        192, 199–200, 201
    integration policy and ethnic
        minority associations 266, 271–2
    Scanzano case, rebellion and 227–8,
        231–2, 238–41
participatory action research (PAR)
    249
participatory planning 303–4
participatory processes 196, 249, 289
participatory projects 57, 291
participatory rhetoric 225

participatory sociality 76
particularism in Italy 234, 236, 240
passive customers 80–81
patronage systems 156
pension reform 7, 14, 16, 136–40, 141–
2, 206, 209–11, 219
  see also Mexico; national pensions
  system in Sweden; Sweden
pension system bureaucracy 210
pensions *see* public pensions systems
Peru 148n1
peso crisis (1994) in Mexico 144–6
planning 21, 41, 134, 190–91, 192, 287,
288–9, 303–4
  International Planning Committee
  (FAO) 285, 287
  systems 21
police (and policing) 16, 20, 40, 44, 90,
96, 177, 239–40, 255
  citizen policing 114
  governance, policing as primary
  mechanism 106, 108
  policing policies, tracking
  transformations in 108
  self-policing 106
  sites of policing 108
  zero tolerance policing in UK 109
policies
  as instruments of governance 15–17,
  20, 169, 172–3, 244–5, 305
  as reflections on regimes of
  governance 180–83
policy
  agency engagement with 17–19
  agency of ideas 55
  authorship of 14, 171
  convergence of 130–48
  covert policy 181–2
  formation 13, 72, 158
  implementation and integration in
  Sweden 271–3
  learning 7–8, 36, 46, 54, 216, 301
  'policy effect' 6, 171–2, 181
  transfer 6–7, 126
policy appropriation 72–3, 74, 80, 81–2
  agency and 30
policy change 136, 147, 192, 226
  from below 246–7, 254, 261n3
  formal change 245, 259
  migrants' citizenship practices and
  244–61

tangible change 260
policy community 11–12
policy convergence, politics of 130–31,
134, 135, 136, 146–8
policy cycle 4
policy domains 14–15, 28, 32, 127
  ethnic minority associations in
  intersection of 266–7
  locations of 33
  weaving together of 34–5, 39, 42, 44
policy enforcement 35–6, 260
policy engagements 45, 147, 223, 224,
226, 245, 246, 247, 259
policy fields 1, 87–8, 169–70, 246, 301
policy ideas 57–8, 59, 60–61, 136
  agency and 55
policy impact 225–6, 245–6, 247,
262n14
policy implementation 44, 86, 101, 158,
224–6, 269, 302, 303, 304–5, 307, 310
  citizenship, policy change and
  migrants' practices of 249, 253–4
  fee-paying students, conflicting
  subjectivities of 72–3, 74, 76–7,
  80, 81–2
  infrastructure and urban resettlement
  in India 188–9, 191, 192–3, 198
  non-state actors of 195–6
  studies of 303
policy makers 7, 8, 30, 35, 62, 86, 101,
138, 169, 206, 212, 245, 246–7, 295,
302, 308
  in Mexico 131, 133, 134, 135, 136,
  139, 142, 143, 146–7, 148
  in United States 181
  World Bank policy makers 147–8
policy neutralisation 226
policy ownership 73–4, 81–2
policy perspective 27–8, 30–31
policy processes, sites of 206, 223
policy regimes, strategy for study of
32–3
policy subjects 11, 223–6
policy transformation 73, 245
policy worlds 1–2, 8, 15, 19, 21, 52,
82–3, 260, 301
political class 239
political fields 136, 142–4, 147, 257
political rationalities 69
political science 4, 6, 223, 300, 301, 303,
307, 309, 310

political strategy 95
political subjects 246–7
political systems 7, 10, 59, 87, 223, 250, 268
political tactics 169–70
political technologies 16, 46, 171, 212, 219
political transformation 11–12, 27, 30–31, 58, 86, 88, 93–4, 101
Portugal 41, 48n1
postcommunist societies 13
poverty 9, 30, 35, 51–2, 107–8, 109–10, 113, 118
  global poverty 58, 148n3
  poverty reduction programmes 59, 134, 148n3, 190–91
  urban poverty 112, 114, 115, 196, 198, 200, 283
  War on Poverty programs 111–12
power
  agency and 77, 305, 308–9
  of bureaucracy (and bureaucrats) 285
  collective power 160–61
  disciplinary mechanisms 17
  governance and 4, 17
  neocons, collective power of 160–61
  networks, dealing with disguised operations and 87–8
  state power 9, 16, 87, 96, 126, 128, 164, 169, 225, 240
  state-private power, intertwining of 154–5
  systems of 86
  tactics of governance and 17
  unelected, power of 182–3
practices
  audit practices 164
  of citizenship, policy change and 244–5, 252–3, 259
  destatalisation of governemtal practices 234–5
  location-specificity of 33
practitioners 6, 303
Premium Pension Authority (PPM) in Sweden 208, 215
privatisation (and reprivatisation) in Mexico 132, 139, 140, 145
professionalism 8, 53–4, 55, 57, 63, 65n1
  fields of professional practice 302

professionals 4, 14, 17, 27–8, 36, 51–2, 60, 61, 62, 63, 90–91, 114, 304
  ethnography of development experts and 52–5
  world of 56–8
protest 9, 18–19, 174, 201, 247, 248–52, 252–5, 261n11
  Scanzano protest 226, 227–42
public administration 75, 300, 302–3
public bureaucracies 310
public health systems 2–3, 56
public pensions systems 130–32, 137–9, 140–41, 143–4, 145–6, 147, 148n1
public policy 6, 51, 64–5, 138, 152, 154, 172–3, 188, 205, 300–301, 305, 310
  and tools of governance 205

Quaderni de Sociologia 242n3
quota systems 287

Radio Free Europe 43
rational choice theories 6, 7
rationality-technology-subjectivity triad 73–4
reflexivity 15, 57, 102, 309
regimes
  audit regimes 20
  of governance 125, 180–83
rehabilitation policy 193
Rektorkollegiet 73
relational systems 108
research
  disciplinary mechanisms 61
  fields of 11–12, 29, 44, 55, 93–4, 125, 265
  strategies for 30–31, 32–4, 34–5, 35–9, 39–44, 45–7, 88
  subjects of 51, 65
resettlement (or relocation)
  infrastructure development and urban resettlement in India, NGOs and 188, 189, 192–3, 194, 196, 199, 200
  sites for 195, 196–7, 198, 199
resettlement policy
  interventions by donors in formulation of 192–3
  World Bank and negotions on 190, 191–4
residential policy 251
resistance 10, 106, 147, 226, 245–6, 309

acts of, tactics for 19
migrants' practices of 245–6, 249–50, 259, 260, 261n2
Scanzano model for 227–8, 231–2, 232–3, 233–6, 236–8
tactics of 19
responsibilisation 215
insecurity in outcomes of 218–20
struggles with process of 217–18
responsibility
agency and, relocation of 209, 212
restrictions
disciplinary mechanisms 308
rhetoric of governance 225
The Right 91, 239, 247, 249, 250–51, 259
right-wing politics 75, 225, 250
rights of customers 74–5, 77
risk 35–6, 131, 134, 155, 176, 205, 231, 233, 259, 266–7, 278
benefits and 286, 294
demographic risk 214
of failure 56
health risk 282
individual risk 61
management of 16, 290–92
rural people. agency of 291, 295, 296

scale 7, 201, 205, 224, 278
large-scale 27, 47, 86–7, 195, 199, 226, 245–6, 257, 260
small-scale 226, 246, 294
transnational scale 200
up-scale (or 'scaling up') 61, 245, 246, 251, 260
of urban resettlement 190
Scanzano revolt in Lucania 225–6, 227–8, 230–31, 232–3, 233, 234–5, 236–7, 238–9, 240–41
Schengen Agreement 39–40, 48n1
Schengen Information System 43
science and technology studies (STS) 20, 170, 309
scientific progress 293–4
security
governance and 120
as organising metaphor 35–9
security state 28, 29, 30, 105–6
urgency in EU, post 11 September 40
sites 7, 114, 125, 189, 227, 228
dispersed sites 45, 87–8, 93, 102

fields and 28
of implementation 72
interactions within 1–2
local, contribution to large-scale transformations 87
migration policy 33–4
multi-sited ethnography 47, 101, 172–3
multi-sited research, in space and time 305–7
national and local 101
for nuclear waste 229–30, 231–2, 233, 236, 238–9, 242n5
pension system bureaucracy 210
of policing 108
of policy processes 206, 223
resettlement (or relocation) 196–7, 198, 199
of study 11, 15, 27, 29, 30, 53, 81–2, 93, 106, 192
unbounded 97
'situated knowledges,' construction of 45
social movements 119, 189, 192, 244–5, 246, 261n5, 268, 287, 296
social-political-economic systems 106
social systems 59
social transformation 62
soft law 127, 187–8, 201
Sogin company in Lucania 228, 229–30, 231, 234–5, 242n8
sovereignty 127, 177–8, 188–90, 193, 201, 240, 287, 295
space
disciplinary mechanisms 11
'space for manoeuvre,' discovery of 135
Spain 177, 260
Barcelona, Sin Papeles protest in 252–5
Canary Islands, Operation Hera in 41
immigration law in 252–5
labour migration quotas, structure of 42–3
migrants in, support by political and civic organisations for 255
'soft' implementation of immigration law in 253–4
state
agencification of 15–16

central planning 153
Crown prerogative 183
'cunning state' 127, 135, 187–202
decentralisation 10
destatalisation of governemtal
    practices in Lucania 234–5
ethnography of 169–70
family and 100
funding 70–71
individual and 1, 2, 205
inter-state cooperation 37
law-and-order state, transformation
    of citizenship in 105–21
masculine prerogative 240
minimum-state policy 127
nation-state 34, 126, 128, 192, 197,
    200, 201, 247, 269, 279n4
neoliberal institutionalism 58–60
private interests and, conflation of
    152, 154–5, 156–7, 159–60, 164
public services and 17–18, 27–8
regulation by 10–11, 13, 51–2, 153
security state 28, 29, 30, 105–6
social relations and 46
state intervention, role of 136
state power 9, 16, 87, 96, 126, 128,
    164, 169, 225, 240
state-sponsored spying 178–9
subsidies, abuse of 70
transformation of, history of 29–30
vertical encompassment 234
Statewatch 43
steering 16, 78
stockbrokers 139
strategy 28, 53, 201, 213
    Beveridge and integration of 20
    de Certeau's perspective on 284
    FAO Strategy Paper (1993) 287
    of internationalisation 70
    for knowledge 11
    methodological strategy 45–7, 101
    for migrants' resistance 249–50,
        252–3, 257–8
    for nuclear waste disposal 229
    political strategy 95
    research strategy 30–31, 32–4, 34–5,
        35–9, 39–44, 45–7, 88
    of 'studying through' 12, 27, 29, 86,
        87–8, 101, 102, 206, 307–8
    of 'studying up' 52, 87, 101, 172,
        307–8

tactics and 19
'street level bureaucrats' 8, 306, 307,
    308
student-customer subjectivity 80, 81
student participation (co-ownership)
    74, 76, 79, 81
study
    sites of 11, 15, 27, 29, 30, 53, 81–2,
        93, 106, 192
    'studying through' strategy 12, 27,
        29, 86, 87–8, 101, 102, 206, 307–8
    'studying up' strategy 52, 87, 101,
        172, 307–8
subjectification 17, 74
subjectivity 82–3, 231, 234, 237, 238,
    240, 261n6
    agency and 80–81
    collective 241
    policy and 68–9, 72, 74, 82
    professional 57
    rationality-technology-subjectivity
        30, 69, 71–2, 73, 77, 81
    student-customer 80, 81
    of students 74, 76
subjects
    audited subjects 20–21
    of governance 17
    of policy 11, 223–6
    of politics 246–7
    of research 51, 65
support systems, institutionalisation of
    117–18
surveillance systems 41
Sweden 16, 18, 205–20, 264–79
    adjustable indexation 212–13
    African women's association 269–71,
        278
    anxiety, pension policy change and
        211–12
    commitment to organisations,
        tradition of 266–7
    democracy as basic value in 276
    depoliticisation of pensions 209–11
    distrust, pension policy change and
        211–12
    ethnic minority associations,
        exploitation of 267–8
    ethnic minority associations, funding
        allocations and 276–7
    ethnic minority associations,
        integration and 275–6

gender equality 273–5, 276
integration of ethnic minorities,
  assimilation or 275–6, 278–9n1
longevity, 'problem' of 213–14
migrants in, origins of 265
national pensions system in 126,
  205–20
national pensions system in, parts of
  208
national pensions system in, scale
  and scope of 205–6
national pensions system in, self-
  regulatory nature of 208–9
National Supplementary Pensions
  Scheme (1963) 207
new public management (NPM)
  philosophy in 266
non-profit associations in 264
Pension Committee in 209, 213, 215,
  216
pension policy in, 'studying through'
  206–7
pension system as instrument of
  governance in 215–16, 217–18
policy, implementation and
  integration of 271–3
political differences, bridging of 208,
  210
political framework, ambiguities in
  277–8
politics of pension systems 207–9
popular movements *(folkrörelser)* in
  266
Premium Pension Authority (PPM)
  208, 215
responsibilisation 215
responsibilisation, insecurity in
  outcomes of 218–20
responsibilisation, struggles with
  process of 217–18
responsible individuals, creation of
  214–16
Social Insurance Agency 208, 216
technicalities within pension system
  in 212–13
technocratic perspective on pension
  system in 210–11
Switzerland 33, 137
systems 12, 16, 19, 55, 59, 65, 251, 259,
  273
  assessment 278
  auditing 111

banking 139
bipolar authority 152
classification 265, 278
complaint 76
constitutional 183
criminal justice 120
decision-making 178–9, 266
defence 41
democratic 17
ecological 59
filtering 43
financial 137, 139
fragmented 155
funds, allocation of 276–7
global (or international) 58, 189,
  282–3
of governance 11, 20–21, 27, 78,
  92, 94–5, 128, 164, 170, 173, 182–3,
  277–8, 279n5, 286, 296
human service 115
identity cards 196
information 28, 43–4
insurance 130
knowledge 62
of law 72, 120
livelihood 295
money exchange 80
national pensions in Sweden 126,
  205–20
networked ecosystem 151–2
omertà 182
patronage 156
pension system in Sweden 126,
  205–20
planning 21
political 7, 10, 59, 87, 223, 250, 268
of power 86
public health 2–3, 56
public pensions 130–32, 137–9,
  140–41, 143–4, 145–6, 147, 148n1
quota 287
relational 108
of representations 63
scientific progress 293–4
social 59
social-political-economic 106
subterranean system, unofficial
  information and 153
support systems, institutionalised
  117–18
surveillance 41
'system goal' 62

systemic division between economy
and culture 241
systemic forces 125–6
systemized self-representation 69
transport 14
unauthorised residents, control and
removal of 250
university 75–6, 78

tactics
discursive tactics 180, 189
operation of 284
of politicians and governments
169–70
of power and governance 17
reduction to 297
of resistance 19
strategy and 19
'techniques of self' 3
technocrats 39, 53, 57, 62, 63, 126, 131,
134–5, 286
actions of, in Mexico 136–40
pension system in Sweden and
210–11, 213–14, 217, 219
technologies
audit 3, 111
biotechnologies 224–5, 286, 294–5
of citizenship 9, 12, 152–3
of governance 15–16, 30, 32, 69, 72,
77, 79, 80–81, 82, 91–2, 125–6
information and communitation
(ICT) 56, 152–3
political 16, 46, 171, 212, 219
territorial governance 59
T&G-Unite 256, 257–8, 259, 260–61
'Third Way' ideology 17–18, 115, 260
top-down transformations 244–5
tracking transformation, methodology
for 108
traditional fieldwork, limitations of
172–3
training 308
transformation
analytical concept 29
citizenship, neo-liberalism and
112–14
concept of 105–9
cultural transformation 101
ecosystem transformation 152–5
historical transformation 92
human subject or consciousness as
operator of 80–81

ideological transformation 29, 91,
94, 102
Latour's perspective on 30
in law-and-order state, citizens and
107–8, 110, 111, 114, 115
local sites and processes of 87–8
micro-processes of 30, 121
moment of, analysis of 106–7
neo-liberalism, authoritarianism and
118–19, 120, 157–8, 161–2
policy neutralisation 226
policy transformation 73, 245
political transformation 11–12, 27,
30–31, 58, 86, 88, 93–4, 101
social transformation 62
top-down transformations 244–5
tracking, methodology for 108
translation (and translations) 14, 30, 73,
80, 81, 308
transport systems 14

United Kingdom (UK) 27, 41, 54, 73,
153
agency and individual, location in
governance regimes 181
British High Court 183
Community Development Project
(CDP) 111–12
covert policy, cultural intimacy and
181–2
deregulation and privatisation in 126
espionage on UN, disclosure of 128,
170, 173–8, 178–80, 180–83
The Future of Higher Education
(White Paper, 2003) 74
governmentality in 180
migrant professionals in,
cosmopolitanism of 56
mobilisations of Latin American
workers in London 255–60
Parliament of 41
pension reform in 206
T&G-Unite 256, 257–8, 259, 260–61
unelected, power of 182–3
war in Iraq, run-up to 169–70,
173–8, 179, 180, 181, 183
welfare policies in, emergence of
109–10
zero tolerance policing in 109
United States
aid program to Russia 60

AID to Families with Dependent
Children (AFDC) 110–11
American-Israeli Public Affairs
Committee (AIPAC) 163
changing character of governance in
183
collective power 160–61
Committee for a Free Lebanon 162
Cuban missile crisis 308
Department of Defense (DoD) 303
deregulation and privatisation in 126
Elk River nuclear reactor in 234
fiscal strength 137
flex nets (covert cabals) in 127, 128,
154, 155–7, 160–61, 161–2, 164
global order, influence on 17
'grassroots authoritarianism' in 109,
114, 118
history 154, 156, 163
incarceration policies in 108, 113–14
Iran-Contra affair 158, 163
Israeli espionage in 160
migrant professionals in,
cosmopolitanism of 56
military assistance to Turkey 161
National Security Agency (NSA)
174, 177
neo-liberal mutation into
authoritarianism in 106–7
neocons in 16–17, 157–8
9/11 terrorist attacks on 40
Personal Responsibility and Work
Opportunity Reconciliation Act
(PRWORA, 1996) 109
policy results, reorganisation of
government for 162–4
policy studies in 302, 306, 307
post 9/11 environment and "war on
terror" 128
post-welfare-state in 9
racialisation of poverty discourse in
113
representational juggling 158–60
security (law-and-order) state in
29–30, 105–21
state-private power, intertwining of
154–5
undocumented workers 118

war in Iraq, run-up to 151, 157–8,
158–9, 175, 176–8, 179, 180, 181,
183
War on Poverty programs 111–12,
116
welfare policies in, dismantling of
110–11
welfare policies in, emergence of
109–10
universalism 56, 171, 214
university reform 12, 30
internationalisation in Denmark
68–83
university systems 75–6, 78
urban infrastructure 107–8, 115–16,
301
urban institutions 195
urban poverty 112, 114, 115, 196, 198,
200, 283
urban resettlement 127
in India 188, 189, 192–3, 194, 196,
197, 198–9, 200, 201
urban transport *see* Mumbai Urban
Transport Project (MUTP)

values, global 288
Visa Information System (EU) 43
vocabulary and grammar of governance
201

war in Iraq, run-up categorised as
history 179
Weber, M.
bureaucracy theory 204–5
Weberian bureaucracy theory 204–5
welfare state, expansion in EU 206
welfare systems 205–6, 220
World Bank 7, 28, 57, 60–62, 63, 64
accountability of, demand for 197,
198–9
governance and 144, 147–8, 202
history of 133–4, 191–2
influence in Mexico 126, 130–31,
132–3, 133–6, 140–42, 142–4, 146–7
Narmada Dam project 191, 192,
193–4, 197
urban resettlement in India and 127,
187, 188–9, 190–91, 191–2, 193–4,
195–6, 197–9, 200, 201, 202

CPSIA information can be obtained at www.ICGtesting.com
Printed in the USA
BVOW03s1104271113

337471BV00006B/56/P